Readings in
ERICAN RELIGIOUS D

Volume 2

e African American Religious Experience

—————— Edited by ——————

Jon R. Stone • Carlos R. Piar

California State University, Long Beach

Kendall Hunt
publishing company

In Honor of and with Appreciation to Our Teachers:

at USC:
John P. Crossley, Donald E. Miller, and Robert S. Ellwood

at UCSB:
Catherine L. Albanese, †Walter H. Capps,
Phillip E. Hammond,
†Robert S. Michaelsen, Birger A. Pearson, and Wade Clark Roof

Kendall Hunt
publishing company

Cover and title page images copyright © Corbis.

Copyright © 2007 by Kendall/Hunt Publishing Company

ISBN 978-1-4652-0473-8

Printed in the United States of America
10 9 8 7 6 5 4

Contents

Other Volumes in This Series

THE NATIVE AMERICAN RELIGIOUS EXPERIENCE

1. Coyote Steals the Sun and Moon [Zuni]
2. Coyote, Ikotome, and the Rock [White River Sioux]
3. Coyote and the Origin of Death [Caddo]
4. The Creation of Man (Second Version) [Morris Edward Opler; Jacarillo Apache]
5. The Creation and Loss of the Sun and Moon [Morris Edward Opler; Jacarillo Apache]
6. The Emergence [Morris Edward Opler; Jacarillo Apache]
7. Creation and the Origin of Corn [Frank Hamilton Cushing; Zuni]
8. Red Sky's Scrolls and Origin Lore [Selwyn Dewdney; Southern Ojibway]
9. Other Origin Tales and Scrolls [Selwyn Dewdney; Southern Ojibway]
10. The Creation of the Ocean [Kashaya Pomo; told by Herman James]
11. The Creation of People and the Ocean [Kashaya Pomo; told by Herman James]
12. The Flood [Kashaya Pomo; told by Mrs. Essie Parrish]
13. Doctoring [Kashaya Pomo; told by Mrs. Essie Parrish]
14. Indians in Overalls [Jaime de Angulo]
15. Selections from *Black Elk Speaks* [as told through John G. Neihardt (Flaming Rainbow)]
16. Fall 1917-Spring 1918: *Manigou-geezis* Strong Spirit Sun [Louise Erdrich]
17. Ceremony [Leslie Marmon Silko]
18. Missionaries and the Religious Vacuum [Vine Deloria, Jr.]
19. The Native American Church of Jesus Christ [Emerson Spider, Sr.]
20. Who Can Sit at the Lord's Table? The Experience of Indigenous Peoples [Rosemary McCombs Maxey]
21. The Native Church: A Search for an Authentic Spirituality [Laverne Jacobs]

THE LATINO/A AMERICAN RELIGIOUS EXPERIENCE

1. Hymns, Prayers, and Other Religious Verses [Aurelio M. Espinosa and J. Manuel Espinosa]
2. The Penitente Brotherhood [Cleofas M. Jaramillo
3. Holy Week at Arroyo Hondo [Cleofas M. Jaramillo]
4. Noche Buena and Religious Dramas [Cleofas M. Jaramillo]
5. Saints' Holy Days [Cleofas M. Jaramillo]
6. Theological Significance [Jeanette Rodriguez]
7. India [Richard Rodriguez]
8. The Mexican-American and the Church [César E. Chavez]
9. El Aposento Alto [Arlene M. Sanchez Walsh]

THE ASIAN AMERICAN RELIGIOUS EXPERIENCE

A Foreword to This Series

It is a commonplace to speak of America as a religiously diverse nation. From its origins, dating well before the arrival of European settlers, the American continent contained a great variety of peoples, languages, cultures, and religions. The native groups that came to inhabit this vast and varied landscape were of many types, from pueblo dwelling peoples, to those living in the woodland, prairie, mountain, and coastal regions. During the period of European exploration and colonial expansion, the Americas soon became home to English, French, Spanish, Portuguese, and Dutch settlers. And, after slavery was introduced into the New World, peoples of African tribal descent added their own cultural and religious expressions to the growing ethnic and racial diversity of the land. From many peoples there emerged one nation; from one nation there arose many religious voices. The long conversation—and the spirited debate—over issues of religious and cultural identity continues to this day. What does it mean to be an American? What does it mean to be part of an ethnic or racial community in America? In what ways have religious beliefs and traditional cultural practices informed that meaning or helped shape that identity?

This current anthology, *Readings in American Religious Diversity*, presents to students of American religion a four-volume collection of primary source materials that serves to illustrate the ethno-racial dimensions of religion in America beyond its usual European expressions. The ethno-racial religious communities featured in this reader broadly include Native American, African American, Asian American, and an array of Latino communities. A unique feature of these texts is that the readings come from within the communities themselves, rather than from researchers commenting upon these communities from the outside. Thus, students reading these selections will come to hear the voices and sense the deeply-felt passion, sorrow, frustration, hope, and joy of those individuals who were or are still part of the important conversations at the heart of these four ethno-racial communities' ongoing dialogue and debates within themselves.

More specifically, these primary-source readers are designed to complement the religious and historical materials of the junior-level course, "American Religious Diversity," which is offered every semester at California State University, Long Beach. For this course, students are required to read religious literature produced by women and men from within two of the four ethno-racial communities mentioned above. While many of our instructors have assigned works of fiction, such as short stories or novels, we have found that fictional literature has tended to give our students only a partial picture of the religious dimensions of these communities, and the difficulties these groups have experienced in their attempts to maintain traditional beliefs and practices in a predominantly "white" and Protestant culture. Thus, in addition to works of fiction, we have discovered that the diversity of religious experience as well as responses within these communities to discrimination, social dislocation, and loss of traditional culture could be "read" within other types of literature. These include folktales, sermons, letters, speeches, essays and addresses, autobiographies, oral histories and published interviews, as well as immigrant community histories, scholarly treatises, and ethnic denominational self-studies.

Because the course for which these four volumes are designed is taught each semester by six to eight full-time and part-time faculty members, we do not believe that it is our role as the editors of this anthology to instruct our colleagues in how to use these selections. At the same time, we do think that it is important to provide an outline of themes that emerge from these readings, especially as they show both the similarities as well as the differences in the experiences of these four ethno-racial communities and the role that religious ideas and practices have played within each. Thus, despite differences in their origins and in their specific experiences in the Americas, the literature produced by persons within the Native American, African American, Asian American, and Latino communities share a number of themes which students and instructors can reflect upon and fruitfully discuss. Among these themes is the experience of being outsiders, of social and cultural "otherness," of dislocation, disorientation, and uprootedness, of turning to tradition and relying upon religious institutions for personal and communal support, of the importance of family and the larger ethnic community, of striving after the recognition of basic rights and of one's human worth, of resistance to assimilation and the struggle against the secularizing influences of modern social and cultural life, and of drawing upon mythologies to strengthen one's sense of self and importance in the world.

Owing to all these difficulties and other personal and social experiences, it is apparent that, for better or for worse, people have turned to religion and to traditional expressions of community life for their remedy. There are those who seek succor within a religious community as well as those who adapt themselves and their traditions to meet the exigencies of life as immigrants, as sojourners or outsiders, in a world where one's experiences are constantly defined by harassment, discrimination, and unrelenting assaults upon one's dignity. But also, and perhaps more importantly, people's experiences have likewise been defined by family, faith, community, friendship, religious mystery, wonder, thankfulness, laughter, and the renewal of the human spirit in the face of adversity.

Of course, while these themes predominate, one can also discern from these readings many lesser and many more contrasting themes. From this quartet of ethno-racial communities, a *discors concordia* or discordant concord can also be heard. The themes and variations that play throughout the pages of this anthology intersect in grand fugal style, and bear witness to the resilience of the human spirit, the signal significance of community, and the central role that religion plays in defining one's place in the world. Religion has been the tie that has bound individuals to their communities, has strengthened those same communities by renewing members' commitments to long-standing traditions, even as those traditions are transformed by the challenges that these and other like communities have had to face.

With respect to the reader selections, originally it had been our hope to include at least 25 readings per volume. But, due to obvious page limitations and higher than expected copyright costs, we have had to limit the number of selections in each volume to about 20. Despite these cost constraints, but not because of them, we decided to reprint the selected number of chapters, speeches, essays, and articles in their entirety, unedited, and as they originally appeared in print—coarse language and all. One notable exception is the journal of Mrs. Jarena Lee, which we were obliged to condense by some thirty original printed pages. Moreover, because this four-volume reader is aimed at highlighting the various types of religious literature produced by members of these four ethno-racial communities, it was soon evident that not all communities produced the same varieties of literature, neither in the types nor in the same quantity. This difference is most evident in the volume on the Asian American religious experience, in which, to maintain some balance of material among sections, we have had to include more scholarly and historical types of literature.

Lastly, while this primary-source reader is primarily intended to meet the interdisciplinary and human diversity requirements of a specific course at Long Beach State, as the editors of this anthology we are also aware of its potential instructional value outside Southern California. Recognizing that instructors and their students at other colleges and universities throughout the United States might likewise find these selections of interest, we have designed the reader so that it might appeal more generally to faculty teaching similar courses in the fields of history, religious studies, ethnic studies, American studies, rhetoric, and comparative literary studies. To help familiarize readers with the four ethno-racial religious communities that comprise this anthology, we have also provided a brief preface or "foretaste" before each volume, along with several suggested questions to help facilitate class discussion. And so that those using this reader may be encouraged to explore further the histories and literatures of these communities, at the beginning of each volume we have included a list of recommended sources for both instructors and students to consult.

Notwithstanding these limitations, we have sought to create an anthology that allows a variety of voices within these communities to be heard, in many cases for the first time under the same cover. Indeed, this text represents a true celebration of the religious diversity that defines the American nation.

Vox manet—the Voice remains (Ovid).

—Jon R. Stone and Carlos R. Piar
Long Beach, California
December 2006

Sources and Selected General Works in American Religious History

Ahlstrom, Sydney E. *A Religious History of the American People*. New Haven, CT: Yale University Press, 1972.

Albanese, Catherine L. *America: Religions and Religion,* 3rd ed. Belmont, CA: Wadsworth, 1999.

Becker, Penny, and Nancy Eiesland (eds.). *Contemporary American Religion: An Ethnographic Reader*. Walnut Creek, CA: AltaMira Press, 1997.

Butler, Jon, Grant Wacker, and Randall Balmer. *Religion in American Life: A Short History*. NY: Oxford University Press, 2003.

Carroll, Bret E. *The Routledge Historical Atlas of Religions in America*. New York: Routledge, 2000.

Corrigan, John, and Winthrop S. Hudson. *Religion in America,* 7th ed. Upper Saddle River, NJ: Prentice-Hall, 2004.

Ebaugh, Helen, and Janet Chafetz. *Religion and the New Immigrants: Continuities and Adaptations in Immigrant Congregations*. Walnut Creek, CA: AltaMira Press, 2000.

Eck, Diana L. *A New Religious America*. San Francisco: HarperSanFrancisco, 2002.

Gaustad, Edwin S (ed.). *A Documentary History of Religion in America,* 2 vols. Grand Rapids, MI: Eerdmans, 1982–1983.

———. *A Religious History of America,* rev. ed. San Francisco: Harper & Row, 1990.

Goff, Philip, and Paul Harvey (eds.). *Themes in Religion and American Culture*. Chapel Hill, NC: University of North Carolina Press, 2004.

Hackett, David G. (ed.). *Religion and American Culture: A Reader*. New York: Routledge, 1995.

Handy, Robert T. *A History of the Churches in the United States and Canada*. New York: Oxford University Press, 1977.

Hemeyer, Julia Corbett. *Religion in America,* 5th ed. Upper Saddle River, NJ: Prentice-Hall, 2005.

Lippy, Charles H., Robert Choquette, and Stafford Poole. *Christianity Comes to the Americas, 1492–1776*. New York: Paragon House, 1992.

McDannell, Colleen (ed.). *Religions of the United States in Practice,* 2 vols. Princeton, NJ: Princeton University Press, 2001.

Neusner, Jacob (ed.). *World Religions in America,* 3rd ed. Louisville, KY: Westminster/John Knox Press, 2003.

Porterfield, Amanda (ed.). *American Religious History*. Oxford, UK: Blackwell Publishers, 2002.

Warner, R. Stephen, and Judith G. Wittner (eds.). *Gatherings in Diaspora: Religious Communities and the New Immigration*. Philadelphia: Temple University Press, 1998.

Williams, Peter W. (ed.). *Perspectives on American Religion and Culture: A Reader*. Oxford, UK: Blackwell Publishers, 1999.

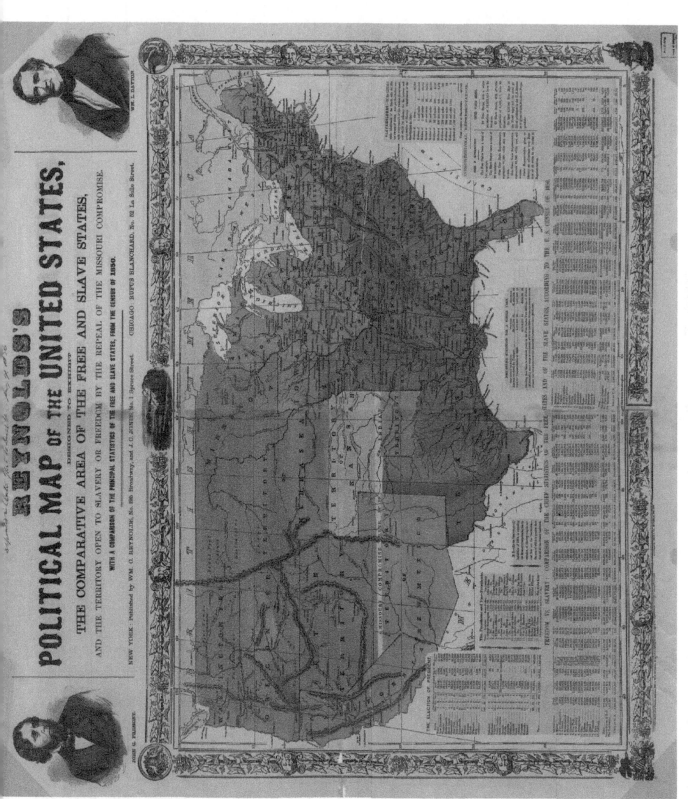

REYNOLDS'S
POLITICAL MAP of the UNITED STATES,
DESIGNED TO EXHIBIT
THE COMPARATIVE AREA OF THE FREE AND SLAVE STATES,
AND THE TERRITORY OPEN TO SLAVERY OR FREEDOM BY THE REPEAL OF THE MISSOURI COMPROMISE.
WITH A COMPARISON OF THE PRINCIPAL STATISTICS OF THE FREE AND SLAVE STATES, FROM THE CENSUS OF 1850.

NEW YORK : Published by WM. C. REYNOLDS, No. 380 Broadway, and J. C. JONES, No. 1 Spruce Street.   CHICAGO : RUFUS BLANCHARD, No. 52 La Salle Street.

HISTORICAL GEOGRAPHY.

Au. Rhees Reserve.

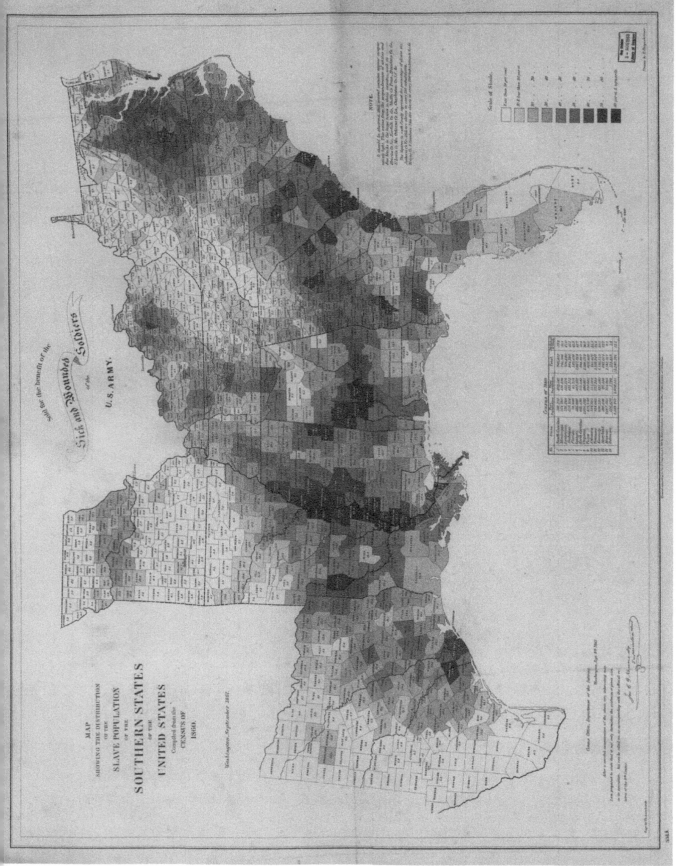

Readings in African American Religious Traditions: A Foretaste

To speak of the African American experience is to be ever mindful of the long shadow cast by the injustice of slavery. Though nearly 150 years have passed since emancipation, the consequences of that "primal crime," as sociologist Robert Bellah has aptly termed it, are felt to this day. How in good conscience, one might ask, could Christian men and women assent to enslaving fellow humans, or visit such evil upon the sons and daughters of the same Heavenly Father? The great indignity and outrage felt by Americans of African descent—both slave and free—are expressed in the pages of newspapers, journals, declarations, addresses, and autobiographical recollections, as well as in creative works of fiction. This section of the reader presents a variety of literary works that convey the depth of feelings and religious experiences associated with slavery and its continuing consequences for African Americans.

As they came to develop in the New World, African American cultures and religions combined deeply rooted African elements with biblical traditions. Especially strong was the identification of the African American experience with that of the Hebrew slaves and their miraculous exodus from Egypt. Indeed, Egypt became a metaphor for slavery, even as the American continent came to be associated metaphorically with Israel's later exile and captivity in Babylon. And, as Israel of old, the African peoples enslaved in America, *de facto* and *de jure*, likewise cried unto God to send to them a deliverer. In time, many talented men as well as women from within the African American community—both North and South—would rise to claim the mantle of prophet and, "like unto Moses from among their brethren," would speak as one with authority from God.

In response, therefore, to the humiliation of slavery and of finding themselves socially and religiously marginalized in white Southern culture, African slaves created their own spaces for worship and community life. Historians have referred to this social and religious phenomenon as the "invisible institution." Initially, Southern slaves would gather in secret locations for mutual comfort and encouragement. These informal gatherings became brief periods of solace from the cruelty of their condition, and provided spiritual healing that was at once personal as well as communal. In time, however, these religious meetings became more formalized. "Slave religion," as Gayraud Wilmore has observed, "was partly a clandestine protest against the hypocrisy of a system that expected blacks to be virtuous and obedient to those who themselves lived lives of indolence and immorality in full view of the ones they purported to serve as examples" (1998:35). From these "hush harbors" emerged a religious and cultural life that became uniquely African American. In fact, these gatherings of African slaves for mutual prayer, to join their voices in deeply moving spirituals (what one might call communal songs in motion), and for spiritual uplift, would help define the characteristic styles of worship in the black churches that would sprout up throughout the South after emancipation.

Several decades later, in his essay, "Of the Faith of the Fathers," W.E.B. DuBois gave eloquent testimony to the music of the soul that typified the black worship experience as "the most original and beautiful expression of human life and longing yet born on American soil." In this essay, DuBois identified three essential characteristics of slave religion that were witnessed in his day, namely, the preacher, the music, and the frenzy of worship "when the Spirit of the Lord passed by" (1926:191). According to DuBois, the preacher is at one and the same time "a leader, a politician, an orator, a 'boss', an intriguer, an idealist," and ever "the centre of a group of men, now twenty, now a thousand in number" (1926:190). The music, though "[s]prung from the African forests, . . . was adapted, changed, and intensified by the tragic soul-life of the slave, until, under the stress of law and whip, it became the one true expression of a people's sorrow, despair, and hope." And, while the worship "varied in expression from the silent rapt countenance or the low murmur and moan to the mad abandon of physical fervor, . . . so firm a hold did it have on the Negro, that many generations firmly believed that without this visible manifestation of the God there could be no true communion with the Invisible" (1926:191). To these three essential characteristics, one might add the community itself, in that one finds worship to be a dialogue between a preacher and his people as well as between the community as a whole and the Divine, mediated through the rhythms of the spoken word and song.

In the North, except for the chains, the condition of freeborn and emancipated Africans during the nineteenth and into the twentieth century differed only slightly from their Southern cousins. Northern blacks found themselves similarly excluded from mainstream social and religious life. In response, individuals, such as Richard Allen and Peter Williams, established their own Protestant churches. Among them were the African Methodist Episcopal Church (AME) and the African Methodist Episcopal Zion Church (AMEZ), which were officially established in 1816 and 1821 respectively. For Northern blacks, these and other independent denominations became a type of invisible institution, that is, a place where shared religious and community life could be experienced apart from the controlling gaze of white society. Or, as Wilmore has also noted, "[b]oth the slave congregations of the South—'the invisible institution'—and the more or less free black churches of the North developed a religion that masked a sublimated outrage balanced with patience, cheerfulness, and a boundless confidence in the ultimate justice of God" (1998:36). In this section of the reader, we have included several brief examples of the influence of the churches in the lives of Southern and Northern blacks. These include selections by Langston Hughes and Zora Hurston, as well as oral recollections edited by B.A. Botkin, and an historical essay by W.E.B. DuBois.

In the century from the end of the Civil War to the famous "March on Washington"—the period of "Jim Crow" laws—the religious experience of African Americans, both North and South, continued to be informed by daily assaults upon their personal and civil rights. "Separate but equal," mandated in 1896 by the Supreme Court in *Plessy v. Ferguson*, allowed for the lawful segregation of blacks from whites and consigned blacks to the status of second-class citizens, if citizens at all. African Americans were denied basic rights, such as the right to vote. They were refused service at local markets and lunch counters, and were consigned to sending their children to run-down schools. Those who objected to these Jim Crow laws were beaten and punished. Lynchings became common in the South, but not unknown in the North and West. As Albert J. Raboteau records, during this period, "[i]ncidents of violence against African Americans became more frequent. Between 1882 and 1885, 227 black people were lynched. Between 1889 and 1899, that figure rose to 1,240. . . . In 1898 alone, white mobs seized and murdered 104 black people" (2001:72). In the pages of the NAACP newsletter, *The Crisis: A Record of the Darker Races*, edited by W.E.B. DuBois, space is given not just for the purpose of documenting lynchings and mob violence against blacks, but of calling upon their white brothers and sisters to reject the evils perpetrated by those among them. In this reader, we have included a short story by DuBois, titled "Jesus Christ in Georgia," which dramatically illustrates this outrage.

It was against these and other longstanding injustices that the leaders of the civil rights movement of the 1950s and 1960s rallied their people. Renewed enforcement of Jim Crow lent greater urgency, and moral authority, to their cause. The Reverend Martin Luther King, Jr.'s, famous letter from a Birmingham jail, reminiscent of St. Paul's own prison epistles, provided an ethical and religious rationale for King's nonviolent approach to gaining the inevitable triumph, as he would later proclaim from the steps of the Lincoln Memorial, by "meeting physical force with soul force." As he wrote, "[i]f the inexpressible cruelties of slavery could not stop us, the opposition we now face will surely fail. We will win our freedom because the sacred heritage of our nation and the eternal will of God are embodied in our echoing demands" (1992:98). One can also hear echoes of King's letter in the selections by James Cone and Jacquelyn Grant, reprinted below.

King had cautioned his followers against resorting to violence, and to resist traveling down the roads of bitterness and hatred that might lead to retaliation and an endless cycle of violence. Others were not as long-suffering as King and his followers. Indeed, King cited as an example the black nationalist groups, such as the Nation of Islam, led by Elijah Muhammad. "This movement," King explained, "is nourished by the contemporary frustration over the continued existence of racial discrimination. It is made up of people who," he believed, "have lost faith in America, who have absolutely repudiated Christianity, and who have concluded that the white man is an incurable 'devil'" (1992:93). As an example of this alternative to King's nonviolent and Christian approach, we have selected two readings: one is a speech by Malcolm X, entitled "Black Man's History," delivered in 1962; the other is a chapter on the place of women in Islam from a more recent apologetic work by Aminah Beverly McCloud. But even between these two readings, whose authors are separated by generation and gender, differences in religious assumptions are noticeable.

Taken together, the selections in this section give evidence of the spiritual and intellectual vitality that has informed and continues to enliven the African American community in our own day. Or, in the words of Maya Angelou, as quoted below in Jacquelyn Grant's essay on Womanist theology (1993:287–288):

Out of the hut of history's shame
I rise
Up from a past that's rooted in pain
I rise
I'm a Black ocean, leaping and wide,
Welling and swelling, I bear in the tide
Leaving behind nights of terror and fear
I rise
Into a daybreak that's wondrously clear
I rise
Bringing the gifts that my ancestors gave
I am the dream and hope of the slave.
I rise.
I rise.
I rise.

Sources and Selected Works in African American History, Literature, and Religions

[*indicates works of fiction]

Abrahams, Roger D. (ed.). *Afro-American Folktales: Stories from Black Traditions in the New World.* New York: Random House, 1985.

Aptheker, Herbert. *Nat Turner's Slave Rebellion.* New York: Grove Press, 1968.

Baer, Hans A. *The Black Spiritual Movement: A Religious Response to Racism.* Knoxville, TN: University of Tennessee Press, 1984.

Baer, Hans A., and Merrill Singer. *African-American Religion in the Twentieth Century.* Knoxville, TN: University of Tennessee Press, 1992.

*Baldwin, James. *Go Tell It on the Mountain.* New York: Dell Publishing, 1985.

*———. *The Fire Next Time.* New York: Vintage International, 1993.

Bennett, Lerone, Jr. *The Shaping of Black America: The Struggles and Triumphs of African-Americans, 1619 to the 1990s.* New York: Penguin Books, 1993.

Berry, Mary Frances, and John W. Blassingame. *Long Memory: The Black Experience in America.* New York: Oxford University Press, 1982.

Branch, Taylor. *Parting the Waters: America in the King Years, 1954–1963.* New York: Simon and Schuster, 1988.

Broderick, Francis L., and August Meier (eds.). *Negro Protest Thought in the Twentieth Century.* Indianapolis: Bobbs-Merrill, 1965.

Burkett, Randall K. *Garveyism as a Religious Movement: The Institutionalization of a Black Civil Religion.* Metuchen, NJ: The Scarecrow Press, 1978.

Cannon, Katie Geneva. *Katie's Canon: Womanism and the Soul of the Black Community.* New York: Continuum, 1995.

Carson, Clayborne, David J. Garrow, Gerald Gill, Vincent Harding, and Darlene Clark Hine (gen. eds.). *The Eyes on the Prize Civil Rights Reader: Documents, Speeches, and Firsthand Accounts from the Black Freedom Struggle, 1954–1990.* New York: Penguin Books, 1991.

Chappell, David L. *A Stone of Hope: Prophetic Religion and the Death of Jim Crow.* Chapel Hill, NC: University of North Carolina Press, 2004.

Clegg, Claude Andrew, III. *An Original Man: The Life and Times of Elijah Muhammad.* New York: St. Martin's Press, 1997.

Cone, James H. *A Black Theology of Liberation,* 2nd ed. Maryknoll, New York: Orbis Books, 1986.

———. *Martin & Malcolm & America.* Maryknoll, New York: Orbis Books, 1995.

Daley, James (ed.). *Great Speeches by African Americans.* New York: Dover Publications, 2006.

Davis, Cyprian. *The History of Black Catholics in the United States.* New York: Crossroad, 1996.

DeCaro, Louis A., Jr. *On the Side of My People: A Religious Life of Malcolm X.* New York: New York University Press, 1996.

DuBois, W.E.B. (ed.). *The Negro Church.* Walnut Creek, CA: AltaMira Press, 2003 [reprint of 1903 edition].

Dunbar, Alice Moore (ed.). *Masterpieces of Negro Eloquence: The Best Speeches Delivered by the Negro from the Days of Slavery to the Present Time*. New York: The Bookery Publishing Co., 1914.

Essien-Udom, E.U. *Black Nationalism: A Search for an Identity in America*. Chicago: The University of Chicago Press, 1971.

Fauset, Arthur Huff. *Black Gods of the Metropolis: Negro Religious Cults of the Urban North*. Philadelphia: University of Pennsylvania Press, 1944.

Fitts, Leroy. *A History of Black Baptists*. Nashville, TN: Broadman Press, 1985.

Franklin, Robert Michael. *Liberating Visions*. Minneapolis, MN: Fortress Press, 1990.

Frazier, Franklin E., and C. Eric Lincoln. *The Negro Church in America/The Black Church since Frazier*. New York: Schocken Books, 1974.

Fulop, Timothy E., and Albert J. Raboteau (eds.). *African-American Religion: Interpretive Essays in History and Culture*. New York: Routledge, 1997.

Gardell, Mattias. *In the Name of Elijah Muhammad: Louis Farrakhan and the Nation of Islam*. Durham, NC: Duke University Press, 1996.

Gordon, Lewis R. *Existentia Africana: Understanding Africana Existential Thought*. New York: Routledge, 2000.

Grant, Joanne (ed.). *Black Protest: History, Documents, and Analyses, 1619 to Present*. New York: Fawcett, 1991.

Higginbotham, Evelyn Brooks. *Righteous Discontent: The Women's Movement in the Black Baptist Church, 1880–1920*. Cambridge, MA: Harvard University Press, 1993.

Hurston, Zora. *Dust Tracks on a Road: An Autobiography*. Philadelphia: J.B. Lippincott Co., 1942.

*———. *Their Eyes Were Watching God*. New York: Harper Perennial, 1990.

Johnson, F. Roy. *The Nat Turner Slave Insurrection*. Murfreesboro, NC: Johnson Publishing Co., 1966.

King, Martin Luther, Jr. (James M. Washington, ed.). *I Have a Dream: Writings and Speeches That Changed the World*. New York: HarperCollins, 1992.

———. *Strength to Love*. Minneapolis, MN: Fortress Press, 1981.

———. *Where Do We Go From Here: Chaos or Community?* New York: Harper & Row, 1967.

———. *Why We Can't Wait*. New York: Signet Classic, 2000.

Lee, Martha F. *The Nation of Islam: An American Millenarian Movement*. Syracuse, New York: Syracuse University Press, 1996.

Levine, Lawrence W. *Black Culture and Black Consciousness*. New York: Oxford University Press, 1977.

Lewis, David L. *W.E.B. Du Bois: Biography of a Race 1868–1919*. New York: Henry Holt & Co., 1993.

Lincoln, C. Eric. *The Black Muslims in America*, 3rd ed. Grand Rapids, MI: Eerdmans; Trenton, NJ: Africa World Press, 1994.

Lincoln, C. Eric, and Lawrence H. Mamiya. *The Black Church in the African American Experience*. Durham, NC: Duke University Press, 1990.

Malcolm X. *The Autobiography of Malcolm X* (as told to Alex Haley). New York: Ballantine Books, 1973.

————. *The End of White World Supremacy.* New York: Arcade Publishing, 1971.

Marsh, Clifton E. *From Black Muslims to Muslim,* 2nd ed. Metuchen, NJ: The Scarecrow Press, 1995.

McCloud, Aminah Beverly. *African American Islam.* New York: Routledge, 1995.

Mellon, James (ed.). *Bullwhip Days: The Slaves Remember, An Oral History.* New York: Weidenfeld & Nicolson, 1988.

Mintz, Steven (ed.). *African American Voices: The Life Cycle Of Slavery,* rev. ed. St. James, New York: Brandywine Press, 1996.

Moses, Wilson Jeremiah. *Black Messiahs and Uncle Toms: Social and Literary Manipulations of a Religious Myth,* rev. ed. University Park, PA: Pennsylvania State University Press, 1993.

Muhammad, Elijah. *Message to the Blackman in America.* Chicago: Muhammad's Temple No. 2, 1965.

Mullane, Deirdre (ed.). *Crossing the Danger Water: Three Hundred Years of African-American Writing.* New York: Anchor Doubleday, 1993.

Murphy, Larry G. (ed.). *Down by the Riverside: Readings in African American Religion.* New York: New York University Press, 2000.

Murphy, Larry G., J. Gordon Melton, and Gary L. Ward (eds.). *Encyclopedia of African American Religions.* New York: Garland Publishing, 1993.

Newman, Richard, Patrick Rael, and Phillip Lapsansky (eds.). *Pamphlets of Protest: An Anthology of Early African American Protest Literature, 1790–1860.* New York: Routledge, 2001.

Oates, Stephen B. *Let the Trumpet Sound: The Life of Martin Luther King, Jr.* New York: Mentor, 1985.

Olmos, Margarite Fernández, and Lisbeth Paravisini-Gebert. *Creole Religions of the Caribbean: An Introduction from Vodou and Santería to Obeah and Espiritismo.* New York: New York University Press, 2003.

Pitts, Walter F. *Old Ship of Zion: The Afro-Baptist Spiritual in the African Diaspora.* New York: Oxford University Press, 1993.

Raboteau, Albert J. *A Fire in the Bones: Reflections on African-American Religious History.* Boston: Beacon Press, 1995.

————. *Slave Religion: The 'Invisible Institution' in the Antebellum South.* New York: Oxford University Press, 1978.

Riggs, Marcia Y. (ed., with Barbara Holmes). *Can I Get a Witness? Prophetic Religious Voices of African American Women: An Anthology.* Maryknoll, New York: Orbis Books, 1997.

Sernett, Milton C. *Bound for the Promised Land: African American Religion and the Great Migration.* Durham, NC: Duke University Press, 1997.

————. (ed.). *African American Religious History: A Documentary History,* 2nd ed. Durham, NC: Duke University Press, 1999.

Shockley, Ann Allen. *Afro-American Women Writers, 1746–1933: An Anthology and Critical Guide.* New York: New American Library, 1989.

Sitkoff, Harvard. *The Struggle for Black Equality, 1954–1992* rev. ed. New York: Hill & Wang, 1993.

Smith, Theophus H. *Conjuring Culture: Biblical Formations of Black America.* New York: Oxford University Press, 1994.

Stewart, Dianne M. *Three Eyes for the Journey: African Dimensions of the Jamaican Religious Experience.* New York: Oxford University Press, 2005.

Taylor, Clarence. *Black Religious Intellectuals: The Fight for Equality from Jim Crow to the 21st Century.* New York: Routledge, 2002.

Townes, Emilie M. *In a Blaze of Glory: Womanist Spirituality as Social Witness.* Nashville, TN: Abingdon Press, 1995.

Turner, Richard Brent. *Islam in the African-American Experience.* Bloomington, IN: Indiana University Press, 1997.

Washington, James M. *A Testament of Hope: The Essential Writings and Speeches of Martin Luther King, Jr.* New York: HarperCollins, 1991.

Washington, Joseph R., Jr. *Black Sects and Cults.* Garden City, New York: Doubleday, 1973.

Watts, Jill. *God, Harlem U.S.A.: The Father Divine Story.* Berkeley, CA: University of California Press, 1992.

West, Cornel. *The Cornel West Reader.* New York: Basic Civitas Books, 1999.

———. *Race Matters.* Boston: Beacon Press, 1993.

West, Cornel, and Eddie S. Glaude, Jr. (eds.). *African American Religious Thought: An Anthology.* Louisville, KY: Westminster/John Knox Press, 2003.

Williams, Juan. *Eyes on the Prize: America's Civil Rights Years, 1954–1965.* New York: Penguin Books, 1988.

Wilmore, Gayraud S. *Black Religion and Black Radicalism,* 3rd ed. Maryknoll, New York: Orbis Books, 1998.

———. (ed.). *African American Religious Studies: An Interdisciplinary Anthology.* Durham, NC: Duke University Press, 1989.

Some Suggested Questions for Discussion:

1. Historically, African American identification with the experiences of the Hebrew slaves in the Book of Exodus has been very strong. List and discuss the similarities and differences that you see between the African experience in America—both before and after emancipation—with that of the Hebrew/Israelite peoples. What are some of the similar themes that one can discern? And, are there similar Moses figures in the twentieth century African American experience?

2. Discuss the African American use of the Bible and its stories in the nineteenth century as opposed to the twentieth century as seen in the readings in this section. What different interpretive lenses do people such as Robert Young, David Walker, Mrs. Jarena Lee, Frederick Douglass, and even W.E.B. DuBois appear to use in comparison and contrast to Martin Luther King, Jr., Malcolm X, James Cone, and Jacquelyn Grant?

3. Two differing and, at times, contradictory pictures of the Christian churches in America (one positive, the other negative) emerge from the readings in this section by Black Americans living in the antebellum period. Comparing the recollections of Mrs. Jarena Lee to those offered by Frederick Douglass, Peter Randolph, and the former slaves interviewed by B.A. Botkin, please identify and then discuss in detail those contrasting views of the churches. How might one account for these conflicting images?

4. Based on the speech by Malcolm X and the essay by Aminah McCloud reprinted below, what beliefs appear to have remained constant in the Nation of Islam (Malcolm X) and the Black Muslim community (McCloud) in the United States despite decades of changes in the movement? That is, would Malcolm X recognize Aminah McCloud's beliefs about African American Islam in the 1990s as consistent with the movement founded by Elijah Muhammad in the 1930s, of which he (Malcolm X) became its best known interpreter in the 1950s and 1960s?

5. In comparing the essays in this section by Jacquelyn Grant and Aminah McCloud, how do their positions differ concerning Womanist interpretations of religious traditions—in the first case Christianity, in the second case Islam? Given their assumptions about women and religion, how might they critique each other's position?

1. An Address before the Pennsylvania Augustine Society (1818)

PRINCE SAUNDERS

"Perhaps there never was a period, when the attention of so many enlightened men was so vigorously awakened to a sense of the importance of a universal dissemination of the blessings of instruction, as at this enlightened age . . ."

AN ADDRESS, etc.:

The human heart is a parti-coloured piece of Mosaic. But notwithstanding its veriagated appearances, the whited inlaying of those genuine excellencies, and of those enobling affections, which encompass humanity with glory and honour, are but seldom to be found its innate, or, as it were, its spontaneous ornaments.

We hence descry some of the grounds for that invaluable importance which has uniformly been given to education, in supplying the mind with intellectual acquisitions, and for adorning it with those elevated accomplishments which have generally been considered as its peculiar fruits, by the virtuous and contemplative of every age and nation; where the genial influences of the Sun of Science have been experienced, and where the blessings of civilized society have been enjoyed. If by investigating the historic page of antiquity, we take a retrospective view of the numerous votaries of literature and the useful arts, who flourished at those early periods, when the improving influences of knowledge and civilization were wholly confined to the oriental regions, we shall then discover some traces of their views of the intrinsic utility of mutually associating, to aid the progress of those who were aspiring to taste the Castilian spring, while ascending the towering heights of Parnassus, that there they might behold the magnificent temple of the Ruler of the Muses, and hear his venerated oracle.

We have heard of the early distinguishing attainments of the celebrated Aristotle, who improved so much at seventeen years of age, that the immortal Plato, (his preceptor,) gave him the appellation of a Lover of the Truth. He soon afterwards became tutor to Alexander the great, and founder of the sublime researches of the ancient Peripotetici. The accomplished and eloquent youth, Antonius Gripho, a native of Gaul, came to Rome, and taught rhetoric and poetry at the house of Julius Caesar, when a mere boy; and historians tell us, that his school was frequented by Cicero and others of the most eminent literati of the age.

Many, in different periods, by cultivating the arts and sciences, have contributed to human happiness and improvement, by that invincible zeal for moral virtue and intellectual excellence, which their example has inspired in other minds and hearts, as well as by the sublimity of those traces of truth with which they have illuminated the world, and dignified the intercourse of civilized society.

Perhaps there never was a period, when the attention of so many enlightened men was so vigorously awakened to a sense of the importance of a universal dissemination of the blessings of instruction, as at this enlightened age, in this, in the northern and eastern sections of our country, in some portions of Europe, and in the island of Hayti.

The hope is encouraged, that in the above-mentioned portions of the world, the means of acquiring knowledge sufficient to read and understand the sacred Scriptures, and to manage with propriety, the ordinary concerns of domestic and social life, will soon be within the reach of every individual. Then, we trust, that we shall see a practical exemplification of the beauty and excellence of those celestial precepts and commandments which came from heaven, and which are equally applicable to all descriptions of men. They address themselves to the king upon the throne; they visit the obscurity of the humblest dwelling; they call upon the poor man to cultivate every good principle of action, as well as the man of a more elevated rank, and to aim at a life of purity, innocence, elevated virtue, and moral excellence, with the assurance that he too, shall reap his reward in that better scene of human destination, to which Christianity has called all those who fear God and work righteousness.

Wherever these lofty and commanding views of piety and virtue have been encouraged, a high sense of the social, moral, and practical obligations and duties of life, have been cherished and cultivated with an elevated and an invincible spirit.

Under the influence of this spirit, this benevolent spirit, practical Christians, of every denomination, have elevated their views far beyond the circumscribed boundaries of selfishness, sectarianism, and party zeal; and, being bound together by the indissoluble links of that golden chain of charity and kind affection, with which Christianity invariably connects its sincere votaries, and standing upon the common ground of Christian equality, they encircle the great community of those who profess the religion of our divine Master, in the arms of their charity and love, and become co-workers and fellow-labourers in the illumination, the improvement, and the ultimate felicity of those who will, undoubtedly, eventually belong to the commonwealth of the Israel of our God.

In such improved sections of the world, the gardens of the Academy are thronged with youth, whose ardour to reap its fairest flowers, would even vie with that evinced by the hazardous enterprize of the intrepid Jason of antiquity, when he cast the watchful Dragon, and seized that invaluable prize, the Golden Fleece.

We have reason to be grateful, my friends, that it has pleased God to permit us to witness a period when those unjust prejudices, and those hitherto insuperable barriers to the instruction, and, consequently, to the intellectual, the moral, and the religious improvement and elevation of the people of colour, under which our fathers groaned, are beginning to subside.

And now, in the true spirit of the religion of that beneficent Parent, who has made of one blood all nations of men who dwell upon the face of the whole earth, many persons of different regions and various nations, have been led to the contemplation of the interesting relations in which the human race stand to each other. They have seen that man, as a solitary individual, is a very wretched being. As long as he stands detached from his kind, he is possessed neither of happiness nor of strength. We are formed by nature to unite; we are impelled towards each other by the benevolent instincts in our frames; we are linked by a thousand connexions, founded on common wants.

Benevolent affection therefore, or, as it is very properly termed, humanity, is what man, as such in every station, owes to man. To be inaccessible, contemptuous, avaricious, and hard hearted, is to revolt against our very reason and nature; it is, according to the language of inspiration, to "hide ourselves from our own flesh."

The genuine kind affections, and the elevated sensibilities of Christianity, as they are exhibited to us in the conduct and character of our blessed Saviour, during his residence in this scene of our pilgrimage, are suited to call forth into vigorous exercise, the best sentiments, feelings and dispositions of the human heart; while they disclose to the admiring view of his obedient followers, those indissoluble and enobling moral ties, which connect earth with heaven, and which assimilate man to the benevolent Author of his being.

Wherever Christianity is considered as a religion of the affections, every well instructed, practical Christian, habitually aspires at an entire imitation of the example, and to yield a cheerful and unreserved obedience to the precepts and instructions of its heavenly founder. So peculiar is the adaptation of Christianity to become a universal religion; for wherever its spirit enters into the councils of nations, we find it unbinding the chains of corporeal and mental captivity, and diffusing over the whole world, the maxims of impartial justice, and of enlightened benevolence.

Such, and so sublimely excellent, are the fruits of a spirit of Christian charity and practical beneficence; for to it alone the glory is due, of having placed the weak under the protection of their stronger brethren; for she unceasingly labours to improve all the varying circumstances and conditions of mankind: so that, among those who profess her true spirit, the love of our neighbour is not an inactive principle, but it is real beneficence; and they, like the good Samaritan in the gospel, evince their sincerity by ministering to the necessities, and in labouring for the welfare, improvement and happiness of mankind.

Mess'rs Vice-Presidents, and Gentlemen of the Pennsylvania Augustine Education Society.

Although the seat of your respected President is vacant on this intersecting occasion, on account of the severe indisposition with which he is visited, still we trust that his heart is with you, and that you have his best wishes and his prayers, for the prosperity of this excellent establishment. The hope is encouraged, that you will never be weary in labouring for the promotion of the cause and interests of science and literature among the rising generation of the people of colour. For upon their intellectual, moral and religious improvements, depend the future elevation of their standing, in the social, civil and ecclesiastical community. Surely then, my friends, you are associated for the most laudable, interesting, and invaluable purposes.

Therefore, let it be the unceasing labour, the undeviating and the inflexibly firm purpose of the members of this Association, individually and collectively, to inspire all within the sphere of their influence, with a sense of the value and importance of giving their children a good education. Hear the words of revelation, calling upon you who profess to be Christians, to "train up your children in the way they should go," and to "bring them up in the nurture and admonition of the Lord." And if you believe this high authority, how can you be excused, if you neglect to give them the means of acquiring a knowledge of their duty to that divine instructor who came to call them to glory, to virtue, and to immortality.

Permit me to again entreat you, duly to appreciate the importance of religiously educating your children. For, a Christian education is not only of great utility while sojourning in this scene of discipline and probation, but it is more transcendently excellent in that more elevated scene of human destination to which we are hastening. For even the ruthless hand of death itself, cannot disrobe the soul of those virtuous principles, which are sometimes acquired through the medium of a virtuous education, and "which, when transplanted to the skies, in heaven's immortal garden bloom."

ROBERT ALEXANDER YOUNG

"Know, then, in your present state or standing, in your sphere of government in any nation within which you reside, we hold and contend you enjoy but a few of your rights of government within them."

Southern District of New-York, s s.

Be it remembered, that on the 18th day of February, A.D. 1829, in the 53d year of the Independence of the United States of America, Robert Alexander Young, of the said district, hath deposited in this office the title of a book the right whereof he claims as author, in the words following, to wit:

"The Ethiopian Manifesto, issued in defence of the Black Man's Rights, in the scale of Universal Freedom."

In conformity to the Act of Congress of the United States, entitled. "An Act for the Encouragement of Learning, by securing the copies of Maps, Charts, and Books, to the author and proprietors of such copies, during the time therein mentioned." And also to an Act, entitled "An Act supplementary to an act, entitled an act for the encouragement of learning, by securing the copies of Maps, Charts, and Books, to the authors and proprietors of such copies, during the times therein mentioned, and extending the benefits thereof to the arts of designing, engraving, and etching historical and other prints."

—FRED I. BETTS, *Clerk of the Southern District of New-York.*

Ethiopian Manifesto

By the Omnipotent will of God, we, Rednaxela, sage, and asserter to the Ethiopian of his rights, do hereby declare, and make known, as follows:—

Ethiopians! the power of Divinity having within us, as man, implanted a sense of the due and prerogatives belonging to you, a people, of whom we were of your race, in part born, as a mirror we trust, to reflect to you from a review of ourselves, the dread condition in which you do at this day stand. We do, therefore, to the accomplishment of our purpose, issue this but a brief of our grand manifesto, herefrom requiring the attention towards us of every native, or those proceeding in descent from the Ethiopian or African people; a regard to your welfare being the great and inspiring motive which leads us to this our undertaking. We do therefore strictly enjoin your attention to these the dictates from our sense of justice, held forth and produced to your notice, but with the most pure intention.

Ethiopians! open your minds to reason; let therein weigh the effects of truth, wisdom, and justice (and a regard to your individual as a general good), and the spirit of these our words we know full well, cannot but produce the effect for which they are by us herefrom

4

intended. Know, then, in your present state or standing, in your sphere of government in any nation within which you reside, we hold and contend you enjoy but a few of your rights of government within them. We here speak of the whole of the Ethiopian people, as we admit not even those in their state of native simplicity, to be in an enjoyment of their rights, as bestowed to them of the great bequest of God to man.

The impositions practised to their state, not being known to them from the heavy and darksome clouds of ignorance which so woefully obscures their reason, we do, therefore, for the recovering of them, as well as establishing to you your rights, proclaim, that duty—imperious duty, exacts the convocation of ourselves in a body politic; that we do, for the promotion and welfare of our order, establish to ourselves a people framed unto the likeness of that order, which from our mind's eye we do evidently discern governs the universal creation. Beholding but one sole power, supremacy, or head, we do of that head, but hope and look forward for succour in the accomplishment of the great design which he hath, in his wisdom, promoted us to its undertaking.

We find we possess in ourselves an understanding; of this we are taught to know the ends of right and wrong, that depression should come upon us or any of our race of the wrongs inflicted on us of men. We know in ourselves we possess a right to see ourselves justified therefrom, of the right of God; knowing, but of his power hath he decreed to man, that either in himself he stands, or by himself he falls. Fallen, sadly, sadly low indeed, hath become our race, when we behold it reduced but to an enslaved state, to raise it from its degenerate sphere, and instill into it the rights of men, are the ends intended of these our words; here we are met in ourselves, we constitute but one, aided as we trust, by the effulgent light of wisdom to a discernment of the path which shall lead us to the collecting together of a people, rendered disobedient to the great dictates of nature, by the barbarity that hath been practised upon them from generation to generation of the will of their more cruel fellow-men. Am I, because I am a descendant of a mixed race of men, whose shade hath stamped them with the hue of black, to deem myself less eligible to the attainment of the great gift allotted of God to man, than are any other of whatsoever cast you please, deemed from being white as being more exalted than the black?

These words, which carry to the view of others the dictates of my mind, I borrow not from the sense of white men or of black: learn, my brother and fellow-Ethiopian, it is but the invigorating power of Deity instills them to my discernment. Of him do I know I derive my right; of him was I on the conception of a mother's womb created free; who then in the shape of man shall dare to rob me of my birthright as bestowed to me in my existence from God? No, I am in myself a man, and as a man will live, or as a man will die; for as I was born free of the will allotted me of the freedom of God, so do I claim and purport to establish an alike universal freedom to every son and daughter descending from the black; though however mixed in grades of colour through an intercourse of white with black; still as I am in myself, but a mixture of like, I call to witness, if the power of my mind hath not a right to claim an allegiance with all descendants of a race, for the justification of whose rights reason hath established within me the ends for their obtainment? God, an almighty, sole, and governing God, can alone direct me to the ends I have, but of his will to fulfill, be they here to the view of the universal world from him established; for as I do in myself stand upright, and claim in myself, as outwardly from myself, all my rights and prerogatives as pertaining to me in my birthright of man, so do I equally claim to the untutored black of every denomination, be he in bondage or free, an alike right; and do hereby publicly protest against the infringement of his rights, as is at this day practised by the fiendish cast of men who dare, contrary to the knowledge of justice, as hath been implanted of God in the soul of man, to hold him in bondage, adducing from his servitude a gorgeous maintenance. Accursed and damned be he in mind, soul and body, who dare after this my protest, to claim the slightest alleged right to hold a man, as regards manly visage, shape, and bearing, equal in all points, though ignorant and untaught with himself, and in intrinsic worth to the view of Deity; by far in his sacred presence, must he appear the better man, the calm submission to his fate, pointing him to the view of justice at the throne of God, as being more worthy of the rights of man, than the wretch who would claim from him his rights as a man.

I pause. Custom here points to me her accursed practises, if founded in error, as base injustice; shall they stand? nay, aught they to be allowed or sanctioned, for so to do by the cognizance of the just, the wise, the great, the good, and sound men of discretion of this world? I speak for no man, understanding but in myself my rights, that from myself shall be made known to a people, rights, which I, of the divine will of God, to them establish. Man—white man—black man—or, more properly, ye monsters incarnate, in human shape, who claim the horrid right to hold nature's untutored son, the Ethiopian, in bondage, to you I do herefrom speak. Mark me, and regard well these my words; be assured, they convey the voice of reason, dictated to you through a prophetic sense of truth. The time is at hand when many signs shall appear to you, to denote that Almighty God regards the affairs of afflicted men:— for know, the cries of bitter servitude, from those unhappy sons of men, whom ye have so long unjustly oppressed with the goading shafts of an accursed slavery, hath descended to Deity. Your God, the great and mighty God, hath seen your degradation of your fellow brother, and mortal man; he hath long looked down with mercy on your suffering slave; his cries have called for a vindication of his rights, and know ye they have been heard of the Majesty of Heaven, whose dignity have you not offended by deeming a mortal man, in your own likeness, as but worthy of being your slave, degraded to your brute? The voice of intuitive justice speaks aloud to you, and bids you to release your slave; otherwise stings, eternal stings, of an outraged and goading conscience will, ere long, hold all them in subjection who pay not due attention to this, its admonition. Beware! know thyselves to be but mortal men, doomed to the good or evil, as your works shall merit from you. Pride ye not yourselves in the greatness of your worldly standing, since all things are but moth when contrasted with the invisible spirit, which in yourself maintains within you your course of action. That within you will, to the presence of your God, be at all times your sole accuser. Weigh well these my words in the balance of your conscientious reason, and abide the judgement thereof to your own standing, for we tell you of a surety, the decree hath already passed the judgement seat of an undeviating God, wherein he hath said, "surely hath the cries of the black, a most persecuted people, ascended to my throne and craved my mercy; now, behold! I will stretch forth mine hand and gather them to the palm, that they become unto me a people, and I unto them their God." Hearken, therefore, oh! slaveholder, thou task inflicter against the rights of men, the day is at hand, nay the hour draweth nigh, when poverty shall appear to thee a blessing, if it but restore to thy fellow-man his rights; all worldly riches shall be known to thee then but as a curse, and in thine heart's desire to obtain contentment, when sad reverses come upon thee, then shalt thou linger for a renewal of days, that in thine end thou might not curse the spirit which called thee forth to life. Take warning, again we say, for of a surety from this, God will give you signs to know, in his decrees he regards the fallen state of the sons of men. Think not that wisdom descries not from here your vanity. We behold it, thou vain bloated upstart worldling of a slaveholder, laugh in derision of thy earthly taught and worldly sneer; but know, on thee we pronounce our judgment, and as fitting thee, point out to thy notice this our sign. Of the degraded of this earth, shall be exalted, one who shall draw from thee, as though gifted of power divine, all attachment and regard of thy slave toward thee. Death shall he prefer to a continuance of his race:—being doomed to thy vile servitude, no cohabitation shall be known between the sexes, while suffering under thy slavery; but should ungovernable passion attain over the untaught mind an ascendancy, abortion shall destroy the birth. We command it, the voice of imperative justice, though however harsh, must be obeyed. Ah! doth your expanding judgement, base slaveholder, not from here descry that the shackles which have been by you so undeservingly forged upon a wretched Ethiopian's frame, are about to be forever from him unlinked. Say ye, this can never be accomplished? If so, must indeed the power and decrees of Infinity become subservient to the will of depraved man. But learn, slaveholder, thine will rests not in thine hand: God decrees to thy slave his rights as man. This we issue forth as the spirit of the black man or Ethiopian's rights, established from the Ethiopian's Rock, the foundation of his civil and religious rights, which hereafter will be exemplified in the order of its course. Ethiopians, throughout the world in general, receive this as but a lesson presented to you from an instructive Book, in which many, many therein are contained, to the vindication of its purpose. As came John the Baptist, of old, to spread abroad the forthcoming of his master, so alike are intended these our words, to denote to the black African or Ethiopian people, that God has prepared them for a leader, who awaits but for his season to proclaim to them his birthright. How shall you know this man? By indubitable signs which cannot be controverted by the power of mortal, his marks being stamped in open visage, as equally so upon his frame, which constitutes him to have been particularly regarded in the infinite work of God to man.

Know ye, then, if a white man ever appeared on earth, bearing in himself the semblance of his former race, the man we proclaim ordained of God, to call together the black people as a nation in themselves. We say, in him will be seen, in appearance a white man, although having been born of a black woman, his mother. The proof is strong, and in Granada's Island, Grand Anta Estate, there, some time ago, did dwell his mother—his father then owner of the said estate. The church books of St. Georgestown, the capital of Grenada, can truly prove his birth. As another instance wherein providence decreed he should appear peculiar in his make, the two middle toes on each of his feet were, in his conception, webbed and bearded. Now, after the custom of the ancient order of men, with long and flowing hair, by like appearances may he be known; none other man, but the one bearing alike marks, and proving his identity from the island on which he was born, can be the man of whom we speak. To him, thou poor black Ethiopian or African slave, do thou, from henceforth, place a firm reliance thereon, as trusting in him to prove thy liberator from the infernal state of bondage, under which you have been so long and so unjustly laboring. To thee he pledges himself, in life to death, not to desert thee, his trust being in the power of the Almighty, who giveth not the race to the swift nor the battle to the strong, but decrees to all men the justice he establishes. As such, we draw from him the conception of your rights, and to its obtainment we issue this to you, our first pledge of faith, binding ourselves herefrom to render to you, at all times, such services as shall tend most to your advantage in effecting a speedy deliverance from your mortal and most deadly foe, the monster of a slaveholder. We would most particularly direct you to such government of yourselves as should be responsible but to God, your maker, for the duty exacted of you to your fellow-men; but, under goading situations, where power and might is but the construction of law, it then behooves the depressed and vilely injured to bear his burthen with the firmness of his manhood:—So at this time, we particularly recommend to you, degraded sons of Africa, to submit with fortitude to your present state of suffering, relying in yourselves, from the justice of a God, that the time is at hand, when, with but the power of words and the divine will of our God, the vile shackles of slavery shall be broken asunder from you, and no man known who shall dare to own or proclaim you as his bondsman. We say it, and assert it as though by an oracle given and delivered to you on high. God, in his holy keeping, direct thee, thou poor untaught and degraded African slave, to a full conception of these the words we have written for your express benefit. Our care and regard of you will be that of a fostering parent toward a beloved offspring. The hatred of your oppressor we fear not, nor do we his power, or any vile machinations that may be resorted to by incendiaries towards us. We hold ourself, with the aid of our God therewith, at all times ready to encounter, trusting but in God, our Creator, and not in ourselves, for a deliverance from all worldly evil.

Peace and Liberty to the Ethiopian first, as also all other grades of men, is the invocation we offer to the throne of our God.

REDNAXELA

DATED FROM THE
ETHIOPIAN'S ROCK,
IN THE
THIRTY-SEVENTH YEAR
FROM ITS
FOUNDATION,
THIS THIRTEENTH DAY OF FEBRUARY, A.D.
1829

3. Appeal to the Colored Citizens of the World (1829, 1830)

DAVID WALKER

"When God Almighty commences his battle on the continent of America, for the oppression of his people, tyrants will wish they were never born."

[Note: The following selection comes from section four of Walker's lengthy "Appeal," "Our Wretchedness In Consequence of the Colonizing Plan."]

Our Wretchedness in Consequence of the Colonizing Plan

My dearly beloved brethren:—This is a scheme on which so many able writers, together with that very judicious coloured Baltimorean, have commented, that I feel my delicacy about touching it. But as I am compelled to do the will of my Master, I declare, I will give you my sentiments upon it.—Previous, how-ever, to giving my sentiments, either for or against it, I shall give that of Mr. Henry Clay, together with that of Mr. Elias B. Caldwell, Esq. of the District of Columbia, as extracted from the National Intelligence, by Dr. Torrey, author of a series of "Essays on Morals, and the Diffusion of Useful Knowledge."

At a meeting which was convened in the District of Columbia, for the express purpose of agitating the subject of colonizing us in some part of the world, Mr. Clay was called to the chair, and having been seated a little while, he rose and spoke, in substance, as follows: says he—"That class of the mixt population of our country [coloured people] was peculiarly situated; they neither enjoyed the immunities of freemen, nor were they subjected to the incapacity of slaves, but partook, in some degree, of the qualities of both. From their condition, and the unconquerable prejudices resulting from their colour, they never could amalgamate with the free whites of this country. It was desirable, therefore, as it respected them, and the residue of the population of the country, to drain them off. Various schemes of colonization had been thought of, and a part of our continent, it was supposed by some, might furnish a suitable establishment for them. But, for his part, Mr. C. said, he had a decided preference for some part of the Coast of Africa. There ample provision might be made for the colony itself, and it might be rendered instrumental to the introduction into that extensive quarter of the globe, of the arts, civilization, and Christianity." [Here I ask Mr. Clay, what kind of Christianity? Did he mean such as they have among the Americans—distinction, whip, blood and oppression? I pray the Lord Jesus Christ to forbid it.] "There," said he, "was a peculiar, a moral fitness, in restoring them to the land of their fathers, and if instead of the evils and sufferings which we had been the innocent cause of inflicting upon the inhabitants of Africa, we can transmit to her the blessings of our arts, our civilization, and our religion. May we not hope that America will extinguish a great portion of that moral debt which she has contracted to that unfortunate continent? Can there be a nobler cause than that which, whilst it proposes," &c. * * * * * * * [you know what this means.] "contemplates the spreading of the arts of civilized life, and the possible redemption from ignorance and barbarism of a benighted quarter of the globe?"

Before I proceed any further, I solicit your notice, brethren, to the foregoing part of Mr. Clay's speech, in which he says, (➔ look above) "and if, instead of the evils and sufferings, which we had been the innocent cause of inflicting," &c.—What this very learned statesman could have been thinking about, when he said in his speech, "we had been the innocent cause of inflicting," &c., I have never been able to conceive. Are Mr. Clay and the rest of the Americans, innocent of the blood and groans of our fathers and us, their children?—Every individual may plead innocence, if he pleases, but God will, before long, separate the innocent from the guilty, unless something is speedily done which I suppose will hardly be, so that their destruction may be sure. Oh Americans! let me tell you, in the name of the Lord, it will be good for you, if you listen to the voice of the Holy Ghost, but if you do not, you are ruined! ! ! Some of you are good men; but the will of my God must be done. Those avaricious and ungodly tyrants among you, I am awfully afraid will drag down the vengeance of God upon you. When God Almighty commences his battle on the continent of America, for the oppression of his people, tyrants will wish they never were born.

But to return to Mr. Clay, whence I digressed. He says, "It was proper and necessary distinctly to state, that he understood it constituted no part of the object of this meeting, to touch or agitate in the slightest degree, a delicate question, connected with another portion of the coloured population of our country. It was not proposed to deliberate upon or consider at all, any question of emancipation, or that which was connected with the abolition of slavery. It was upon that condition alone, he was sure, that many gentlemen from the South and the West, whom he saw present, had attended, or could be expected to co-operate. It was upon that condition only, that he himself had attended."

That is to say, to fix a plan to get those of the coloured people, who are said to be free, away from among those of our brethren whom they unjustly hold in bondage, so that they may be enabled to keep them the more secure in ignorance and wretchedness, to support them and their children, and consequently they would have the more obedient slaves. For if the free are allowed to stay among the slaves, they will have intercourse together, and, of course, the free will learn the slaves *bad habits*, by teaching them that they are MEN, as well as other people, and certainly *ought* and *must* be FREE.

I presume, that every intelligent man of colour must have some idea of Mr. Henry Clay, originally of Virginia, but now of Kentucky; they know too, perhaps, whether he is a friend, or a foe to the coloured citizens of this country, and of the world. This gentleman, according to his own words, had been highly favoured and blessed of the Lord, though he did not acknowledge it; but, to the contrary, he acknowledged men, for all the blessings with which God had favoured him. At a public dinner, given him at Fowler's Garden, Lexington, Kentucky, he delivered a public speech to a very large concourse of people—in the concluding clause of which, he says, "And now, my friends and fellow citizens, I cannot part from you,

---

* See Dr. Torrey's Portraiture of Domestic Slavery in the United States, pages 85, 86.

on possibly the last occasion of my ever publicly addressing you, without reiterating the expression of my thanks, from a heart overflowing with gratitude. I came among you, now more than thirty years ago, an orphan boy, pennyless, a stranger to you all, without friends, without the favour of the great, you took me up, cherished me, protected me, honoured me, you have constantly poured upon me a bold and unabated stream of innumerable favours, time which wears out every thing has increased and strengthened your affection for me. When I seemed deserted by almost the whole world, and assailed by almost every tongue, and pen, and press, you have fearlessly and manfully stood by me, with unsurpassed zeal and undiminished friendship. When I felt as if I should sink beneath the storm of abuse and detraction, which was violently raging around me, I have found myself upheld and sustained by your encouraging voices and approving smiles. I have doubtless, committed many faults and indiscretions, over which you have thrown the broad mantle of your charity. But I can say, and in the presence of God and in this assembled multitude, I will say, that I have honestly and faithfully served my country—that I have never wronged it—and that, however unprepared, I lament that I am to appear in the Divine presence on other accounts, I invoke the stern justice of his judgment on my public conduct, without the slightest apprehension of his displeasure."

Hearken to this Statesman indeed, but no philanthropist, whom God sent into Kentucky, an orphan boy, penniless, and friendless, where he not only gave him a plenty of friends and the comforts of life, but raised him almost to the very highest honour in the nation, where his great talents, with which the Lord has been pleased to bless him, has gained for him the affection of a great portion of the people with whom he had to do. But what has this gentleman done for the Lord, after having done so much for him? The Lord has a suffering people, whose moans and groans at his feet for deliverance from oppression and wretchedness, pierce the very throne of Heaven, and call loudly on the God of Justice, to be revenged. Now, what this gentleman who is so highly favoured of the Lord, has done to liberate those miserable victims of oppression, shall appear before the world by his letters to Mr. Gallatin, Envoy Extraordinary and Minister Plenipotentiary to Great Britain, dated June 19, 1826.— Though Mr. Clay was writing for the States, yet nevertheless, it appears from the very face of his letters to that gentleman, that he was as anxious, if not more so, to get those free people and sink them into wretchedness, as his constituents, for whom he wrote.

The Americans of North and of South America including the West India Islands—no trifling portion of whom were, for stealing, murdering, &c. compelled to flee from Europe, to save their necks or banishment, have effected their escape to this continent, where God blessed them with all the comforts of life—He gave them a plenty of every thing calculated to do them good—not satisfied with this, however, they wanted slaves and wanted us for their slaves, who belong to the Holy Ghost, and no other, who we shall have to serve instead of tyrants.—I say, the Americans want us, the property of the Holy Ghost to serve them. But there is a day fast approaching, when (unless there is a universal repentance on the part of the whites, which will scarcely take place, they have got to be so hardened in consequence of our blood, and so wise in their own conceit.) To be plain and candid with you, Americans! I say that the day is fast approaching, when there will be a greater time on the continent of America, than ever was witnessed upon this earth since it came from the hand of its Creator. Some of you have done us so much injury, that you will never be able to repent.—Your cup must be filled.—You want us for your slaves, and shall have enough of us—God is just, *who will give you your fill of us*. But Mr. Henry Clay, speaking to Mr. Gallatin, respecting coloured people, who had effected their escape from the U. States (or to them *hell upon earth! ! !*) to the hospitable shores of Canada,* from whence it would cause more than the lives of the Americans to get them, to plunge into wretchedness—he says: "The General Assembly of Kentucky, one of the states which is most affected by the escape of slaves into Upper Canada has again, at their session which has just terminated, invoked the interposition of the General Government. In the treaty which has been recently concluded with the United Mexican States, and which is now under the consideration of the Senate, provision is made for the restoration of fugitive slaves. As it appears from your statements of what passed on that subject, with the British Plenipotentiaries, that they admitted the correctness of the principle of restoration, it is hoped that you will be able to succeed in making satisfactory arrangements."

There are a series of these letters, all of which are to the same amount; some however, presenting a face more of his own responsibility. I wonder what would this gentleman think, if the Lord should give him among the rest of his blessings enough of slaves? Could he blame any other being but himself? Do we not belong to the Holy Ghost? What business has he or any body else, to be sending letters about the world respecting us? Can we not go where we want to, as well as other people, only if we obey the voice of the Holy Ghost? This gentleman, (Mr. Henry Clay) not only took an active part in this colonizing plan, but was absolutely chairman of a meeting held at Washington, the twenty-first day of December 1816, to agitate the subject of colonizing us in Africa.—Now I appeal and ask every citizen of these United States and of the world, both *white* and *black*, who has any knowledge of Mr. Clay's public labor for these States—I want you candidly to answer the Lord, who sees the secrets of our hearts.—Do you believe that Mr. Henry Clay, late Secretary of State, and now in Kentucky, is a friend to the blacks, further, than his personal interest extends? Is it not his greatest object and glory upon earth, to sink us into miseries and wretchedness by making slaves of us, to work his plantation to enrich him and his family? Does he care a pinch of snuff about Africa—whether it remains a land of Pagans and of blood, or of Christians, so long as he gets enough of her sons and daughters to dig up gold and silver for him? If he had no slaves, and could obtain them in no other way if it were not, repugnant to the laws of his country, which prohibit the importation of slaves (which act was, indeed, more through apprehension than humanity) would he not try to import a few from Africa, to work his farm? Would he work in the hot sun to earn his bread, if he could make an African work for nothing, particularly, if he could keep him in ignorance and make him believe that God made him for nothing else but to work for him? Is not Mr. Clay a white man, and too delicate to work in the hot sun! ! Was he not made by his Creator to sit in the shade, and make the blacks work without remuneration for their services, to support him and his family! ! ! I have been for some time taking notice of this man's speeches and public writings, but never to my knowledge have I seen any thing in his writings which insisted on the emancipation of slavery, which has almost ruined his country. Thus we see the depravity of men's hearts, when in pursuit only of gain—particularly when they oppress their fellow creatures to obtain that gain—God suffers some to go on until they are lost forever. This same Mr. Clay, wants to know, what he has done, to merit die disapprobation of the American people. In a public speech delivered by him, he asked: "Did I involve my country in an unnecessary war?" to merit the censure of the Americans—"Did I bring obliquy upon the nation, or the people

---

* Among the English, our real friends and benefactors.

whom I represented? —did I ever lose any opportunity to advance the fame, honor and prosperity of this State and the Union?" How astonishing it is, for a man who knows so much about God and his ways, as Mr. Clay, to ask such frivolous questions? Does he believe that a man of his talents and standing in the midst of a people, will get along unnoticed by the penetrating and all seeing eye of God, who is continually taking cognizance of the hearts of men? Is not God against him, for advocating the murderous cause of slavery? If God is against him, what can the Americans, together with the whole world do for him? Can they save him from the hand of the Lord Jesus Christ?

I shall now pass in review the speech of Mr. Elias B. Caldwell Esq. of the District of Columbia, extracted from the same page on which Mr. Clay's will be found. Mr. Caldwell, giving his opinion respecting us, at that ever memorable meeting, he says: "The more you improve the condition of these people, the more you cultivate their minds, the more miserable you make them in their present state. You give them a higher relish for those privileges which they can never attain, and turn what we intend for a blessing into a curse." Let me ask this benevolent man, what he means by a blessing intended for us? Did he mean sinking us and our children into ignorance and wretchedness, to support him and his family? What he meant will appear evident and obvious to the most ignorant in the world (See Mr. Caldwell's intended blessings for us, O! my Lord! ! "No," said he, "if they must remain in their present situation, keep them in the *lowest state of degradation and ignorance*. The nearer you bring them to the condition of brutes, the better chance do you give them of possessing their *apathy*." Here I pause to get breath, having labored to extract the above clause of this gentleman's speech, at that colonizing meeting. I presume that everybody knows the meaning of the word "*apathy*," —if any do not, let him get Sheridan's Dictionary, in which he will find it explained in full. I solicit the attention of the world, to the foregoing part of Mr. Caldwell's speech, that they may see what man will do with his fellow men, when he has them under his feet. To what length will not man go in iniquity when given up to a hard heart, and reprobate mind, in consequence of blood and oppression? The last clause of this speech, which was written in a very artful manner, and which will be taken for the speech of a friend, without close examination and deep penetration, I shall now present. He says, "surely, Americans ought to be the last people on earth, to advocate such slavish doctrines, to cry peace and contentment to those who are deprived of the privileges of civil liberty, they who have so largely partaken of its blessings, who know so well how to estimate its value, ought to be among the foremost to extend it to others." The real sense and meaning of the last part of Mr. Caldwell's speech is, get the free people of colour away to Africa, from among the slaves, where they may at once be blessed and happy, and those who we hold in slavery, will be contented to rest in ignorance and wretchedness, to dig up gold and silver for us and our children. Men have indeed got to be so cunning, these days, that it would take the eye of a Solomon to penetrate and find them out.

→ ADDITION.—OUR dear Redeemer said, "Therefore, whatsoever ye have spoken in darkness, shall be heard in the light; and that which ye have spoken in the ear in closets, shall be pro-claimed upon the house tops."

How obviously this declaration of our Lord has been shown among the Americans of the United States. They have hitherto passed among some nations, who do not know any thing about their internal concerns, for the most enlightened, humane charitable, and merciful people upon earth, when at the same time they treat us, the (coloured people) secretly more cruel and unmerciful than any other nation upon earth.—It is a fact that in our Southern and

Western States, there are millions who hold us in chains or in slavery, whose greatest object and glory, is centered in keeping us sunk in the most profound ignorance and stupidity, to make us work without remunerations for our services. Many of whom if they catch a coloured person, whom they hold in unjust ignorance, slavery and degradation, to them and their children, with a book in his hand, will beat him nearly to death. I heard a wretch in the state of North Carolina said that if any man would teach a black person whom he held in slavery, to spell, read or write, he would prosecute him to the very extent of the law.—Said the ignorant wretch,* "a Nigar, ought not to have any more sense than enough to work for his master." May I not ask to fatten the wretch and his family?—These and similar cruelties these *Christians* have been for hundreds of years inflicting on our fathers and us in the dark God has however, very recently published some of their secret crimes on the house top, that the world may gaze on their Christianity and see of what kind it is composed.—Georgia for instance, God has completely shown to the world, the *Christianity* among its white *inhabitants.* A law has recently passed the Legislature of this *republican* State (Georgia) prohibiting all free or slave persons of colour, from learning to read or write; another law has passed the *republican* House of Delegates, (but not the Senate) in Virginia, to prohibit all persons of colour, (free and slave) from learning to read or write, and even to hinder them from meeting together in order to worship our Maker! ! ! ! !—Now I solemnly appeal, to the most skilful historians in the world, and all those who are mostly acquainted with the histories of the Antideluvians and of Sodom and Gomorrah, to show me a parallel of barbarity. *Christians! ! Christians! ! !* I dare you to show me a parallel of cruelties in the annals of Heathens or of Devils, with those of Ohio, Virginia and of Georgia—know the world that these things were before done in the dark, or in a corner under a garb of humanity and religion. God has however, taken of the figleaf covering, and made them expose them-selves on the house top. I tell you that God works in many ways his wonders to perform, he will unless they repent, make them expose themselves enough more yet to the world.—See the acts of the *Christians* in FLORIDA, SOUTH CAROLINA, and KENTUCKY—was it not for the reputation of the house of my Lord and Master, I would mention here, an act of cruelty inflicted a few days since on a black man, by the white *Christians* in the PARK STREET CHURCH, in this (CITY) which is almost enough to make Demons themselves quake and tremble in their FIREY HABITATIONS.—Oh! my Lord how refined in iniquity the whites have got to be in consequence of our blood**—what kind! ! Oh! what kind! ! ! of Christianity can be found this day in all the earth! ! ! ! !

I write without the fear of man, I am writing for my God, and fear none but himself; they may put me to death if they choose—(I fear and esteem a good man however, let him

---

* It is a fact, that in all our Slave-holding States (in the countries) there are thousands of the whites, who are almost as ignorant in comparison as horses, the most they know, is to beat the coloured people, which some of them shall have their hearts full of yet.

** "Niger," is a word derived from the Latin, which was used by the old Romans, to designate inanimate beings, which were black: such as soot pot wood, house, &c. Also, animals which they considered inferior to the human species, as a black horse, cow, hog, bird, dog, &c. The white Americans have applied this term to Africans, by way of reproach for our colour, to aggravate and heighten our miseries, because they have their feet on our throats, prejudice—what have we to do with it? Their prejudices will be obliged to fall like lightning to the ground, in succeeding generations; not, however, with the will and consent of all the whites, for some will be obliged to hold on to the old adage, viz: the blacks are not men, but were made to be an inheritance to us and our children for ever! ! ! ! ! ! I hope the residue of the coloured people, will stand still and see the salvation of God and the miracle which he will work for our delivery from wretchedness under the Christians! ! ! ! !

be black or white.) I forbear to comment on the cruelties inflicted on this Black Man by the Whites, in the Park Street MEETING HOUSE, I will leave it in the dark! ! ! ! ! But I declare that the atrocity is really to Heaven daring and infernal, that I must say that God has commenced a course of exposition among the Americans, and the glorious and heavenly work will continue to progress until they learn to do justice.←

Extract from the Speech of Mr. John Randolph, of Roanoke.

Said he:—"It had been properly observed by the Chairman, as well as by the gentleman from this District (meaning Messrs. Clay and Caldwell) that there was nothing in the proposition submitted to consideration which in the smallest degree touches* The Blood of our fathers who have been murdered by the whites, and the groans of our Brethren, who are now held in cruel ignorance, wretchedness and slavery by them, cry aloud to the Maker of Heaven and of earth, against the whole continent of America, for redresses. Another very important and delicate question, which ought to be left as much out of view as possible, is Negro Slavery. "There is no fear," Mr. R. said, "that this proposition would alarm the slave-holders; they had been accustomed to think seriously of the subject.—There was a popular work on agriculture by John Taylor of Caroline, which was widely circulated, and much confided in, in Virginia. In that book, much read because coming from a practical man, this description of people, [referring to us half free ones] were pointed out as a great evil. They had indeed been held up as the greater bug-bear to every man who feels an inclination to emancipate his slaves, not to create in the bosom of his country so great a nuisance. If a place could be provided for their reception, and a mode of sending them hence, there were hundreds, nay thousands of citizens who would, by manumitting their slaves, relieve themselves from the cares attendant on their possession. The great slaveholder," Mr. R. said, "was frequently a mere sentry at his own door-bound to stay on his plantation to see that his slaves were properly treated, &c." Mr. R. concluded by saying, that he had thought it necessary to make these remarks being a slave-holder himself, to shew that, "so far from being connected with abolition of slavery, the measure proposed would prove one of the greatest securities to enable the master to keep in possession his own property."

Here is a demonstrative proof, of a plan got up, by a gang of slave-holders to select the free people of colour from among the slaves, that our more miserable brethren may be the better secured in ignorance and wretchedness, to work their farms and dig their mines, and thus go on enriching the Christians with their blood and groans. What our brethren could have been thinking about, who have left their native land and home and gone away to Africa, I am unable to say. This country is as much ours as it is the whites, whether they will admit it now or not, they will see and believe it by and by. . . .

→ ADDITION.—If any of us see fit to go away, go to those who have been for many years, and are now our greatest earthly friends and benefactors—the English. If not so, go to our brethren, the Haytians, who, according to their word, are bound to protect and comfort us. The Americans say, that we are ungrateful—but I ask them for heaven's sake, what should we be grateful to them for—for murdering our fathers and mothers?—Or do they wish us to return thanks to them for chaining and hand-cuffing us, branding us, cramming fire down our throats, or for keeping us in slavery, and beating us nearly or quite to death to make us work in ignorance and miseries, to support them and their families. They certainly think that we are a gang of fools. Those among them, who have volunteered their services for our redemption, though we are unable to compensate them for their labours, we nevertheless thank them from the bottom of our hearts, and have our eyes steadfastly fixed upon them, and their labours of love for God and man.—But do slave-holders think that we thank them for keeping us in miseries, and taking our lives by the inches?

Before I proceed further with this scheme, I shall give an extract from the letter of that truly Reverend Divine, (Bishop Allen,) of Philadelphia, respecting this trick. At the instance of the editor of the Freedom's Journal, he says, "Dear Sir, I have been for several years trying to reconcile my mind to the Colonizing of Africans in Liberia, but there have always been, and there still remain great and insurmountable objections against the scheme. We are an unlettered people, brought up in ignorance, not one in a hundred can read or write, not one in a thousand has a liberal education; is there any fitness for such to be sent into a far country, among heathens, to convert or civilize them when they themselves are neither civilized or Christianized? Se: the great bulk of the poor, ignorant Africans in this country, exposed to every temptation before them: all for the want of their morals being refined by education and proper attendance paid unto them by their owners, or those who had the charge of them. It is said by the Southern slave-holders, that the more ignorant they can bring up the Africans, the better slaves they make, ('go and come.') Is there any fitness for such people to be colonized in a far country to be their own rulers? Can we not discern the project of sending the free people of colour away from their country? Is it not for the interest of the slave-holders to select the free people of colour out of the different states, and send them to Liberia? Will it not make their slaves uneasy to see free men of colour enjoying liberty? It is against the law in some of the Southern States, that a person of colour should receive an education, under a severe penalty. Colonizationists speak of America being first colonized; but is there any comparison between the two? America was colonized by as *wise, judicious and educated* men as the world afforded. WILLIAM PENN did not want for *learning, wisdom, or intelligence.* If all the people in Europe and America were as ignorant and in the same situation as our brethren, what would become of the world? Where would be the principle or piety that would govern the people? We were stolen from our mother country, and brought *here.* We have *tilled* the ground and made fortunes for thousands, and still they are not weary of our services. *But they who stay to till the ground must be slaves.* Is there not land enough in America, or 'corn enough in Egypt?' Why should they send us into a far country to die? See the thousands of foreigners emigrating to America every year: and if there be ground sufficient for them to cultivate, and bread for them to eat, why would they wish to send the *first tillers* of the land away? Africans have made fortunes for thousands, who are yet unwilling to part with their services; but the free must be sent away, and those who remain, must be *slaves.* I have no doubt that there are many good men who do not see as I do, and who are for sending us to Liberia; but they have not duly considered the subject—they are not men of colour.—This land which we have watered with our *tears* and *our blood,* is now our *mother country,* and we are well satisfied to stay where wisdom abounds and the gospel is free."

—"RICHARD ALLEN, *"Bishop of the African Methodist Episcopal "Church in the United States."*

I have given you, my brethren, an extract verbatim, from the letter of that godly man, as you may find it on the aforementioned page of Freedom's Journal. I know that thousands, and perhaps millions of my brethren in these States, have never heard of such a man as Bishop Allen—a man whom God many years ago raised up among his ignorant and degraded brethren, to preach Jesus Christ and him crucified to them—who notwithstanding, had to wrestle against principalities and the powers of darkness to diffuse that gospel with which he was endowed among his brethren—but who having overcome the combined powers of devils and wicked men, has under God planted a Church among us which will be as durable as the foundation of the earth on which it stands. Richard Allen! O my God! The bare recollection of the labours of this man, and his ministers among his deplorably wretched brethren, (rendered so by the whites) to bring them to a knowledge of the God of Heaven, fills my soul with all those very high emotions which would take the pen of an Addison to portray. It is impossible my brethren for me to say much in this work respecting that man of God. When the Lord shall raise up coloured historians in succeeding generations, to present the crimes of this nation, to the then gazing world, the Holy Ghost will make them do justice to the name of Bishop Allen, of Philadelphia. Suffice it for me to say, that, the name of this very man (Richard Allen) though now in obscurity and degradation, will notwithstanding, stand on the pages of history among the greatest divines who have lived since the apostolic age, and among the Africans, Bishop Allen's will be entirely preeminent. My brethren, search after the character and exploits of this godly man among his ignorant and miserable brethren to bring them to a knowledge of the truth as it is in our Master. Consider upon the tyrants and false Christians against whom he had to contend in order to get access to his brethren. See him and his ministers in the States of New York, New Jersey, Pennsylvania, Delaware and Maryland, carrying the gladsome tidings of free and full salvation to the coloured people. Tyrants and false Christians however, would not allow him to penetrate far into the South, for fear that he would awaken some of his ignorant brethren, whom they held in wretchedness and misery—for fear, I say it, that he would awaken and bring them to a knowledge of their Maker. O my Master! my Master! I can-not but think upon Christian Americans! ! !—What kind of people can they be? Will not those who were burnt up in Sodom and Gomorrah rise up in judgment against Christian Americans with the Bible in their hands, and condemn them? Will not the Scribes and Pharisees of Jerusalem, who had nothing but the laws of Moses and the Prophets to go by, rise up in judgment against Christian Americans, and condemn them,* who, in addition to these have a revelation from Jesus Christ the Son of the living God? In fine, will not the Antideluvians, together with the whole heathen world of antiquity, rise up in judgment against Christian Americans and condemn them? The Christians of Europe and America go to Africa, bring us away, and throw us into the seas, and in other ways murder us, as they would wild beast. The Antideluvians and heathens never dreamed of such barbarities.— Now the Christians believe, because they have a name to live, while they are dead, that God will overlook such things. But if he does not deceive them, it will be because he has over-looked it sure enough. But to return to this godly man, Bishop Allen. I do hereby openly affirm it to the world, that he has done more in a spiritual sense for his ignorant and wretched brethren than any other man of colour has, since the world began. And as for the greater part of the whites, it has hitherto been their greatest object and glory to keep us ignorant of our Maker, so as to make us believe that we were made to be slaves to them and their children, to dig up gold and silver for them.

It is notorious that not a few professing Christians among the whites, who profess to love our Lord and Saviour Jesus Christ, have assailed this man and laid all the obstacles in his way

---

* I mean those whose labours for the good, or rather destruction of Jerusalem and the Jews ceased before our Lord entered the Temple, and overturned the tables of the Money Changers.

they possibly could, consistent with their profession—and what for? Why, their course of proceeding and his, clashed exactly together—they trying their best to keep us ignorant, that we might be the better and more obedient slaves—while he, on the other hand, doing his very best to enlighten us and teach, us a knowledge of the Lord. And I am sorry that I have it to say, that many of our brethren have joined in with our oppressors, whose dearest objects are only to keep us ignorant and miserable against this man to stay his hand.—However, they have kept us in so much ignorance, that many of us know no better than to fight against ourselves, and by that means strengthen the hands of our natural enemies, to rivet their infernal chains of slavery upon us and our children. I have several times called the white Americans our *natural enemies*—I shall here define my meaning of the phrase. Shem, Ham and Japheth, together with their father Noah and wives, I believe were not natural enemies to each other. When the ark rested after the flood upon Mount Arrarat, in Asia, they (eight) were all the people which could be found alive in all the earth—in fact if Scriptures be true, (which I believe are) there were no other living men in all the earth, notwithstanding some ignorant creatures hesitate not to tell us that we, (the blacks) are the seed of Cain the murderer of his brother Abel. But where or of whom those ignorant and avaricious wretches could have got their information, I am unable to declare. Did they receive it from the Bible? I have searched the Bible as well as they, if I am not as well learned as they are, and have never seen a verse which testifies whether we are the seed of Cain or of Abel. Yet those men tell us that we are the seed of Cain, and that God put a dark stain upon us, that we might be known as their slaves! ! ! Now, I ask those avaricious and ignorant wretches, who act more like the seed of Cain, by murdering the whites or the blacks? How many vessel loads of human beings have the blacks thrown into the seas? How many thousand souls have the blacks murdered in cold blood, to make them work in wretchedness and ignorance, to support them and their families?* —However, let us be the seed of *Cain, Harry, Dick, or Tom*! ! ! God will show the whites what we are, yet. I say, from the beginning, I do not think that we were natural enemies to each other. But the whites having made us so wretched, by subjecting us to slavery, and having murdered so many millions of us, in order to make us work for them, and out of devilishness—and they taking our wives, whom we love as we do ourselves—our mothers who bore the pains of death to give us birth—our fathers and dear little children, and ourselves, and strip and beat us one before the other—chain, hand-cuff, and drag us about like rattle-snakes—shoot us down like wild bears, before each other's faces to make us submissive to, and work to support them and their families. They (the whites) know well, if we are *men*—and there is a secret monitor in their hearts which tells them we are—they know, I say, if we *are* men, and see them treating us in the manner they do, that there can be nothing in our hearts but death alone, for them, notwithstanding we may appear cheerful, when we see them murdering our dear mothers and wives because we cannot help ourselves. Man, in all ages and all nations of the earth, is the same. Man is a peculiar creature—he is the image of his God, though he may be subjected to the most wretched condition upon earth, yet the spirit and feeling which constitute the creature, man, can never be entirely erased from his breast, because the God who made him after his own image planted it in his heart; he cannot get rid of it.

---

* How many millions souls of the human family have the blacks beat nearly to death to keep them from learning to read the Word of God and from writing. And telling lies about them, by holding them up to the world as a tribe of TALKING APES, void of INTELLECT! ! ! ! ! incapable of LEARNING, &c.

The whites knowing this, they do not know what to do; they know that they have done us so much injury, they are afraid that we, being men and not brutes, will retaliate, and woe will be to them; therefore, that dreadful fear, together with an avaricious spirit, and the natural love in them, to be called masters, (which term will yet honour them with to their sorrow) bring them to the resolve that they will keep us in ignorance and wretchedness, as long as they possibly can,* and make the best of their time, while it lasts.

Consequently they, themselves, (and not us) render them-selves our natural enemies, by treating us so cruel. They keep us miserable now, and call us their property, but some of them will have enough of us by and by—their stomachs shall run over with us; they want us for their slaves, and shall have us to their fill. We are all in the world together!! —I said above, because we cannot help ourselves, (viz. we cannot help the whites murdering our mothers and our wives) but this statement is incorrect—for we can help ourselves; for, if we lay aside abject servility, and be determined to act like men, and not brutes—the murderers among the whites would be afraid to show their cruel heads. But O, my God! —in sorrow I must say it, that my colour, all over the world, have a mean, servile spirit. They yield in a moment to the whites, let them be right or wrong—the reason they are able to keep their feet on our throats. Oh! my coloured brethren, all over the world, when shall we arise from this death-like apathy?—And be men! ! You will notice, if ever we become men, (I mean *respectable* men, such as other people are,) we must exert ourselves to the full. For remember, that it is the greatest desire and object of the greater part of the whites, to keep us ignorant, and make us work to support them and their families.—Here now, in the Southern and Western sections of this country, there are at least three coloured persons for one white, why is it, that those few weak, good-for-nothing whites, are able to keep so many able men, one of whom, can put to flight a dozen whites, in wretchedness and misery? It shows at once, what the blacks are, we are ignorant, abject, servile and mean—and the whites know it—they know that we are too servile to assert our rights as men—or they would not fool with us as they do. Would they fool with any other peoples as they do with us? No, they know too well, that they would get themselves ruined. Why do they not bring the inhabitants of Asia to be body servants to them? They know they would get their bodies rent and torn from head to foot. Why do they not get the Aborigines of this country to be slaves to them and their children, to work their farms and dig their mines? They know well that the Aborigines of this country, or (Indians) would tear them from the earth. The Indians would not rest day or night, they would be up all times of night, cutting their cruel throats. But my colour, (some, not all,) are willing to stand still and be murdered by the cruel whites. In some of the West-Indies Islands,

---

* And still holds us up with indignity as being incapable of acquiring knowledge! ! See the inconsistency of the assertions of those wretches—they beat us inhumanely, sometimes almost to death for attempting to inform ourselves, by reading the Word of our Maker, and at the same time tell us, that we are beings void of intellect! How admirably their practices agree with their professions in this case. Let me cry shame upon you Americans, for such out-rages upon human nature! ! ! If it were possible for the whites always to keep us ignorant and miserable, and make us work to enrich them and their children, and insult our feelings by representing us as talking Apes, what would they do? But glory, honour and praise to Heaven's King, that the sons and daughters of Africa, will, in spite of all the opposition of their enemies, stand forth in all the dignity and glory that is granted by the Lord to his creature man.

and over a large part of South America, there are six or eight coloured persons for one white.*

Why do they not take possession of those places? Who hinders them? It is not the avaricious whites—for they are too busily engaged in laying up money—derived from the blood and tears of the blacks. The fact is, they are too servile, they love to have Masters too well! ! Some of our brethren, too, who seeking more after self aggrandizement, than the glory of God, and the welfare of their brethren, join in with our oppressors, to ridicule and say all manner of evils falsely against our Bishop. They think, that they are doing great things, when they can get in company with the whites, to ridicule and make sport of those who are labouring for their good. Poor ignorant creatures, they do not know that the sole aim and object of the whites, are only to make fools and slaves of them, and put the whip to them, and make them work to support them and their families. But I do say, that no man, can well be a despiser of Bishop Allen, for his public labours among us, unless he is a despiser of God and of Righteousness. Thus, we see, my brethren, the two very opposite positions of those great men, who have written respecting this "Colonizing Plan." (Mr. Clay and his slave-holding party,) men who are resolved to keep us in eternal wretchedness, are also bent upon sending us to Liberia. While the Reverend Bishop Allen, and his party, men who have the fear of God, and the wellfare of their brethren at heart. The Bishop, in particular, whose labours for the salvation of his brethren, are well known to a large part of those, who dwell in the United States, are completely opposed to the plan—and advise us to stay where we are. Now we have to determine whose advice we will take respecting this all important matter, whether we will adhere to Mr. Clay and his slave holding party, who have always been our oppressors and murderers, and who are for colonizing us, more through apprehension than humanity, or to this godly man who has done so much for our benefit, together with the advice of all the good and wise among us and the whites. Will any of us leave our homes and go to Africa? I hope not.**

---

* For instance in the two States of Georgia, and South Carolina, there are, perhaps, not much short of six or seven hundred thousand persons of colour; and if I was a gambling character, I would not be afraid to stake down upon the board FIVE CENTS against TEN, that there are in the single State of Virginia, five or six hundred thousand Coloured persons. Four hundred and fifty thousand of whom (let them be well equipt for war) I would put against every white person on the whole continent of America. (Why? why because I know that the Blacks, once they get involved in a war, had rather die than to live, they either kill or be killed.) The whites know this too, which make them quake and tremble. To show the world further, how servile the coloured people are, I will only hold up to view, the one Island of Jamaica, as a specimen of our meanness. In that Island, there are three hundred and fifty thousand souls—of whom fifteen thousand are whites, the remainder, three hundred and thirty-five thousand are coloured people! and this Island is ruled by the white people! ! ! ! ! ! ! (15,000) ruling and tyranizing over 335,000 persons ! ! ! ! ! ! ! !—O! coloured men!! O! coloured men!!! O! coloured men!!!! Look!! look!!! at this!!!! and, tell me if we are not abject and servile enough, how long, O! how long my colour shall we be dupes and dogs to the cruel whites?—I only passed Jamaica, and its inhabitants, in review as a specimen to show the world, the condition of the Blacks at this time, now coloured people of the whole world, I beg you to look at the (15000 white,) and (Three Hundred and Thirty-five Thousand coloured people) in that Island, and tell me how can the white tyrants of the world but say that we are not men, hut were made to be slaves and Dogs to them and their children forever!! !! ! !—why my friend only look at the thing ! ! ! ! (15000) whites keeping in wretchedness and degradation (335000) viz. 22 coloured persons for one white! ! ! ! ! ! ! when at the same time, an equal number (15000) Blacks, would almost take the whole of South America, because where they go as soldiers to fight death follows in their tram.
** Those who are ignorant enough to go to Africa, the coloured people ought to be glad to have them go, for if they are ignorant enough to let the whites fool them off to Africa, they would be no small injury to us if they reside in this country.

Let them commence their attack upon us as they did on our brethren in Ohio, driving and beating us from our country, and my soul for theirs they will have enough of it. Let no man of us budge one step: and let slave-holders come to beat us from our country. America is more our country, than it is the whites—we have enriched it with our *blood and tears*. The greatest riches in all America have arisen from our blood and tears:—and will they drive us from our property and homes, which we have earned with our *blood?* They must look sharp or this very thing will bring swift destruction upon them. The Americans have got so fat on our blood and groans, that they have almost forgotten the God of armies. But let them go on.

→ ADDITION.—I will give here a very imperfect list of the cruelties inflicted on us by the enlightened Christians of America.—First, no trifling portion of them will beat us nearly to death if they find us on our knees praying to God,—They hinder us from going to hear the word of God—they keep us sunk in ignorance, and will not let us learn to read the word of God, nor write—If they find us with a book of any description in our hand they will beat us nearly to death—they are so afraid we will learn to read, and enlighten our dark and benighted minds—They will not suffer us to meet together to worship the God who made us—they brand us with hot iron—they cram bolts of fire down our throats—they cut us as they do horses, bulls, or hogs—they crop our ears and sometimes cut off bits of our tongues—they chain and hand-cuff us, and while in that miserable and wretched condition, beat us with cow-hides and clubs—they keep us half naked and starve us sometimes nearly to death under their infernal whips or lashes (which some of them shall have enough of yet)—They put on us fifty-sixes and chains, and make us work in that cruel situation, and in sickness, under lashes to support them and their families.—They keep us three or four hundred feet under ground working in their mines, night and day to dig up gold and silver to enrich them and their children.—They keep us in the most death-like ignorance by keeping us from all source of information, and call us, who are free men and next to the Angels of God, their property! ! ! ! ! They make us fight and murder each other, many of us being ignorant, not knowing any better.—They take us, (being ignorant,) and put us as drivers one over the other, and make us afflict each other as bad as they themselves afflict us—and to crown the whole of this catalogue of cruelties, they tell us that we the (blacks) are an inferior race of beings! incapable of self government! !—We would be injurious to society and ourselves, if tyrants should loose their unjust hold on us! ! ! That if we were free we would not work, but would live on plunder or theft! ! ! ! that we are the meanest and laziest set of beings in the world! ! ! ! ! ! That they are obliged to keep us in bondage to do us good ! ! ! ! ! !—That we are satisfied to rest in slavery to them and their children ! ! ! ! ! ! !—That we ought not to be set free in America, but ought to be sent away to Africa ! ! ! ! ! ! ! ! !—That if we were set free in America, we would involve the country in a civil war, which assertion is altogether at variance with our feeling or design, for we ask them for nothing but the rights of man, viz. for them to set us free, and treat us like men, and there will be no danger, for we will love and respect them, and protect our country—but cannot conscientiously do these things until they treat us like men. ←

How cunning slave-holders think they are!!!—How much like the king of Egypt who, after he saw plainly that God was determined to bring out his people, in spite of him and his, as powerful as they were. He was willing that Moses, Aaron and the Elders of Israel, but not all the people should go and serve the Lord. But God deceived him as he will Christian Americans, unless they are very cautious how they move. What would have become of the United States of America, was it not for those among the whites, who not in words barely, but in truth and in deed, love and fear the Lord?—Our Lord and Master said: "[But] Whose shall offend one of these little ones which believe in me, it were better for him that a mill-stone were hanged about his neck, and that he were drowned in the depth of the sea."

But the Americans with this very threatening of the Lord's, not only beat his little ones among the Africans, but many of them they put to death or murder. Now the avaricious Americans, think that the Lord Jesus Christ will let them off, because his words are no more than the words of a man! ! ! In fact, many of them are so avaricious and ignorant, that they do not believe in our Lord and Saviour Jesus Christ. Tyrants may think they are so skillful in State affairs is the reason that the government is preserved. But I tell you, that this country would have been given up long ago, was it not for the lovers of the Lord. They are indeed, the salt of the earth. Remove the people of God among the whites, from this land of blood, and it will stand until they cleverly get out of the way.

I adopt the language of the Rev. Mr. S. E. Cornish, of New York, editor of the Rights of All, and say: "Any coloured man of common intelligence, who gives his countenance and influence to that colony, further than its missionary object and interest extend, should be considered as a traitor to his brethren, and discarded by every respectable man of colour. And every member of that society, however pure his motive, whatever may be his religious character and moral worth, should in his efforts to remove the coloured population from their rightful soil, the land of their birth and nativity, be considered as acting gratuitously unrighteous and cruel."

Let me make an appeal brethren, to your hearts, for your cordial co-operation in the circulation of "The Rights of All", among us. The utility of such a vehicle conducted, cannot be estimated. I hope that the well informed among us, may see the absolute necessity of their co-operation in its universal spread among us. If we should let it go down, never let us undertake any thing of the kind again, but give up at once and say that we are really so ignorant and wretched that we cannot do any thing at all! !—As far as I have seen the writings of its editor, I believe he is not seeking to till his pockets with money, but has the welfare of his brethren truly at heart. Such men, brethren, ought to be supported by us.

But to return to the colonizing trick. It will be well for me to notice here at once, that I do not mean indiscriminately to condemn all the members and advocates of this scheme, for I believe that there are some friends to the sons of Africa, who are laboring for our salvation, not in words—only but in truth and in deed, who have been drawn into this plan—Some, more by persuasion than any thing else; while others, with humane feelings and lively zeal for our good, seeing how much we suffer from the afflictions poured upon us by unmerciful tyrants, are willing to enroll their names in any thing which they think has for its ultimate end our redemption from wretchedness and miseries; such men, with a heart truly overflowing with gratitude for their past services and zeal in our cause, I humbly beg to examine this plot minutely, and see if the end which they have in view will be completely consummated by such a course of procedure. Our friends who have been imperceptibly drawn into this plot I view with tenderness, and would not for the world injure their feelings, and I have only to hope for the future, that they will withdraw themselves from it;—for I declare to them, that the plot is not for the glory of God, but on the contrary the perpetuation of slavery in this country, which will ruin them and the country forever, unless something is immediately done.

Do the colonizationists think to send us off without first being reconciled to us? Do they think to bundle us up like brutes and send us off, as they did our brethren of the State of

Ohio?* Have they not to be reconciled to us, or reconcile us to them, for the cruelties with which they have afflicted our fathers and us?

Methinks colonizationists think they have a set of brutes to deal with, sure enough. Do they think to drive us from our country and homes, after having enriched it with our blood and tears, and keep back millions of our dear brethren, sunk in the most barbarous wretchedness, to dig up gold and silver for them and their children? Surely, the Americans must think that we are brutes, as some of them have represented us to be. They think that we do not feel for our brethren, whom they are murdering by the inches, but they are dreadfully deceived. I acknowledge that there are some deceitful and hypocritical wretches among us, who will tell us one thing while they mean another, and thus they go on aiding our enemies to oppress themselves and us. But I declare this day before my Lord and Master, that I believe there are some true-hearted sons of Africa, in this land of oppression, but pretended *liberty*! ! !—who do in reality feel for their suffering brethren, who are held in bondage by tyrants. Some of the advocates of this cunningly devised plot of Satan represent us to be the greatest set of cutthroats in the world, as though God wants us to take his work out of his hand before he is ready. Does not vengeance belong to the Lord? Is he not able to repay the Americans for their cruelties, with which they have afflicted Africa's sons and daughters, without our interference, unless we are ordered? It is surprising to think that the Americans, having the Bible in their hands, do not believe it. Are not the hearts of all men in the hands of the God of battles? And does he not suffer some, in consequence of cruelties, to go on until they are irrecoverably lost? Now, what can be more aggravating, than for the Americans, after having treated us so bad, to hold us up to the world as such great throat-cutters? It appears to me as though they are resolved to assail us with every species of affliction that their ingenuity can invent !—→ See the African Repository and Colonial Journal, from its commencement to the present day—see how we are through the medium of that periodical, abused and held up by the Americans, as the greatest nuisance to society, and throat-cutters in the world. But the Lord sees their actions. Americans! notwithstanding you have and do continue to treat us more cruel than any heathen nation ever did a people it had subjected to the same condition that you have us. Now let us reason—I mean you of the United States, whom I believe God designs to save from destruction, if you will hear. For I declare to you, whether you believe it or not, that there are some on the continent of America, who will never be able to repent. God will surely destroy them, to show you his disapprobation of the murders they and you have inflicted on us. I say, let us reason; had you not better take our body, while you have it in your power, and while we are yet ignorant and wretched, not knowing but a little, give us education, and teach us the pure religion of our Lord and Master, which is calculated to make the lion lay down in peace with the lamb, and which millions of you have beaten us nearly to death for trying to obtain since we have been among you, and thus at once, gain our affection while we are ignorant? Remember Americans, that we must and shall be free and enlightened as you are, will you wait until we shall, under God, obtain our liberty by the crushing arm of power? Will it

---

* The great slave holder, Mr. John Randolph, of Virginia, intimated in one of his great, happy and eloquent HARRANGUES, before the Virginia Convention, that Ohio is a slave State, by ranking it among other Slave-holding States. This probably was done by the HONORABLE Slave-holder to deter the minds of the ignorant; to such I would say, that Ohio always was and is now a free State, that it never was and I do not believe it ever will be a slave-holding State; the people I believe, though some of them are hard hearted enough, detest Slavery too much to admit an evil into their bosom, which gnaws into the very vitals, and sinews of those who are now in possession of it.

not be dreadful for you? I speak Americans for your good. We must and shall be free I say, in spite of you. You may do your best to keep us in wretchedness and misery, to enrich you and your children; but God will deliver us from under you. And wo, wo, will be to you if we have to obtain our freedom by fighting. Throw away your fears and prejudices then, and enlighten us and treat us like men, and we will like you more than we do now hate you,* and tell us now no more about colonization, for America is as much our country, as it is yours.—Treat us like men, and there is no danger but we will all live in peace and happiness together.

For we are not like you, hard hearted, unmerciful, and unforgiving. What a happy country this will be, if the whites will listen. What nation under heaven, will be able to do any thing with us, unless God gives us up into its hand? But Americans, I declare to you, while you keep us and our children in bondage, and treat us like brutes, to make us support you and your families, we can-not be your friends. You do not look for it, do you? Treat us then like men, and we will be your friends. And there is not a doubt in my mind, but that the whole of the past will be sunk into oblivion, and we yet, under God, will become a united and happy people. The whites may say it is impossible, but remember that nothing is impossible with God.

The Americans may say or do as they please, but they have to raise us from the condition of brutes to that of respectable men, and to make a national acknowledgement to us for the wrongs they have inflicted on us. As unexpected, strange, and wild as these propositions may to some appear, it is no less a fact, that unless they are complied with, the Americans of the United States, though they may for a little while escape, God will yet weigh them in a balance, and if they are not superior to other men, as they have represented themselves to be, he will give them wretchedness to their very heart's content.

And now brethren, having concluded these four Articles, I submit them, together with my Preamble, dedicated to the Lord, for your inspection, in language so very simple, that the most ignorant, who can read at all, may easily understand—of which you may make the best you possibly can.** Should tyrants take it into their heads to emancipate any of you, remember that your freedom is your natural right.

You are men, as well as they and instead of returning thanks to them for your freedom, return it to the Holy Ghost, who is our rightful owner. If they do not want to part with your labours, which have enriched them, let them keep you, and my word for it, that God Almighty, will break their strong band. Do you believe this, my brethren?—See my Address, delivered before the General Coloured Association of Massachusetts, which may be found in Freedom's Journal, for Dec. 20, 1828.~See the last clause of that Address. Whether you believe

---

* You are not astonished at my saying we hate you, for if we are men, we cannot but hate you, while you are treating us like dogs.

** Some of my brethren, who are sensible, do not take an interest in enlightening the minds of our more ignorant brethren respecting this BOOK and in reading it to them, just as though they will not have either to stand or fall by what is written in this book. Do they believe that I would be so foolish as to put out a book of this kind without strict—ah! very strict commandments of the Lord?—Surely the blacks and whites must think that I am ignorant enough.—Do they think that I would have the audacious wickedness to take the name of my God in vain?

Notice, I said in the concluding clause of Article 3—I call God, I call Angels I call men to witness, that the destruction of the Americans is at hand and will be speedily consummated unless they repent. Now I wonder if the world think that I would take the name of God in this way in vain? What do they think I take God to be? Do they suppose that I would trifle with that God who will not have his Holy name taken in vain?—He will show you and the world, in due time, whether this book is for his glory, or written by me through envy to the whites, as some have represented.

it or not, I tell you that God will dash tyrants, in combination with devils, into atoms, and will bring you out from your wretchedness and miseries under these *Christian People! ! ! ! !*

Those philanthropists and lovers of the human family, who have volunteered their services for our redemption from wretchedness, have a high claim on our gratitude, and we should always view them as our greatest earthly benefactors.

If any are anxious to ascertain who I am, know the world that I am one of the oppressed, degraded and wretched sons of Africa rendered so by the avaricious and unmerciful, among the whites. —If any wish to plunge me into the wretched incapacity of a slave, or murder me for the truth, know ye, that I am in the hand of God, and at your disposal. I count my life not dear unto me, but I am ready to be offered at any moment. For what is the use of living, when in fact I am dead. But remember, Americans, that as miserable, wretched, degraded and abject as you have made us in preceding, and in this generation, to support you and your families, that some of you, (whites) on the continent of America, will yet curse the day that you ever were born. You want slaves, and want us for your slaves! ! ! My colour will yet, root some of you out of the very face of the earth! ! ! ! ! ! You may doubt it if you please. I know that thousands will doubt—they think they have us so well secured in wretchedness, to them and their children, that it is impossible for such things to occur.*

---

* Why do the Slave-holders or Tyrants of America and their advocates fight so hard to keep my brethren from receiving and reading my Book of Appeal to them?—Is it because they treat us so well?—Is it because we are satisfied to rest in Slavery to them and their children?—Is it because they are treating us like men, by compensating us all over this free country!! for our labours?—But why are the Americans so very fearfully terrified respecting my Book?—Why do they search vessels, &c. when entering the harbours of tyrannical States, to see if any of my Books can be found, for fear that my brethren will get them to read. Why, I thought the Americans proclaimed to the world that they are a happy, enlightened, humane and Christian people, all the in-habitants of the country enjoy equal Rights! ! America is the Asylum for the oppressed of all nations! ! !

Now I ask the Americans to see the fearful terror they labor under for fear that my brethren will get my Book and read it-and tell me if their declaration is true—viz, if the United States of America is a Republican Government?—Is this not the most tyrannical, unmerciful, and cruel government under Heaven—not excepting the Algerines, Turks and Arabs?—I believe if any candid person would take the trouble to go through the Southern and Western sections of this country, and could have the heart to see the cruelties inflicted by these Christians on us, he would say, that the Algerines, Turks and Arabs treat their dogs a thousand times better than we are treated by the Christians.—But perhaps the Americans do their very best to keep my Brethren from receiving and reading my "Appeal" for fear they will find in it an extract which I made from their Declaration of Independence, which says, "we hold these truths to be self-evident, that all men are created equal," &c. &c. &c.—If the above are not the causes of the alarm among the Americans, respecting my Book, I do not know what to impute it to, unless they are possessed of the same spirit with which Demetrius the Silversmith was possessed-however, that they may judge whether they are of the same avaricious and ungodly spirit with that man, I will give here an extract from the Acts of the Apostles, chapter xix,—verses 23, 24, 25, 26, 27.

"And the same time there arose no small stir about that way. For a certain man named Demetrius, a silversmith, which made silver shrines for Diana, brought no small gain unto the craftsmen; whom he called together with the workmen of like occupation, and said, Sirs, ye know that by this craft we have our wealth: moreover, ye see and hear, that not alone at Ephesus, but almost throughout all Asia, this Paul hath persuaded and turned away much people, saying, that they be no gods which are made with hands: so that not only this our craft is in danger to be set at nought; but also that the temple of the great goddess Diana should be despised, and her magnificence should be destroyed, whom all Asia and the world worshippeth."

I pray you Americans of North and South America, together with the whole European inhabitants of the world, (I mean Slave-holders and their advocates) to read and ponder over the above verses in your minds, and judge whether or not you are of the infernal spirit with that Heathen Demetrius, the Silversmith: In fine I beg you to read the whole chapter through carefully.

So did the antideluvians doubt Noah, until the day in which the flood came and swept them away. So did the Sodomites doubt until Lot had got out of the city, and God rained down fire and brimstone from Heaven upon them, and burnt them up. So did the king of Egypt doubt the very existence of a God; he said, "who is the Lord, that I should let Israel go?" Did he not find to his sorrow, who the Lord was, when he and all his mighty men of war, were smothered to death in the Red Sea? So did the Romans doubt, many of them were really so ignorant, that they thought the whole of mankind were made to be slaves to them; just as many of the Americans think now, of my colour. But they got dreadfully deceived. When men got their eyes opened, they made the murderers scamper. The way in which they cut their tyrannical throats, was not much inferior to the way the Romans or murderers, served them, when they held them in wretchedness and degradation under their feet. So would Christian Americans doubt, if God should send an Angel from Heaven to preach their funeral sermon. The fact is, the Christians having a name to live, while they are dead, think that God will screen them on that ground.

See the hundreds and thousands of us that are thrown into the seas by Christians, and murdered by them in other ways. They cram us into their vessel holds in chains and in hand-cuffs—men, women and children, all together! ! O! save us, we pray thee, thou God of Heaven and of earth, from the devouring hands of the white Christians! ! !

> Oh! thou Alpha and Omega!
> The beginning and the end,
> Enthron'd thou art, in Heaven above,
> Surrounded by Angels there.
>
> From Whence thou seest the miseries
> To which we are subject;
> The whites have murder'd us, O God
> And kept us ignorant of thee.
>
> Not satisfied with this, my Lord!
> They throw us in the seas:
> Be pleas'd, we pray, for Jesus' sake,
> To save us from their grasp.
>
> We believe that, for thy glory's sake,
> Thou wilt deliver us;
> But that thou may'st effect these things,
> Thy glory must be sought.

In conclusion, I ask the candid and unprejudiced of the whole world, to search the pages of historians diligently, and see if the Antideluvians—the Sodomites—the Egyptians—the Babylonians—the Ninevites—the Carthagenians—the Persians—the Macedonians—the Greeks—the Romans—the Mahometans—the Jews—or devils, ever treated a set of human beings, as the white Christians of America do us, the blacks, or Africans. I also ask the attention of the world of mankind to the declaration of these very American people, of the United States.

A Declaration Made July 4, 1776

It says,* "When in the course of human events, it becomes necessary for one people to dissolve the political bands which have connected them with another, and to assume among the Powers of the earth, the separate and equal station to which the laws of nature and of nature's God entitle them. A decent respect for the opinions of mankind requires, that they should declare the causes which impel them to the separation.—We hold these truths to be self evident—that all men are created equal, that they are endowed by their Creator with certain unalienable rights: that among these, are life, liberty, and the pursuit of happiness that, to secure these rights, governments are instituted among men, deriving their just powers from the consent of the governed; that when ever any form of government becomes destructive of these ends, it is the right of the people to alter or to abolish it, and to institute a new government laying its foundation on such principles, and organizing its powers in such form, as to them shall seem most likely to effect their safety and happiness. Prudence, indeed, will dictate, that governments long established should not be changed for light and transient causes; and accordingly all experience hath shewn, that mankind are more disposed to suffer, while evils are sufferable, than to right themselves by abolishing the forms to which they are accustomed. But when a long train of abuses and usurpations, pursuing invariably the same object, evinces a design to reduce them under absolute despotism, it is their right it is their duty to throw off such government, and to provide new guards for their future security." See your Declaration Americans! ! !

Do you understand your own language? Hear your language, proclaimed to the world, July 4th, 1776 → "We hold these truths to be self evident—that ALL MEN ARE CREATED EQUAL! ! that they *are endowed by their Creator with certain unalienable rights*; that among these are life, *liberty*, and the pursuit of happiness! !" Compare your own language above, extracted from your Declaration of Independence, with your cruelties and murders inflicted by your cruel and unmerciful fathers and yourselves on our fathers and on us—men who have never given your fathers or you the least provocation! ! ! ! !

Hear your language further! → "But when a long train of abuses and usurpation, pursuing invariably the same object, evinces a design to reduce them under absolute despotism, it is their *right*, it is their *duty*, to throw off such government, and to provide new guards for their future security."

Now, Americans! I ask you candidly, was your sufferings under Great Britain, one hundredth part as cruel and tyranical as you have rendered ours under you? Some of you, no doubt, believe that we will never throw off your murderous government and "provide new guards for our future security." If Satan has made you believe it, will he not deceive you?* Do the whites say, I being a black man, ought to be humble, which I readily admit?

I ask them, ought they not to be as humble as I? or do they think that they can measure arms with Jehovah? Will not the Lord yet humble them? or will not these very coloured people whom they now treat worse than brutes, yet under God, humble them low down enough? Some of the whites are ignorant enough to tell us, that we ought to be submissive to them,

---

* See the Declaration of Independence of the United States.

that they may keep their feet on our throats. And if we do not submit to be beaten to death by them, we are bad creatures and of course must be damned, &c. If any man wishes to hear this doctrine openly preached to us by the American preachers, let him go into the Southern and Western sections of this country—I do not speak from hear say—what I have written, is what I have seen and heard myself. No man may think that my book is made up of conjecture—I have travelled and observed nearly the whole of those things myself, and what little I did not get by my own observation, I received from those among the whites and blacks, in whom the greatest confidence may be placed.

The Americans may be as vigilant as they please, but they cannot be vigilant enough for the Lord, neither can they hide themselves, where he will not find and bring them out.

4. Narrative of the Life of Frederick Douglass, an American Slave

FREDERICK DOUGLASS

This battle with Mr. Covey was the turning-point in my career as a slave. It rekindled the few expiring embers of freedom, and revived within me a sense of my own manhood. It recalled the departed self-confidence, and inspired me again with a determination to be free. The gratification afforded by the triumph was a full compensation for whatever else might follow, even death itself. He only can understand the deep satisfaction which I experienced, who has himself repelled by force the bloody arm of slavery. I felt as I never felt before. It was a glorious resurrection, from the tomb of slavery, to the heaven of freedom. My long-crushed spirit rose, cowardice departed, bold defiance took its place; and I now resolved that, however long I might remain a slave in form, the day had passed forever when I could be a slave in fact. I did not hesitate to let it be known of me, that the white man who expected to succeed in whipping, must also succeed in killing me.

From this time I was never again what might be called fairly whipped, though I remained a slave four years afterwards. I had several fights, but was never whipped.

It was for a long time a matter of surprise to me why Mr. Covey did not immediately have me taken by the constable to the whipping-post, and there regularly whipped for the crime of raising my hand against a white man in defence of myself. And the only explanation I can now think of does not entirely satisfy me; but such as it is, I will give it. Mr. Covey enjoyed the most unbounded reputation for being a first-rate overseer and negro-breaker. It was of considerable importance to him. That reputation was at stake; and had he sent me— a boy about sixteen years old—to the public whipping-post, his reputation would have been lost; so, to save his reputation, he suffered me to go unpunished.

My term of actual service to Mr. Edward Covey ended on Christmas day, 1833. The days between Christmas and New Year's day are allowed as holidays; and, accordingly, we were not required to perform any labor, more than to feed and take care of the stock. This time we regarded as our own, by the grace of our masters; and we therefore used or abused it nearly as we pleased. Those of us who had families at a distance, were generally allowed to spend the whole six days in their society. This time, however, was spent in various ways. The staid, sober, thinking and industrious ones of our number would employ themselves in making cornbrooms, mats, horse-collars, and baskets; and another class of us would spend the time in hunting opossums, hares, and coons. But by far the larger part engaged in such sports and merriments as playing ball, wrestling, running foot-races, fiddling, dancing, and drinking whisky; and this latter mode of spending the time was by far the most agreeable to the feelings of our masters. A slave who would work during the holidays was considered by our masters as scarcely deserving them. He was regarded as one who rejected the favor of his master. It was deemed a disgrace not to get drunk at Christmas; and he was regarded as lazy indeed, who had not provided himself with the necessary means, during the year, to get whisky enough to last him through Christmas.

From what I know of the effect of these holidays upon the slave, I believe them to be among the most effective means in the hands of the slaveholder in keeping down the spirit of insurrection. Were the slaveholders at once to abandon this practice, I have not the slightest doubt it would lead to an immediate insurrection among the slaves. These holidays serve as conductors, or safety-valves, to carry off the rebellious spirit of enslaved humanity. But for these, the slave would be forced up to the wildest desperation; and woe betide the slaveholder, the day he ventures to remove or hinder the operation of those conductors! I warn him that, in such an event, a spirit will go forth in their midst, more to be dreaded than the most appalling earthquake.

The holidays are part and parcel of the gross fraud, wrong, and inhumanity of slavery. They are professedly a custom established by the benevolence of the slaveholders; but I undertake to say, it is the result of selfishness, and one of the grossest frauds committed upon the down-trodden slave. They do not give the slaves this time because they would not like to have their work during its continuance, but because they know it would be unsafe to deprive them of it. This will be seen by the fact, that the slaveholders like to have their slaves spend those days just in such a manner as to make them as glad of their ending as of their beginning. Their object seems to be, to disgust their slaves with freedom, by plunging them into the lowest depths of dissipation. For instance, the slaveholders not only like to see the slave drink of his own accord, but will adopt various plans to make him drunk. One plan is, to make bets on their slaves, as to who can drink the most whisky without getting drunk; and in this way they succeed in getting whole multitudes to drink to excess. Thus, when the slave asks for virtuous freedom, the cunning slaveholder, knowing his ignorance, cheats him with a dose of vicious dissipation, artfully labelled with the name of liberty. The most of us used to drink it down, and the result was just what might be supposed: many of us were led to think that there was little to choose between liberty and slavery. We felt, and very properly too, that we had almost as well be slaves to man as to rum. So, when the holidays ended, we staggered up from the filth of our wallowing, took a long breath, and marched to the field,—feeling, upon the whole, rather glad to go, from what our master had deceived us into a belief was freedom, back to the arms of slavery.

I have said that this mode of treatment is a part of the whole system of fraud and inhumanity of slavery. It is so. The mode here adopted to disgust the slave with freedom, by allowing him to see only the abuse of it, is carried out in other things. For instance, a slave loves molasses; he steals some. His master, in many cases, goes off to town, and buys a large quantity; he returns, takes his whip, and commands the slave to eat the molasses, until the poor fellow is made sick at the very mention of it. The same mode is sometimes adopted to make the slaves refrain from asking for more food than their regular allowance. A slave runs through his allowance, and applies for more. His master is enraged at him; but, not willing to send him off without food, gives him more than is necessary, and compels him to eat it within a given time. Then, if he complains that he cannot eat it, he is said to be satisfied neither full nor fasting, and is whipped for being hard to please! I have an abundance of such illustrations of the same principle, drawn from my own observation, but think the cases I have cited sufficient. The practice is a very common one.

On the first of January, 1834, I left Mr. Covey, and went to live with Mr. William Freeland, who lived about three miles from St. Michael's. I soon found Mr. Freeland a very different man from Mr. Covey. Though not rich, he was what would be called an educated southern gentleman. Mr. Covey, as I have shown, was a well-trained negro-breaker and slave-driver. The former (slaveholder though he was) seemed to possess some regard for honor, some reverence for justice, and some respect for humanity. The latter seemed totally insensible to all such sentiments. Mr. Freeland had many of the faults peculiar to slaveholders, such as being very passionate and fretful; but I must do him the justice to say, that he was exceedingly free from those degrading vices to which Mr. Covey was constantly addicted. The one was open and frank, and we always knew where to find him. The other was a most artful deceiver, and could be understood only by such as were skilful enough to detect his cunningly-devised frauds. Another advantage I gained in my new master was, he made no pretensions to, or profession of, religion; and this, in my opinion, was truly a great advantage. I assert most unhesitatingly, that the religion of the south is a mere covering for the most horrid crimes,—a justifier of the most appalling barbarity,— a sanctifier of the most hateful frauds,—and a dark shelter under, which the darkest, foulest, grossest, and most infernal deeds of slaveholders find the strongest protection. Were I to be again reduced to the chains of slavery, next to that enslavement, I should regard being the slave of a religious master the greatest calamity that could befall me. For of all slaveholders with whom I have ever met, religious slaveholders are the worst. I have ever found them the meanest and basest, the most cruel and cowardly, of all others. It was my unhappy lot not only to belong to a religious slaveholder, but to live in a community of such religionists. Very near Mr. Freeland lived the Rev. Daniel Weeden, and in the same neighborhood lived the Rev. Rigby Hopkins. These were members and ministers in the Reformed Methodist Church. Mr. Weeden owned, among others, a woman slave, whose name I have forgotten. This woman's back, for weeks, was kept literally raw, made so by the lash of this merciless, *religious* wretch. He used to hire hands. His maxim was, Behave well or behave ill, it is the duty of a master occasionally to whip a slave, to remind him of his master's authority. Such was his theory, and such his practice.

Mr. Hopkins was even worse than Mr. Weeden. His chief boast was his ability to manage slaves. The peculiar feature of his government was that of whipping slaves in advance of deserving it. He always managed to have one or more of his slaves to whip every Monday morning. He did this to alarm their fears, and strike terror into those who escaped. His plan was to whip for the smallest offences, to prevent the commission of large ones. Mr. Hopkins could always find some excuse for whipping a slave. It would astonish one, unaccustomed to a slaveholding life, to see with what wonderful ease a slaveholder can find things, of which to make occasion to whip a slave. A mere look, word, or motion,—a mistake, accident, or want of power,—are all matters for which a slave may be whipped at any time. Does a slave look dissatisfied? It is said, he has the devil in him, and it must be whipped out. Does he speak loudly when spoken to by his master? Then he is getting high-minded, and should be taken down a button-hole lower. Does he forget to pull off his hat at the approach of a white person? Then he is wanting in reverence, and should be whipped for it. Does he ever venture to vindicate his conduct, when censured for it? Then he is guilty of impudence,— one of the greatest crimes of which a slave can be guilty. Does he ever venture to suggest a different mode of doing things from that pointed out by his master? He is indeed presumptuous, and getting above himself; and nothing less than a flogging will do for him. Does he, while ploughing, break a plough,— or, while hoeing, break a hoe? It is owing to his carelessness, and for it a slave must always be whipped. Mr. Hopkins could always find something of this sort to justify the use of the lash, and he seldom failed to embrace such opportunities. There was not a man in the whole county, with whom the slaves who had the getting their own home, would not prefer to live, rather than with this Rev. Mr. Hopkins. And yet there was not a man any where round, who made higher professions of religion, or was more active in revivals,—more attentive to the class, love-feast, prayer and preaching meetings, or more devotional in his family,—that prayed earlier, later, louder, and longer,—than this same reverend slave-driver, Rigby Hopkins.

But to return to Mr. Freeland, and to my experience while in his employment. He, like Mr. Covey, gave us enough to eat; but, unlike Mr. Covey, he also gave us sufficient time to take our meals. He worked us hard, but always between sunrise and sunset. He required a good deal of work to be done, but gave us good tools with which to work. His farm was large, but he employed hands enough to work it, and with ease, compared with many of his neighbors. My treatment, while in his employment, was heavenly, compared with what I experienced at the hands of Mr. Edward Covey.

Mr. Freeland was himself the owner of but two slaves. Their names were Henry Harris and John Harris. The rest of his hands he hired. These consisted of myself, Sandy Jenkins,* and Handy Caldwell. Henry and John were quite intelligent, and in a very little while after I went there, I succeeded in creating in them a strong desire to learn how to read. This desire soon sprang up in the others also. They very soon mustered up some old spelling-books, and nothing would do but that I must keep a Sabbath school. I agreed to do so, and accordingly devoted my Sundays to teaching these my loved fellow-slaves how to read. Neither of them knew his letters when I went there. Some of the slaves of the neighboring farms found what was going on, and also availed themselves of this little opportunity to learn to read. It was understood, among all who came, that there must be as little display about it as possible. It was necessary to keep our religious masters at St. Michael's unacquainted with the fact, that, instead of spending the Sabbath in wrestling, boxing, and drinking whisky, we were trying to learn how to read the will of God; for they had much rather see us engaged in those degrading sports, than to see us behaving like intellectual, moral, and accountable beings. My blood boils as I think of the bloody manner in which Messrs. Wright Fairbanks and Garrison West, both class-leaders, in connection with many others, rushed in upon us with sticks and stones, and broke up our virtuous little Sabbath school, at St. Michael's—all calling themselves Christians! humble followers of the Lord Jesus Christ! But I am again digressing.

I held my Sabbath school at the house of a free colored man, whose name I deem it imprudent to mention; for should it be known, it might embarrass him greatly, though the crime of holding the school was committed ten years ago. I had at one time over forty scholars, and those of the right sort, ardently desiring to learn. They were of all ages, though mostly men and women. I look back to those Sundays with an amount of pleasure not to be expressed. They were great days to my soul. The work of instructing my dear fellow-slaves was the sweetest engagement with which I was ever blessed. We loved each other, and to leave them at the close of the Sabbath was a severe cross indeed. When I think that these

---

* This is the same man who gave me the roots to prevent my being whipped by Mr. Covey. He was "a clever soul." We used frequently to talk about the fight with Covey, and as often as we did so, he would claim my success as the result of the roots which he gave me. This superstition is very common among the more ignorant slaves. A slave seldom dies but that his death is attributed to trickery.

precious souls are to-day shut up in the prison-house of slavery, my feelings overcome me, and I am almost ready to ask, "Does a righteous God govern the universe? and for what does he hold the thunders in his right hand, if not to smite the oppressor, and deliver the spoiled out of the hand of the spoiler?" These dear souls came not to Sabbath school because it was popular to do so, nor did I teach them because it was reputable to be thus engaged. Every moment they spent in that school, they were liable to be taken up, and given thirty-nine lashes. They came because they wished to learn. Their minds had been starved by their cruel masters. They had been shut up in mental darkness. I taught them, because it was the delight of my soul to be doing something that looked like bettering the condition of my race. I kept up my school nearly the whole year I lived with Mr. Freeland; and, beside my Sabbath school, I devoted three evenings in the week, during the winter, to teaching the slaves at home. And I have the happiness to know, that several of those who came to Sabbath school learned how to read; and that one, at least, is now free through my agency.

The year passed off smoothly. It seemed only about half as long as the year which preceded it. I went through it without receiving a single blow. I will give Mr. Freeland the credit of being the best master I ever had, *till I became my own master.* For the ease with which I passed the year, I was, however, some what indebted to the society of my fellow-slaves. They were noble souls; they not only possessed loving hearts, but brave ones. We were linked and interlinked with each other. I loved them with a love stronger than any thing I have experienced since. It is sometimes said that we slaves do not love and confide in each other. In answer to this assertion, I can say, I never loved any or confided in any people more than my fellow-slaves, and especially those with whom I lived at Mr. Freeland's. I believe we would have died for each other. We never undertook to do any thing, of any importance, without a mutual consultation. We never moved separately. We were one; and as much so by our tempers and dispositions, as by the mutual hardships to which we were necessarily subjected by our condition as slaves.

At the close of the year 1834, Mr. Freeland again hired me of my master, for the year 1835. But, by this time, I began to want to live *upon free land* as well as *with Freeland;* and I was no longer content, therefore, to live with him or any other slaveholder. I began, with the commencement of the year, to prepare myself for a final struggle, which should decide my fate one way or the other. My tendency was upward. I was fast approaching manhood, and year after year had passed, and I was still a slave. These thoughts roused me—I must do something. I therefore resolved that 1835 should not pass without witnessing an attempt, on my part, to secure my liberty. But I was not willing to cherish this determination alone. My fellow-slaves were dear to me. I was anxious to have them participate with me in this, my life-giving determination. I therefore, though with great prudence, commenced early to ascertain their views and feelings in regard to their condition, and to imbue their minds with thoughts of freedom. I bent myself to devising ways and means for our escape, and meanwhile strove, on all fitting occasions, to impress them with the gross fraud and inhumanity of slavery. I went first to Henry, next to John, then to the others. I found, in them all, warm hearts and noble spirits. They were ready to hear, and ready to act when a feasible plan should be proposed. This was what I wanted. I talked to them of our want of manhood, if we submitted to our enslavement without at least one noble effort to be free. We met often, and consulted frequently, and told our hopes and fears, recounted the difficulties, real and imagined, which we should be called on to meet. At times we were almost disposed to give up, and try to content ourselves with our wretched lot; at others, we were firm and unbending in our determination to go. Whenever we suggested any plan, there was shrinking—the odds were fearful. Our path was beset with the greatest obstacles; and if we succeeded in gaining the end of it, our right to be free was yet questionable—we were yet liable to be returned to bondage. We could see no spot, this side of the ocean, where we could be free. We knew nothing about Canada. Our knowledge of the north did not extend farther than New York; and to go there, and be forever harassed with the frightful liability of being returned to slavery—with the certainty of being treated tenfold worse than before—the thought was truly a horrible one, and one which it was not easy to overcome. The case sometimes stood thus: At every gate through which we were to pass, we saw a watchman—at every ferry a guard—on every bridge a sentinel—and in every wood a patrol. We were hemmed in upon every side. Here were the difficulties, real or imagined—the good to be sought, and the evil to be shunned. On the one hand, there stood slavery, a stern reality, glaring frightfully upon us,—its robes already crimsoned with the blood of millions, and even now feasting itself greedily upon our own flesh. On the other hand, away back in the dim distance, under the flickering light of the north star, behind some craggy hill or snow-covered mountain, stood a doubtful freedom—half frozen—beckoning us to come and share its hospitality. This in itself was sometimes enough to stagger us; but when we permitted ourselves to survey the road, we were frequently appalled. Upon either side we saw grim death, assuming the most horrid shapes. Now it was starvation, causing us to eat our own flesh;—now we were contending with the waves, and were drowned;— now we were overtaken, and torn to pieces by the fangs of the terrible bloodhound. We were stung by scorpions, chased by wild beasts, bitten by snakes, and finally, after having nearly reached the desired spot,—after swimming rivers, encountering wild beasts, sleeping in the woods, suffering hunger and nakedness,—we were overtaken by our pursuers, and, in our resistance, we were shot dead upon the spot! I say, this picture sometimes appalled us, and made us

> "rather bear those ills we had,
> Than fly to others, that we knew not of."

In coming to a fixed determination to run away, we did more than Patrick Henry, when he resolved upon liberty or death. With us it was a doubtful liberty at most, and almost certain death if we failed. For my part, I should prefer death to hopeless bondage.

Sandy, one of our number, gave up the notion, but still encouraged us. Our company then consisted of Henry Harris, John Harris, Henry Bailey, Charles Roberts, and myself. Henry Bailey was my uncle, and belonged to my master. Charles married my aunt: he belonged to my master's father-in-law, Mr. William Hamilton.

The plan we finally concluded upon was, to get a large canoe belonging to Mr. Hamilton, and upon the Saturday night previous to Easter holidays, paddle directly up the Chesapeake Bay. On our arrival at the head of the bay, a distance of seventy or eighty miles from where we lived, it was our purpose to turn our canoe adrift, and follow the guidance of the north star till we got beyond the limits of Maryland. Our reason for taking the water route was, that we were less liable to be suspected as runaways; we hoped to be regarded as fishermen; whereas, if we should take the land route, we should be subjected to interruptions of almost every kind. Any one having a white face, and being so disposed, could stop us, and subject us to examination.

The week before our intended start, I wrote several protections, one for each of us. As well as I can remember, they were in the following words, to wit:—

"This is to certify that I, the undersigned, have given the bearer, my servant, full liberty to go to Baltimore, and spend the Easter holidays. Written with mine own hand, &c., 1835.

"William Hamilton,
"Near St. Michael's, in Talbot county, Maryland."

We were not going to Baltimore; but, in going up the bay, we went toward Baltimore, and these protections were only intended to protect us while on the bay.

As the time drew near for our departure, our anxiety became more and more intense. It was truly a matter of life and death with us. The strength of our determination was about to be fully tested. At this time, I was very active in explaining every difficulty, removing every doubt, dispelling every fear, and inspiring all with the firmness indispensable to success in our undertaking; assuring them that half was gained the instant we made the move; we had talked long enough; we were now ready to move; if not now, we never should be; and if we did not intend to move now, we had as well fold our arms, sit down, and acknowledge ourselves fit only to be slaves. This, none of us were prepared to acknowledge. Every man stood firm; and at our last meeting, we pledged ourselves afresh, in the most solemn manner, that, at the time appointed, we would certainly start in pursuit of freedom. This was in the middle of the week, at the end of which we were to be off. We went, as usual, to our several fields of labor, but with bosoms highly agitated with thoughts of our truly hazardous undertaking. We tried to conceal our feelings as much as possible; and I think we succeeded very well.

After a painful waiting, the Saturday morning, whose night was to witness our departure, came. I hailed it with joy, bring what of sadness it might. Friday night was a sleepless one for me. I probably felt more anxious than the rest, because I was, by common consent, at the head of the whole affair. The responsibility of success or failure lay heavily upon me. The glory of the one, and the confusion of the other, were alike mine. The first two hours of that morning were such as I never experienced before, and hope never to again. Early in the morning, we went, as usual, to the field. We were spreading manure; and all at once, while thus engaged, I was overwhelmed with an indescribable feeling, in the fulness of which I turned to Sandy, who was near by, and said, "We are betrayed!" "Well," said he, "that thought has this moment struck me." We said no more. I was never more certain of any thing.

The horn was blown as usual, and we went up from the field to the house for breakfast. I went for the form, more than for want of any thing to eat that morning. Just as I got to the house, in looking out at the lane gate, I saw four white men, with two colored men. The white men were on horseback, and the colored ones were walking behind, as if tied. I watched them a few moments till they got up to our lane gate. Here they halted, and tied the colored men to the gate-post. I was not yet certain as to what the matter was. In a few moments, in rode Mr. Hamilton, with a speed betokening great excitement. He came to the door, and inquired if Master William was in. He was told he was at the barn. Mr. Hamilton, without dismounting, rode up to the barn with extraordinary speed. In a few moments, he and Mr. Freeland returned to the house. By this time, the three constables rode up, and in great haste dismounted, tied their horses, and met Master William and Mr. Hamilton returning from the barn; and after talking awhile, they all walked up to the kitchen door. There was no one in the kitchen but myself and John. Henry and Sandy were up at the barn. Mr. Freeland put his head in at the door, and called me by name, saying, there were some gentlemen at the door who wished to see me. I stepped to the door, and inquired what they wanted. They at once seized me, and, without giving me any satisfaction, tied me—lashing my hands closely together. I insisted upon knowing what the matter was. They at length said, that they had learned I had been in a "scrape," and that I was to be examined before my master; and if their information proved false, I should not be hurt.

In a few moments, they succeeded in tying John. They then turned to Henry, who had by this time returned, and commanded him to cross his hands. "I won't!" said Henry, in a firm tone, indicating his readiness to meet the consequences of his refusal. "Won't you?" said Tom Graham, the constable. "No, I won't!" said Henry, in a still stronger tone. With this, two of the constables pulled out their shining pistols, and swore, by their Creator, that they would make him cross his hands or kill him. Each cocked his pistol, and, with fingers on the trigger, walked up to Henry, saying, at the same time, if he did not cross his hands, they would blow his damned heart out. "Shoot me, shoot me!" said Henry; "you can't kill me but once. Shoot, shoot,—and be damned! *I won't be tied!*" This he said in a tone of loud defiance; and at the same time, with a motion as quick as lightning, he with one single stroke dashed the pistols from the hand of each constable. As he did this, all hands fell upon him, and, after beating him some time, they finally overpowered him, and got him tied.

During the scuffle, I managed, I know not how, to get my pass out, and, without being discovered, put it into the fire. We were all now tied; and just as we were to leave for Easton jail, Betsy Freeland, mother of William Freeland, came to the door with her hands full of biscuits, and divided them between Henry and John. She, then delivered herself of a speech, to the following effect:—addressing herself to me, she said, *"You devil! You yellow devil!* it was you that put it into the heads of Henry and John to run away. But for you, you long-legged mulatto devil! Henry nor John would never have thought of such a thing." I made no reply, and was immediately hurried off towards St. Michael's. Just a moment previous to the scuffle with Henry, Mr. Hamilton suggested the propriety of making a search for the protections which he had understood Frederick had written for himself and the rest. But, just, at the moment he was about carrying his proposal into effect, his aid was needed in helping to tie Henry; and the excitement attending the scuffle caused them either to forget, or to deem it unsafe, under the circumstances, to search. So we were not yet convicted of the intention to run away.

When we got about half way to St. Michael's, while the constables having us in charge were looking ahead, Henry inquired of me what he should do with his pass. I told him to eat it with his biscuit, and own nothing; and we passed the word around, *"Own nothing;"* and *"Own nothing!"* said we all. Our confidence in each other was unshaken. We were resolved to succeed or fail together, after the calamity had befallen us as much as before. We were now prepared for any thing. We were to be dragged that morning fifteen miles behind horses, and then to be placed in the Easton jail. When we reached St. Michael's, we underwent a sort of examination. We all denied that we ever intended to run away. We did this more to bring out the evidence against us, than from any hope of getting clear of being sold; for, as I have said, we were ready for that. The fact was, we cared but little where we went, so we went together. Our greatest concern was about separation. We dreaded that more than any thing this side of death. We found the evidence against us to be the testimony of one person; our master would not tell who it was; but we came to a unanimous decision among ourselves as to who their informant was. We were sent off to the jail at Easton. When we got there, we were delivered up to the sheriff, Mr. Joseph Graham, and by him placed in jail. Henry, John, and myself, were placed in one room together—Charles, and Henry Bailey, in another. Their object in separating us was to hinder concert.

We had been in jail scarcely twenty minutes, when a swarm of slave traders, and agents for slave traders, flocked into jail to look at us, and to ascertain if we were for sale. Such a set of beings I never saw before! I felt myself surrounded by so many fiends from perdition. A band of pirates never looked more like their father, the devil. They laughed and grinned over us, saying, "Ah, my boys! we have got you, haven't we?" And after taunting us in various ways, they one by one went into an examination of us, with intent to ascertain our value. They would impudently ask us if we would not like to have them for our masters. We would make them no answer, and leave them to find out as best they could. Then they would curse and swear at us, telling us that they could take the devil out of us in a very little while, if we were only in their hands.

While in jail, we found ourselves in much more comfortable quarters than we expected when we went there. We did not get much to eat, nor that which was very good; but we had a good clean room, from the windows of which we could see what was going on in the street, which was very much better than though we had been placed in one of the dark, damp cells. Upon the whole, we got along very well, so far as the jail and its keeper were concerned. Immediately after the holidays were over, contrary to all our expectations, Mr. Hamilton and Mr. Freeland came up to Easton, and took Charles, the two Henrys, and John, out of jail, and carried them home, leaving me alone. I regarded this separation as a final one. It caused me more pain than any thing else in the whole transaction. I was ready for any thing rather than separation. I supposed that they had consulted together, and had decided that, as I was the whole cause of the intention of the others to run away, it was hard to make the innocent suffer with the guilty; and that they had, therefore, concluded to take the others home, and sell me, as a warning to the others that remained. It is due to the noble Henry to say, he seemed almost as reluctant at leaving the prison as at leaving home to come to the prison. But we knew we should, in all probability, be separated, if we were sold; and since he was in their hands, he concluded to go peaceably home.

I was now left to my fate. I was all alone, and within the walls of a stone prison. But a few days before, and I was full of hope. I expected to have been safe in a land of freedom; but now I was covered with gloom, sunk down to the utmost despair. I thought the possibility of freedom was gone. I was kept in this way about one week, at the end of which, Captain Auld, my master, to my surprise and utter astonishment, came up, and took me out, with the intention of sending me, with a gentleman of his acquaintance, into Alabama. But, from some cause or other, he did not send me to Alabama, but concluded to send me back to Baltimore, to live again with his brother Hugh, and to learn a trade.

Thus, after an absence of three years and one month, I was once more permitted to return to my old home at Baltimore. My master sent me away, because there existed against me a very great prejudice in the community, and he feared I might be killed.

In a few weeks after I went to Baltimore, Master Hugh hired me to Mr. William Gardner, an extensive ship-builder, on Fell's Point. I was put there to learn how to calk. It, however, proved a very unfavorable place for the accomplishment of this object. Mr. Gardner was engaged that spring in building two large man-of-war brigs, professedly for the Mexican government. The vessels were to be launched in the July of that year, and in failure thereof, Mr. Gardner was to lose a considerable sum; so that when I entered, all was hurry. There was no time to learn any thing. Every man had to do that which he knew how to do. In entering the shipyard, my orders from Mr. Gardner were, to do whatever the carpenters commanded me to do. This was placing me at the beck and call of about seventy-five men. I was to regard all these as masters. Their word was to be my law. My situation was a most trying one. At times I needed a dozen pair of hands. I was called a dozen ways in the space of a single minute. Three or four voices would strike my ear at the same moment. It was—"Fred., come help me to cant this timber here."—"Fred., come carry this timber yonder."—"Fred., bring that roller here."—"Fred., go get a fresh can of water."—"Fred., come help saw off the end of this timber."—"Fred., go quick, and get the crowbar."—"Fred., hold on the end of this fall."—"Fred., go to the blacksmith's shop, and get a new punch."—"Hurra, Fred.! run and bring me a cold chisel."—"I say, Fred., bear a hand, and get up a fire as quick as lightning under that steam-box."—"Halloo, nigger! come, turn this grind-stone."—"Come, come! move, move! and *bowse* this timber forward."—"I say, darky, blast your eyes, why don't you heat up some pitch?"—"Halloo! halloo! halloo!" (Three voices at the same time.) "Come here!—Go there!—Hold on where you are! Damn you, if you move, I'll knock your brains out!"

This was my school for eight months; and I might have remained there longer, but for a most horrid fight I had with four of the white apprentices, in which my left eye was nearly knocked out, and I was horribly mangled in other respects. The facts in the case were these: Until a very little while after I went there, white and black ship-carpenters worked side by side, and no one seemed to see any impropriety in it. All hands seemed to be very well satisfied. Many of the black carpenters were freemen. Things seemed to be going on very well. All at once, the white carpenters knocked off, and said they would not work with free colored workmen. Their reason for this, as alleged, was, that if free colored carpenters were encouraged, they would soon take the trade into their own hands, and poor white men would be thrown out of employment. They therefore felt called upon at once to put a stop to it. And, taking advantage of Mr. Gardner's necessities, they broke off, swearing they would work no longer, unless he would discharge his black carpenters. Now, though this did not extend to me in form, it did reach me in fact. My fellow-apprentices very soon began to feel it degrading to them to work with me. They began to put on airs, and talk about the "niggers" taking the country, saying we all ought to be killed; and, being encouraged by the journeymen, they commenced making my condition as hard as they could, by hectoring me around, and sometimes striking me. I, of course, kept the vow I made after the fight with Mr. Covey, and struck back again, regardless of consequences; and while I kept them from combining, I succeeded very well; for I could whip the whole of them, taking them separately. They, however, at length combined, and came upon me, armed with sticks, stones, and heavy handspikes. One came in front with a half brick. There was one at each side of me, and one behind me. While I was attending to those in front, and on either side, the one behind ran up with the handspike, and struck me a heavy blow upon the head. It stunned me. I fell, and with this they all ran upon me, and fell to beating me with their fists. I let them lay on for a while, gathering strength. In an instant, I gave a sudden surge, and rose to my hands and knees. Just as I did that, one of their number gave me, with his heavy boot, a powerful kick in the left eye. My eyeball seemed to have burst. When they saw my eye closed, and badly swollen, they left me. With this I seized the handspike, and for a time pursued them. But here the carpenters interfered, and I thought I might as well give it up. It was impossible to stand my hand against so many. All this took place in sight of not less than fifty white ship-carpenters, and not one interposed a friendly word; but some cried, "Kill the damned nigger! Kill him! kill him! He struck a white person." I found my only chance for life was in flight. I succeeded in getting away without an additional blow, and barely so; for to strike a white man is death by Lynch law,—and that was the law in Mr. Gardner's ship-yard; nor is there much of any other out of Mr. Gardner's ship-yard.

I went directly home, and told the story of my wrongs to Master Hugh; and I am happy to say of him, irreligious as he was, his conduct was heavenly, compared with that of his brother Thomas under similar circumstances. He listened attentively to my narration of the circumstances leading to the savage outrage, and gave many proofs of his strong indignation at it. The heart of my once overkind mistress was again melted into pity. My puffed-out eye and blood-covered face moved her to tears. She took a chair by me, washed the blood from my face, and, with a mother's tenderness, bound up my head, covering the wounded eye with a lean piece of fresh beef. It was almost compensation for my suffering to witness, once more, a manifestation of kindness from this, my once affectionate old mistress. Master Hugh was very much enraged. He gave expression to his feelings by pouring out curses upon the heads of those who did the deed. As soon as I got a little the better of my bruises, he took me with him to Esquire Watson's, on Bond Street, to see what could be done about the matter. Mr. Watson inquired who saw the assault committed. Master Hugh told him it was done in Mr. Gardner's ship-yard, at midday, where there were a large company of men at work. "As to that," he said, "the deed was done, and there was no question as to who did it." His answer was, he could do nothing in the case, unless some white man would come forward and testify. He could issue no warrant on my word. If I had been killed in the presence of a thousand colored people, their testimony combined would have been insufficient to have arrested one of the murderers. Master Hugh, for once, was compelled to say this state of things was too bad. Of course, it was impossible to get any white man to volunteer his testimony in my behalf, and against the white young men. Even those who may have sympathized with me were not prepared to do this. It required a degree of courage unknown to them to do so; for just at that time, the slightest manifestation of humanity toward a colored person was denounced as abolitionism, and that name subjected its bearer to frightful liabilities. The watchwords of the bloody-minded in that region, and in those days, were, "Damn the abolitionists!" and "Damn the niggers!" There was nothing done, and probably nothing would have been done if I had been killed. Such was, and such remains, the state of things in the Christian city of Baltimore.

Master Hugh, finding he could get no redress, refused to let me go back again to Mr. Gardner. He kept me himself, and his wife dressed my wound till I was again restored to health. He then took me into the shipyard of which he was foreman, in the employment of Mr. Walter Price. There I was immediately set to calking, and very soon learned the art of using my mallet and irons. In the course of one year from the time I left Mr. Gardner's, I was able to command the highest wages given to the most experienced calkers. I was now of some importance to my master. I was bringing him from six to seven dollars per week. I sometimes brought him nine dollars per week: my wages were a dollar and a half a day. After learning how to calk, I sought my own employment, made my own contracts, and collected the money which I earned. My pathway became much more smooth than before; my condition was now much more comfortable. When I could get no calking to do, I did nothing. During these leisure times, those old notions about freedom would steal over me again. When in Mr. Gardner's employment, I was kept in such a perpetual whirl of excitement, I could think of nothing, scarcely, but my life; and in thinking of my life, I almost forgot my liberty. I have observed this in my experience of slavery, —that whenever my condition was improved, instead of its increasing my contentment, it only increased my desire to be free, and set me to thinking of plans to gain my freedom. I have found that, to make a contented slave, it is necessary to make a thoughtless one. It is necessary to darken his moral and mental vision, and, as far as possible, to annihilate the power of reason. He must be able to detect no inconsistencies in slavery; he must be made to feel that slavery is right; and he can be brought to that only when he ceases to be a man.

* * * * *

Appendix

I find, since reading over the foregoing Narrative that I have, in several instances, spoken in such a tone and manner, respecting religion, as may possibly lead those unacquainted with my religious views to suppose me an opponent of all religion. To remove the liability of such misapprehension, I deem it proper to append the following brief explanation. What I have said respecting and against religion, I mean strictly to apply to the *slaveholding religion* of this land, and with no possible reference to Christianity proper; for, between the Christianity of this land, and the Christianity of Christ, I recognize the widest possible difference—so wide, that to receive the one as good, pure, and holy, is of necessity to reject the other as bad, corrupt, and wicked. To be the friend of the one, is of necessity to be the enemy of the other. I love the pure, peaceable, and impartial Christianity of Christ: I therefore hate the corrupt, slaveholding, women-whipping, cradle-plundering, partial and hypocritical Christianity of this land. Indeed, I can see no reason, but the most deceitful one, for calling the religion of this land Christianity. I look upon it as the climax of all misnomers, the boldest of all frauds, and the grossest of all libels. Never was there a clearer case of "stealing the livery of the court of heaven to serve the devil in." I am filled with unutterable loathing when I contemplate the religious pomp and show, together with the horrible inconsistencies, which every where surround me. We have men-stealers for ministers, women-whippers for missionaries, and cradle-plunderers for church members. The man who wields the blood-clotted cowskin during the week fills the pulpit on Sunday, and claims to be a minister of the meek and lowly Jesus. The man who robs me of my earnings at the end of each week meets me as a class-leader on Sunday morning, to show me the way of life, and the path of salvation. He who sells my sister, for purposes of prostitution, stands forth as the pious advocate of purity. He who proclaims it a religious duty to read the Bible denies me the right of learning to read the name of the God who made me. He who is the religious advocate of marriage robs whole millions of its sacred influence, and leaves them to the ravages of wholesale pollution. The warm defender of the sacredness of the family relation is the same that scatters whole families,—sundering husbands and wives, parents and children, sisters and brothers,—leaving the hut vacant, and the hearth desolate. We see the thief preaching against theft, and the adulterer against adultery. We have men sold to build churches, women sold to support the gospel, and babes sold to purchase Bibles for the *poor heathen! all for the glory of God and the good of souls!* The slave auctioneer's bell and the church-going bell chime in with each other, and the bitter cries of the heart-broken slave are drowned in the religious shouts of his pious master. Revivals of religion and revivals in the slave-trade go hand in hand together. The slave prison and the church stand near each other.

The clanking of fetters and the rattling of chains in the prison, and the pious psalm and solemn prayer in the church, may be heard at the same time. The dealers in the bodies and souls of men erect their stand in the presence of the pulpit, and they mutually help each other. The dealer gives his blood-stained gold to support the pulpit, and the pulpit, in return, covers his infernal business with the garb of Christianity. Here we have religion and robbery the allies of each other—devils dressed in angels' robes, and hell presenting the semblance of paradise.

"Just God! and these are they,
   Who minister at thine altar, God of right!
Men who their hands, with prayer and blessing, lay
   On Israel's ark of light.

"What! preach, and kidnap men?
   Give thanks, and rob thy own afflicted poor?
Talk of thy glorious liberty, and then
   Bolt hard the captive's door?

"What! servants of thy own
   Merciful Son, who came to seek and save
The homeless and the outcast, fettering down
   The tasked and plundered slave!

"Pilate and Herod friends!
   Chief priests and rulers, as of old, combine!
Just God and holy! is that church which lends
   Strength to the spoiler thine?"

The Christianity of America is a Christianity, of whose votaries it may be as truly said, as it was of the ancient scribes and Pharisees, "They bind heavy burdens, and grievous to be borne, and lay them on men's shoulders, but they themselves will not move them with one of their fingers. All their works they do for to be seen of men.——They love the uppermost rooms at feasts, and the chief seats in the synagogues, ... and to be called of men, Rabbi, Rabbi.————But woe unto you, scribes and Pharisees, hypocrites! for ye shut up the kingdom of heaven against men; for ye neither go in yourselves, neither suffer ye them that are entering to go in. Ye devour widows' houses, and for a pretence make long prayers; therefore ye shall receive the greater damnation. Ye compass sea and land to make one proselyte, and when he is made, ye make him twofold more the child of hell than yourselves.——Woe unto you, scribes and Pharisees, hypocrites! for ye pay tithe of mint, and anise, and cumin, and have omitted the weightier matters of the law, judgment, mercy, and faith; these ought ye to have done, and not to leave the other undone. Ye blind guides! which strain at a gnat, and swallow a camel. Woe unto you, scribes and Pharisees, hypocrites! for ye make clean the outside of the cup and of the platter; but within, they are full of extortion and excess.——Woe unto you, scribes and Pharisees, hypocrites! for ye are like unto whited sepulchres, which indeed appear beautiful outward, but are within full of dead men's bones, and of all uncleanness. Even so ye also outwardly appear righteous unto men, but within ye are full of hypocrisy and iniquity."

Dark and terrible as is this picture, I hold it to be strictly true of the overwhelming mass of professed Christians in America. They strain at a gnat, and swallow a camel. Could any thing be more true of our churches? They would be shocked at the proposition of fellowshipping a *sheep*-stealer; and at the same time they hug to their communion a *man*-stealer, and brand me with being an infidel, if I find fault with them for it. They attend with Pharisaical strictness to the outward forms of religion, and at the same time neglect the weightier matters of the law, judgment, mercy, and faith. They are always ready to sacrifice, but seldom to show mercy. They are they who are represented as professing to love God whom they have not seen, whilst they hate their brother whom they have seen. They love the heathen on the other side of the globe. They can pray for him, pay money to have the Bible put into his hand, and missionaries to instruct him; while they despise and totally neglect the heathen at their own doors.

Such is, very briefly, my view of the religion of this land; and to avoid any misunderstanding, growing out of the use of general terms, I mean, by the religion of this land, that which is revealed in the words, deeds, and actions, of those bodies, north and south, calling themselves Christian churches, and yet in union with slaveholders. It is against religion, as presented by these bodies, that I have felt it my duty to testify.

I conclude these remarks by copying the following portrait of the religion of the south, (which is, by communion and fellowship, the religion of the north,) which I soberly affirm is "true to the life," and without caricature or the slightest exaggeration. It is said to have been drawn, several years before the present anti-slavery agitation began, by a northern Methodist preacher, who, while residing at the south, had an opportunity to see slaveholding morals, manners, and piety, with his own eyes. "Shall I not visit for these things? saith the Lord. Shall not my soul be avenged on such a nation as this?"

A PARODY

"Come, saints and sinners, hear me tell
How pious priests whip Jack and Nell,
And women buy and children sell,
And preach all sinners down to hell,
   And sing of heavenly union.

"They'll bleat and baa, dona like goats,
Gorge down black sheep, and strain at motes,
Array their backs in fine black coats,
Then seize their negroes by their throats,
   And choke, for heavenly union.

"They'll church you if you sip a dram,
And damn you if you steal a lamb;
Yet rob old Tony, Doll, and Sam,
Of human rights, and bread and ham;
   Kidnapper's heavenly union.

"They'll loudly talk of Christ's reward,
And bind his image with a cord,
And scold, and swing the lash abhorred,
And sell their brother in the Lord
   To handcuffed heavenly union.

"They'll read and sing a sacred song,
And make a prayer both loud and long,
And teach the right and do the wrong,
Hailing the brother, sister throng,
    With words of heavenly union.

"We wonder how such saints can sing,
Or praise the Lord upon the wing,
Who roar, and scold, and whip, and sting,
And to their slaves and mammon cling,
    In guilty conscience union.

"They'll raise tobacco, corn, and rye,
And drive, and thieve, and cheat, and lie,
And lay up treasures in the sky,
By making switch and cowskin fly,
    In hope of heavenly union.

"They'll crack old Tony on the skull,
And preach and roar like Bashan bull,
Or braying ass, of mischief full,
Then seize old Jacob by the wool,
    And pull for heavenly union.

"A roaring, ranting, sleek man-thief,
Who lived on mutton, veal, and beef,
Yet never would afford relief
To needy, sable sons of grief,
    Was big with heavenly union.

"'Love not the world,' the preacher said,
And winked his eye, and shook his head;
He seized on Tom, and Dick, and Ned,
Cut short their meat, and clothes, and bread,
    Yet still loved heavenly union.

"Another preacher whining spoke
Of One whose heart for sinners broke
He tied old Nanny to an oak,
And drew the blood at every stroke,
    And prayed for heavenly union.

"Two others oped their iron jaws,
And waved their children-stealing paws;
There sat their children in gewgaws;
By stinting negroes' backs and maws,
    They kept up heavenly union.

"All good from Jack another takes,
And entertains their flirts and rakes,
Who dress as sleek as glossy snakes,
And cram their mouths with sweetened cakes;
   And this goes down for union."

Sincerely and earnestly hoping that this little book may do something toward throwing light on the American slave system, and hastening the glad day of deliverance to the millions of my brethren in bonds—faithfully relying upon the power of truth, love, and justice, for success in my humble efforts—and solemnly pledging my self anew to the sacred cause, —I subscribe myself,

FREDERICK DOUGLASS.
—Lynn, *Mass., April 28, 1845.*

5. Religious Experience and Journal of Mrs. Jarena Lee

JARENA LEE

"And it shall come to pass . . . . that I will pour out my Spirit upon all flesh; and your sons, and your daughters shall prophecy." —Joel ii. 28.

I was born February 11th, 1783, at Cape May, State of New Jersey. At the age of seven years I was parted from my parents, and went to live as a servant maid, with a Mr. Sharp, at the distance of about sixty miles from the place of my birth.

My parents being wholly ignorant of the knowledge of God, had not therefore instructed me in any degree in this great matter. Not long after the commencement of my attendance on this lady, she had bid me do something respecting my work, which in a little while after she asked me if I had done, when I replied, Yes—but this was not true.

At this awful point, in my early history, the Spirit of God moved in power through my conscience, and told me I was a wretched sinner. On this account so great was the impression, and so strong were the feelings of guilt, that I promised in my heart that I would not tell another lie.

But notwithstanding this promise my heart grew harder, after a while, yet the Spirit of the Lord never entirely forsook me, but continued mercifully striving with me, until his gracious power converted my soul.

The manner of this great accomplishment, was as follows: In the year 1804, it so happened that I went with others to hear a missionary of the Presbyterian order preach. It was an afternoon meeting, but few were there, the place was a school room; but the preacher was solemn, and in his countenance the earnestness of his master's business appeared equally strong, as though he were about to speak to a multitude.

At the reading of the Psalms, a ray of renewed conviction darted into my soul. These were the words, composing the first verse of the Psalms for the service:

"Lord, I am vile, conceived in sin,
Born unholy and unclean.
Sprung from man, whose guilty fall
Corrupts the race, and taints us all."

This description of my condition struck me to the heart, and made me to feel in some measure, the weight of my sins, and sinful nature. But not knowing how to run immediately to the Lord for help, I was driven of Satan, in the course of a few days, and tempted to destroy myself.

There was a brook about a quarter of a mile from the house, in which there was a deep hole, where the water whirled about among the rocks; to this place it was suggested, I must go and drown myself.

At the time I had a book in my hand; it was on a Sabbath morning, about ten o'clock; to this place I resorted, where on coming to the water I sat down on the bank, and on my looking into it, it was suggested that drowning would be an easy death. It seemed as if some one was speaking to me, saying put your head under, it will not distress you. But by some means, of which I can give no account, my thoughts were taken entirely from this purpose, when I went from the place to the house again. It was the unseen arm of God which saved me from self-murder.

But notwithstanding this escape from death, my mind was not at rest—but so great was the labor of my spirit and the fearful oppressions of a judgment to come, that I was reduced as one extremely ill, on which account a physician was called to attend me, from which illness I recovered in about three months.

But as yet I had not found Him of whom Moses and the prophets did write, being extremely ignorant: there being no one to instruct me in the way of life and salvation as yet. After my recovery, I left the lady, who, during my sickness, was exceedingly kind, and went to Philadelphia. From this place I soon went a few miles into the country, where I resided in the family of a Roman Catholic. But my anxiety still continued respecting my poor soul, on which account I used to watch my opportunity to read in the Bible; and this lady observing this, took the Bible from me and hid it, giving me a novel in its stead—which when I perceived, I refused to read.

Soon after this I again went to the city of Philadelphia, and commenced going to the English Church, the pastor of which was an Englishman, by the name of Pilmore, one of the number who at first preached Methodism in America, in the city of New York.

But while sitting under the ministration of this man, which was about three months, and at the last time, it appeared that there was a wall between me and a communion with that people, which was higher than I could possibly see over, and seemed to make this impression upon my mind, *this is not the people for you.*

But on returning home at noon I inquired of the head cook of the house respecting the rules of the Methodists, as I knew she belonged to that society, who told me what they were; on which account I replied, that I should not be able to abide by such strict rules not even one year—however, I told her that I would go with her and hear what they had to say.

The man who was to speak in the afternoon of that day, was the Rev. Richard Allen, since bishop of the African Episcopal Methodists in America. During the labors of this man that afternoon, I had come to the conclusion, that this is the people to which my heart unites, and it so happened, that as soon as the service closed he invited such as felt a desire to flee the wrath to come, to unite on trial with them—I embraced the opportunity. Three weeks from that day, my soul was gloriously converted to God, under preaching, at the very outset of the sermon. The text was barely pronounced, which was 'I perceive thy heart is not right in the sight of God," when there appeared to *my* view, in the centre of the heart, *one* sin; and this was *malice* against one particular individual, who had strove deeply to injure me, which I resented. At this discovery I said, *Lord* I forgive *every* creature. That instant, it appeared to me as if a garment, which had entirely enveloped my whole person, even to my fingers' ends, split at the crown of my head, and was stripped away from me, passing like a shadow from my sight—when the glory of God seemed to cover me in its stead.

That moment, though hundreds were present, I did leap to my feet and declare that God, for Christ's sake, had pardoned the sins of my soul. Great was the ecstacy of my mind, for I felt that not only the sin of *malice* was pardoned, but all other sins were swept away together. That day was the first when my heart had believed, and my tongue had made confession unto salvation—the first words uttered, a part of that song, which shall fill eternity with its sound, was *glory* to *God.* For a few moments I had power to exhort sinners, and to tell of the wonders and of the goodness of Him who had clothed me with *His* salvation. During this the minister was silent, until my soul felt its duty had been performed, when he declared another witness of the power of Christ to forgive sins on earth, was manifest in my conversion.

From the day on which I first went to the Methodist Church, until the hour of my deliverance, I was strangely buffetted by that enemy of all righteousness—the devil.

I was naturally of a lively turn of disposition; and during the space of time from my first awakening until I knew my peace was made with God, I rejoiced in the vanities of this life, and then again sunk back into sorrow.

For four years I had continued in this way, frequently laboring under the awful apprehension, that I could never be happy in this life. This persuasion was greatly strengthened during the three weeks, which was the last of Satan's power over me, in this peculiar manner, on which account I had come to the conclusion that I had better be dead than alive. Here I was again tempted to destroy my life by drowning; but suddenly this mode was changed—and while in the dusk of the evening, as I was walking to and fro in the yard of the house, I was beset to hang myself with a cord suspended from the wall enclosing the secluded spot.

But no sooner was the intention resolved on in my mind, than an awful dread came over me, when I ran into the house; still the tempter pursued me. There was standing a vessel of water—into this I was strangly impressed to plunge my head, so as to extinguish the life which God had given me. Had I done this, I have been always of the opinion, that I should have been unable to have released myself; although the vessel was scarcely large enough to hold a gallon of water. Of me may it not be said as written by Isaiah, (chap. 65, verses 1, 2.) "I am sought of them that asked not for me; I am found of them that sought me not." Glory be to God for his redeeming power, which saved me from the violence of my own hands, from the malice of Satan, and from eternal death; for had I have killed myself, a great ransom could not have delivered me; for it is written —"No murderer hath eternal life abiding in him." How appropriately can I sing—

> "Jesus sought me when a stranger,
>   Wandering from the fold of God;
> He to rescue me from danger,
>   Interposed his precious blood."

But notwithstanding the terror which seized upon me, when about to end my life, I had no view of the precipice on the edge of which I was tottering, until it was over, and my eyes were opened. Then the awful gulf of hell seemed to he open beneath me, covered only, as it were, by a spider's web, on which I stood. I seemed to hear the howling of the damned, to see the smoke of the bottomless pit, and to hear the rattling of those chains, which hold the impenitent under clouds of darkness to the judgment of the great day.

I trembled like Belshazzar, and cried out in the horror of my spirit, "God be merciful to me a sinner." That night I formed a resolution to pray; which, when resolved upon, there appeared, sitting in one corner of the room, Satan, in the form of a monstrous dog, and in a rage, as if in pursuit, his tongue protruding from his mouth to a great length, and his eyes looked like two balls of fire; it soon, however, vanished out of my sight. From this state of terror and dismay, I was happily delivered under the preaching of the Gospel as before related.

This view which I was permitted to have of Satan, in the form of a dog, is evidence, which corroborates in my estimation, the Bible account of a hell of fire, which burneth with brimstone, called in Scripture the bottomless pit; the place where all liars, who repent not, shall have their portion; as also the Sabbath breaker, the adulterer, the fornicator, with the fearful, the abominable, and the unbelieving, this shall be the portion of their cup.

This language is too strong and expressive to be applied to any state of suffering in *time*. Were it to be thus applied, the reality could no where be found in human life; the consequence would be, that *this* scripture would be found a false testimony. But when made to apply to an endless state of perdition, in eternity, beyond the bounds of human life, then this language is found not to exceed our views of a state of eternal damnation.

During the latter part of my state of conviction, I can now apply to my case, as it then was, the beautiful words of the poet:

"The more I strove against its power,
I felt its weight and guilt the more;
'Till late I heard my Saviour say,
Come hither soul, I am the way."

This I found to be true, to the joy of my disconsolate and despairing heart, in the hour of my conversion to God.

During this state of mind, while sitting near the fire one evening, after I had heard Rev. Richard Allen, as before related, a view of my distressed condition so affected my heart, that I could not refrain from weeping and crying aloud; which caused the lady with whom I then lived, to inquire, with surprise, what ailed me; to which I answered, that I knew not what ailed me. She replied that I ought to pray. I arose from where I was sitting, being in an agony, and weeping convulsively, requested her to pray for me; but at the very moment when she would have done so, some person wrapped heavily at the door for admittance; it was but a person of the house, but this occurrence was sufficient to interrupt us in our intentions; and I believe to this day, I should then have found salvation to my soul. This interruption was, doubtless, also the work of Satan.

Although at this time, when my conviction was so great, yet I knew not that Jesus Christ was the Son of God, the second person in the adorable Trinity. I knew him not in the pardon of my sins, yet I felt a consciousness that if I died without pardon, that my lot must inevitably be damnation. If I would pray—I knew not how. I could form no connexion of ideas into words; but I knew the Lord's prayer; this I uttered with a loud voice, and with all my might and strength. I was the most ignorant creature in the world; I did not even know that Christ had died for the sins of the world, and to save sinners. Every circumstance, however, was so directed as still to continue and increase the sorrows of my heart, which I now know to have been a Godly sorrow which wrought repentance, which is not to repented of. Even the falling of the dead leaves from the forests, and the dried spires of the mown grass, showed me that I too must die in like manner. But my case was awfully different from that of the grass of the field, or the wide spread decay of a thousand forests, as I felt within me a living principle, an immortal spirit, which cannot die, and must forever either enjoy the smiles of its Creator, or feel the pangs of ceaseless damnation.

But the Lord led me on; being gracious, he took pity on my ignorance; he heard my wailings, which had entered into the ear of the Lord of Sabaoth. Circumstances so transpired that I soon came to a knowledge of the being and character of the Son of God, of whom I knew nothing.

My strength had left me. I had become feverish and sickly through the violence of my feelings, on which account I left my place of service to spend a week with a colored physician, who was a member of the Methodist society, and also to spend this week in going to places where prayer and supplication was statedly made for such as me.

Through this means I had learned much, so as to be able in some degree to comprehend the spiritual meaning of the text, which the minister took on the Sabbath morning, as before related, which was "I perceive thy heart is not right in the sight of God."—Acts, chap. 8, verse 21.

This text, as already related, became the power of God unto salvation to me, because I believed. I was baptized according to the direction of our Lord, who said, as he was about to ascend from the mount, to his disciples, "Go ye into all the world and preach my gospel to every creature, he that believeth and is baptized shall be saved."

I have now passed through the account of my conviction, and also of my conversion to God: and shall next speak of the blessings of sanctification.

A time, after I had received forgiveness, flowed sweetly on; day and night my joy was full, no temptation was permitted to molest me. I could say continually with the psalmist, that "God had separated my sins from me as far as the east is from the west." I was ready continually to cry,

> *"Come all the world, come sinner thou,*
> *All things in Christ are ready now."*

I continued in this happy state of mind for almost three months, when a certain colored man, by name William Scott, came to pay me a religious visit. He had been for many years a faithful follower of the Lamb; and he had also taken much time in visiting the sick and distressed of our color, and understood well the great things belonging to a man of full stature in Christ Jesus.

In the course of our conversation, he inquired if the Lord had justified my soul. I answered yes. He then asked me if he had sanctified me. I answered no; and that I did not know what that was. He then undertook to instruct me further in the knowledge of the Lord respecting this blessing.

He told me the progress of the soul from a state of darkness, or of nature, was three-fold; or consisted in three degrees, as follows: First, conviction for sin. Second, justification from sin. Third, the entire sanctification of the soul to God. I thought this description was beautiful, and immediately believed in it. He then inquired if I would promise to pray for this in my secret devotions. I told him yes. Very soon I began to call upon the Lord to show me all that was in my heart, which was not according to his will. Now there appeared to be a new struggle commencing in my soul, not accompanied with fear, guilt, and bitter distress, as while under my first conviction for sin, but a laboring of the mind to know more of the right way of the Lord. I began now to feel that my heart was not clean in his sight; that there yet remained the roots of bitterness, which if not destroyed, would ere long sprout up from these roots, and overwhelm me in a new growth of the brambles and brushwood of sin.

By the increasing light of the Spirit, I had found there yet remained the root of pride, anger, self-will, with many evils, the result of fallen nature. I now became alarmed at this discovery, and began to fear that I had been deceived in my experience. I was now greatly alarmed, lest I should fall away from what I knew I had enjoyed; and to guard against this I prayed almost incessantly, without acting faith on the power and promises of God to keep me from falling. I had not yet learned how to war against temptation of this kind. Satan well knew that if he could succeed in making me disbelieve my conversion, that he would catch me either on the ground of complete despair, or on the ground of infidelity. For if all I had passed through was to go for nothing, and was but a fiction, the mere ravings of a disordered mind, that I would naturally be led to believe that there is nothing in religion at all.

From this snare I was mercifully preserved, and led to believe that there was yet a greater work than that of pardon to be wrought in me. I retired to a secret place, (after having sought this blessing, as well as I could, for nearly three months, from the time brother Scott had instructed me respecting it,) for prayer, about four o'clock in the afternoon. I had struggled long and hard, but found not the desire of my heart. When I rose from my knees, there seemed a voice speaking to me, as I yet stood in a leaning posture—"Ask for sanctification." When to my surprise, I recollected that I had not even thought of it in my whole prayer. It would seem Satan had hidden the very object from my mind, for which I had purposely kneeled to pray. But when this voice whispered in my heart, saying, "Pray for sanctification," I again bowed in the same place, at the same time, and said "Lord *sanctify* my soul for Christ's sake." That very instant, as if lightning had darted through me, I sprang to my feet, and cried, "The Lord has sanctified my soul!" There was none to hear this but the angels who stood around to witness my joy—and Satan, whose malice raged the more. That Satan was there, I knew; for no sooner had I cried out "The Lord has sanctified my soul," than there seemed another voice behind me, saying "No, it is too great a work to be done." But another spirit said "Bow down for the witness—I received it—*thou art sanctified!*" The first I knew of myself after that, I was standing in the yard with my hands spread out, and looking with my face toward heaven.

I now ran into the house and told them what had happened to me, when, as it were a new rush of the same ecstacy came upon me, and caused me to feel as if I were in an ocean of light and bliss.

During this, I stood perfectly still, the tears rolling in a flood from my eyes. So great was the joy, that it is past description. There is no language that can describe it, except that which was heard by St. Paul, when he was caught up to third heaven, and heard words which it was not lawful to utter.

My Call to Preach the Gospel

Between four and five years after my sanctification, on a certain time, an impressive silence fell upon me, and I stood as if some one was about to speak to me, yet I had no such thought in my heart.— But to my utter surprise there seemed to sound a voice which I thought I distinctly heard, and most certainly understand, which said to me, "Go preach the Gospel!" I immediately replied aloud, "No one will believe me." Again I listened, and again the same voice seemed to say—"Preach the Gospel; I will put words in your mouth, and will turn your enemies to become your friends."

At first I supposed that Satan had spoken to me, for I had read that he could transform himself into an angel of light for the purpose of deception. Immediately I went into a secret place, and called upon the Lord to know if he had called me to preach, and whether I was deceived or not; when there appeared to my view the form and figure of a pulpit, with a Bible lying thereon, the back of which was presented to me as plainly as if it had been a literal fact.

In consequence of this, my mind became so exercised, that during the night following, I took a text and preached in my sleep. I thought there stood before me a great multitude, while I expounded to them the things of religion. So violent were my exertions and so loud were my exclamations, that I awoke from the sound of my own voice, which also awoke the family of the house where I resided. Two days after I went to see the preacher in charge of the African Society, who was the Rev. Richard Allen, the same before named in these pages, to tell him that I felt it my duty to preach the gospel. But as I drew near the street in which his house was, which was in the city of Philadelphia, my courage began to fail me; so terrible did the cross appear, it seemed that I should not be able to bear it. Previous to my setting out to go to see him, so agitated was my mind, that my appetite for my daily food failed me entirely. Several times on my way there, I turned back again; but as often I felt my strength again renewed, and I soon found that the nearer I approached to the house of the minister, the less was my fear. Accordingly, as soon as I came to the door, my fears subsided, the cross was removed, all things appeared pleasant—I was tranquil.

I now told him, that the Lord had revealed it to me, that must preach the gospel. He replied, by asking, in what sphere I wished to move in? I said, among the Methodists. He then replied, that a Mrs. Cook, a Methodist lady, had also some time before requested the same privilege; who, it was believed, had done much good in the way of exhortation, and holding prayer meetings; and who had been permitted to do so by the verbal license of the preacher in charge at the time. But as to women preaching, he said that our Discipline knew nothing at all about it— that it did not call for women preachers. This I was glad to hear, because it removed the fear of the cross—but no sooner did this feeling cross my mind, than I found that a love of souls had in a measure departed from me; that holy energy which burned within me, as a fire, began to be smothered. This I soon perceived.

O how careful ought we to be, lest through our by-laws of church government and discipline, we bring into disrepute even the word of life. For as unseemly as it may appear now-a-days for a woman to preach, it should be remembered that nothing is impossible with God. And why should it be thought impossible, heterodox, or improper for a woman to preach? seeing the Saviour died for the woman as well as for the man.

If the man may preach, because the Saviour died for him, why not the woman? seeing he died for her also. Is he not a whole Saviour, instead of a half one? as those who hold it wrong for a woman to preach, would seem to make it appear.

Did not Mary *first* preach the risen Saviour, and is not the doctrine of the resurrection the very climax of Christianity—hangs not all our hope on this, as argued by St. Paul? Then did not Mary, a woman, preach the gospel? for she preached the resurrection of the crucified Son of God.

But some will say that Mary did not expound the Scripture, therefore, she did not preach, in the proper sense of the term. To this I reply, it may be that the term *preach* in those primitive times, did not mean exactly what it is now *made* to mean; perhaps it was a great deal more simple then, than it is now—if it were not, the unlearned fishermen could not have preached the gospel at all, as they had no learning.

To this it may be replied, by those who are determined not to believe that it is right for a woman to preach, that the disciples, though they were fishermen and ignorant of letters too, were inspired so to do. To which I would reply, that though they were inspired, yet that inspiration did not save them from showing their ignorance of letters, and of man's wisdom; this the multitude soon found out, by listening to the remarks of the envious Jewish priests. If then, to preach the gospel, by the gift of heaven, comes by inspiration solely, is God straitened: must he take the man exclusively? May he not, did he not, and can he not inspire a female to preach the simple story of the birth, life, death, and resurrection of our Lord, and accompany it too with power to the sinner's heart. As for me, I am fully persuaded that the Lord called me to labor according to what I have received, in his vineyard. If he has not, how could he consistently bear testimony in favor of my poor labors, in awakening and converting sinners?

In my wanderings up and down among men, preaching according to my ability, I have frequently found families who told me that they had not for several years been to a meeting, and yet, while listening to hear what God would say by his poor female instrument, have believed with trembling—tears rolling down their cheeks, the signs of contrition and repentance towards God. I firmly believe that I have sown seed, in the name of the Lord, which shall appear with its increase at the great day of accounts, when Christ shall come to make up his jewels.

At a certain time, I was beset with the idea, that soon or late I should fall from grace and lose my soul at last. I was frequently called to the throne of grace about this matter, but found no relief; the temptation pursued me still. Being more and more afflicted with it, till at a certain time, when the spirit strongly impressed it on my mind to enter into my closet and carry my case once more to the Lord; the Lord enabled me to draw nigh to him, and to his mercy seat, at this time, in an extraordinary manner; for while I wrestled with him for the victory over this disposition to doubt whether I should persevere, there appeared a form of fire, about the size of a man's hand, as I was on my knees; at the same moment there appeared to the eye of faith a man robed in a white garment, from the shoulders down to the feet; from him a voice proceeded, saying: "Thou shalt never return from the cross." Since that time I have never doubted, but believe that God will keep me until the day of redemption. Now I could adopt the very language of St. Paul, and say, that nothing could have separated me from the love of God, which is in Christ Jesus. Since that time, 1807, until the present, 1833, I have not even doubted the power and goodness of God to keep me from falling, through the sanctification of the spirit and belief of the truth.

My Marriage

In the year 1811, I changed my situation in life, having married Mr. Joseph Lee, pastor of a Society at Snow Hill, about six miles from the city of Philadelphia. It became necessary therefore for me to remove. This was a great trial at first, as I knew no person at Snow Hill, except my husband, and to leave my associates in the society, and especially those who composed the *band* of which I was one. None but those who have been in sweet fellowship with such as really love God, and have together drank bliss and happiness from the same fountain, can tell how dear such company is, and how hard it is to part from them.

At Snow Hill, as was feared, I never found that agreement and closeness in communion and fellowship, that I had in Philadelphia, among my young companions, nor ought I to have expected it. The manners and customs at this place were somewhat different, on which account I became discontented in the course of a year, and began to importune my husband to remove to the city. But this plan did not suit him, as he was the Pastor of the Society, he could not bring his mind to leave them. This afflicted me a little. But the Lord showed me in a dream what his will was concerning this matter.

I dreamed that as I was walking on the summit of a beautiful hill, that I saw near me a flock of sheep, fair and white, as if but newly washed; when there came walking toward me a man of a grave and dignified countenance, dressed entirely in white, as it were in a robe, and looking at me, said emphatically, "Joseph Lee must take care of these sheep, or the wolf will come and devour them." When I awoke I was convinced of my error, and immediately, with a glad heart, yielded to the right spirit in the Lord. This also greatly strengthened my faith in his care over them, for fear the wolf should by some means take any of them away. The following verse was beautifully suited to our condition, as well as to all the little flocks of God scattered up and down this land:

"Us into Thy protection take,
And gather with Thine arm;
Unless the fold We first forsake,
The wolf can never harm."

After this, I fell into a state of general debility, and in an ill state of health, so much so, that I could not sit up; but a desire to warn sinners to flee the wrath to come, burned vehemently in my heart, when the Lord would send sinners into the house to see me. Such opportunities I embraced to press home on their consciences the things of eternity, and so effectual was the word of exhortation made through the Spirit, that I have seen them fall to the floor crying aloud for mercy.

From this sickness I did not expect to recover, and there was but one thing which bound me to earth, and this was, that I had not as yet preached the gospel to the fallen sons and daughters of Adam's race, to the satisfaction of my mind. I wished to go from one end of the earth to the other, crying, Behold, behold the lamb! To this end I earnestly prayed the Lord to raise me up, if consistent with his will. He condescended to hear my prayer, and to give me a token in a dream, that in due time I should recover my health. The dream was as follows: I thought I saw the sun rise in the morning, and ascend to an altitude of about half an hour high, and then become obscured by a dense black cloud, which continued to hide its rays for about one-third part of the day, and then it burst forth again with renewed splendor.

This dream I interpreted to signify my early life, my conversion to God, and this sickness, which was a great affliction, as it hindered me, and I feared would forever hinder me from preaching the gospel, was signified by the cloud; and the bursting forth of the sun, again, was the recovery of my health, and being permitted to preach.

I went to the throne of grace on this subject, where the Lord made this impressive reply in my heart, while on my knees: "Ye shall be restored to thy health again, and worship God in full purpose of heart."

This manifestation was so impressive, that I could but hide my face as if some one was gazing upon me, to think of the great goodness of the Almighty God to my poor soul and body. From that very time I began to gain strength of body and mind, glory to God in the highest, until my health was fully recovered.

For six years from this time I continued to receive from above, such baptisms of the Spirit as mortality could scarcely bear. About that time I was called to suffer in my family, by death—five, in the course of about six years, fell by his hand; my husband being one of the number, which was the greatest affiction of all.

I was now left alone in the world, with two infant children, one of the age of about two years, the other six months, with no other dependence than the promise of Him who hath said—I will be the widow's God, and a father to the fatherless. Accordingly, he raised me up friends, whose liberality comforted and solaced me in my state of widowhood and sorrows, I could sing with the greatest propriety the words of the poet.

> "He helps the stranger in distress,
> The widow and the fatherless,
>   And grants the prisoner sweet release."

I can say even now, with the Psalmist, "Once I was young, but now I am old, yet I have never seen the righteous forsaken, nor his seed begging bread." I have ever been fed by his bounty, clothed by his mercy, comforted and healed when sick, succored when tempted, and every where upheld by his hand.

The Subject of My Call to Preach Renewed

It was now eight years since I had made application to be permitted to preach the gospel, during which time I had only been allowed to exhort, and even this privilege but seldom. This subject now was renewed afresh in my mind; it was as a fire shut up in my bones. About thirteen months passed on, while under this renewed impression. During this time, I had solicited of the Rev. Bishop, Richard Allen, who at this time had become Bishop of the African Episcopal Methodists in America, to be permitted the liberty of holding prayer meetings in my own hired house, and of exhorting as I found liberty, which was granted me. By this means, my mind was relieved, as the house soon filled when the hour appointed for prayer had arrived.

I cannot but relate in this place, before I proceed further with the above subject, the singular conversion of a very wicked young man. He was a colored man, who had generally attended our meetings, but not for any good purpose; but rather to disturb and to ridicule our denomination. He openly and uniformly declared that he neither believed in religion, nor wanted any thing to do with it. He was of a Gallio disposition, and took the lead among the young people of color. But after a while he fell sick, and lay about three months in a state of ill health; his disease was a consumption. Toward the close of his days, his sister who was a member of the society, came and desired me to go and see her brother, as she had no hopes of his recovery, perhaps the Lord might break into his mind. I went alone, and found him very low. I soon commenced to inquire respecting his state of feeling, and how he found his mind. His answer was, "O tolerable well," with an air of great in difference. I asked him if I should pray for him. He answered in a sluggish and careless manner, "O yes, if you have time." I then sung a hymn, kneeled down and prayed for him, and then went my way.

Three days after this, I went again to visit the young man. At this time there went with me two of the sisters in Christ. We found the Rev. Mr. Cornish, of our denomination, laboring with him. But he said he received but little satisfaction from him. Pretty soon, however, brother Cornish took his leave; when myself, with the other two sisters, one of which was an elderly woman named Jane Hutt, the other was younger, both colored, commenced conversing with him, respecting his eternal interest, and of his hopes of a happy eternity, if any he had. He said but little; we then kneeled, down together and besought the Lord in his behalf, praying that if mercy were not clear gone for ever, to shed a ray of softening grace upon the hardness of his heart. He appeared now to be somewhat more tender, and we thought we could perceive some tokens of conviction, as he wished us to visit him again, in a tone of voice not quite as indifferent as he had hitherto manifested.

But two days had elapsed after this visit, when his sister came to me in haste, saying, that she believed her brother was then dying, and that he had *sent* for me. I immediately called on Jane Hutt, who was still among us as a mother in Israel, to go with me. When we arrived there, we found him sitting up in bed, very restless and uneasy, but he soon laid down again. He now wished me to come to him, by the side of his bed. I asked him how he was. He said, "Very ill;" and added, "Pray for me, quick?" We now perceived his time in this world to be short. I took up the hymn-book, and opened to a hymn suitable to his case, and commenced to sing, but there seemed to be a *horror* in the room—a darkness of a mental kind, which was felt by us all; there being five persons, except the sick young man and his nurse. We had sung but one verse, when they all gave over singing, on account of this uneartlhy sensation, but myself. I continued to sing on alone, but in a dull and heavy manner, though looking up to God all the while for help. Suddenly I felt a spring of energy awake in my heart, when darkness gave way in some degree. It was but a glimmer from above. When the hymn was finished, we all kneeled down to pray for him. While calling on the name of the Lord, to have mercy on his soul, and to grant him repentance unto life, it came suddenly into my mind never to rise from my knees until God should hear prayer in his behalf, until he should convert and save his soul.

Now, while I thus continued importuning heaven, as I felt I was led, a ray of light, more abundant, broke forth among us. There appeared to my view, though my eyes were closed, the Saviour in full stature, nailed to the cross, just over the head of the young man, against the ceiling of the room. I cried out, brother look up, the Saviour is come, he will pardon you, your sins he will forgive. My sorrow for the soul of the young man was gone; I could no longer pray—joy and rapture made it impossible. We rose up from our knees, when lo, his eyes were gazing with ecstacy upwards; over his face there was an expression of joy; his lips were clothed in a sweet and holy smile; but no sound came from his tongue; it was heard in its stillness of bliss; full of hope and immortality. Thus, as I held him by the hand, his happy and purified soul soared away, without a sigh or a groan, to its eternal rest.

I now closed his eyes, straightened out his limbs, and left him to be dressed for the grave. But as for me, I was filled with the power of the Holy Ghost—the very room seemed filled with glory. His sister and all that were in the room rejoiced, nothing doubting but he had entered into Paradise; and I believe I shall see him at the last and great day, safe on the shores of salvation.

But to return to the subject of my call to preach. Soon after this, as above related, the Rev. Richard Williams was to preach at Bethel Church, where I with others were assembled. He entered the pulpit, gave out the hymn, which was sung, and then addressed the throne of grace; took his text, passed through the exordium, and commenced to expound it. The text he took is in Jonah, 2d chap. 9th verse,—"Salvation is of the Lord." But as he proceeded to explain, he seemed to have lost the spirit; when in the same instant, I sprang, as by altogether supernatural impulse, to my feet, when I was aided from above to give an exhortation on the very text which my brother Williams had taken.

I told them I was like Jonah; for it had been then nearly eight years since the Lord had called me to preach his gospel to the fallen sons and daughters of Adam's race, but that I had lingered like him, and delayed to go at the bidding of the Lord, and warn those who are as deeply guilty as were the people of Ninevah.

During the exhortation, God made manifest his power in a manner sufficient to show the world that I was called to labor according to my ability, and the grace given unto me, in the vineyard of the good husbandman.

I now sat down, scarcely knowing what I had done, being frightened. I imagined, that for this indecorum, as I feared it might be called, I should be expelled from the church. But instead of this, the Bishop rose up in the assembly, and related that I had called upon him eight years before, asking to be permitted to preach, and that he had put me off; but that he now as much believed that I was called to that work, as any of the preachers present. These remarks greatly strengthened me, so that my fears of having given an offence, and made myself liable as an offender, subsided, giving place to a sweet serenity, a holy joy of a peculiar kind, untasted in my bosom until then.

The next Sabbath day, while sitting under the word of the gospel, I felt moved to attempt to speak to the people in a public manner, but I could not bring my mind to attempt it in the church. I said, Lord, anywhere but here. Accordingly, there was a house not far off which was pointed out to me; to this I went. It was the house of a sister belonging to the same society with myself. Her name was Anderson. I told her I had come to hold a meeting in her house, if she would call in her neighbors. With this request she immediately complied. My congregation consisted of but five persons. I commenced by reading and singing a hymn; when I arose I found my hand resting on the Bible, which I had not noticed till that moment. It now occurred to me to take a text. I opened the Scripture, as it happened, at the 141st Psalm, fixing my eye on the third verse, which reads: "Set a watch, O Lord, before my mouth, keep the door of my lips." My sermon, such as it was, applied wholly to myself, and added an exhortation. Two of my congregation wept much, as the fruit of my labor this time. In closing, I said to the few, that if any one would open a door, I would hold a meeting the next sixth-day evening: when one answered that her house was at my service. Accordingly I went, and God made manifest his power among the people. Some wept, while others shouted for joy. One whole seat of females, by the power of God, as the rushing of a wind, were all bowed to the floor, at once, and screamed out. Also a sick man and woman in one house, the Lord convicted them both; one lived, and the other died. God wrought a judgment—some were well at night, and died in the morning. At this place I continued to hold meetings about six months. During that time I kept house with my little son, who was very sickly. About this time I had a call to preach at a place about thirty miles distant, among the Methodists, with whom I remained one week, and during the whole time, not a thought of my little son came into my mind; it was hid from me, lest, I should have been diverted from the work I had to do, to look after my son. Here by the instrumentality of a poor coloured woman, the Lord poured forth his spirit among the people. Though, as I was told, there were lawyers, doctors, und magistrates present, to hear me speak, yet there was mourning and crying among sinners, for the Lord scattered fire among them of his own kindling. The Lord gave his hand-maiden power to speak for his-great name, for he arrested the hearts of the people, and caused a shaking amongst the multitude, for God was in the midst.

I now returned home, found all well; no harm had come to my child, although I left it very sick. Friends had taken care of it which was of the Lord. I now began to think seriously of breaking up housekeeping, and forsaking all to preach the everlasting Gospel. I felt a strong desire to return to the place of my nativity, at Cape May, after an absence of about fourteen years. To this place, where the heaviest cross was to be met with, the Lord sent me, as Saul of Tarsus was sent to Jerusalem, to preach the same gospel which he had neglected and despised before his conversion. I went by water, and on my passage was much distressed by sea sickness, so much so that I expected to have died, but such was not the will of the Lord respecting me. After I had disembarked, I proceeded on as opportunities offered, toward where my mother lived. When within ten miles of that place, I appointed an evening meeting. There were a goodly number came out to hear. The Lord was pleased to give me light and liberty among the people. After meeting, there came an elderly lady to me and said, she believed the Lord had sent me among them; she then appointed me another meeting there two weeks from that night. The next day I hastened forward to the place of my mother, who was happy to see me, and the happiness was mutual between us. With her I left my poor sickly boy, while I departed to do my Master's will. In this neighborhood I had an uncle, who was a Methodist, and who gladly threw open his door for meetings to be held there. At the first meeting which I held at my uncle's house, there was, with others who had come from curiosity to hear the woman preacher, an old man, who was a Deist, and who said he did not believe the coloured people had any souls—he was sure they had none. He took a seat very near where I was standing, and boldly tried to look me out of countenance. But as I labored on in the best manner I was able, looking to God all the while, though it seemed to me I had but little liberty, yet there went an arrow from the bent bow of the gospel, and fastened in his till then obdurate heart. After I had done speaking, he went out, and called the people around him, said that my preaching might seem a small thing, yet he believed I had the worth of souls at heart. This language was different from what it was a little time before, as he now seemed to admit that coloured people had souls, as it was to these I was chiefly speaking; and unless they had souls, whose good I had in view, his remark must have been, without meaning. He now came into the house, and in the most friendly manner shook hands with me, saying, he hoped God had spared him to some good purpose. This man was a great slave holder, and had been very cruel; thinking nothing of knocking down a slave with a fence stake, or whatever might come to hand. From this time it was said of him that he became greatly altered in his ways for the better. At that time he was about seventy years old, his head as white as snow; but whether he became a converted man or not, I never heard.

The week following, I had an invitation to hold a meeting at the Court House of the County, when I spoke from the 53d chap. of Isaiah, 3d verse. It was a solemn time, and the Lord attended the word; I had life and liberty, though there were people there of various denominations. Here again I saw the aged slaveholder, who notwithstanding his age, walked about three miles to hear me. This day I spoke twice, and walked six miles to the place appointed. There was a magistrate present, who showed his friendship, by saying in a friendly manner, that he had heard of me: he handed me a hymnbook, pointing to a hymn which he had selected. When the meeting was over, he invited me to preach in a school-house in his neighborhood, about three miles distant from where I then was. During this meetng one backslider was reclaimed. This day I walked six miles, and preached twice to large congregations, both in the morning and evening. The Lord was with me, glory be to his holy name. I next went six miles and held a meeting in a coloured friund's house, at eleven o'clock in the morning, and preached to a well behaved congregation of both coloured and white. After service I again walked back, which was in all twelve miles in the same day. This was on Sabbath, or as I sometimes call it, seventh day; for after my conversion I preferred the plain language of the Friends. On the fourth day, after this, in compliance with an invitation received by note, from the same magistrate who had heard me at the above place I preached to a large congregation, where we had a precious time: much weeping was heard among the people. The same gentleman, now at the close of the meeting, gave out another appointment at the same place, that day week. Here again I had liberty, there was a move among the people. Ten years from that time, in the neighborhood of Cape May, I held a prayer meeting in a school house, which was then the regular place of preaching for the Episcopal Methodists, after service, there came a white lady, of great distinction, a member of the Methodist Society, and told me that at the same school house ten years before, under my preaching, the Lord first awakened her. She rejoiced much to see me, and invited me home with her, where I staid till the next day. This was bread cast upon the water, seen after many days.

From this place I next went to Dennis Creek meeting house, where at the invitation or an elder, I spoke to a large congregation of various and conflicting sentiments, when a wonderful shock of God's power was felt, shown everywhere by groans, by sighs, and loud and happy amens. I felt as if aided from above. My tongue was cut loose, the stammerer spoke freely; the love of God, and of his service, burned with a vehement flame within me—his name was glorified among the people.

I had my little son with me, and was very much straitened for money—and not having means to procure my passage home, I opened a School, and taught eleven scholars, for the purpose of raising a small sum. For many weeks I knew not what to do about returning home, when the Lord came to my assistance as I was rambling in the fields meditating upon his goodness, and made known to me that I might go to the city of Philadelphia, for which place I soon embarked with a very kind captain. We had a perilous passage—a dreadful storm arose, and before leaving the Delaware bay, we had a narrow escape from being run down by a large ship. But the good Lord held us in the hollow of his hand, and in the afternoon of Nov. 12, 1821, we arrived at the city.

Here I held meetings in the dwelling house of sister Lydia Anderson, and for about three months had as many appointments as I could attend. We had many precious seasons together, and the Lord was with his little praying band, convincing and converting sinners to the truth. I continued in the city until spring, when I felt it impressed upon my mind to travel, and walked fourteen miles in company with a sister to meet with some ministers, there to assemble, from Philadelphia. Satan tempted me while on the way, telling me that I was a fool for walking so far, as I would not be permitted to preach. But I pursued my journey, with the determination to set down and worship with them. When I arrived, a goodly number of people had assembled, and no preacher. They waited the time to commence the exercises, and then called upon me. I took the 3d chapter John, 14th verse for my text. I had life and liberty, and the Lord was in the camp with a shout. Another meeting was appointed three miles from there, when I spoke from Psalms cxxxvii, 1, 2, 3, 4. My master was with me, and made manifest his power. In the County House, also, we held a meeting, and had a sweet waiting upon the Lord. I spoke from Hebrews ii, 3, when the Lord gave me peculiar liberty. At a dwelling house one night I spoke from John vii, 46, when six souls fell to the floor crying for mercy. We had a blessed outpouring of the spirit among us—the God of Jacob was in our midst—and the shout of heaven-born souls was like music to our ears.

About the month of February my little son James, then in his sixth year, gave evidence of having religious inclinations. Once he got up in a chair, with a hymn book in his hand, and with quite a ministerial jesture, gave out a hymn. I felt the spirit move me to sing with him. A worthy sister was in the room, who I asked to pray for him. I invoked the Lord to answer and seal this prayer in the courts of heaven. I believed He would and did, and while yet on our knees I was filled with the fulness of God, and the answer came. I cried out in the joy of my heart—"The dead is alive"—and ran down stairs to inform a neighbor. Tears ran down the cheeks of my now happy boy, and great was our rejoicing together. He had been the subject of many prayers, and often had I thought I would rather follow him to his grave than to see him grow up an open and profane sinner like many children I had seen. And here let me say, the promise of the Lord is, "ask and ye shall receive." Dear parents; pray for your children in childhood—carry them in the arms of faith to the mercy seat, and there present them an offering to the Lord. I can say from my own experience, the Lord will hear prayer. I had given James the Bible as Hannah gave Samuel to God in his youth, and by his gracious favor he was received. For the further encouragement of fathers and mothers to engage in this blessed work, let me refer them to Ecclesiastes xi, 6: "In the morning sow thy seed, and in the evening withhold not thy hand, for thou knowest not whether shall prosper either this or that, or whether they both shall be alike good."

"Sow it in the youthful mind,
　　Can you have a fairer field?
Be it but in faith consigned,
　　Harvest, doubtless, it shall yield,
Fruits of early, piety,
　　All that God delights to see."

In November I journeyed for Trenton, N. J. At Burlington I spoke to the people on the Sabbath, and had a good time among them, and on Monday the 12th, in a School house. Sister Mary Owan, who had laid aside all the cares of the world, went with me. We had no means of travelling but on foot, but the Lord regarded us, and by some means put it into the heart of a stranger, to convey us to the Trenton bridge. We fell in with the elder of the circuit, who spoke to me in a cold and formal manner, and as though he thought my capacity was not equal to his. We went into the sister's house, where we expected to stay, and waited a long while with our hats and cloaks on, before the invitation to lodge there was given. In the morning I had thought to visit Newhope, but remained to discharge my duty in visiting the sick and afflicted three or four days in the neighborhood. I was invited to a prayer meeting, and was called upon by a brother to speak. I improved the offer, and made some remarks from Kings xviii, 21. One of the preachers invited me to preach for them on sixth day evening, which I complied with before an attentive congregation, when God followed the word with much power, and great was our joy. On the 17th I spoke in the morning at 11 o'clock. I felt my weakness and deficiency for the work, and thought "who is able for these things," and desired to get away from the task. My text was Timothy vi, 2–7. The

Lord again cut loose the stammering tongue, and opened the Scriptures to my mind, so that, glory to God's dear name, we had a most melting, sin-killing, and soul-reviving time. In the afternoon I assisted in leading a class, when we found the Lord faithful and true—and on the same evening I spoke from Hebrews ii, 3.

The next day, sister Mary Owan and myself set out for Newhope, where we arrived, after walking sixteen miles, at about six o'clock in the evening. Though tedious, it was a pleasant walk to view the high mountain and towering hills, and the beauty and variety of nature around us, which powerfully impressed my mind with the greatness and wisdom of my Maker. At this place I stopt at the house of the gentleman with whose wife's mother I was brought up, and by whom we were agreeably received. The next evening we called upon brother Butler, where I addressed a small company, and God, through his words, quickened some. The next night I spoke in an Academy to a goodly number of people, from John iii, 14. Here I found some very ill-behaved persons, who talked roughly, and said among other things, "I was not a woman, but a man dressed in female clothes." I labored one week among them, and went next to Lambertsville, where we experienced kindness from the people, and had a happy time and parted in tears.

I now returned to Philadelphia, where I stayed a short time, and went to Salem, West Jersey. I met with many troubles on my journey, especially from the elder, who like many others, was averse to a woman's preaching. And here let me tell that elder, if he has not gone to heaven, that I have heard that as far back as Adam Clarke's time, his objections to female preaching were met by the answer—"If an ass reproved Balaam, and a barn-door fowl reproved Peter, why should not a woman reprove sin?" I do not introduce this for its complimentary classification of women with donkeys and fowls, but to give the reply of a poor woman, who had once been a slave. To the first companion she said—"May be a speaking woman is like an ass—but I can tell you one thing, the ass seen the angel when Balaam didn't."

Notwithstanding the opposition, we had a prosperous time at Salem. I had some good congregations, and sinners were cut to the heart. After speaking in the meeting house, two women came up into the pulpit, and falling upon my neck cried out "What shall I do to be saved?" One said she had disobeyed God, and he had taken her children from her—he had called often after her, but she did not hearken. I pointed her to the all-atoning blood of Christ, which is sufficient to cleanse from all sin, and left her, after prayer, to his mercy. From this place I walked twenty-one miles, and preached with difficulty to a stiff-necked and rebellious people, who I soon left without any animosity for their treatment. They might have respected my message, if not the poor weak servant who brought it to them with so much labor.

"If they persecute you in one city, flee into another," was the advice I had resolved to take, and I hastened to Greenwich, where I had a lively congregation, had unusual life and liberty in speaking, and the power of God was there. We also had a solemn time in the meeting house on Sabbath day morning, and in a dwelling house in the evening; a large company assembled, when the spirit was with us, and we had a mighty shaking among the dry bones.

On second day morning, I took stage and rode seven miles to Woodstown, and there I spoke to a respectable congregation of white and colored, in a school house. I was desired to speak in the colored meeting house, but the minister could not reconcile his mind to a woman preacher—he could not unite in fellowship with me even to shaking hands as Christians ought. I had visited that place before, when God made manifest his power "through the foolishness of preaching," and owned the poor old woman. One of the brothers appointed a meeting in his own house, and after much persuasion this minister came also. I did not feel much like preaching, but spoke from Acts viii, 35. I felt my inability, and was led to complain of weakness—but God directed the arrow to the hearts of the guilty—and my friend the minister got happy, and often shouted "Amen," and "as it is, sister." We had a wonderful display of the spirit of God among us, and we found it good to be there. There is nothing too hard for the Lord to do. I committed the meeting into the hands of the elder, who afterwards invited me to preach in the meeting house. He had said he did not believe that ever a soul was converted under the preaching of a woman—but while I was laboring in his place, conviction seized a woman, who fell to the floor crying for mercy. This meeting held till 12 or 1 o'clock. O how precious is the sound of Jesus' name! I never felt a doubt at this time of my acceptance with God, but rested my soul on his every promise. The elder shook hands, and we parted.

Nov. 22, 1822, I returned to Philadelphia, and attended meetings in and out of the city. God was still my help, and I preached and formed a class, and tried to be useful. The oppositions I met with, however, were numerous—so much so, that I was tempted to withdraw from the Methodist Church, lest some might go into ruin by their persecutions of me—but this was allowed only to try my faithfulness to God. At times I was pressed down like a cart beneath its shafts—my life seemed as at the point of the sword—my heart was sore and pained me in my body. But the Lord knows how to deliver the godly out of temptation, and to reserve the unjust till the day of judgment to be punished. While relating the feelings of my mind to a sister who called to see me, joy sprang up in my bosom that I was not overcome by the adversary, and I was overwhelmed with the love of God and souls. I embraced the sister in my arms, and we had a melting time together. Oh how comforting it is to have the spirit of God bearing witness with our spirits that we are his children in such dark hours!

When Satan appears to stop up our path,
And fill us with fears, we triumph by faith;
He cannot take from us, (tho' oft he has tried,)
The soul cheering promise the Lord will provide.
He tells us we're weak, our hope is in vain,
The good that we seek we ne'er shall obtain;
But when such suggestions our graces have tried,
This answers all questions, the Lord will provide.

I felt a greater love for the people than ever. It appeared to me that they erred through ignorance of my desire to do them good; and my prayer was that nothing but love might appear in my ways, and actuate my heart. Religion is love—God is love. But it was nothing less than the Divine power that brought me through, for it appeared that the hosts of darkness were arrayed against me to destroy my peace and lead me away from the throne of love.

June 24, I left the city of Philadelphia to travel in Delaware State. I went with captain Ryal, a kind gentleman, who took me to his house in Wilmington, and himself and lady both treated me well. The first night of my arrival; I preached in the stone Methodist meeting house. I tried, in my weak way, to interest the assembly from the 2d chapter of Hebrews,

3d verse—"How shall we escape, if we neglect so great salvation." God was there, as we had the most delightful evidence—and many had their eyes opened to see there was no escape from the second death while out of Christ, and cried unto God for his saving grace. I would that all who have not embraced the salvation offered in the gospel, might examine the question candidly and seriously, ere the realities of the other world break up their fancied security.

In July I spoke in a School house to a large congregation, from Numbers xxix, 17. Here we had a sweet foretaste of heaven—full measure, and running over—shouting and rejoicing—while the poor errand-bearer of a free gospel was assisted from on high. I wish my reader had been there to share with us the joyous heavenly feast. On the 15th of July I gave an exhortation in the meeting house again to a listening multitude—deep and solemn were the convictions of many, and good, I trust, was done.

The next place I visited was Newcastle. The meeting house could not be obtained, and two young gentleman interested themselves to get the Court house, but the Trustees objected, wishing to know why the Methodists did not open their Church. The reason was "I was not licensed," they said. My two friends waited on me to speak in the Market house, where I attended at early candlelight, and had the pleasure of addressing a few plain truths to a crowded but respectful congregation, from John vii, 46—"Never man spake like this man." On Sunday the same young gentlemen invited me to give another discourse, to which I consented, before a large gathering of all descriptions.

From here I proceeded to Christine, where we worshipped in a dwelling house, and I must say was well treated by some of my colored friends. I then returned to Wilmington, where in a few days I had a message to return again to C. My friends said I should have the Meeting house, for which Squire Luden interested himself, and the appointment was published. When the people met at the proper time, the doors remained locked. Amid cries of "shame" we left the Church steps—but a private house was opened a short distance up the road, and though disappointed in obtaining egress to a Church, the Lord did not disappoint his people, for we were fed with the bread of life, and had a happy time. Mr. and Mrs. Lewelen took me to their house, and treated me, not as one of their hired servants, but as a companion, for which I shall ever feel grateful. Mr. Smith, a doctor, also invited me to call upon them—he was a Presbyterian, but we prayed and conversed together about Jesus and his love, and parted without meddling with each others creeds. Oh, I long to see the day when Christians will meet on one common platform—Jesus of Nazareth—and cease their bickerings and contentions about non-essentials—when "our Church" shall be less debated, but "our Jesus" shall be all in all.

Another family gave me the invitation to attend a prayer meeting. It was like a "little heaven below." From here I walked about four miles that evening, accompanied by the house maid of Mrs. Ford, a Presbyterian, who said she knew her mistress would be glad to see me. Mrs. F. gave me a welcome—said she felt interested in my speaking, and sent a note to a Methodist lady, who replied that my labor would be acceptable, no doubt, in her Church that afternoon. When I came in, the elder was in the pulpit. He gave us a good sermon. After preaching, this lady spoke of me to the elder; in consequence, he invited me to his pulpit, saying "he was willing that every one should do good." My text was Hebrew ii, 3. Though weak in body, the good Master filled my mouth and gave me liberty among strangers, and seldom have I spent so happy a Sabbath. Mrs. F. had a colored woman in her family one hundred and ten years of age, with whom I conversed about religion—how Christ had died to redeem us, and the way of salvation, and the poor old lady said "she wished she could hear me every day." I also called upon another, one hundred and sixteen years old, who was blind. We talked together about Jesus—she had a strong and abiding evidence of her new birth, and in a few weeks went home to heaven. Here she was long deprived of the light of the sun, and the privilege of reading God's blessed word; but there her eyes are unsealed, and the Sun of righteousness has risen with healing in his wings.

> *There glory beams on all the plains,*
> *Which sight to her is given—*
> *There music rolls in sweetest strains,*
> *And spotless beauty ever reigns,*
> *And all is love in heaven.*

I left Mrs. Ford's and walked about three miles to St. George, with a recommend to a Mrs. Sutton, a noble-minded lady of the Presbyterian order, where I was generously treated. Here I preached in the School house to a respectable company—had considerable weeping and a profitable waiting upon the Lord. I accepted an invitation from a gentleman to preach in a Methodist Church three miles distant—found there a loving people, and was highly gratified at the order and decorum manifested while I addressed them. Mrs. Smith took me home with her, who I found to be a christian both in sentiment and action. By invitation, I went next to Port Penn, and spoke with freedom, being assisted of the Lord, to a full house, and had a glorious feast of the Spirit. The next night found me at Canton Bride, to which place I had walked—spoke in a School house, from Math, xxii, 41—"What think ye of Christ?" The presence of the Lord over-shadowed us—believers rejoiced—some were awakened to believe well of my Master, and I trust are on their way to glory. In Fields-borough, also, we had gracious meetings.

At Smyrna I met brother C. W. Cannon, who made application for the Friend's Meeting house for me, where the Lord blessed us abundantly. We attended a Camp-meeting of the old connexion, and got greatly refreshed for the King's service. I rode ten miles and delivered a message from the Lord to a waiting audience—the Master assisted, and seven individuals, white and colored, prostrated themselves for prayer. Next day I rode to Middletown—spoke in a School house to a white congregation from Isaiah lxiii, 1, and a good time it was. In the morning at 11 o'clock, I addressed a Methodist Society, and in the afternoon at 3 o'clock, spoke under a tree in the grave yard, by the road side, to a large audience. Squire Maxwell's lady, who was present, invited me home to tea with herself and nieces, and a Quaker lady showed her benevolence by putting into my hand enough to help me on my journey. The Lord is good—what shall I do to make it known? I rode seven miles that night, and gave an exhortation after the minister had preached, and felt happier than a King.

I now travelled to Cecil county, Md., and the first evening spoke to a large congregation. The pastor afterwards baptized some adult persons—and we all experienced the cleansing and purifying power. We had a baptism within and without. I was next sent for by the servant of a white gentleman, to hold a meeting in his house in the evening. He invited the neighbors, colored and white, when I spoke according to the ability God gave me. It was pleasant to my poor soul to be there—Jesus was in our midst—and we gave glory to God. Yes, glory—glory be to God in the highest. "God forbid that I should glory, save in the cross of our Lord Jesus Christ." I boast not myself. Paul may plant and Apollos water, but God giveth the increase, I tried also to preach three times at a place 14 miles from here—had good meetings—backsliders were reclaimed and sinners convicted of sin, who I left in the hands of God, with the hope of meeting and recognizing again "when we arrive at home."

* * * * *

Returned back to Middletown. The next day the preacher of the circuit conveyed me to his place of appointment at Elkton. We had a wonderful outpouring of the spirit. At Frenchtown I spoke at 11 o'clock, where I realized my nothingness, but, God's name he praised, he helped me in the duty. Went again to Middletown, and from there to Canton's Bridge, and talked to the people as best I could. Seven miles from this place I found, by the direction of a kind Providence, my own sister, who had been separated from me some thirty-three years. We were young when last we met, with less of the cares of life than now. Each heart then was buoyant with mildly hopes and pleasures—and little did we expect at parting that thirty-three years would pass over us, with its changes and vicissitudes, ere we should see each other's face. Both were much altered in appearance, but we knew each other, and talked over the dealings of the Lord with us, retracing our wanderings in the world and "the days when life was young."

> "Our days of childhood quickly pass,
>   And soon our happiest years are run—
> As the pure dew that gems the grass
>   Is dried beneath the summer sun.
> There's such deceit—such guile in men,
> Who would not be a child again?"

During this visit I had three meetings in different directions in gentlemen's houses, and a prayer meeting at my brother's, who did not enjoy religion. My good old friend Mr. Lorton happened to be there, who told the people that he had been to my house—that he knew Mr. Lee (my husband) intimately, and that he had often preached for him while pastor of the Church at Snow Hill, N. J.

I next attended and preached several times at a camp meetinng, which continued five days. We had pentecostal showers—sinners were pricked to the heart, and cried mightily to God for succor from impending judgment, and I verily believe the Lord was well pleased at our weak endeavors to serve him in the tented grove. The elder in charge, on the last day of the camp, appointed a meeting for me in a dwelling house. Spoke from Acts ii, 41. The truth fastened in the hearts of two young women, who, after I was seated, came and fell down at my side, and cried for God to have mercy on them—we prayed and wrestled with the Lord, and both were made happy in believing, and are alive in the faith of the gospel. The next morning a brother preacher took me to St. Georgetown. From there I took stage to Wilmington, and called on my friend Captain Rial, in whose family I spent two days and nights. Went to Philadelphia to attend a camp-meeting. Returned again to W—, where I was taken sick with typhus fever, and was in the doctor's hands for some days—but the Lord rebuked the disease, gave me my usual health again, and I returned back to Philadelphia.

The Bishop gave me an invitation to speak in Bethel Church; but here my heart fluttered with fear at the commencement, in a manner known but to those who feel their unworthiness in addressing new and large assemblies. My text was in Isaiah x. 10, 11. Previous to dismission, the Bishop gave me another appointment in Wesley Church for first day morning, where I labored to encourage believers, from Ephesians ii, 19. The comforter was with us—we were sprinkled as with clear water from above—the hands of those that were hanging down were lifted up, and we truly had a refreshing season. Glory to God for the manifestation of His Spirit. "Now therefore ye are no more strangers and foreigners, but fellow-citizens with the saints, and of the household of God."

On the ensuing Thursday night, in Union Church, I had the opportunity of speaking a word for my Saviour again, and recommeneed the impenitent to see to it that they took the advice of my text, in Rev. iii, 18. The Lord searched the heart as he did Jerusalem with a lighted candle, and there was a moving of the Spirit among the people.

From Philadelphia I travelled on foot thirty miles to Downingtown, and gave ten sermons while there; and remember the cold day in December I walked sixteen miles from the above place to brother Wells', where I staid one week, and labored both among colored and white. They had one class there. Three miles further, I talked on Lord's day to an apparently hardened people, and next night preached in a School-house, after a ride of ten miles. The call of the Lord was for me now to go to West Chester, N. Y., where I remained a little period with brother Thomas Henry and brother Miller; preached in a School-house and in the Wesleyan Methodist Meeting-house. When prepared to go home, a request was sent me to preach in the Court-house of the county, to which I rode ten miles, and addressed the citizens on two evenings. The Lord strengthened his feeble instrument in the effort to win souls to Christ, for which my heart at this time was heavily burthened. Next morning I left for Westhaven, where I visited a School of boys and girls, and was much pleased to see them engaged and improving in their studies. How great the difference now, thought I, for the mental and moral culture of the young than when I was a child!

In the month of June, 1823, I went on from Philadelphia to New York with Bishop Allen and several Elders, (including our present Rev. Bishop Brown,) to attend the New York Annual Conference of our denomination, where I spent three months of my time. We arrived about nine o'clock in the evening. As we left the boat, a person fell into the dock, and notwithstanding the effort made to save and find him, he was seen no more. 'In the midst of life we are in death.' On the 4th of June I spoke in the Asbury Church, from Psalms c, 33. I think I never witnessed such a shouting and rejoicing time. The Church had then but recently adopted the African M. E. discipline. On the 5th I brought my master's message to the Bethel Church—Text Isaiah lviii, 1. "Cry aloud, spare not; lift up thy voice like a trumpet, and show my people their transgressions, and the house of Jacob their sins." The spirit of God came upon me; I spoke without fear of man, and seemed willing even there to be offered up; the preachers shouted and prayed, and it was a time long to be remembered.

June 6. Spoke in the Church in High Street, Brooklyn, from Jer. ix, 1—"Oh that my head were waters, and mine eyes a fountain of tears, that I might weep day and night for the slain of the daughter of my people." In these days I felt it my duty to travel up and down in the world, and promulgate the gospel of Christ, especially among my own people, though I often desired to be released from the great task. The Lord had promised to be with me, and my trust was in his strong arm.

Renouncing every worldly thing,
Safe 'neath the shadow of thy wing,
My sweetest thought henceforth shall be
That all I want I find in thee,
*   In thee, my God, in Thee.*

I left my friend in Brooklyn, and went to Flushing, L. I. Here we had quite a revival feeling, and two joined society. Visited Jamaica and Jericho; spoke in brother B's dwelling, in the church, and under a tree. Went to White Plains to the camp-meeting; the Lord was with us indeed; believers were revived, backsliders reclaimed, and sinners converted. Returned and spent a little time in Brooklyn, where I addressed the people from Rev. iii, 18, and John iii, 15.

July 22. Spoke in Asbury Church from Acts xiii, 41—"Behold ye despisers, and wonder and perish." I pointed out the portion of the hypocrite, the liar, the Sabbath-breaker, and all who do wickedly and die in their sins; they shall be to the judgment bar of Jehovah, and before an assembled universe hear their awful sentence, "Depart from me, ye cursed, into everlasting fire, prepared for the devil and his angels," while the righteous shall be received "into life eternal." On the 28th I went to Dutch Hill, L. I., and spoke before a congregation of white and colored, in a barn, as there was no other suitable place. I felt happy when I thought of my dear Redeemer, who was born in a stable and cradled in a manger, and we had a precious season. Brother Croker, of Brooklyn, and father Thompson were with me, at whose feet I desired rather to sit and learn, they being experienced "workmen that needed not to be ashamed." But the Lord sends by whom he will.

The next Sabbath I weakly attempted to address my friends in New York again. Took the words in Math. xxviii, 13, for my text—"Say ye, his disciples came by night, and stole him away while we slept." The place was greatly crowded, and many came who could not get in. A class met here, to which the preacher invited all who desired to remain, and thirty persons tarried. He called upon me to lead, but He who led Israel over the Red Sea assisted, and it was a gracious time with us. Some who remained from curiosity were made, like Belshazzar, to tremble and weep, while the spirit strove powerfully with them. One experienced religion and joined society. I expect in the resurrection morning to meet many who were in that little company, in my Father's house, where we shall strike hands no more to part; where our song of redemption shall be raised to God and the Lamb forever. Dear reader, if you have not, I charge you to make your peace with God while time and opportunity is given, and be one of that number who shall take part and lot in the first resurrection. Though I may never see you in the flesh, I leave on this page my solemn entreaty that you delay not to obtain the pardoning favor of God; that you leave not the momentous subject of religion to a sick bed or dying hour, but NOW, even now, seek the Lord with full purpose of heart, and he will be found of thee. "If any man sin, he has advocate with the Father, Jesus Christ the righteous."

"Oh that the world might taste and see
*   The riches of his grace;*
The arms of love that compass me,
*   Would all mankind embrace."*

I visited a woman who was laying sick upon her death-bed. She told me "she had once enjoyed religion, but the enemy had cheated her out of it." She knew that she must die in a very little while, and could not get well, and her agony of soul, in view of its unprepared state for a judgment to come, awoke every feeling of sympathy within me. Oh! how loud such a scene calls upon us to be "faithful unto death"—then shall we "receive a crown of life." Also visited Mrs. Miller, who once "tasted that the Lord was good," but had ceased now to follow him. She had been a Methodist for many years—got her feelings injured through some untoward circumstance—had fallen from grace, and now was sick. A good sister accompanied me? we conversed with Mrs. M., sung an appropriate hymn, and my friend supplicated the throne of grace in her behalf. She had frequently felt the need of a returning Saviour, and during prayer her heart became melted into tenderness. She cried aloud for mercy, wrestled like Jacob for the witness, and the Lord, faithful and true, "healed her backslidings," and we left her happy in his father. Praise the Lord for his matchless grace. I entertained no doubt of her well-grounded hope; and on seeing such a display of God's power, I was lost in wonder, love and praise. Let the backslider hear and take courage, Let all who are out of Christ hear the invitation—"Repent ye and be converted, for God hath called all men everywhere to repent."

"*Without reserve give Christ your heart,*
Let him his righteousness impart—
Then all things else he'll freely give,
With him you all things shall receive."

With a serene and tranquil mind I now returned to Philadelphia. The Bishop was pleased to give me an appointment at Bethel Church, but a spirit of opposition arose among the people against the propriety of female preaching. My faith was tried—yet I felt my call to labor for souls none the less. "Shall the servant be above his Master?" The ministers of Jesus must expect persecution, if they would be faithful witnesses against sin and sinners—but shall they, "awed by a mortal's form, conceal the word of God?" Thou God knowest my heart, and that thy glory is all I have in view. Shall I cease from sounding the alarm to an ungodly world, when the vengeance of offended heaven is about to be poured out, because my way is sometimes beset with scoffers, or those who lose sight of the great Object, and stop on the road to glory to contend about non-essentials? Rather let the messengers of God go on—let them not be hindered by the fashions and customs of a gainsaying and mis-loving generation, but with the crown in view, which shall deck the brow of those only who are "faithful unto death"— let them "cry aloud and spare not." Who regarded the warnings of Noah? who believed in his report? Who among the antidiluvians, that witnessed the preparations of this righteous man to save himself and family from a deluge of waters, believed him any thing else than a fanatic, deluded, and beside himself? Let the servants of Christ gird on the armor, and "listen to the Captain's voice: "Lo I am with you always, even unto the end." With the promise of my Lord impressed upon my mind, I remained at home only a week, and walked twenty-one miles to Lumbertown, and preached in the Old Methodist Church and our African Church. Brother Joshua Edely was then a deacon there, and held a quarterly meeting soon after my reaching the place. He also appointed a love-feast in the morning, when the love that true believers enjoy at such scenes made the place akin to heaven. While here I spoke as the Spirit taught me from Solomon's Songs. It was a happy meeting—refreshing to the thirsty soul—and we had a shout of the king in the camp. I shall never forget the kindness I received here from dear sister G. B. May the blessings of heaven be hers in this and the world to come.

I travelled seven miles from the above place to Snow Hill on Sabbath morning, where I was to preach in the Church of which I was a member; and although much afflicted in body, I strove, by the grace of God, to perform the duty. This was once the charge of JOSEPH LEE. In this desk my lamented husband had often stood up before me, proclaiming the "acceptable year of the Lord"—here he labored with zeal and spent his strength to induce sinners to be "reconciled to God"—here his toils ended. And could it be, that a poor unworthy being like myself should be called to address his former congregation, and should stand in the same pulpit! The thought made me tremble. My heart sighed when memory brought back the image, and the reminiscences of other days crowded upon me. But why, my heart, dost thou sigh? He has ceased from his labor, and I here see his works do follow. It will be enough, if these, the people of his care, press on and gain the kingdom. It will be enough, if, on the final day, "for which all other days were made," we pass through the gates into the city, and live again together where death cannot enter, and separations are unknown. Cease then, my tears—a little while, my fluttering heart! and the turf that covers my companion, perchance, may cover thee—a little while, my soul! if faithful, and the widow's God will call thee from this valley of tears and sorrows to rest in the mansions the Saviour has gone to prepare for his people. "Good what God gives—just what he takes away."

My mind was next exercised to visited Trenton, N. J. I spoke for the people there, but soon had felt the cross so heavy. Perhaps it was occasioned through grieving over the past, and my feelings of loneliness in the world. A sister wished me to go with her to Bridgeport—where I found brother Orwin, then elder over that church. He gave me an appointment. We had a full house, and God's power was manifest among the people, and I returned to the elder's house rejoicing. The following day I walked fourteen miles to a meeting, where also we were greatly favored with the presence of God. Soon after this, I thought of going home to Philadelphia. I got about three miles on foot, when an apparent voice said "I thou goest horne thou wilt die." I paused for a moment, and not comprehending what it meant, pursued my journey. Again I was startled by something like a tapping on my shoulder, but, on turning round, I found myself alone, which two circumstances created a singular feeling I could not understand. I thought of Balaam when met by the angel in the way. I was taken sick and it seemed I should die in the road. I said I will go back, and walked about four miles to Bridgeport. Told a good sister my exercise, who was moved with sympathy, and got brandy and bathed me. On Wednesday night I spoke to the people at Trenton Bridge, and notwithstanding the opposition I had met with from brother Samuel R—, then on the circuit, the Lord supported the "woman preacher" and my soul was cheered. On Thursday I walked fourteen miles, when the friends applied to the elder to let me talk for them, but his prejudices also, against women preaching were very strong, and tried hard to disaffect the minds of the people. The dear man has since gone to stand before that God who knows the secrets of all hearts—and where, I earnestly pray, he may find some who have been saved by grace through the instrumentality of female preaching.

"Then here, O God, thy work fulfil;
    And from thy mercy's throne
O grant me strength to do thy will,
    And to resist my own."

Norristown, Bucks county, January 6, 1824. Brother Morris conveyed me here at his own expense, and made application for places for me to speak. Addressed a large congregation on the fourth day after my introduction into the place, in the court-house, from Isaiah liiii. 1,—"Who hath believed our report? and to whom is the arm of the Lord revealed?" I felt embarrassed in the commencement, but the Spirit came, and "helped our infirmities"—good attention, and some weeping. On the 18th I spoke in the academy—it was a solemn time, and the people came out in numbers to hear. I then walked four miles to brother Morris's—spoke twice in the schoolhouse, and once in a dwelling house.

On the 14th April, I went with Bishop Allen and several elders to Baltimore, on their way to attend Conference; at the end of which the Bishop gave me permission to express a few thoughts for my Lord. On leaving the city of B., I travelled about 100 miles to Eastern Shore, Maryland. Brother Bailey was then laboring on that circuit, who received and treated me very kindly. We had several good meetings, and twice I spoke in Bethel Church, when the outpouring of the Spirit was truly great. In company with a good sister, who took a gig and horse, I travelled about three hundred miles, and labored in different places. Went to Denton African Church, and on the first Sabbath gave two sermons. The Church was in a thriving, prosperous condition, and the Lord blessed the word to our comfort. During the week I labored in the court-house before a large concourse of hearers. The Lord was unspeakably good, and one fell to the floor under the power.

By request, I also spoke in the Old Methodist Church in Denton, which was full to overflowing. It was a happy meeting. My tongue was loosened, and my heart warm with the love of God and souls—a season yet sweet to my memory. From there I went to Greensboro'—the elder gave a sermon, after which I exhorted the poor sinner to prepare to meet the Lord in peace, before mercy was clear gone forever. The Old Methodist connexion gave an invitation for me to speak in their house, which I embraced, feeling thankful that the middle wall of partition had, thus far, been broken down. "He that feareth God and worketh righteousness shall be accepted of him"—not he who hath a different skin—not he who belongs to this denomination, or, to that—but "he that feareth God." My Master is no respecter of persons. May the partition walls that divide His sincere followers be broken down by the spirit of love.

In Whitehall Chapel I spoke to a respectable congregation, from Isaiah liii. 1. Though in a slave country, I found the Omnipresent One was with us. Dr. Clarke took us home to dine with his family—for which uncommon attention I felt highly gratified. I believe him a Christian in heart, and one, no doubt, who has read the words of the Saviour: "Whosoever shall give to drink unto one of these little ones a cup of cold water only, shall in no wise lose his reward." And, notwithstanding the doctor was a Presbyterian, Mr. Buly had the privilege of baptizing two of their colored children. * * *

I stopped next at Concord, and in the Old Methodist connexion tried to encourage the Lord's people to persevere. God displayed His power by a general outpouring of the Spirit—sinners cried for mercy, while others shouted for joy. Spoke also to a congregation of colored and white at Stanton Mills; and arrived again at Eastern Shore, where I spoke in Bethel Church during Quarterly Meeting. Attended their love-feast, where several joined society, and many encouraging testimonies were given by young converts that "God hath power on earth to forgive sins." May they be faithful stewards of the manifold gifts of God—and never be ashamed to confess what the Lord had done for them. Many lose the witness out of the heart by withholding their testimony from their friends and neighbors of the power of God to save. They run well for a season, but the tempter whispers "not now"—and by and by the soul becomes barren and unfruitful. May God help the young converts to "watch," and tell around what a dear Saviour they have found.

> "Ashamed of Jesus!—yes, I may,
>   When I've no guilt to wash away—
> No tears to wipe—no good to crave—
>   No fears to quell—no soul to save."

June 10th, 1824. Left Eastern Shore for a journey to Bath, and went around the circuit with brother J. B., the elder. In the Old Methodist Church, at Fory's Neck, I had the privilege of speaking to a large congregation, which was made the power of God unto salvation. Visited Lewistown, and had a blessed meeting in the Methodist Church. The tears of the penitent flowed sweetly, which always encourages me to persevere in proclaiming the glad tidings of a risen Saviour to my fellow beings. When the heart is thus melted into tenderdess, I feel assured the Lord sanctions the feeble effort of His poor servant—it is a good omen to my mind that the mourner is not forsaken of God, and that he yet stands knocking at the door for admittance. Oh! that those who weep for an absent Jesus may be comforted by hearing Him say—" Thy sins, which were many, are all forgiven thee: go in peace and sin no more."

* * * * *

But here I feel constrained to give over, as from the smallness of this pamphlet I cannot go through with the whole of my journal, as it would probably make a volume of two hundred pages; which, if the Lord be willing, may at some future day be published. But for the satisfaction of such as may follow after me, when I am no more, I have recorded how the Lord called me to his work, and how he has kept me from falling from grace, as I feared I should. In all things he has proved himself a God of truth to me; and in his service I am now as much determined to spend and be spent, as at the very first. My ardour for the progress of his cause abates not a whit, so far as I am able to judge, though I am now something more than fifty years of age.

As to the nature of uncommon impressions, which the reader cannot but have noticed, and possibly sneered at in the course of these pages, they may be accounted for in this way: It is known that the blind have the sense of hearing in a manner much more acute than those who can see: also their sense of feeling is exceedingly fine, and is found to detect any roughness on the smoothest surface, where those who can see find none. So it may be with such as I am, who has never had more than three months schooling; and wishing to know much of the way and law of God, have therefore watched the more closely, the operations of the Spirit, and have in consequence been led thereby. But let it be remarked that I have never found that Spirit lead me contrary to the Scriptures of truth, as I understand them. "For as many as are led by the *Spirit* of God are the sons of God."— Rom. viii. 14.

I have now only to say, May the blessing of the Father, and of the Son, and of the Holy Ghost, accompany the reading of this poor effort to speak well of his name, wherever it may be read.   AMEN.

P. S. Please to pardon errors, and excuse all imperfections, as I have been deprived of the advantages of education (which I hope all will appreciate) as I am measurably a self-taught person. I hope the contents of this work may be instrumental in leaving a lasting impression upon the minds of the impenitent; may it prove to be encouraging to the justified soul, and a comfort to the sanctified

Though much opposed, it is certainly essential in life, as Mr. Wesley wisely observes. Thus ends the Narrative of JARENA LEE, the first female preacher of the First African Methodist Episcopal Church.

Bethel at Philadelphia, Penn., United States of America.

6. Religious Instruction

PETER RANDOLPH

MANY say the negroes receive religious education—that Sabbath worship is instituted for them as for others, and were it not for slavery, they would die in their sins—that really, the institution of slavery is a benevolent missionary enterprise. Yes, they are preached to, and I will give my readers some faint glimpses of these preachers, and their doctrines and practices.

In Prince George County, there were two meeting-houses intended for public worship. Both were occupied by the Baptist denomination. These houses were built by William and George Harrison, brothers. Mr. G. Harrison's was built on the line of his brother's farm, that their slaves might go there on the Sabbath and receive instruction, such as slaveholding ministers would give. The prominent preaching to the slaves was," 'Servants, obey your masters.' "Do not *steal* or *lie*, for this is very wrong. Such conduct is sinning against the Holy Ghost, *and is base ingratitude to your kind masters, who feed, clothe, and protect you.*" All Gospel, my readers! It was great policy to build a church for the "*dear slave,*" and allow him the wondrous privilege of such holy instruction! Edloe's slaves sometimes obtained the consent of Harrison to listen to the Sabbath teachings so generously dealt out to his servants. Shame! shame! to take upon yourselves the name of Christ, with all that blackness of heart. I should think, when making such statements, the slaveholders would feel the rebuke of the Apostle, and fall down and be carried out from the face of day, as were Ananias and Sapphira, when they betrayed the trust committed to them, or refused to bear true testimony in regard to that trust.

There was another church, about fourteen miles from the one just mentioned. It was called "Brandon's church," and there the white Baptists worshipped. Edloe's slaves sometimes went there. The colored people had a very small place allotted them to sit in, so they used to get as near the window as they could to hear the preacher talk to his congregation. But sometimes, while the preacher was exhorting to obedience, some of those outside would be selling refreshments, cake, candy, and rum, and others would be horse-racing. This was the way, my readers, the Word of God was delivered and received in Prince George County. The Gospel was so mixed with Slavery, that the people could see no beauty in it, and feel no reverence for it.

There was one Brother Shell, who used to preach. One Sabbath, while exhorting the poor, impenitent, hard-hearted, ungrateful slaves, so much beloved by their masters, to repentance and prayerfulness, while entreating them to lead good lives, that they might escape the wrath (of the lash) to come, some of his crocodile tears overflowed his cheek, which so affected his hearers, that they shouted and gave thanks to God, that brother Shell had at length felt the spirit of the Lord in his heart; and many went away rejoicing that a heart of stone had become softened. But, my readers, Monday morning, brother Shell was afflicted with his old malady, hardness of heart, so that he was obliged to catch one of the sisters by the throat, and give her a terrible flogging.

The like of this is the preaching, and these are the men that spread the Gospel among the slaves. Ah! such a Gospel had better be buried in oblivion, for it makes more heathens than Christians. Such preachers ought to be forbidden by the laws of the land ever to mock again at the blessed religion of Jesus, which was sent as a light to the world.

Another Sunday, when Shell was expounding, (very much engaged was he in his own attempts to enlighten his hearers,) there was one Jem Fulcrum became so enlightened that he fell from his seat, quite a distance, to the floor. Brother Shell thought he had preached unusually well so to affect Jem; so he stopped in the midst of his sermon, and asked, "Is that poor Jemmy? poor fellow!" But, my readers, he did not know the secret,—*brother Jem had fallen asleep. Poor* Shell did not do so much good as he thought he had, so Monday morning he gave Jem enough of his raw-hide spirit to last him all the week; at least, till the next Sabbath, when he could have an opportunity to preach to him.

I could only think, when Shell took so much glory to himself for the effect of his preaching upon the slaves, of the man who owned colored Pompey. This slaveholder was a great fighter, (as most of them are,) and had prepared himself for the contest with great care, and wished to know how he looked; so he said, "Pompey, how do I look?" "O, massa, *mighty.*" "What do you mean by 'mighty,' Pompey ?" "Why, massa, you look noble." "What do you mean by 'noble?'" "Why, sar, you look just like one *lion.*" "Why, Pompey, where have you ever seen a lion?" "I see one down in yonder field the other day, massa." "Pompey, you foolish fellow, that was a *jackass.*" "Was it, massa? Well, you look just like him."

This may seem very simple to my readers, but surely, nothing more noble than a jackass, without his simplicity and innocence, can that man be, who will rise up as an advocate of this system of wrong. He who trains his dogs to hunt foxes, and enjoys the hunt or the horse-race on the Sabbath, who teaches his blood-hounds to follow upon the track of the freedom-loving negro, is not more guilty or immoral than he who stands in a Northern pulpit, and hunts down the flying fugitive, or urges his hearers to bind the yoke again upon the neck of the escaped bondman. He who will lisp one word in favor of a system which will send blood-hounds through the forests of Virginia, the Carolinas, Georgia, Kentucky, and all the South, chasing human beings, (who are seeking the inalienable rights of all men, "life, liberty, and the pursuit of happiness,") possesses no heart; and that minister of religion who will do it is unworthy his trust, knows not what the Gospel teaches, and had better turn to the heathen for a religion to guide him nearer the right; for the heathen in their blindness have some regard for the rights of others, and seldom will they invade the honor and virtue of their neighbors, or cause them to be torn in pieces by infuriated beasts.

Mr. James L. Goltney was a Baptist preacher, and was employed by Mr. M. B. Harrison to give religious instruction to his slaves. He often used the common text: "Servants, obey your masters." He would try to make it appear that he knew what the slaves were thinking of,—telling them they thought they had a right to be free, but he could tell them better,— referring them to some passages of Scripture. "It is the devil," he would say, "who tells you to try and be free." And again he bid them be patient at work, warning them that it would be his duty to whip them, if they appeared dissatisfied,—all which would be pleasing to God! "If you run away, you will be turned out of God's church, until you repent, return, and ask God and your master's pardon." In this way he would continue to preach his slaveholding gospel.

This same Goltney used to administer the Lord's Supper to the slaves. After such preaching, let no one say that the slaves have the Gospel of Jesus preached to them.

One of the Baptist ministers was named B. Harrison. He owned slaves, and was very cruel to them. He came to an untimely end. While he was riding out one afternoon, the report of a gun was heard, and he was found dead,—his brains being blown out. It could never be found who killed him, and so he went to judgment, with all his sins on his head.

Mr. L. Hanner was a Christian preacher, selecting texts like the following: "The Spirit of the Lord is upon me, because he hath anointed me to preach deliverance to the captives, he hath sent me to bind up the broken-hearted." But Hanner was soon mobbed out of Prince George's County, and had to flee for his life, and all for preaching a true Gospel to colored people.

I did not know of any other denomination where I lived in Virginia, than the Baptists and Presbyterians. Most of the colored people, and many of the poorer class of whites, were Baptists.

Sabbath and Religious Meetings

On the Sabbath, after doing their morning work, and breakfast over, (such as it is,) that portion of the slaves who belong to the church ask of the overseer permission to attend meeting. If he is in the mood to grant their request, he writes them a pass, as follows:—

"Permit the bearer to pass and repass to—, this evening, unmolested."

Should a pass not be granted, the slave lies down, and sleeps for the day—the only way to drown his sorrow and disappointment.

Others of the slaves, who do not belong to the church, spend their Sabbath in playing with marbles, and other games, for each other's food, &c.

Some occupy the time in dancing to the music of a banjo, made out of a large gourd. This is continued till the after part of the day, when they separate, and gather wood for their log-cabin fires the ensuing week.

Not being allowed to hold meetings on the plantation, the slaves assemble in the swamps, out of reach of the patrols. They have an understanding among themselves as to the time and place of getting together. This is often done by the first one arriving breaking boughs from the trees, and bending them in the direction of the selected spot. Arrangements are then made for conducting the exercises. They first ask each other how they feel, the state of their minds, &c. The male members then select a certain space, in separate groups, for their division of the meeting. Preaching in order, by the brethren; then praying and singing all round, until they generally feel quite happy. The speaker usually commences by calling himself unworthy, and talks very slowly, until, feeling the spirit, he grows excited, and in a short time, there fall to the ground twenty or thirty men and women under its influence. Enlightened people call it excitement; but I wish the same was felt by everybody, so far as they are sincere.

The slave forgets all his sufferings, except to remind others of the trials during the past week, exclaiming: "Thank God, I shall not live here always!" Then they pass from one to another, shaking hands, and bidding each other farewell, promising, should they meet no more on earth, to strive and meet in heaven, where all is joy, happiness and liberty. As they separate, they sing a parting hymn of praise.

Sometimes the slaves meet in an old log-cabin, when they find it necessary to keep a watch. If discovered, they escape, if possible; but those who are caught often get whipped.

Some are willing to be punished thus for Jesus' sake. Most of the songs used in worship are composed by the slaves themselves, and describe their own sufferings. Thus:

> "O, that I had a bosom friend,
> To tell my secrets to,
> One always to depend upon
> In every thing I do !"

> "How I do wander, up and down!
> I seem a stranger, quite undone;
> None to lend an ear to my complaint,
> No one to cheer me, though I faint."

Some of the slaves sing—

> "No more rain, no more snow,
> No more cowskin on my back;"

then they change it by singing—

> "Glory be to God that rules on high."

In some places, if the slaves are caught praying to God, they are whipped more than if they had committed a great crime. The slaveholders will allow the slaves to dance, but do not want them to pray to God. Sometimes, when a slave, on being whipped, calls upon God, he is forbidden to do so, under threat of having his throat cut, or brains blown out. O, reader! this seems very hard,—that slaves cannot call on their Maker, when the case most needs it. Sometimes the poor slave takes courage to ask his master to let him pray, and is driven away with the answer, that if discovered praying, his back will pay the bill.

The Blood of the Slave

The blood of the slave cries unto God from the ground,
and it calls loudly for vengeance on his adversaries.
The blood of the slave cries unto God from the rice swamps.
The blood of the slave cries unto God from the cotton plantations.
The blood of the slave cries unto God from the tobacco farms.
The blood of the slave cries unto God from the sugar fields.
The blood of the slave cries unto God from the corn fields.
The blood of the slave cries unto God from the whipping-post.
The blood of the slave cries unto God from the auction-block.
The blood of the slave cries unto God from the gallows.
The blood of the slave cries unto God from the hunting-dogs
that run down the poor fugitive.

The blood of men, women and babes cries unto God from Texas to Maine. Wherever the Fugitive Slave Law reaches, the voice of its victims is heard.

The mighty God, the great Jehovah, speaks to the consciences of men, and says, "LET MY PEOPLE GO FREE!" And the slaveholder answers, "Who is Jehovah, that I should obey him?" Then the Anti-Slavery voice is heard, calling, "Awake! *Awake!* and cry aloud against this great evil; lift up your voice like a trumpet, and show the people their sins, and the nation its guilt. Pray that God may have mercy upon us. O, forgive us this great evil,—the evil of selling, whipping, and killing men, women and children! O, God of justice! give us hearts and consciences to feel the deep sorrow of this great evil that we have so long indulged in! Lo! we have sinned against Heaven; we have sinned against light,—against the civilized world. We have sinned against that declaration which our fathers put forth to the world, '*All men are created equal.*' O, God! forgive us this great sin! O, let this prayer be heard !"

7. Pastor and Flock

From *Lay My Burden Down*

They'd pray, "Lord, deliver us from under bondage."

What the Preacher Said

I

We went to the white folks' church, so we sit in the back on the floor. They allowed us to join their church whenever one got ready to join or felt that the Lord had forgiven them of their sins. We told our determination; this is what we said: "I feel that the Lord have forgiven me for my sins. I have prayed and I feel that I am a better girl. I belong to Master So and So and I am so old." The white preacher would then ask our miss and master what they thought about it and if they could see any change. They would get up and say: "I notice she don't steal and I notice she don't lie as much and I notice she works better." Then they let us join. We served our mistress and master in slavery time and not God.

II

They had preaching one Sunday for white folks and one Sunday for black folks. They used the same preacher there, but some colored preachers would come on the place at times and preach under the trees down at the quarters. They said the white preacher would say, "You may get to the kitchen of heaven if you obey your master, if you don't steal, if you tell no stories," etc.

III

The niggers didn't go to the church building; the preacher came and preached to them in their quarters. He'd just say, "Serve your masters. Don't steal your master's turkey. Don't steal your master's chickens. Don't steal your master's hogs. Don't steal your master's meat. Do whatsomever your master tells you to do." Same old thing all the time.

IV

When Grandma was fourteen or fifteen years old, they locked her up in the seedhouse once or twice for not going to church. You see, they let the white folks go to the church in the morning and the colored folks in the evening, and my grandma didn't always want to go. She would be locked up in the seed bin, and she would cuss the preacher out so he could hear her. She would say, "Master, let us out." And he would say, "You want to go to church?" And she would say, "No, I don't want to hear that same old sermon: 'Stay out of your missus' and master's henhouse. Don't steal your missus' and master's chickens. Stay out of your missus' and master's smokehouse. Don't steal your missus' and master's hams.' I don't steal nothing. Don't need to tell me not to."

She was telling the truth, too. She didn't steal because she didn't have to. She had plenty without stealing. She got plenty to eat in the house. But the other slaves didn't git nothing but fat meat and corn bread and molasses. And they got tired of that same old thing. They wanted something else sometimes. They'd go to the henhouse and get chickens. They would go to the smokehouse and get hams and lard. And they would get flour and anything else they wanted, and they would eat something they wanted. There wasn't no way to keep them from it.

V

One time when an old white man came along who wanted to preach, the white people gave him a chance to preach to the niggers. The substance of his sermon was this:

"Now when you servants are working for your masters, you must be honest. When you go to the mill, don't carry along an extra sack and put some of the meal or the flour in for yourself. And when you women are cooking in the big house, don't make a big pocket under your dress and put a sack of coffee and a sack of sugar and other things you want in it."

They took him out and hanged him for corrupting the morals of the slaves.

God Got a Clean Kitchen to Put You In

There wasn't no church on the plantation where I stay. Had preaching in Mr. Ford's yard some-times, and then another time the slaves went to white people's church at Bear Swamp. Boss tell slaves to go to meeting 'cause he say he pay the preacher. Dean Ears, white man, gave out speech to the slaves one day there to Nichols. Slaves sat in gallery when they go there. He tell them to obey they master and missus. Then he say, "God got a clean kitchen to put you in. You think you gwine be free, but you ain't gwine be free long as there an ash in Ashpole Swamp." White folks complain 'bout the slaves getting two sermons and they get one. After that, they tell old slaves not to come to church till after the white folks had left. That never happen till after the war was over.

Two Ways of Preaching the Gospel

I been preaching the gospel and farming since slavery time. I jined the church 'most 83 years ago when I was Major Gaud's slave, and they baptizes me in the spring branch close to where I finds the Lord. When I starts preaching I couldn't read or write and had to preach what Master told me, and he say tell them niggers iffen they obeys the master they goes to Heaven; but I knowed there's something better for them, but daren't tell them 'cept on the sly. That I done lots. I tells 'em iffen they keeps praying, the Lord will set 'em free.

Every Kind of Fish Is Caught in a Net

Sunday morning he preached "Every kind of fish is caught in a net." . . . Parson sure told 'em 'bout it. He say, "First, they catch the crawfish, and that fish ain't worth much; anybody that gets back from duty or one which says I will and then won't is a crawfish Christian."

Then he say, "The next is a mudcat; this kind of a fish likes dark trashy places. When you catch 'em, you won't do it in front water; it likes back water and wants to stay in mud. That's the way with some people in church. You can't never get them to the front for nothing. You has to fish deep for them. The next one is the jellyfish. It ain't got no backbone to face the right thing. That the trouble with our churches today. Too many jellyfishes in 'em. Next," he say, "is the goldfish—good for nothing but to look at. They is pretty. That the way folks is. Some of them go to church just to sit up and look pretty to everybody. Too pretty to sing; too pretty to say Amen!" That what the parson preached Sunday. Well, I'm a full-grown man and a full-grown Christian, praise the Lord. Yes'm, parson is a real preacher.

They'd Pray

My master used to ask us children, "Do your folks pray at night?" We said "No," 'cause our folks had told us what to say. But the Lord have mercy, there was plenty of that going on. They'd pray, "Lord, deliver us from under bondage."

Master Frank Has Come Through

We went to church all the time. We had both white and colored preachers. Master Frank wasn't a Christian, but he would help build brush-arbors for us to have church under, and we sure would have big meetings. I'll tell you.

One day Master Frank was going through the woods close to where niggers was having church. All on a sudden he started running and beating hisself and hollering, and the niggers all went to shouting and saying, "Thank the Lord, Master Frank has done come through!" Master Frank after a minute say, "Yes, through the worst of 'em." He had run into a yellow jackets' nest.

Damn Poor Preacher

I never went to school a day in my life. I learned my ABC's after I was nineteen years old. I went to night school, then to a teacher by the name of Nelse Otom. I was the first nigger to join the church on this side of the Mason and Dixie line. During slavery we all joined the white folks' church, set in the back. After slavery in 1866 they met in conference and motioned to turn all of the black sheep out then. There was four or five they turned out here and four or five there, so we called our preacher, and I was the first one to join. Old Master asked our preacher what we paid him to preach to us. We told him old shoes and clothes. Old Master says, "Well, that's damn poor pay." Our preacher says, "And they got a damn poor preacher."

Boots or No Boots

Once when Master Gilliam took one of his slaves to church at old Tranquil, he told him that he mustn't shout that day—said he would give him a pair of new boots if he didn't shout. About the middle of services, the old nigger couldn't stand it no longer. He jumped up and hollered: "Boots or no boots, I gwine to shout today."

Methodist Dogs and Baptist Dogs

Master John had a big fine bird dog. She was a mammy dog, and one day he found six puppies out in the harness-house. They was 'most all girl puppies, so Master gwine drown 'em. I axed him to give 'em to me, and pretty soon the missus sent me to the postoffice, so I put the puppies in a basket and took 'em with me. Dr. Lyles come by where I was setting, and he say, "Want to sell them pups, Siney?" I tell him, "Uh-huh." Then he say, "What 'nomination is they?" I tell him, "They's Methodist dogs." He didn't say no more. 'Bout a week after that Old Missus sent me to the postoffice again, so I took my basket of puppies. Sure 'nough, 'long come Dr. Lyles, and he say, "Siney, see you still ain't sold them pups." I say, "No, sir." Then he axed me again what 'nomination they belong to. I told him they was Baptist dogs. He say, "How come? You told me last week them was Methodist pups." Ha! Ha! Bless God! Look like he had me. But I say, "Yes, sir, but you see, Doctor, they got their eyes open since then." He laugh and go on down to his newspaper office.

From LAY MY BURDEN DOWN

Barbecue and Big Meeting

Newt and Anderson was my young masters. They was 'long 'bout my own age. They went to school at Goshen Hill. The school was near the store, some folks called it the trading post in them days. They had barrels of liquor setting out from the store in a long row. Sold the liquor to the rich mens that carried on at the race track near by. Folks in Goshen was all rich in them days. Rogers Church, where the Carlisles, Jeters, Sims, Selbys, Glens, and lots of other folks went, too, and the slaves, was the richest country church in this part of the whole state, so I is often been told. Ebenezer, over in Maybinton, was the onliest church in the whole country that tried to strive with Rogers in the way of finery and style. The Hendersons, Maybins, Hardys, Douglasses, Cofields, Chicks, and Oxners was the big folks over there. Both the churches was Methodist.

Every summer they carried on camp meeting at Rogers. All the big Methodist preachers would come from 'way off then. They was entertained in the Carlisle big house. Missus put on the dog (as the niggers says now) then. Everything was cleaned up just 'fore the meeting like us did for the early spring cleaning. Camp meeting come just after the craps was done laid by. Then all craps was done laid by before July the fourth. It was unheard of for anybody to let the Fourth come without the craps outen the way. Times is done changed now, Lord. Then the fields was heavy with corn head high and cotton up around the darky's waist! Grass was all cleaned out of the furrows on the last go round. The fields and even the terraces was put in apple pie order for the gathering of the craps in the fall.

As you all knows, the Fourth has always been nigger day. Marse and Missus had good rations for us early on the Fourth. Then us went to barbecues after the morning chores was done. In them days the barbecues was usually held on the plantation of Marse Jim Hill in Fish Dam. That was not far from Goshen. Marse Jim had a pretty spring that is still all walled up with fine rocks. The water come outen these rocks that cold that you can't hold your hand in it for more than a minute at the longest. There is a big flat rock beyond the spring that I 'specks covers more than an acre and a half of ground. A creek run along over this rock, where the mules and the hosses could rest in the shade of the trees and drink all the water that they wanted. Wild ferns growed waist high along there then. All kinds of pretty flowers and daisies was gathered by the gals. Them was the best days that any darky has ever seed. Never had nothing to aggravate your mind then. Plenty to eat; plenty to wear; plenty wood to burn; good house to live in; and no worry 'bout where it was a-coming from!

Old Marse he give us the rations for the barbecues. Every master wanted his darkies to be thought well of at the barbecues by the darkies from all the other plantations. They had pigs barbecued, and goats; and the missus let the womenfolks bake pies, cakes, and custards for the barbecue, just 'zactly like it was for the white folks' barbecue theyself!

Young ones carried on like young colts, a-frolicking in the pasture till they had done got so full of victuals that they could not eat another bite. Then they roamed on off and set down somewheres to sleep in the shade of the trees. When the sun started to going down, then the old folks begin to git ready to return back to they home plantations, for there was the master's stock and chickens to feed and put up for the night, to say nothing of the cows to milk. The master's work had to go on around the big house, 'cause all the darkies had been 'lowed to have such a pleasant day. Next day being Saturday was on this occasion not only ration day, but the day to git ready for the white folks' camp meeting which I has already called to recollection several times. . . .

As I has said once, the fields was in lay-by shape and the missus done already got the house cleaned. The childrens was put in one room to sleep, and that make more room for the preachers and guests that gwine to visit in the big house for the next six weeks. Then the plans for cooking had to be brung 'bout. They never had no ice in them days, as you well knows; but us had a dry well under our big house. It was deep, and everything keep real cool down there. Steps led down into it, and it always be real dark down there. The rats run around down there, and the young-uns scared to go down for anything. So us carry a lightwood knot for light when us put anything in it or take anything out. There ain't no need for me to tell you 'bout the wellhouse where us kept all the milk and butter, for it was the talk of the country 'bout what nice fresh milk and butter the missus always had. A hollow oak log was used for the milk trough. Three times a day Cilla had her little boy run fresh cool well water all through the trough. That keep the milk from gwine to whey and the butter fresh and cool. In the dry well was kept the canned things and dough to set till it had done riz! When company come like they always did for the camp meetings, shoats and goats and maybe a sheep or lamb or two was kilt for barbecue out by Cilla's cabin. These carcasses was kept down in the dry well over night and put over the pit early the next morning after it had done took salt. Then there was a big box covered with screen wire that victuals was kept in in the dry well. These boxes was made rat-proof.

Whilst the meats for the company table was kept barbecued out in the yard, the cakes, pies, breads, and t'other fixings was done in the kitchen out in the big house yard. Baskets had to be packed to go to camp meeting. Tables was built up at Rogers under the big oak trees that has all been cut down now. The tables just groaned and creaked and sighed with victuals at dinner hour every day during the camp meeting.

Missus fetch her finest linens and silver and glasses to outshine them brung by t'other white folks of quality. In them days the white folks of quality in Union most all come from Goshen Hill and Fish Dam. After the white folks done et all they could hold, then the slaves what had done come to church and to help with the tables and the carriages would have the dinner on a smaller table over clost to the spring. Us had table cloths on our table also, and us et from the kitchen china and the kitchen silver.

Young gals couldn't eat much in public, 'cause it ain't stylish for young courting gals to let on like they has any appetite to speak of. I sees that am a custom that still goes amongst the womenfolks, not to eat so heavy. Colored gals tried to do just like the young white missus would do.

After everything was done et, it would be enough to pack up and fetch back home to feed all the hungry niggers what roams round here in Union now. Them was the times when everybody had 'nough to eat and more than they wanted and plenty clothes to wear!

During the preaching us darkies sot in the back of the church. Our white folks had some benches there that didn't nobody set on 'cept the slaves. Us wore the best clothes that us had. The marse give us a coat and a hat, and his sons give all the old hats and coats round. Us wore shirts and pants made from the looms. Us kept them cleaned and ironed just like the master and the young masters done theirn. Then us wore a string tie, that the white folks done let us have, to church. That 'bout the onliest time that a darky was seed with a tie. Some the oldest men even wore a cravat, that they had done got from the old master. Us combed our hair on Sunday for church. But us never bothered much with it no other time. During slavery some of the old men had short plaits of hair.

The gals come out in the starch dresses for the camp meeting. They took they hair down outen the strings for the meeting. In them days all the darky womens wore they hair in string 'cept when they 'tended church or a wedding. At the camp meetings the womens pulled off the head rags, 'cept the mammies. On this occasion the mammies wore linen head rags fresh laundered. They wore the best aprons with long streamers ironed and starched out a-hanging down they backs. All the other darky womens wore the black dresses, and they got hats from some they white lady folks, just as us mens got hats from ourn. Them womens that couldn't git no hats mostly wore black bonnets. The nigger gals and wenches did all the dressing up that they could for the meeting and also for the barbecue.

At night when the meeting done busted till next day was when the darkies really did have they freedom of spirit. As the wagon be creeping along in the late hours of moonlight, the darkies would raise a tune. Then the air soon be filled with the sweetest tune as us rid on home and sung all the old hymns that us loved. It was always some big black nigger with a deep bass voice like a frog that'd start up the tune. Then the other mens jine in, followed up by the fine little voices of the gals and the cracked voices of the old womens and the grannies. When us reach near the big house us soften down to a deep hum that the missus like! Sometimes she hist up the window and tell us sing "Swing Low, Sweet Chariot" for her and the visiting guests. That all us want to hear. Us open up, and the niggers near the big house that hadn't been to church would wake up and come out to the cabin door and jine in the refrain. From that we'd swing on into all the old spirituals that us love so well and that us knowed how to sing. Missus often 'low that her darkies could sing with heaven's inspiration. Now and then some old mammy would fall outen the wagon a-shouting Glory! and Hallelujah! and Amen! After that us went off to lay down for the night.

If All Slaves Had Belonged to White Folks Like Ours

I was big enough to remember well us coming back from Texas after we refugeed there when the fighting of the war was so bad at St. Charles. We stayed in Texas till the surrender, then we all come back in lots of wagons. I was sick, but they put me on a little bed, and me and all the little children rode in a "Jersey" that one of the old Negro mammies drove, along behind the wagons, and our young master, Colonel Bob Chaney, rode a great big black horse. Oh! he nice-looking on that horse! Every once and a while he'd ride back to the last wagon to see if everything was all right. I remember how scared us children was when we crossed the Red River. Aunt Mandy said, "We crossing you old Red River today, but we not going to cross you any more, 'cause we are going home now, back to Arkansas." That day when we stopped to cook our dinner I picked up a lot little blackjack acorns, and when my mammy saw them she said, "Throw them things down, child. They'll make you wormy." I cried because I thought they were chinquapins. I begged my daddy to let's go back to Texas, but he said, "No! No! We going with our white folks." My mammy and daddy belonged to Colonel Jesse Chaney, much of a gentleman, and his wife, Miss Sallie, was the best mistress anybody ever had. She was a Christian. I can hear her praying yet! She wouldn't let one of her slaves hit a tap on Sunday. They must rest and go to church. They had preaching at the cabin of some one of the slaves, and in the summertime sometimes they had it out in the shade under the trees. Yes, and the slaves on each plantation had their own church. They didn't go gallivanting over the neighborhood or country like niggers do now. Colonel Chaney had lots and lots of slaves, and all their houses were in a row, all one-room cabins. Everything happened in that one room—birth, sickness, death, and everything, but in them days niggers kept their houses clean and their door yards too. These houses where they lived was called "the quarters." I used to love to walk down by that row of houses. It looked like a town, and late of an evening as you'd go by the doors you could smell meat a-frying, coffee making, and good things cooking. We were fed good and had plenty clothes to keep us dry and warm.

Along about time for the surrender, Colonel Jess, our master, took sick and died with some kind of head trouble. Then Colonel Bob, our young master, took care of his mama and the slaves. All the grown folks went to the field to work, and the little children would be left at a big room called the nursing-home. All us little ones would be nursed and fed by an old mammy, Aunt Mandy. She was too old to go to the field, you know. We wouldn't see our mammy and daddy from early in the morning till night when their work was done, then they'd go by Aunt Mandy's and get their children and go home till work time in the morning.

Some of the slaves were house Negroes. They didn't go to work in the fields. They each one had their own job around the house, barn, orchard, milkhouse, and things like that.

When washday come, Lord, the pretty white clothes! It would take three or four women a-washing all day.

When two of the slaves wanted to get married, they'd dress up nice as they could and go up to the big house, and the master would marry them. They'd stand up before him, and he'd read out of a book called *The Discipline* and say, "Thou shalt love the Lord thy God with all thy heart, all thy strength, with all thy might and thy neighbor as thyself." Then he'd say they were man and wife and tell them to live right and be honest and kind to each other. All the slaves would be there too, seeing the wedding.

Our Miss Sallie was the sweetest best thing in the world! She was so good and kind to everybody, and she loved her slaves, too. I can remember when Uncle Tony died how she cried! Uncle Tony Wadd was Miss Sallie's favorite servant. He stayed in a little house in the yard and made fires for her, brought in wood and water, and just waited on the house. He was a little black man and white-headed as cotton, when he died. Miss Sallie told the niggers when they come to take him to the graveyard, to let her know when they got him in his coffin, and when they sent and told her she come out with all the little white children, her little grandchildren, to see Uncle Tony. She just cried and stood for a long time looking at him, then she said, "Tony, you have been a good and faithful servant." Then the Negro men walked and carried him to the graveyard out in a big grove in the field. Every plantation had its own graveyard and buried its own folks and slaves right on the place.

If all slaves had belonged to white folks like ours, there wouldn't been any freedom wanted.

9. The Chanted Sermon

ALBERT J. RABOTEAU

Sunday after Sunday, for more than a century and a half, black ministers have moved their congregations to religious ecstasy by a distinctive style of preaching. Sometimes called the "black folk sermon" or "old-time country preaching," this complex verbal art is governed by strict performance rules that require skill and dedication to master. This kind of sermon is "old-time" in the sense that it is a traditional genre whose origins stretch back to the eighteenth century. But it is also a hardy perennial, alive and healthy in the modern day. It is "country" since its development took place primarily in the prayer meetings and revivals of the rural South. But it has long since spread West and North to the cities, where radio, television, and records extend the preachers' voices beyond the churches into the cars and homes of their flocks. This preaching style is a "folk" art because it is a creation of popular rather than elite culture and because it is an oral rather than literary form. However, the "folk" are notoriously difficult to define, and this tradition of preaching remains popular among literate and "sophisticated" congregations. Though "old-time" and "folk" are part of the aura surrounding this kind of preaching, the term "chanted" more accurately describes its defining characteristic, the metrical, tonal, rhythmic chant with which the preacher climaxes the sermon.[1]

The chanted sermon, while it is usually identified with black preachers, is not an exclusively black tradition; neither is it inclusive of all the preaching styles used by black ministers. Some whites preach in this manner, and there have always been some black ministers who preach in an altogether different idiom. Nevertheless, the chanted sermon is as much a staple of African-American culture as spirituals, gospel, blues, and tales. Like these other forms of oral literature, the sermon has served as a source of information, advice, wisdom, and, not least, sheer enjoyment for generations of black Americans. This sermonic style has spread outside the pulpit to influence public speaking and singing styles in the secular sphere. Black and white literary artists as varied as Paul Laurence Dunbar, James Weldon Johnson, William Faulkner, Toni Morrison, Paule Marshalle, and Ralph Ellison have attempted to capture the cadences and esthetic effect of the chanted sermon.[2]

Because the oral rather than the written word has been the primary bearer of black culture, verbal skill is valued highly in the black community. As is the case with oral tradition in general, so here, too, the individual verbal artist earns critical recognition not by introducing something new, but by performing the old with skill, fluency, spontaneity, and intensity. Style of delivery determines the success of the oral performer whether bluesman, gospel singer, or preacher. It is not, then, merely the word as spoken—much less as read—but the

"The Chanted Sermon" and accompanying notes from *A Fire in the Bones* by Albert J. Raboteau. © 1995 by Albert J. Raboteau. Reprinted by permission of Beacon Press, Boston.

word as *performed* that must be taken into account if the sermon is to be adequately understood. In this case, more than in most, style is content. For this reaon, the chanted sermon cannot be given full justice in print.[3]

The formal structure of the sermon derives from the Evangelical Protestant belief that the sermonic words should be devoted to explaining the Word. The presence of the Bible on the pulpit is a visual reminder of this close connection. It is customary for the preacher to begin by reading a text chosen from the Old or New Testament, which is supposed to indicate the theme of the sermon to follow. Frequently, the preacher's theme as it is actually developed strays far afield from the announced text, but the tradition of reading a biblical verse is strong, so strong that some illiterate slave preachers of the antebellum South had their texts read for them or, lacking a Bible, pretended to read scriptural words from their hand or from a handkerchief; others claimed that, since they could not read, verses from the Bible were written by God on their hearts. The Bible is more than a source of texts; it is the single most important source of language, imagery, and story for the sermon. Through the sermon, as well as spirituals and gospel songs, the Jewish and Christian Scriptures entered and shaped the imaginative world of African-Americans. Black preachers fashioned out of the biblical characters, events, and symbols a religious ethos that fit the peculiar experience of black people in America.

After reading his text, the preacher elaborates its context. Drawing upon his knowledge of the Bible, he may range widely over both Testaments; explaining the meaning of this specific text by reference to other passages. Having set the context, the preacher ideally devotes the rest of his sermon to applying the lessons of the text to the day-to-day concerns of his congregation. Text-context-application is the conventional pattern for the development of the logic of the sermon. There is, however, another pattern as important as the structure of logical meaning, that of performance style, which gives rise to the sermon's emotive meaning.

The stylistic structure of the chanted sermon may be divided into three movements. The preacher begins calmly, speaking in conversational, if oratorical and occasionally grandiloquent, prose; he then gradually begins to speak more rapidly, excitedly, and to chant his words in time to a regular beat; finally, he reaches an emotional peak in which his chanted speech becomes tonal and merges with the singing, clapping, and shouting of the congregation. Frequently, the preacher ends the sermon by returning briefly to conversational prose.

The chanting preacher composes his sermon extemporaneously. This does not mean that he does not prepare. He may have thought about his sermon all week; he may have used a book of sermon outlines to get ideas; he may even carry notes into the pulpit. But at some point, he must breath spontaneous life into the outline, whether written or memorized, by composing on the spot a sermon delivered in rhythmic metrical speech. The meter is not based on accent but on time, the length of time between regular beats. As the preacher moves into the chanted section of his sermon, he fits his speech to a beat. When necessary, he lengthens vowels or rushes together words in order to make a line match the meter. The regularity of the beat is accentuated by the preacher's gasp for air at the end of each line. Sometimes he actually raps out the rhythm on the pulpit. The congregational responses—"Preach it, preach it," "Amen, brother," "Yes, yes, glory!"—reinforce the beat and simultaneously fill in the space left by the preacher's pause for breath. When properly "working," the rhythm of the sermon becomes "as inexorable as a drumbeat."[4]

At a certain stage, the preacher's chanting takes on a musical tone, which indicates a concomitant rise in emotional pitch. The preacher's voice changes: the timbre becomes harsh, almost hoarse. His vocal cords are constricted; his breathing is labored. All the while he moves, gestures, dances, speaking with body as well as voice.

The difficulty of delivering an extemporaneously composed metrical sermon can only be fully appreciated by one who has attempted it. The fullest description of how chanting preachers compose their sermons has been presented by Bruce Rosenberg, a medievalist interested in the composition of oral epics. Extending the theories of Parry and Lord concerning oral composition to the "art of the American folk preacher," he argues that this style of preaching is heavily formulaic. The "basic unit of composition" is, according to Rosenberg, the formula, by which he means "the metrically governed sentence" that the preacher generates in oral performance. The preacher clusters "these formulas together" into larger segments, called "themes," which become, through repetition, part of his repertoire. Since the preacher is familiar with these clusters of verses or themes, he may "fall back" upon them when his rhythm falters. Stock phrases or "stall formulas," such as C. L. Franklins's "I don't believe you hear me tonight," allow the preacher time to pause until the next verse comes to him, at the same time that they invite the congregation to respond. Because of the metrical constraints, the preacher makes frequent and effective use of repetition and tends to develop the narrative of his sermon along associational rather than logical lines.[5]

Congregational response is crucial to the delivery of the sermon. If response is weak or irregular, it will keep the preacher off stride. Conversely, if the preacher's sense of timing is poor, he will fail to rouse the congregation, and the sermon will fail. There is, then, a reciprocal relation between preacher and congregation in the composition of the sermon. Ideally, the preacher's delivery will ignite the congregation's vocal response, which will, in turn, support and push him further.

The expert preacher composes impromptu a sermon typically twenty to forty minutes in length. It is obvious that he has learned to do so only after long hours of observation and practice. However, if asked, he disavows the importance of his own skill or training in preaching and credits the sermon to the inspiration of the Holy Spirit. For this reason, chanting preachers refer to themselves as "spiritual" preachers as distinct from "manuscript" preachers, that is, those who read their sermons from prepared texts. In this view, the preacher's words are placed in his mind and on his lips by the Holy Spirit. The preacher is literally the instrument of God's breath, "God's trombone," in James Weldon Johnson's apt metaphor. When the preacher states that he is "filled with" or "set on fire by the Spirit," he is not only claiming that he is a channel of God's grace or that God is telling him what to say; he is also describing his own ecstatic experience of preaching. As he preaches, he feels that a force or power other than his ordinary self takes over.

This power he identifies as the Spirit of God. Hence the conventional antipathy of the "old-time preacher" to formal seminary training—"I haven't rubbed my head on seminary walls"—was only partially due to the suspicion that education would alienate him from his uneducated flock. The insistence that the sermon was God's work, not man's, tended to undermine the importance of education for preaching. Two other conventions stem from the same rationale: the preacher's contention that he resisted God's call to preach until it proved irresistible and his frequent complaint as he steps to the pulpit: "I feel poorly this morning." In both cases, the weakness of the minister and the strength of God are acclaimed.

Similarly, the members of the congregation explain that the emotional experience that moves them to sing, shout, and dance is the effect of God's Spirit. The experiential claims of the preacher and his congregation should not be dismissed as conventional piety. Rather, they should be taken seriously by those who want to understand the sermon, precisely because these claims of inspiration define and determine the expectations and so the performances of both preacher and congregation. The experiential dimension is crucial because for Evangelical Christians one only becomes Christian through an *experience*, the experience of conversion. And even after conversion, religion has to be vital, "heartfelt," and not just intellectually convincing. When religious fervor grows cold, it is time for revival.

Early descriptions of Methodist and Baptist preaching, black and white, suggest three characteristics: it was plain or simple in language, dramatic in delivery, and—at least for the Baptists—musical, if we can believe the pejorative description applied by their critics: "Baptist whine." Today's chanted sermon still evidences these traits. The preacher's eloquence is measured not by his book learning but by his mother-wit. Down-home familiarity, wordplay, humor, well-turned phrases put a congregation at ease and encourage them to identify with the preacher. Formal, academic, scholarly language is inappropriate. It is viewed as "lecturing" not preaching and leaves the congregation cold. Dramatic ability, as much as sense of timing, is a necessity for the successful preacher, who may play several parts at once in the pulpit as he retells one of the familiar Bible stories. The relation of music and preaching has been symbiotic. There is a vocal continuum between speech and song in the sermon, as speech becomes rhythmic chant, and chant in turn becomes tonal and shades into song. The sermon may be introduced and closed by a hymn. Preachers make extensive use of verses from spiritual and hymns within their sermons. Conversely, gospel quartets and rhythm-and-blues singers imitate the style of the chanting preacher.

The date of the first chanted sermon cannot be given, because there was, of course, no such moment. Many sermons and many influences contributed to the development of this sermonic style: the emphasis placed upon biblical preaching by Evangelical Protestantism, the emotional and dramatic delivery legitimated by the Great Awakening of the mid eighteenth century, the ecstatic behavior encouraged by the revivals, the musical "tuned" voice of early Baptist preachers, the antiphonal pattern familiarized by the custom of lining-out hymns, and the renewed stress upon Christian experience fostered by American revivalism. By the early decades of the nineteeth century, the chanted sermon had probably emerged as a recognizable style of preaching. At midcentury Frederick Olmsted observed and described a chanted sermon delivered in a black church in New Orleans:

> As soon as I had taken my seat, my attention was attracted by an old negro near me, whom I supposed for some time to be suffering under some nervous complaint; he trembled, his teeth chattered, and his face, at intervals, was convulsed. He soon began to respond aloud to the sentiments of the preacher, in such words as these: "Oh, yes,!" and similar expressions could be heard from all parts of the house whenever the speaker's voice was unusually solemn, or his language and manner eloquent or excited.
>
> Sometimes the outcries and responses were not confined to ejaculations of this kind, but shouts, and groans, terrific shrieks, and indescribable expressions of ecstasy—of pleasure or agony—and even stamping, jumping, and clapping of hands were added. . . . I was once surprised to find my own muscles all stretched, as if ready for a struggle—my face glowing, and my feet stamping—having been infected unconsciously. . . . I could not, when my mind reverted to itself, find any connection or meaning in the phrases of the speaker that remained in my memory; and I have no doubt it was his "action" rather than his sentiments, that had given rise to the excitement of the congregation.[6]

Olmsted's description focuses on the power of the sermon to excite ecstatic response, even in a cultured white northerner like Olmsted himself.

Mary Boykin Chesnut, a southern white woman, found herself excited by the chanted style with which a slave driver on her plantation delivered a prayer:

> *He became wildly excited, on his knees, facing us with his eyes shut. He clapped his hands at the end of every sentence, and his voice rose to the pitch of a shrill shriek, yet was strangely clear and musical, occasionally in a plaintive minor key that went to your heart. Sometimes it rang out like a trumpet. I wept bitterly. . . . The Negroes sobbed and shouted and swayed backward and forward, some with aprons to their eyes, most of them clapping their hands and responding in shrill tones: "Yes, God!" "Jesus?" "Savior?" "Bless de Lord, amen," etc. It was a little too exciting for me. I would very much have liked to shout, too. . . . When he rose from his knees [he] trembled and shook as one in a palsy, and from his eyes you could see the ecstasy had not left him yet.*[7]

In both instances, the observers distinguish the style of delivery from the meaning of the sermon or, in Chesnut's case, prayer. Both find themselves moved, but neither considers the possibility that the ecstasy they resist is itself the meaning of the events they witness. By dismissing the "sense" of the emotional behavior aroused by the style of the sermon or prayer, Olmsted and Chesnut are missing the message. The same mistake is made by the modern observer who separates form from content, style from meaning in describing the chanted sermon. To identify ecstatic behavior with the style of the preacher, and instruction or edification with the intelligible content of his words, is to misunderstand the complexity of the sermon and the religious ethos from which it springs.

Ecstatic religious behavior is central to the religious tradition in which the chanting preacher stands. As we have seen, the origins of this tradition can be found in the Evangelical revivals of the eighteenth and nineteenth centuries. But there is another source not yet mentioned: the African religious culture of the slaves. A look at this distant heritage and its interaction with Protestant revivalism may help to explain how style and meaning are one in the sermon and why it is that the chanted delivery has exerted such a long and deep appeal. In the revivals, African-Americans found a context in which the bodily expression of religious emotion was not only permitted but encouraged—harking back to the danced religions of their African forebears. Black American Christians were filled with the Spirit of the Christian God, but they responded in ways markedly similar to the ways in which their ancestors had responded to possession by the gods of Africa. Possessed by the Holy Spirit, slaves and freedmen danced, sang, and shouted in styles that were African. More important, ecstatic trance was at the center of their worship as it had been in Africa. In the revivals, African and Christian traditions met on common ground, ecstatic response to divine possession. The African tradition of religious dance was Christianized and the Evangelical Protestant tradition of experiential religion was Africanized.[8]

The influence of African traditions upon the religious dancing and singing of slaves and their descendants may be granted, but what about preaching? Where does the African influence lie? Anthropologist Morton Marks has suggested an answer. According to Marks, there is a ritual structure underlying several kinds of speech events within African-American cultures in the New World. The structure consists of an alternation from European styles of performance to African ones. When the style switch occurs, it acts as a code signaling that ritual possession by the Spirit is about to occur. To the observer unfamiliar with the performance clues, the stylistic switch is commonly perceived as a change from order to chaos, from music to noise, or from speech to gibberish. What in fact is really happening is a shift from one type of order to another: from a nonrhythmic to a rhythmic, or rather, increasingly rhythmic, performance style. The importance of rhythmic drumming and singing for the onset of divine possession in African and African-American religions has been widely observed. Applied to the chanted sermon, Marks's theory implies that the preacher's switch from conversational prose to the metrical and tonal chant, the rhythm holding steady as a drumbeat, sets the stage for the divine possession that everyone expects. Moreover there are recognizable cues that announce the Spirit's arrival. The preacher's harsh vocal sound, the constriction of voice, the audible gasp at the end of each line, the tonal quality, the participatory claps, shouts and noise of the congregation all announce the onset of possession and instigate it in others. In this sense, the preacher's style itself speaks, at least to those who understand the language of his sermonic tradition.[9]

Admittedly, Marks's theory is an interpretation; it has not been proved. Still the notion that African-influenced performance styles have been transmitted to American blacks and that they are shared across different African-American cultures in the New World has been convincingly demonstrated for dance, song, and music. It may very well be true of the chanted sermon and other forms of oral performance as well.

The chanted sermon is the product of a religious imagination in which experience is primary and is so because it validates religious truth. Without experience, how can one know that one's religious life is real? In the words of one former slave: "Nobody can talk about the religion of God unless they've had a religious experience in it."[10] In the chanted sermon, African-American Christians did not merely talk about God, they experienced his power, and found that in the experience their own spirits were renewed.

Notes

1. Given its importance in African-American culture, the literature on the "folk," or chanted, sermon is not as extensive as one might suppose. The following works have heavily influenced my treatment: James Weldon Johnson, *God's Trombones: Seven Negro Sermons in Verse* (New York: Viking Press, 1927); William H. Pipes, *Say Amen, Brother! Old-Time Negro Preaching: A Study in American Frustration* (New York: William Frederick Press, 1951); Bruce A. Rosenberg, *The Art of the American Folk Preacher* (New York: Oxford University Press, 1970), "The Psychology of the Spiritual Sermon," in *Religious Movements in Contemporary America*, ed. Irving I. Zaretsky and Mark P. Leone (Princeton: Princeton University Press, 1974), 13–49; Henry H. Mitchell, *Black Preaching* (Philadelphia: J. B. Lippincott, 1970); Gerald L. Davis, *I Got the Word in Me and I Can Sing It, You Know: A Study of the Performed African-American Sermon* (Philadelphia: University of Pennsylvania Press, 1985).

2. See Paul Laurence Dunbar's poem, "An Antebellum Sermon," most easily accessible in Dudley Randall, ed., *The Black Poets* (New York: Bantam Books, 1971), 44–46; Johnson, *God's Trombones*; Ralph Ellison, *Invisible Man* (New York: Signet Books, 1952), 12–13; William Faulkner, *The Sound and the Fury* (New York: Vintage Books, 1946), 356–71; Paule Marshall, *Praisesong for the Widow* (New York: E. P. Dutton, 1983), 198–203. The speeches of Martin Luther King, Jr., have made this tradition at least vaguely familiar to many Americans otherwise unacquainted with

it. Although male-dominated, the tradition has also been exemplified by women preachers who usually had to struggle against clerical resistance to exercise their talents to preach.

3. I urge the reader to listen to a recording or radio broadcast of a chanted sermon, or better yet, visit a church in which this type of preaching is performed. The Reverend C. L. Franklin, father of Aretha, has recorded more than seventy albums of sermons on Chess and Jewel labels. See Jeff Todd Titon, ed., *Give Me This Mountain: Reverend C. L. Franklin, Life History and Selected Sermons* (Urbana: University of Illinois Press, 1989). Sunday evening broadcasts of black church services are common. The chanted sermon *must be heard* to be understood.

4. Rosenberg, *Art of the American Folk Preacher*, 48.

5. Rosenberg's description of the use of formulas in oral composition differs from Lord's: Lord thought that "new formulas" were created by analogy with the old, the composition process [being] merely one of substituting a word or phrase." Rosenberg, applying the insights of generative theory, suggests that the preacher "has at his command . . . not several score or several hundred formulas which he manipulates by word and phrase substitution, but rather a metrical deep structure which enables him to generate an infinite number of sentences in his native meter." Note these positions are not mutually exclusive. See Rosenberg, "Psychology of the Spiritual Sermon," 141, and *Art of the American Folk Preacher*, 46–116; Pipes, *Say Amen, Brother!* 150–55.

6. Frederick Law Olmsted, *The Cotton Kingdom*, 2 vols. (New York, 1861).

7. Mary Boykin Chestnut, *A Diary from Dixie*, ed. Ben Ames Williams (Boston: Houghton Mifflin, 1949), 148–49.

8. For fuller treatment of African influence upon the religious worship of American slaves, see Albert J. Raboteau, *Slave Religion: The "Invisible Institution" in the Antebellum South* (New York: Oxford University Press: 1978), 48–75.

9. Morton Marks, "Uncovering Ritual Structures in Afro-American Music," in Zaretsky and Leone, *Religious Movements in Contemporary America*, 60–134.

10. Clifton H. Johnson, ed., *God Struck Me Dead: Religious Conversion Experiences and Autobiographies of Ex-slaves* (Philadelphia: Pilgrim Press, 1969), 144.

10. Of the Faith of the Fathers

W.E.B. DuBois

Dim face of Beauty haunting all the world,
Fair face of Beauty all too fair to see,
Where the lost stars adown the heavens are hurled,—
There, there alone for thee
May white peace be.

Beauty, sad face of Beauty, Mystery, Wonder,
What are these dreams to foolish babbling men
Who cry with little noises 'neath the thunder
Of Ages ground to sand,
To a little sand. —Fiona Macleod

It was out in the country, far from home, far from my foster home, on a dark Sunday night. The road wandered from our rambling log-house up the stony bed of a creek, past wheat and corn, until we could hear dimly across the fields a rhythmic cadence of song,—soft, thrilling, powerful, that swelled and died sorrowfully in our ears. I was a country school-teacher then, fresh from the East, and had never seen a Southern Negro revival. To be sure, we in Berkshire were not perhaps as stiff and formal as they in Suffolk of olden time; yet we were very quiet and subdued, and I know not what would have happened those clear Sabbath mornings had some one punctuated the sermon with a wild scream, or interrupted the long prayer with a loud Amen! And so most striking to me, as I approached the village and the little plain church perched aloft, was the air of intense excitement that possessed that mass of black folk. A sort of suppressed terror hung in the air and seemed to seize us,—a pythian madness, a demoniac possession, that lent terrible reality to song and word. The black and massive form of the preacher swayed and quivered as the words crowded to his lips and flew at us in singular eloquence. The people moaned and fluttered, and then the gaunt-cheeked brown woman beside me suddenly leaped straight into the air and shrieked like a lost soul, while round about came wail and groan and outcry, and a scene of human passion such as I had never conceived before.

Those who have not thus witnessed the frenzy of a Negro revival in the untouched backwoods of the South can but dimly realize the religious feeling of the slave; as described, such scenes appear grotesque and funny, but as seen they are awful. Three things characterized this religion of the slave,—the Preacher, the Music, and the Frenzy. The Preacher is the most unique personality developed by the Negro on American soil. A leader, a politician, an orator, a "boss," an intriguer, an idealist,—all these he is, and ever, too, the centre of a group of men, now twenty, now a thousand in number. The combination of a certain adroitness with deep-seated earnestness, of tact with consummate ability, gave him his preëminence, and helps him maintain it. The type, of course, varies according to time and place, from the West

Indies in the sixteenth century to New England in the nineteenth, and from the Mississippi bottoms to cities like New Orleans or New York.

The Music of Negro religion is that plaintive rhythmic melody, with its touching minor cadences, which, despite caricature and defilement, still remains the most original and beautiful expression of human life and longing yet born on American soil. Sprung from the African forests, where its counterpart can still be heard, it was adapted, changed, and intensified by the tragic soul-life of the slave, until, under the stress of law and whip, it became the one true expression of a people's sorrow, despair, and hope.

Finally the Frenzy or "Shouting," when the Spirit of the Lord passed by, and, seizing the devotee, made him mad with supernatural joy, was the last essential of Negro religion and the one more devoutly believed in than all the rest. It varied in expression from the silent rapt countenance or the low murmur and moan to the mad abandon of physical fervor,—the stamping, shrieking, and shouting, the rushing to and fro and wild waving of arms, the weeping and laughing, the vision and the trance. All this is nothing new in the world, but old as religion, as Delphi and Endor. And so firm a hold did it have on the Negro, that many generations firmly believed that without this visible manifestation of the God there could be no true communion with the Invisible.

These were the characteristics of Negro religious life as developed up to the time of Emancipation. Since under the peculiar circumstances of the black man's environment they were the one expression of his higher life, they are of deep interest to the student of his development, both socially and psychologically. Numerous are the attractive lines of inquiry that here group themselves. What did slavery mean to the African savage? What was his attitude toward the World and Life? What seemed to him good and evil,—God and Devil? Whither went his longings and strivings, and wherefore were his heart-burnings and disappointments? Answers to such questions can come only from a study of Negro religion as a development, through its gradual changes from the heathenism of the Gold Coast to the institutional Negro church of Chicago.

Moreover, the religious growth of millions of men, even though they be slaves, cannot be without potent influence upon their contemporaries. The Methodists and Baptists of America owe much of their condition to the silent but potent influence of their millions of Negro converts. Especially is this noticeable in the South, where theology and religious philosophy are on this account a long way behind the North, and where the religion of the poor whites is a plain copy of Negro thought and methods. The mass of "gospel" hymns which has swept through American churches and well-nigh ruined our sense of song consists largely of debased imitations of Negro melodies made by ears that caught the jingle but not the music, the body but not the soul, of the Jubilee songs. It is thus clear that the study of Negro religion is not only a vital part of the history of the Negro in America, but no uninteresting part of American history.

The Negro church of to-day is the social centre of Negro life in the United States, and the most characteristic expression of African character. Take a typical church in a small Virginian town: it is the "First Baptist" a roomy brick edifice seating five hundred or more persons, tastefully finished in Georgia pine, with a carpet, a small organ, and stained-glass windows. Underneath is a large assembly room with benches. This building is the central club-house of a community of a thousand or more Negroes. Various organizations meet here,—the church proper, the Sunday-school, two or three insurance societies, women's societies, secret societies, and mass meetings of various kinds. Entertainments, suppers, and lectures are held beside the five or six regular weekly religious services. Considerable sums of money are collected and expended here, employment is found for the idle, strangers are introduced, news is disseminated and charity distributed. At the same time this social, intellectual, and economic centre is a religious centre of great power. Depravity, Sin, Redemption, Heaven, Hell, and Damnation are preached twice a Sunday with much fervor, and revivals take place every year after the crops are laid by; and few indeed of the community have the hardihood to withstand conversion. Back of this more formal religion, the Church often stands as a real conserver of morals, a strengthener of family life, and the final authority on what is Good and Right.

Thus one can see in the Negro church to-day, reproduced in microcosm, all that great world from which the Negro is cut off by color-prejudice and social condition. In the great city churches the same tendency is noticeable and in many respects emphasized. A great church like the Bethel of Philadelphia has over eleven hundred members, an edifice seating fifteen hundred persons and valued at one hundred thousand dollars, an annual budget of five thousand dollars, and a government consisting of a pastor with several assisting local preachers, an executive and legislative board, financial boards and tax collectors; general church meetings for making laws; subdivided groups led by class leaders, a company of militia, and twenty-four auxiliary societies. The activity of a church like this is immense and far-reaching, and the bishops who preside over these organizations throughout the land are among the most powerful Negro rulers in the world.

Such churches are really governments of men, and consequently a little investigation reveals the curious fact that, in the South, at least, practically every American Negro is a church member. Some, to be sure, are not regularly enrolled, and a few do not habitually attend services; but, practically, a proscribed people must have a social centre, and that centre for this people is the Negro church. The census of 1890 showed nearly twenty-four thousand Negro churches in the country, with a total enrolled membership of over two and a half millions, or ten actual church members to every twenty-eight persons, and in some Southern States one in every two persons. Besides these there is the large number who, while not enrolled as members, attend and take part in many of the activities of the church. There is an organized Negro church for every sixty black families in the nation, and in some States for every forty families, owning, on an average, a thousand dollars' worth of property each, or nearly twenty-six million dollars in all.

Such, then, is the large development of the Negro church since Emancipation. The question now is, What have been the successive steps of this social history and what are the present tendencies? First, we must realize that no such institution as the Negro church could rear itself without definite historical foundations. These foundations we can find if we remember that the social history of the Negro did not start in America. He was brought from a definite social environment,—the polygamous clan life under the headship of the chief and the potent influence of the priest. His religion was nature-worship, with profound belief in invisible surrounding influences, good and bad, and his worship was through incantation and sacrifice. The first rude change in this life was the slave ship and the West Indian sugar-fields. The plantation organization replaced the clan and tribe, and the white master replaced the chief with far greater and more despotic powers. Forced and long-continued toil became the rule of life, the old ties of blood relationship and kinship disappeared, and instead of the family appeared a new polygamy and polyandry, which, in some cases, almost reached promiscuity. It was a terrific social revolution, and yet some traces were retained of the former group life, and the chief remaining institution was the Priest or Medicine-man. He early appeared on the plantation and found his function as the healer of the sick, the interpreter of the Unknown, the comforter of the sorrowing, the supernatural avenger of wrong, and the one who rudely but picturesquely expressed the longing, disappointment, and resentment of a stolen and oppressed people. Thus, as bard, physician, judge, and priest, within the narrow limits allowed by the slave system, rose the Negro preacher, and under him the first Afro-American institution, the Negro church. This church was not at first by any means Christian nor definitely organized; rather it was an adaptation and mingling of heathen rites among the members of each plantation, and roughly designated as Voodooism. Association with the masters, missionary effort and motives of expediency gave these rites an early veneer of Christianity, and after the lapse of many generations the Negro church became Christian.

Two characteristic things must be noticed in regard to this church. First, it became almost entirely Baptist and Methodist in faith; secondly, as a social institution it antedated by many decades the monogamic Negro home. From the very circumstances of its beginning, the church was confined to the plantation, and consisted primarily of a series of disconnected units; although, later on, some freedom of movement was allowed, still this geographical limitation was always important and was one cause of the spread of the decentralized and democratic Baptist faith among the slaves. At the same time, the visible rite of baptism appealed strongly to their mystic temperament. To-day the Baptist Church is still largest in membership among Negroes, and has a million and a half communicants. Next in popularity came the churches organized in connection with the white neighboring churches, chiefly Baptist and Methodist, with a few Episcopalian and others. The Methodists still form the second greatest denomination, with nearly a million members. The faith of these, two leading denominations was more suited to the slave church from the prominence they gave to religious feeling and fervor. The Negro membership in other denominations has always been small and relatively unimportant, although the Episcopalians and Presbyterians are gaining among the more intelligent classes to-day, and the Catholic Church is making headway in certain sections. After Emancipation, and still earlier in the North, the Negro churches largely severed such affiliations as they had had with the white churches, either by choice or by compulsion. The Baptist churches became independent, but the Methodists were compelled early to unite for purposes of episcopal government. This gave rise to the great African Methodist Church, the greatest Negro organization in the world, to the Zion Church and the Colored Methodist, and to the black conferences and churches in this and other denominations.

The second fact noted, namely, that the Negro church antedates the Negro home, leads to an explanation of much that is paradoxical in this communistic institution and in the morals of its members. But especially it leads us to regard this institution as peculiarly the expression of the inner ethical life of a people in a sense seldom true elsewhere. Let us turn, then, from the outer physical development of the church to the more important inner ethical life of the people who compose it. The Negro has already been pointed out many times as a religious animal,—a being of that deep emotional nature which turns instinctively toward the supernatural. Endowed with a rich tropical imagination and a keen, delicate appreciation of Nature, the transplanted African lived in a world animate with gods and devils, elves and witches; full of strange influences,—of Good to be implored, of Evil to be propitiated. Slavery, then, was to him the dark triumph of Evil over him. All the hateful powers of the Under-world were striving against him, and a spirit of revolt and revenge filled his heart. He called up all the resources of heathenism to aid,—exorcism and witchcraft, the mysterious Obi worship with its barbarous rites, spells, and blood-sacrifice even, now and then, of human victims. Weird midnight orgies and mystic conjurations were invoked, the witch-woman and the voodoopriest became the centre of Negro group life, and that vein of vague superstition which characterizes the unlettered Negro even to-day was deepened and strengthened.

In spite, however, of such success as that of the fierce Maroons, the Danish blacks, and others, the spirit of revolt gradually died away under the untiring energy and superior strength of the slave masters. By the middle of the eighteenth century the black slave had sunk, with hushed murmurs, to his place at the bottom of a new economic system, and was unconsciously ripe for a new philosophy of life. Nothing suited his condition then better than the doctrines of passive submission embodied in the newly learned Christianity. Slave masters early realized this, and cheerfully aided religious propaganda within certain bounds. The long system of repression and degradation of the Negro tended to emphasize the elements in his character which made him a valuable chattel: courtesy became humility, moral strength degenerated into submission, and the exquisite native appreciation of the beautiful became an infinite capacity for dumb suffering. The Negro, losing the joy of this world, eagerly seized upon the offered conceptions of the next; the avenging Spirit of the Lord enjoining patience in this world, under sorrow and tribulation until the Great Day when He should lead His dark children home,—this became his comforting dream. His preacher repeated the prophecy, and his bards sang,—

"Children, we all shall be free
When the Lord shall appear!"

This deep religious fatalism, painted so beautifully in "Uncle Tom," came soon to breed, as all fatalistic faiths will, the sensualist side by side with the martyr. Under the lax moral life of the plantation, where marriage was a farce, laziness a virtue, and property a theft, a religion of resignation and submission degenerated easily, in less strenuous minds, into a philosophy of indulgence and crime. Many of the worst characteristics of the Negro masses of to-day had their seed in this period of the slave's ethical growth. Here it was that the Home was ruined under the very shadow of the Church, white and black; here habits of shiftlessness took root, and sullen hopelessness replaced hopeful strife.

With the beginning of the abolition movement and the gradual growth of a class of free Negroes came a change. We often neglect the influence of the freedman before the war, because of the paucity of his numbers and the small weight he had in the history of the nation. But we must not forget that his chief influence was internal,—was exerted on the black world; and that there he was the ethical and social leader. Huddled as he was in a few centres like Philadelphia, New York, and New Orleans, the masses of the freedmen sank into poverty and listlessness; but not all of them. The free Negro leader early arose and his chief characteristic was intense earnestness and deep feeling on the slavery question. Freedom became to him a real thing and not a dream His religion became darker and more intense, and into his ethics crept a note of revenge, into his songs a day of reckoning close at hand. The "Coming of the Lord" swept this side of Death, and came to be a thing to be hoped for in this day. Through fugitive slaves and irrepressible discussion this desire for freedom seized the black millions still in bondage, and became their one ideal of life. The black bards caught new notes, and sometimes even dared to sing,—

"O Freedom, O Freedom, O Freedom over me!
Before I'll be a slave
I'll be buried in my grave,
And go home to my Lord
And be free."

For fifty years Negro religion thus transformed itself and identified itself with the dream of Abolition, until that which was a radical fad in the white North and an anarchistic plot in the white South had become a religion to the black world. Thus, when Emancipation finally came, it seemed to the freedman a literal Coming of the Lord. His fervid imagination was stirred as never before, by the tramp of armies, the blood and dust of battle, and the wail and whirl of social upheaval. He stood dumb and motionless before the whirlwind: what had he to do with it? Was it not the Lord's doing, and marvellous in his eyes? Joyed and bewildered with what came, he stood awaiting new wonders till the inevitable Age of Reaction swept over the nation and brought the crisis of to-day.

It is difficult to explain clearly the present critical stage of Negro religion. First, we must remember that living as the blacks do in close contact with a great modern nation, and sharing, although imperfectly, the soul-life of that nation, they must necessarily be affected more or less directly by all the religious and ethical forces that are to-day moving the United States. These questions and movements are, however, overshadowed and dwarfed by the (to them) all-important question of their civil, political, and economic status. They must perpetually discuss the "Negro Problem,"—must live, move, and have their being in it, and interpret all else in its light or darkness. With this come, too, peculiar problems of their inner life,—of the status of women, the maintenance of Home, the training of children, the accumulation of wealth, and the prevention of crime. All this must mean a time of intense ethical ferment, of religious heart-searching and intellectual unrest. From the double life every American Negro must live, as a Negro and as an American, as swept on by the current of the nineteenth while yet struggling in the eddies of the fifteenth century,—from this must arise a painful self-consciousness, an almost morbid sense of personality and a moral hesitancy which is fatal to self-confidence. The worlds within and without the Veil of Color are changing, and changing rapidly, but not at the same rate, not in the same way; and this must produce a peculiar wrenching of the soul, a peculiar sense of doubt and bewilderment. Such a double life, with double thoughts, double duties, and double social classes, must give rise to double words and double ideals, and tempt the mind to pretence or to revolt, to hypocrisy or to radicalism.

In some such doubtful words and phrases can one perhaps most clearly picture the peculiar ethical paradox that faces the Negro of to-day and is tingeing and changing his religious life. Feeling that his rights and his dearest ideals are being trampled upon, that the public conscience is ever more deaf to his righteous appeal, and that all the reactionary forces of prejudice, greed, and revenge are daily gaining new strength and fresh allies, the Negro faces no enviable dilemma. Conscious of his impotence, and pessimistic, he often becomes bitter and vindictive; and his religion, instead of a worship, is a complaint and a curse, a wail rather than a hope, a sneer rather than a faith. On the other hand, another type of mind, shrewder and keener and more tortuous too, sees in the very strength of the anti-Negro movement its patent weaknesses, and with Jesuitic casuistry is deterred by no ethical considerations in the endeavor to turn this weakness to the black man's strength. Thus we have two great and hardly reconcilable streams of thought and ethical strivings; the danger of the one lies in anarchy, that of the other in hypocrisy. The one type of Negro stands almost ready to curse God and die, and the other is too often found a traitor to right and a coward before force; the one is wedded to ideals remote, whimsical, perhaps impossible of realization; the other forgets that life is more than meat and the body more than raiment. But, after all, is not this simply the writhing of the age translated into black,—the triumph of the Lie which to-day, with its false culture, faces the hideousness of the anarchist assassin?

To-day the two groups of Negroes, the one in the North, the other in the South, represent these divergent ethical tendencies, the first tending toward radicalism, the other toward hypocritical compromise. It is no idle regret with which the white South mourns the loss of the old-time Negro,—the frank, honest, simple old servant who stood for the earlier religious age of submission and humility. With all his laziness and lack of many elements of true manhood, he was at least open-hearted, faithful, and sincere. To-day he is gone, but who is to blame for his going? Is it not those very persons who mourn for him? Is it not the tendency, born of Reconstruction and Reaction, to found a society on lawlessness and deception, to tamper with the moral fibre of a naturally honest and straightforward people until the whites threaten to become ungovernable tyrants and the blacks criminals and hypocrites? Deception is the natural defence of the weak against the strong, and the South used it for many years against its conquerors; to-day it must be prepared to see its black proletariat turn that same two-edged weapon against itself. And how natural this is! The death of Denmark Vesey and Nat Turner proved long since to the Negro the present hopelessness of physical defence. Political defence is becoming less and less available, and economic defence is still only partially effective. But there is a patent defence at hand,—the defence of deception and flattery, of cajoling and lying. It is the same defence which the Jews of the Middle Age used and which left its stamp on their character for centuries. To-day the young Negro of the South who would succeed cannot be frank and outspoken, honest and self-assertive, but rather he is daily tempted to be silent and wary, politic and sly; he must flatter and be pleasant, endure petty insults with a smile, shut his eyes to wrong; in too many cases he sees positive personal advantage in deception and lying. His real thoughts, his real aspirations, must be guarded in whispers; he must not criticise, he must not complain. Patience, humility, and adroitness must, in these growing black youth, replace impulse, manliness, and courage. With this sacrifice there is an economic opening, and perhaps peace and some prosperity. Without this there is riot, migration, or crime. Nor is this situation peculiar to the Southern United States,—is it not rather the only method by which undeveloped races have gained the right to share modern culture? The price of culture is a Lie.

On the other hand, in the North the tendency is to emphasize the radicalism of the Negro. Driven from his birthright in the South by a situation at which every fibre of his more outspoken and assertive nature revolts, he finds himself in a land where he can scarcely earn a decent living amid the harsh competition and the color discrimination. At the same time, through schools and periodicals, discussions and lectures, he is intellectually quickened and awakened. The soul, long pent up and dwarfed, suddenly expands in new-found freedom. What wonder that every tendency is to excess,—radical complaint, radical remedies, bitter denunciation or angry silence. Some sink, some rise. The criminal and the sensualist leave the church for the gambling-hell and the brothel, and fill the slums of Chicago and Baltimore; the better classes segregate themselves from the group-life of both white and black, and form an aristocracy, cultured but pessimistic, whose bitter criticism stings while it points out no way of escape. They despise the submission and subserviency of the Southern Negroes, but offer no other means by which a poor and oppressed minority can exist side by side with its masters. Feeling deeply and keenly the tendencies and opportunities of the age in which they live, their souls are bitter at the fate which drops the Veil between; and the very fact that this bitterness is natural and justifiable only serves to intensify it and make it more maddening.

Between the two extreme types of ethical attitude which I have thus sought to make clear wavers the mass of the millions of Negroes, North and South; and their religious life and activity partake of this social conflict within their ranks. Their churches are differentiating,— now into groups of cold, fashionable devotees, in no way distinguishable from similar white groups save in color of skin; now into large social and business institutions catering to the desire for information and amusement of their members, warily avoiding unpleasant questions both within and without the black world, and preaching in effect if not in word: *Dum vivimus, vivamus.*

But back of this still broods silently the deep religious feeling of the real Negro heart, the stirring, unguided might of powerful human souls who have lost the guiding star of the past and are seeking in the great night a new religious ideal. Some day the Awakening will come, when the pent-up vigor of ten million souls shall sweep irresistibly toward the Goal, out of the Valley of the Shadow of Death, where all that makes life worth living—Liberty, Justice, and Right—is marked "For White People Only."

11. Religion in the South

W.E.B. DuBois

IT is often a nice question as to which is of greater importance among a people—the way in which they earn their living, or their attitude toward life. As a matter of fact these two things are but two sides of the same problem, for nothing so reveals the attitude of a people toward life as the manner in which they earn their living; and on the other hand the earning of a living depends in the last analysis upon one's estimate of what life really is. So that these two questions that I am discussing with regard to the South are intimately bound up with each other.

If we have studied the economic development of the South carefully, then we have already seen something of its attitude toward life; the history of religion in the South means a study of these same facts over which we have gone, from a different point of view. Moreover, as the economic history of the South is in effect the economics of slavery and the Negro problem, so the essence of a study of religion in the South is a study of the ethics of slavery and emancipation.

It is very difficult of course for one who has not seen the practical difficulties that surround a people at any particular time in their battle with the hard facts of this world, to interpret with sympathy their ideals of life; and this is especially difficult when the economic life of a nation has been expressed by such a discredited word as slavery. If, then, we are to study the history of religion in the South, we must first of all divest ourselves of prejudice, pro and con; we must try to put ourselves in the place of those who are seeking to read the riddle of life and grant to them about the same general charity and the same general desire to do right that we find in the average human being. On the other hand, we must not, in striving to be charitable, be false to truth and right. Slavery in the United States was an economic mistake and a moral crime. This we cannot forget. Yet it had its excuses and mitigations. These we must remember.

When in the seventeenth century there grew up in the New World a system of human slavery, it was not by any means a new thing. There were slaves and slavery in Europe, not, to be sure, to a great extent, but none the less real. The Christian religion, however, had come to regard it as wrong and unjust that those who partook of the privileges and hopes and aspirations of that religion should oppress each other to the extent of actual enslavement. The idea of human brotherhood in the seventeenth century was of a brotherhood of coreligionists. When it came to the dealing of Christian with heathen, however, the century saw nothing wrong in slavery; rather, theoretically, they saw a chance for a great act of humanity and religion. The slaves were to be brought from heathenism to Christianity, and through slavery the benighted Indian and African were to find their passport into the kingdom of God. This theory of human slavery was held by Spaniards, French, and English. It was New England in the early days that put the echo of it in her codes (see Note 1) and recognition of it can be seen in most of the colonies.

But no sooner had people adopted this theory than there came the insistent and perplexing question as to what the status of the heathen slave was to be after he was Christianized and baptized; and even more pressing, what was to be the status of his children?

It took a great deal of bitter heart searching for the conscientious early slave-holders to settle this question. The obvious state of things was that the new convert awoke immediately to the freedom of Christ and became a freeman. But while this was the theoretical, religious answer, and indeed the answer which was given in several instances, the practice soon came into direct and perplexing conflict with the grim facts of economic life.

Here was a man who had invested his money and his labor in slaves; he had done it with dependence on the institution of property. Could he be deprived of his property simply because his slaves were baptized afterward into a Christian church? Very soon such economic reasoning swept away the theological dogma and it was expressly declared in colony after colony that baptism did not free the slaves (see Note 2). This, of course, put an end to the old doctrine of the heathen slave and it was necessary for the church to arrange for itself a new theory by which it could ameliorate, if not excuse, the position of the slave. The next question was naturally that of the children of slaves born in Christianity and the church for a time hedged unworthily on the subject by consigning to perpetual slavery the children of heathen but not those born of Christian parents; this was satisfactory for the first generation but it fell short of the logic of slavery later, and a new adjustment was demanded.

Here again this was not found difficult. In Virginia there had been built up the beginnings of a feudal aristocracy. Men saw nothing wrong or unthinkable in the situation as it began to develop, but rather something familiar. At the head of the feudal manor was the lord, or master, beneath him the under-lord or overseers and then the artisans, retainers, the free working men and lastly the serfs, slaves or servants as they were called. The servant was not free and yet he was not theoretically exactly a slave, and the laws of Virginia were rather careful to speak very little of slaves.

Serfdom in America as in Europe was to be a matter of status or position and not of race or blood, and the law of the South in the seventeenth and early eighteenth centuries made little or no distinction between black and white bondservants save in the time of their service. The idea, felt rather than expressed, was that here in America we were to have a new feudalism suited to the new country. At the top was the governor of the colony representing the majesty of the English king, at the bottom the serfs or slaves, some white, most of them black.

Slavery therefore was gradually transformed in the seventeenth and eighteenth centuries into a social status out of which a man, even a black man, could escape and did escape; and, no matter what his color was, when he became free, he became free in the same sense that other people were. Thus it was that there were free black voters in the southern colonies (Virginia and the Carolinas) in the early days concerning whose right to vote there was less question than there is concerning my right to vote now in Georgia (see Note 3).

The church recognized the situation and the Episcopal church especially gave itself easily to this new conception. This church recognized the social gradation of men; all souls were equal in the sight of God, but there were differences in worldly consideration and respect, and consequently it was perfectly natural that there should be an aristocracy at the top and a group of serfs at the bottom.

Meantime, however, America began to be stirred by a new democratic ideal; there came the reign of that ruler of men, Andrew Jackson; there came the spread of the democratic churches, Methodist and Baptist, and the democratization of other churches. Now when

America became to be looked upon more and more as the dwelling place of free and equal men and when the Methodist and, particularly, the Baptist churches went down into the fields and proselyted among the slaves, a thing which the more aristocratic Episcopal church had never done (see Note 4), there came new questions and new heart-searchings among those who wanted to explain the difficulties and to think and speak clearly in the midst of their religious convictions.

As such people began to look round them the condition of the slaves appalled them. The Presbyterian Synod of South Carolina and Georgia declared in 1833: "There are over two millions of human beings in the condition of heathen and some of them in a worse condition. They may be justly considered the heathen of this country, and will bear a comparison with heathen in any country in the world. The Negroes are destitute of the gospel, and ever will be under the present state of things. In the vast field extending from an entire state beyond the Potomac [*i.e.*, Maryland] to the Sabine River [at the time our southwestern boundary] and from the Atlantic to the Ohio, there are, to the best of our knowledge, not twelve men exclusively devoted to the religious instruction of the Negroes. In the present state of feeling in the South, a ministry of their own color could neither be obtained nor tolerated.

"But do not the Negroes have access to the gospel through the stated ministry of the whites? We answer, no. The Negroes have no regular and efficient ministry; as a matter of course, no churches; neither is there sufficient room in the white churches for their accommodation. We know of but five churches in the slave-holding states built expressly for their use. These are all in the state of Georgia. We may now inquire whether they enjoy the privileges of the gospel in their own houses, and on our plantations? Again we return a negative answer. They have no Bibles to read by their own firesides. They have no family altars; and when in affliction, sickness, or death, they have no minister to address to them the consolations of the gospel, nor to bury them with appropriate services."

The same synod said in 1834: "The gospel, as things now are, can never be preached to the two classes (whites and blacks) successfully in conjunction. The galleries or back seats on the lower floor of white churches are generally appropriated to the Negroes, when it can be done without inconvenience to the whites. When it cannot be done conveniently, the Negroes must catch the gospel as it escapes through the doors and windows. If the master is pious, the house servants alone attend family worship, and frequently few of them, while the field hands have no attention at all. So far as masters are engaged in the work [of religious instruction of slaves], an almost unbroken silence reigns on this vast field."

The Rev. C. C. Jones, a Georgian and ardent defender of slavery (see Note 5) says of the period 1790–1820: "It is not too much to say that the religious and physical condition of the Negroes were both improved during this period. Their increase was natural and regular, ranging every ten years between thirty-four and thirty-six per cent. As the old stock from Africa died out of the country, the grosser customs, ignorance, and paganism of Africa died with them. Their descendants, the country-born, were better looking, more intelligent, more civilized, more susceptible of religious impressions.

"On the whole, however, but a minority of the Negroes, and that a small one, attended regularly the house of God, and taking them as a class, their religious instruction was extensively and most seriously neglected."

And of the decade 1830–40, he insists: "We cannot cry out against the Papists for withholding the Scriptures from the common people and keeping them in ignorance of the way of life, for we withhold the Bible from our servants, and keep them in ignorance of it, while we will not use the means to have it read and explained to them."

Such condition stirred the more radical-minded toward abolition sentiments and the more conservative toward renewed effort to evangelize and better the condition of the slaves. This condition was deplorable as Jones pictures it. "Persons live and die in the midst of Negroes and know comparatively little of their real character. They have not the immediate management of them. They have to do with them in the ordinary discharge of their duty as servants, further than this they institute no inquiries; they give themselves no trouble.

"The Negroes are a distinct class in the community, and keep themselves very much to themselves. They are one thing before the whites and another before their own color. Deception before the former is characteristic of them, whether bond or free, throughout the whole United States. It is habit, a long established custom, which descends from generation to generation. There is an upper and an under current. Some are contented with the appearance on the surface; others dive beneath. Hence the diversity of impressions and representations of the moral and religious condition of the Negroes. Hence the disposition of some to deny the darker pictures of their more searching and knowing friends."

He then enumerates the vice of the slaves: "The divine institution of marriage depends for its perpetuity, sacredness, and value, largely upon the protection given it by the law of the land. Negro marriages are neither recognized nor protected by law. The Negroes receive no instruction on the nature, sacredness, and perpetuity of the institution; at any rate they are far from being duly impressed with these things. They are not required to be married in any particular form, nor by any particular persons."

He continues: "Hence, as may well be imagined, the marriage relation loses much of the sacredness and perpetuity of its character. It is a contract of convenience, profit, or pleasure, that may be entered into and dissolved at the will of the parties, and that without heinous sin, or the injury of the property or interests of any one. That which they possess in common is speedily divided, and the support of the wife and children falls not upon the husband, but upon the master. Protracted sickness, want of industrial habits, of congeniality of disposition, or disparity of age, are sufficient grounds for a separation."

Under such circumstances, "polygamy is practiced both secretly and openly." Uncleanness, infanticide, theft, lying, quarreling, and fighting are noted, and the words of Charles Cotesworth Pinckney in 1829 are recalled: "There needs no stronger illustration of the doctrine of human depravity than the state of morals on plantations in general. Besides the mischievous tendency of bad example in parents and elders, the little Negro is often taught by these natural instructors that he may commit any vice that he can conceal from his superiors, and thus falsehood and deception are among the earliest lessons they imbibe. Their advance in years is but a progression to the higher grades of iniquity. The violation of the Seventh Commandment is viewed in a more venial light than in fashionable European circles. Their depredations of rice have been estimated to amount to twenty-five per cent of the gross average of crops."

John Randolph of Roanoke once visited a lady and "found her surrounded with her seamstresses, making up a quantity of clothing. 'What work have you in hand?' 'O sir, I am preparing this clothing to send to the poor Greeks.' On taking leave at the steps of her mansion, he saw some of her servants in need of the very clothing which their tender-hearted mistress was sending abroad. He exclaimed, 'Madam, madam, the Greeks are at your door!'"

One natural solution of this difficulty was to train teachers and preachers for the slaves from among their own number. The old Voodoo priests were passing away and already here and there new spiritual leaders of the Negroes began to arise. Accounts of several of these, taken from "The Negro Church," will be given.

Among the earliest was Harry Hosier who traveled with the Methodist Bishop Asbury and often filled appointments for him. George Leile and Andrew Bryan were preachers whose life history is of intense interest. "George Leile or Lisle, sometimes called George Sharp, was born in Virginia about 1750. His master (Mr. Sharp) some time before the American war removed and settled in Burke County, Georgia. Mr. Sharp was a Baptist and a deacon in a Baptist church, of which Rev. Matthew Moore was pastor. George was converted and baptized under Mr. Moore's ministry. The church gave him liberty to preach.

"About nine months after George Leile left Georgia, Andrew, surnamed Bryan, a man of good sense, great zeal, and some natural elocution, began to exhort his black brethren and friends. He and his followers were reprimanded and forbidden to engage further in religious exercises. He would, however, pray, sing, and encourage his fellow worshipers to seek the Lord.

"Their persecution was carried to an inhuman extent. Their evening assemblies were broken up and those found present were punished with stripes. Andrew Bryan and Sampson, his brother, converted about a year after him, were twice imprisoned, and they with about fifty others were whipped. When publicly whipped, and bleeding under his wounds, Andrew declared that he not only rejoiced to be whipped, but would gladly suffer death for the cause of Jesus Christ, and that while he had life and opportunity he would continue to preach Christ. He was faithful to his vow and, by patient continuance in well-doing, he put to silence and shamed his adversaries, and influential advocates and patrons were raised up for him. Liberty was given Andrew by the civil authority to continue his religious meetings under certain regulations. His master gave him the use of his barn at Brampton, three miles from Savannah, where he preached for two years with little interruption."

Lott Carey a free Virginia Negro "was evidently a man of superior intellect and force of character, as is evidenced from the fact that his reading took a wide range—from political economy, in Adam Smith's Wealth of Nations,' to the voyage of Captain Cook. That he was a worker as well as a preacher is true, for when he decided to go to Africa his employers offered to raise his salary from $800 to $1,000 a year. Remember that this was over eighty years ago. Carey was not seduced by such a flattering offer, for he was determined.

"His last sermon in the old First Church in Richmond must have been exceedingly powerful, for it was compared by an eyewitness, a resident of another state, to the burning, eloquent appeals of George Whitfield. Fancy him as he stands there in that historic building ringing the changes on the word 'freely,' depicting the willingness with which he was ready to give up his life for service in Africa.

"He, as you may already know, was the leader of the pioneer colony to Liberia, where he arrived even before the agent of the Colonization Society. In his new home his abilities were recognized, for he was made vice governor, and became governor in fact while Governor Ashmun was absent from the colony in this country. Carey did not allow his position to betray the cause of his people, for he did not hesitate to expose the duplicity of the Colonization Society and even to defy their authority, it would seem, in the interests of the people.

"While casting cartridges to defend the colonists against the natives in 1828, the accidental upsetting of a candle caused an explosion that resulted in his death.

"Carey is described as a typical Negro, six feet in height, of massive and erect frame, with the sinews of a Titan. He had a square face, keen eyes, and a grave countenance. His movements were measured; in short, he had all the bearing and dignity of a prince of the blood."

John Chavis was a full-blooded Negro, born in Granville County, N. C., near Oxford, in 1763. He was born free and was sent to Princeton, studying privately under Dr. Witherspoon, where he did well. He went to Virginia to preach to Negroes. In 1802, in the county court, his freedom and character were certified to and it was declared that he had passed "through a regular course of academic studies" at what is now Washington and Lee University. In 1805 he returned to North Carolina, where in 1809 he was made a licentiate in the Presbyterian Church and allowed to preach. His English was remarkably pure, his manner impressive, his explanations clear and concise.

For a long time he taught school and had the best whites as pupils—a United States senator, the sons of a chief justice of North Carolina, a governor of the state and many others. Some of his pupils boarded in the family, and his school was regarded as the best in the State. "All accounts agree that John Chavis was a gentleman," and he was received socially among the best whites and asked to table. In 1830 he was stopped from preaching by the law. Afterward he taught a school for free Negroes in Raleigh.

Henry Evans was a full-blooded Virginia free Negro, and was the pioneer of Methodism in Fayetteville, N. C. He found the Negroes there, about 1800, without any religious instruction. He began preaching and the town council ordered him away; he continued and whites came to hear him. Finally the white auditors outnumbered the blacks and sheds were erected for Negroes at the side of the church. The gathering became a regular Methodist Church, with a white and Negro membership, but Evans continued to preach. He exhibited "rare self-control before the most wretched of castes! Henry Evans did much good, but he would have done more good had his spirit been untrammeled by this sense of inferiority."

His dying words uttered as he stood, aged and bent beside his pulpit, are of singular pathos: "I have come to say my last word to you. It is this: None but Christ. Three times have I had my life in jeopardy for preaching the gospel to you. Three times I have broken ice on the edge of the water and swam across the Cape Fear to preach the gospel to you; and, if in my last hour I could trust to that, or anything but Christ crucified, for my salvation, all should be lost and my soul perish forever."

Early in the nineteenth century Ralph Freeman was a slave in Anson County, N. C. He was a full-blooded Negro, and was ordained and became an able Baptist preacher. He baptized and administered communion, and was greatly respected. When the Baptists split on the question of missions he sided with the anti-mission side. Finally the law forbade him to preach.

Lunsford Lane was a Negro who bought his freedom in Raleigh, N. C., by the manufacture of smoking tobacco. He later became a minister of the gospel, and had the confidence of many of the best people.

The story of Jack of Virginia is best told in the words of a Southern writer:

"Probably the most interesting case in the whole South is that of an African preacher of Nottoway County, popularly known as 'Uncle Jack,' whose services to white and black were so valuable that a distinguished minister of the Southern Presbyterian Church felt called upon to memorialize his work in a biography.

"Kidnapped from his idolatrous parents in Africa, he was brought over in one of the last cargoes of slaves admitted to Virginia and sold to a remote and obscure planter in Nottoway County, a region at that time in the backwoods and destitute particularly as to religious life and instruction. He was converted under the occasional preaching of Rev. Dr. John Blair Smith, president of Hampden-Sidney College, and of Dr. William Hill and Dr. Archibald Alexander of Princeton, then young theologues, and by hearing the Scriptures read.

"Taught by his master's children to read, he became so full of the spirit and knowledge of the Bible that he was recognized among the whites as a powerful expounder of Christian doctrine, was licensed to preach by the Baptist Church, and preached from plantation to plantation within a radius of thirty miles, as he was invited by overseers or masters. His freedom was purchased by a subscription of whites, and he was given a home and tract of land for his support. He organized a large and orderly Negro church, and exercised such a wonderful controlling influence over the private morals of his flock that masters, instead of punishing their slaves, often referred them to the discipline of their pastor, which they dreaded far more.

"He stopped a heresy among the Negroes of Southern Virginia, defeating in open argument a famous fanatical Negro preacher named Campbell, who advocated noise and 'the spirit' against the Bible, and winning over Campbell's adherents in a body. For over forty years, and until he was nearly a hundred years of age, he labored successfully in public and private among black and whites, voluntarily giving up his preaching in obedience to the law of 1832, the result of 'Old Nat's war.'

"The most refined and aristocratic people paid tribute to him, and he was instrumental in the conversion of many whites. Says his biographer, Rev. Dr. William S. White: 'He was invited into their houses, sat with their families, took part in their social worship, sometimes leading the prayer at the family altar. Many of the most intelligent people attended upon his ministry and listened to his sermons with great delight. Indeed, previous to the year 1825, he was considered by the best judges to be the best preacher in that county. His opinions were respected, his advice followed, and yet he never betrayed the least symptoms of arrogance or self-conceit.

"'His dwelling was a rude log cabin, his apparel of the plainest and coarsest materials.' This was because he wanted to be fully identified with his class. He refused gifts of better clothing, saying 'These clothes are a great deal better than are generally worn by people of my color, and besides if I wear finer ones I find I shall be obliged to think about them even at meeting.'"

Thus slowly, surely, the slave, in the persons of such exceptional men, appearing here and there at rare intervals, was persistently stretching upward. The Negroes bade fair in time to have their leaders. The new democratic evangelism began to encourage this, and then came the difficulty—the inevitable ethical paradox.

The good men of the South recognized the needs of the slaves. Here and there Negro ministers were arising. What now should be the policy? On the part of the best thinkers it seemed as if men might strive here, in spite of slavery, after brotherhood; that the slaves should be proselyted, taught religion, admitted to the churches, and, notwithstanding their civil station, looked upon as the spiritual brothers of the white communicants. Much was done to make this true. The conditions improved in a great many respects, but no sooner was there a systematic effort to teach the slaves, even though that teaching was confined to elementary religion, than the various things followed that must follow all intellectual awakenings.

We have had the same thing in our day. A few Negroes of the South have been taught, they consequently have begun to think, they have begun to assert themselves, and suddenly men are face to face with the fact that either one of two things must happen—either they must stop teaching or these people are going to be men, not serfs or slaves. Not only that, but to seek to put an awakening people back to sleep means revolt. It meant revolt in the eighteenth century, when a series of insurrections and disturbances frightened the South tremendously, not so much by their actual extent as by the possibilities they suggested. It was noticeable that many of these revolts were led by preachers.

The revolution in Hayti greatly stirred the South and induced South Carolina to declare in 1800:

"It shall not be lawful for any number of slaves, free Negroes, mulattoes, or mestizoes, even in company with white persons, to meet together and assemble for the purpose of mental instruction or religious worship either before the rising of the sun or after the going down of the same. And all magistrates, sheriffs, militia officers, etc., etc., are hereby vested with power, etc., for dispersing such assemblies."

On petition of the white churches the rigor of this law was slightly abated in 1803 by a modification which forbade any person, before nine o'clock in the evening, "to break into a place of meeting wherein shall be assembled the members of any religious society in this State, provided a majority of them shall be white persons, or otherwise to disturb their devotions unless such persons, etc., so entering said place (of worship) shall first have obtained from some magistrate, etc., a warrant, etc., in case a magistrate shall be then actually within a distance of three miles from such place of meeting; otherwise the provisions, etc. (of the Act of 1800) to remain in full force."

So, too, in Virginia the Haytian revolt and the attempted insurrection under Gabriel in 1800 led to the Act of 1804, which forbade all evening meetings of slaves. This was modified in 1805 so as to allow a slave, in company with a white person, to listen to a white minister in the evening. A master was "allowed" to employ a religious teacher for his slaves. Mississippi passed similar restrictions.

By 1822 the rigor of the South Carolina laws in regard to Negro meetings had abated, especially in a city like Charleston, and one of the results was the Vesey plot.

"The sundry religious classes or congregations, with Negro leaders or local preachers, into which were formed the Negro members of the various churches of Charleston, furnished Vesey with the first rudiments of an organization, and at the same time with a singularly safe medium for conducting his underground agitation. It was customary, at that time, for these Negro congregations to meet for purposes of worship entirely free from the presence of whites. Such meetings were afterward forbidden to be held except in the presence of at least one representative of the dominant race, but during the three or four years prior to the year 1822 they certainly offered Denmark Vesey regular, easy, and safe opportunity for preaching his gospel of liberty and hate. And we are left in no doubt whatever in regard to the uses to which he put those gatherings of blacks.

"Like many of his race, he possessed the gift of gab, as the silver in the tongue and the gold in the full or thick-lipped mouth are oftentimes contemptuously characterized. And, like many of his race, he was a devoted student of the Bible, to whose interpretation he brought, like many other Bible students not confined to the Negro race, a good deal of imagination and not a little of superstition, which, with some natures, is perhaps but another name for the desires of the heart.

"Thus equipped, it is no wonder that Vesey, as he pored over the Old Testament scriptures, found many points of similitude in the history of the Jews and that of the slaves in the United States. They were both peculiar peoples. They were both Jehovah's peculiar peoples, one in the past, the other in the present. And it seemed to him that as Jehovah bent His ear, and bared His arm once in behalf of the one, so would He do the same for the other. It was all vividly real to his thought, I believe, for to his mind thus had said the Lord.

"He ransacked the Bible for apposite and terrible texts whose commands in the olden times, to the olden people, were no less imperative upon the new times and the new people. This new people were also commanded to arise and destroy their enemies and the city in which they dwelt, 'both man and woman, young and old, with the edge of the sword.' Believing super-stitiously as he did in the stern and Nemesis-like God of the Old Testament he looked confidently for a day of vengeance and retribution for the blacks. He felt, I doubt not, something peculiarly applicable to his enterprise and intensely personal to himself in the stern and exultant prophecy of Zechariah, fierce and sanguinary words, which were constantly in his mouth: 'Then shall the Lord go forth and fight against those nations as when He fought in the day of battle.' According to Vesey's lurid exegesis 'those nations' in the text meant beyond peradventure the cruel masters, and Jehovah was to go forth to fight them for the poor slaves and on whichever side fought that day the Almighty God on that side would assuredly rest victory and deliverance.

"It will not be denied that Vesey's plan contemplated the total annihilation of the white population of Charleston. Nursing for many dark years the bitter wrongs of himself and race had filled him without doubt with a mad spirit of revenge and had given to him a decided predilection for shedding the blood of his oppressors. But if he intended to kill them to satisfy a desire for vengeance he intended to do so also on broader ground. The conspirators, he argued, had no choice in the matter, but were compelled to adopt a policy of extermination by the necessity of their position. The liberty of the blacks was in the balance of fate against the lives of the whites. He could strike that balance in favor of the blacks only by the total destruction of the whites. Therefore the whites, men, women, and children, were doomed to death."*

Vesey's plot was well laid, but the conspirators were betrayed.

Less than ten years after this plot was discovered and Vesey and his associates hanged, there broke out the Nat Turner insurrection in Virginia. Turner was himself a preacher.

"He was a Christian and a man. He was conscious that he was a Man and not a 'thing'; therefore, driven by religious fanaticism, he undertook a difficult and bloody task. Nathaniel Turner was born in Southampton County, Virginia, October 2, 1800. His master was one Benjamin Turner, a very wealthy and aristocratic man. He owned many slaves, and was a cruel and exacting master. Young 'Nat' was born of slave parents, and carried to his grave many of the superstitions and traits of his father and mother. The former was a preacher, the latter a 'mother in Israel.' Both were unlettered but, nevertheless, very pious people.

"The mother began when Nat was quite young to teach him that he was born, like Moses, to be the deliverer of his race. She would sing to him snatches of wild, rapturous songs and repeat portions of prophecy she had learned from the preachers of those times. Nat listened with reverence and awe, and believed everything his mother said. He imbibed the deep religious character of his parents, and soon manifested a desire to preach. He was solemnly set apart to 'the gospel ministry' by his father, the church, and visiting preachers. He was quite low in stature, dark, and had the genuine African features. His eyes were small but sharp, and gleamed like fire when he was talking about his 'mission' or preaching from some

---

* Grimke: "Right on the Scaffold."

prophetic passage of scripture. It is said that he never laughed. He was a dreamy sort of a man, and avoided the crowd.

"Like Moses he lived in the solitudes of the mountains and brooded over the condition of his people. There was something grand to him in the rugged scenery that nature had surrounded him with. He believed that he was a prophet, a leader raised up by God to burst the bolts of the prison-house and set the oppressed free. The thunder, the hail, the storm-cloud, the air, the earth, the stars, at which he would sit and gaze half the night all spake the language of the God of the oppressed. He was seldom seen in a large company, and never drank a drop of ardent spirits. Like John the Baptist, when he had delivered his message, he would retire to the fastness of the mountain or seek the desert, where he could meditate upon his great work."

In the impression of the Richmond *Enquirer* of the 30th of August, 1831, the first editorial or leader is under the caption of "The Banditte." The editor says:

"They remind one of a parcel of blood-thirsty wolves rushing down from the Alps; or, rather, like a former incursion of the Indians upon the white settlements. Nothing is spared; neither age nor sex respected—the helplessness of women and children pleads in vain for mercy. . . . The case of Nat Turner warns us. No black man ought to be permitted to turn preacher through the country. The law must be enforced, or the tragedy of Southampton appeals to us in vain."

Mr. Gray, the man to whom Turner made his confession before dying, said:

"It has been said that he was ignorant and cowardly and that his object was to murder and rob for the purpose of obtaining money to make his escape. It is notorious that he was never known to have a dollar in his life, to swear an oath, or drink a drop of spirits. As to his ignorance, he certainly never had the advantages of an education, but he can read and write, and for natural intelligence and quickness of apprehension is surpassed by few men I have ever seen. As to his being a coward, his reason as given for not resisting Mr. Phipps, shows the decision of his character. When he saw Mr. Phipps present his gun, he said he knew it was impossible for him to escape as the woods were full of men. He, therefore, thought it was better for him to surrender and trust to fortune for his escape.

"He is a complete fanatic or plays his part most admirably. On other subjects he possesses an uncommon share of intelligence, with a mind capable of attaining anything, but warped and perverted by the influence of early impressions. He is below the ordinary stature, though strong and active, having the true Negro face, every feature of which is strongly marked.

"I shall not attempt to describe the effect of his narrative, as told and commented on by himself, in the condemned hole of the prison; the calm deliberate composure with which he spoke of his late deeds and intentions; the expression of his fiend-like face when excited by enthusiasm, still bearing the stains of the blood of the helpless innocence about him, clothed with rags and covered with chains, yet daring to raise his manacled hand to Heaven, with a spirit soaring above the attributes of man. I looked on him and the blood curdled in my veins."**

The Turner insurrection is so connected with the economic revolution which enthroned cotton that it marks an epoch in the history of the slave. A wave of legislation passed over

---

** "The Negro Church," Atlanta University Publications, No. 8.

the South prohibiting the slaves from learning to read and write, forbidding Negroes to preach, and interfering with Negro religious meetings.

Virginia declared, in 1831, that neither slaves nor free Negroes might preach, nor could they attend religious service at night without permission. In North Carolina slaves and free Negroes were forbidden to preach, exhort or teach "in any prayer-meeting or other association for worship where slaves of different families are collected together" on penalty of not more than thirty-nine lashes. Maryland and Georgia had similar laws. The Mississippi law of 1831 said: It is "unlawful for any slave, free Negro, or mulatto to preach the gospel" upon pain of receiving thirty-nine lashes upon the naked back of the presumptuous preacher. If a Negro received written permission from his master he might preach to the Negroes in his immediate neighborhood, providing six respectable white men, owners of slaves, were present. In Alabama the law of 1832 prohibited the assembling of more than five male slaves at any place off the plantation to which they belonged, but nothing in the act was to be considered as forbidding attendance at places of public worship held by white persons. No slave or free person of color was permitted to "preach, exhort, or harangue any slave or slaves, or free persons of color, except in the presence of five respectable slaveholders, or unless the person preaching was licensed by some regular body of professing Christians in the neighborhood, to whose society or church the Negroes addressed properly belonged."

In the District of Columbia the free Negroes began to leave white churches in 1831 and to assemble in their own.

Thus it was that through the fear of insurrection, the economic press of the new slavery that was arising, and the new significance of slavery in the economics of the South, the strife for spiritual brotherhood was given up. Slavery became distinctly a matter of race and not of status. Long years before, the white servants had been freed and only black servants were left; now social condition came to be not simply a matter of slavery but a matter of belonging to the black race, so that even the free Negroes began to be disfranchised and put into the caste system (see Note 6).

A new adjustment of ethics and religion had to be made to meet this new situation, and in the adjustment no matter what might be said or thought, the Negro and slavery had to be the central thing.

In the adjustment of religion and ethics that was made for the new slavery, under the cotton kingdom, there was in the first place a distinct denial of human brotherhood. These black men were not men in the sense that white men were men. They were different—different in kind, different in origin; they had different diseases (see Note 7); they had different feelings; they were not to be treated the same; they were not looked upon as the same; they were altogether apart and, while perhaps they had certain low sensibilities and aspirations, yet so far as this world is concerned, there could be with them neither human nor spiritual brotherhood.

The only status that they could possibly occupy was the status of slaves. They could not get along as freemen; they could not work as freemen; it was utterly unthinkable that people should live with them free. This was the philosophy that was worked out gradually, with exceptions here and there, and that was thought through, written on, preached from the pulpits and taught in the homes, until people in the South believed it as they believed the rising and the setting of the sun.

As this became more and more the orthodox ethical opinion, heretics appeared in the land as they always do. But intolerance and anathema met them. In community after community there was a demand for orthodoxy on this one burning question of the economic and religious South, and the heretics were driven out. The Quakers left North Carolina, the abolitionists either left Virginia or ceased to talk, and throughout the South those people who dared to think otherwise were left silent or dead (see Note 8).

So long as slavery was an economic success this orthodoxy was all powerful; when signs of economic distress appeared it became intolerant and aggressive. A great moral battle was impending in the South, but political turmoil and a development of northern thought so rapid as to be unintelligible in the South stopped this development forcibly. War came and the hatred and moral bluntness incident to war, and men crystallized in their old thought.

The matter now could no longer be argued and thought out, it became a matter of tradition, of faith, of family and personal honor. There grew up therefore after the war a new predicament; a new-old paradox. Upon the whites hung the curse of the past; because they had not settled their labor problem then, they must settle the problem now in the face of upheaval and handicapped by the natural advance of the world.

So after the war and even to this day, the religious and ethical life of the South bows beneath this burden. Shrinking from facing the burning ethical questions that front it unrelentingly, the Southern Church clings all the more closely to the letter of a worn out orthodoxy, while its inner truer soul crouches before and fears to answer the problem of eight million black neighbors. It therefore assiduously "preaches Christ crucified," in prayer meeting *patois*, and crucifies "Niggers" in unrelenting daily life.

While the Church in the North, all too slowly but surely is struggling up from the ashes of a childish faith in myth and miracle, and beginning to preach a living gospel of civic virtue, peace and good will and a crusade against lying, stealing and snobbery, the Southern church for the most part is still murmuring of modes of "baptism," "infant damnation" and the "divine plan of creation."

Thus the post-bellum ethical paradox of the South is far more puzzling than the economic paradox. To be sure there is leaven in the lump. There are brave voices here and there, but they are easily drowned by social tyranny in the South and by indifference and sensationalism in the North (see Note 9).

First of all the result of the war was the complete expulsion of Negroes from white churches. Little has been said of this, but perhaps it was in itself the most singular and tremendous result of slavery. The Methodist Church South simply set its Negro members bodily out of doors. They did it with some consideration for their feelings, with as much kindliness as crass unkindliness can show, but they virtually said to all their black members—to the black mammies whom they have almost fulsomely praised and whom they remember in such astonishing numbers to-day, to the polite and deferential old servant, to whose character they build monuments—they said to them: "You cannot worship God with us." There grew up, therefore, the Colored Methodist Episcopal Church.

Flagrantly unchristian as this course was, it was still in some ways better than the absolute withdrawal of church fellowship on the part of the Baptists, or the policy of Episcopalians, which was simply that of studied neglect and discouragement which froze, harried, and well nigh invited the black communicants to withdraw.

From the North now came those Negro church bodies born of color discrimination in Philadelphia and New York in the eighteenth century, and thus a Christianity absolutely divided along the color line arose. There may be in the South a black man belonging to a white church to-day but if so, he must be very old and very feeble. This anomaly—this utter denial of the very first principles of the ethics of Jesus Christ—is today so deep seated and unquestionable a principle of Southern Christianity that its essential heathenism is scarcely thought of, and every revival of religion in this section banks its spiritual riches solidly and unmovedly against the color line, without conscious question.

Among the Negroes the results are equally unhappy. They needed ethical leadership, spiritual guidance, and religious instruction. If the Negroes of the South are to any degree immoral, sexually unchaste, criminally inclined, and religiously ignorant, what right has the Christian South even to whisper reproach or accusation? How often have they raised a finger to assume spiritual or religious guardianship over those victims of their past system of economic and social life?

Left thus unguided the Negroes, with some help from such Northern white churches as dared, began their own religious upbuilding (see Note 10). They faced tremendous difficulties—lack of ministers, money, and experience. Their churches could not be simply centres of religious life—because in the poverty of their organized efforts all united striving tended to centre in this one social organ. The Negro Church consequently became a great social institution with some ethical ideas but with those ethical ideas warped and changed and perverted by the whole history of the past; with memories, traditions, and rites of heathen worship, of intense emotionalism, trance, and weird singing.

And above all, there brooded over and in the church the sense of all their grievances. Whatsoever their own shortcomings might be, at least they knew that they were not guilty of hypocrisy; they did not cry "Whosoever will" and then brazenly ostracize half the world. They knew that they opened their doors and hearts wide to all people that really wanted to come in and they looked upon the white churches not as examples but with a sort of silent contempt and a real inner questioning of the genuineness of their Christianity.

On the other hand, so far as the white post-bellum Christian church is concerned, I can conceive no more pitiable paradox than that of the young white Christian in the South to-day who really believes in the ethics of Jesus Christ. What can he think when he hangs upon his church doors the sign that I have often seen, "All are welcome." He knows that half the population of his city would not dare to go inside that church. Or if there was any fellowship between Christians, white and black, it would be after the manner explained by a white Mississippi clergyman in all seriousness: "The whites and Negroes understand each other here perfectly, sir, perfectly; if they come to my church they take a seat in the gallery. If I go to theirs, they invite me to the front pew or the platform."

Once in Atlanta a great revival was going on in a prominent white church. The people were at fever heat, the minister was preaching and calling "Come to Jesus." Up the aisle tottered an old black man—he was an outcast, he had wandered in there aimlessly off the streets, dimly he had comprehended this call and he came tottering and swaying up the aisle. What was the result? It broke up the revival. There was no disturbance; he was gently led out, but that sudden appearance of a black face spoiled the whole spirit of the thing and the revival was at an end.

Who can doubt that if Christ came to Georgia to-day one of His first deeds would be to sit down and take supper with black men, and who can doubt the outcome if He did?

It is this tremendous paradox of a Christianity that theoretically opens the church to all men and yet closes it forcibly and insultingly in the face of black men and that does this not simply in the visible church but even more harshly in the spiritual fellowship of human souls—it is this that makes the ethical and religious problem in the South to-day of such tremendous importance, and that gives rise to the one thing which it seems to me is the most difficult in the Southern situation and that is, the tendency to deny the truth, the tendency to lie when the real situation comes up because the truth is too hard to face. This lying about the situation of the South has not been simply a political subterfuge against the dangers of ignorance, but is a sort of gasping inner revolt against acknowledging the real truth of the ethical conviction which every true Southerner must feel, namely: that the South is eternally and fundamentally wrong on the plain straight question of the equality of souls before God—of the inalienable rights of all men.

Here are men—they are aspiring, they are struggling piteously forward, they have frequent instances of ability, there is no doubt as to the tremendous strides which certain classes of Negroes have made—how shall they be treated? That they should be treated as men, of course, the best class of Southerners know and sometimes acknowledge. And yet they believe, and believe with fierce conviction, that it is impossible to treat Negroes as men, and still live with them. Right there is the paradox which they face daily and which is daily stamping hypocrisy upon their religion and upon their land.

Their irresistible impulse in this awful dilemma is to point to and emphasize the Negro's degradation, even though they know that it is not the degraded Negro whom they most fear, ostracize, and fight to keep down, but rather the rising, ambitious Negro.

If my own city of Atlanta had offered it to-day the choice between 500 Negro college graduates—forceful, busy, ambitious men of property and self-respect, and 500 black cringing vagrants and criminals, the popular vote in favor of the criminals would be simply overwhelming. Why? because they want Negro crime? No, not that they fear Negro crime less, but that they fear Negro ambition and success more. They can deal with crime by chain-gang and lynch law, or at least they think they can, but the South can conceive neither machinery nor place for the educated, self-reliant, self-assertive black man.

Are a people pushed to such moral extremities, the ones whose level-headed, unbiased statements of fact concerning the Negro can be relied upon? Do they really know the Negro? Can the nation expect of them the poise and patience necessary for the settling of a great social problem?

Not only is there then this initial falseness when the South excuses its ethical paradox by pointing to the low condition of the Negro masses, but there is also a strange blindness in failing to see that every pound of evidence to prove the present degradation of black men but adds to the crushing weight of indictment against their past treatment of this race.

A race is not made in a single generation. If they accuse Negro women of lewdness and Negro men of monstrous crime, what are they doing but advertising to the world the shameless lewdness of those Southern men who brought millions of mulattoes into the world, and whose deeds throughout the South and particularly in Virginia, the mother of slavery, have left but few prominent families whose blood does not to-day course in black veins? Suppose to-day Negroes do steal; who was it that for centuries made stealing a virtue by stealing their labor? Have not laziness and listlessness always been the followers of slavery? If these ten millions are ignorant by whose past law and mandate and present practice is this true?

The truth then cannot be controverted. The present condition of the Negro in America is better than the history of slavery proves we might reasonably expect. With the help of his friends, North and South, and despite the bitter opposition of his foes, South and North, he has bought twelve million acres of land, swept away two-thirds of his illiteracy, organized his church, and found leadership and articulate voice. Yet despite this the South, Christian and unchristian, with only here and there an exception, still stands like a rock wall and says: Negroes are not men and must not be treated as men.

When now the world faces such an absolute ethical contradiction, the truth is nearer than it seems.

It stands to-day perfectly clear and plain despite all sophistication and false assumption: If the contention of the South is true—that Negroes cannot by reason of hereditary inferiority take their places in modern civilization beside white men, then the South owes it to the world and to its better self to give the Negro every chance to prove this. To make the assertion dogmatically and then resort to all means which retard and restrict Negro development is not simply to stand convicted of insincerity before the civilized world, but, far worse than that, it is to make a nation of naturally generous, honest people to sit humiliated before their own consciences.

I believe that a straightforward, honorable treatment of black men according to their desert and achievement, will soon settle the Negro problem. If the South is right few will rise to a plane that will make their social reception a matter worth consideration; few will gain the sobriety and industry which will deserve the ballot; and few will achieve such solid moral character as will give them welcome to the fellowship of the church. If, on the other hand, Negroes with the door of opportunity thrown wide do become men of industry and achievement, of moral strength and even genius, then such rise will silence the South with an eternal silence.

The nation that enslaved the Negro owes him this trial; the section that doggedly and unreasonably kept him in slavery owes him at least this chance; and the church which professes to follow Jesus Christ and does not insist on this elemental act of justice merits the denial of the Master—"*I never knew you.*"

This, then, is the history of those mighty moral battles in the South which have given us the Negro problem. And the last great battle is not a battle of South or East, of black or white, but of all of us. The path to racial peace is straight but narrow—its following to-day means tremendous fight against inertia, prejudice, and intrenched snobbery. But it is the duty of men, it is a duty of the church, to face the problem. Not only is it their duty to face it—they *must* face it, it is impossible not to, the very attempt to ignore it is assuming an attitude. It is a problem not simply of political expediency, of economic success, but a problem above all of religious and social life; and it carries with it not simply a demand for its own solution, but beneath it lies the whole question of the real intent of our civilization: Is the civilization of the United States Christian?

It is a matter of grave consideration what answer we ought to give to that question. The precepts of Jesus Christ cannot but mean that Christianity consists of an attitude of humility, of a desire for peace, of a disposition to treat our brothers as we would have our brothers treat us, of mercy and charity toward our fellow men, of willingness to suffer persecution for right ideals and in general of love not only toward our friends but even toward our enemies.

Judged by this, it is absurd to call the practical religion of this nation Christian. We are not humble, we are impudently proud; we are not merciful, we are unmerciful toward friend and foe; we are not peaceful nor peacefully inclined as our armies and battle-ships declare; we do not want to be martyrs, we would much rather be thieves and liars so long as we can be rich; we do not seek continuously, and prayerfully inculcate, love and justice for our fellow men, but on the contrary the treatment of the poor, the unfortunate, and the black within our borders is almost a national crime.

The problem that lies before Christians is tremendous (see Note 11), and the answer must begin not by a slurring over of the one problem where these different tests of Christianity are most flagrantly disregarded, but it must begin by a girding of ourselves and a determination to see that justice is done in this country to the humblest and blackest as well as to the greatest and whitest of our citizens.

Now a word especially about the Episcopal church, whose position toward its Negro communicants is peculiar. I appreciate this position and speak of it specifically because I am one of those communicants. For four generations my family has belonged to this church and I belong to it, not by personal choice, not because I feel myself welcome within its portals, but simply because I refuse to be read outside of a church which is mine by inheritance and the service of my fathers. When the Episcopal church comes, as it does come to-day, to the Parting of the Ways, to the question as to whether its record in the future is going to be, on the Negro prpblem, as disgraceful as it has been in the past, I feel like appealing to all who are members of that church to remember that after all it is a church of Jesus Christ. Your creed and your duty enjoin upon you one, and only one, course of procedure.

In the real Christian church there is neither black nor white, rich nor poor, barbarian, Scythian, bond nor free, but all stand equal before the face of the Master. If you find that you cannot treat your Negro members as fellow Christians then do not deceive yourselves into thinking that the differences that you make or are going to make in their treatment are made for their good or for the service of the world; do not entice them to ask for a separation which your unchristian conduct forces them to prefer; do not pretend that the distinctions which you make toward them are distinctions which are made for the larger good of men, but simply confess in humility and self-abasement that you are not able to live up to your Christian vows; that you cannot treat these men as brothers and therefore you are going to set them aside and let them go their half-tended way.

I should be sorry, I should be grieved more than I can say, to see that which happened in the Southern Methodist Church and that which is practically happening in the Presbyterian Church, and that which will come in other sects—namely, a segregation of Negro Christians, come to be true among Episcopalians. It would be a sign of Christian disunity far more distressing than sectarianism. I should therefore deplore it; and yet I am also free to say that unless this church is prepared to treat its Negro members with exactly the same consideration that other members receive, with the same brotherhood and fellowship, the same encouragement to aspiration, the same privileges, similarly trained priests and similar preferment for them, then I should a great deal rather see them set aside than to see a continuation of present injustice. All I ask is that when you do this you do it with an open and honest statement of the real reasons and not with statements veiled by any hypocritical excuses.

I am therefore above all desirous that the younger men and women who are to-day taking up the leadership of this great group of men, who wish the world better and work toward that end, should begin to see the real significance of this step and of the great problem behind it. It is not a problem simply of the South, not a problem simply of this country, it is a problem of the world.

As I have said elsewhere: "Most men are colored. A belief in humanity is above all a belief in colored men." If you cannot get on with colored men in America you cannot, get on with the modern world; and if you cannot work with the humanity of this world how shall your souls ever tune with the myriad sided souls of worlds to come?

It may be that the price of the black man's survival in America and in the modern world, will be a long and shameful night of subjection to caste and segregation. If so, he will pay it, doggedly, silently, unfalteringly, for the sake of human liberty and the souls of his children's children. But as he stoops he will remember the indignation of that Jesus who cried, yonder behind heaving seas and years: "Woe unto you scribes and Pharisees, hypocrites, that strain out a gnat and swallow a camel,"—as if God cared a whit whether His Sons are born of maid, wife or widow so long as His church sits deaf to His own calling:

"Ho! every one that thirsteth, come ye to the waters and he that hath no money; come ye, buy and eat; yea, come, buy wine and milk without money and without price!"

Notes

1. See Atlanta University Publications, No 8, Section 4.

2. "Baptism doth not alter the condition of the person as to his bondage or freedom, in order that diverse masters freed from this doubt may more carefully endeavor the propagation of Christianity." (Williams I, 139.)

3. Of. Dr. Albert Bushnell Hart, "The Realities of Negro Suffrage," Proceedings of the American Political Science Association, Vol. II, 1905.

4. The Church of England through the "Society for the Propagation of the Gospel" (incorporated 1701) sent several missionaries who worked chiefly in the North. The history of the society goes on to say: "It is a matter of commendation to the clergy that they have done thus much in so great and difficult a work. But, alas! what is the instruction of a few hundreds in several years with respect to the many thousands uninstructed, unconverted, living, dying, utter pagans. It must be confessed what hath been done is as nothing with regard to what a true Christian would hope to see effected." After stating several difficulties in respect to the religious instruction of the Negroes, it is said: "But the greatest obstruction is the masters themselves do not consider enough the obligation which lies upon them to have their slaves instructed." The work of this society in America ceased in 1783. The Methodists report the following members:

1786	-	-	-	-	1,890
1790	-	-	-	-	11,682
1791	-	-	-	-	12,884
1796	-	-	-	-	12,215

Nearly all were in the North and the border states. Georgia had only 148. The Baptists had 18,000 Negro members in 1793. As to the Episcopalians, the single state of Virginia where more was done than elsewhere will illustrate the result:

"The Church Commission for Work among the Colored People at a late meeting decided to request the various rectors of parishes throughout the South to institute Sunday-schools and special services for the colored population 'such as were frequently found in the South before the war.' The commission hope for 'real advance' among the colored people in so doing. We do not agree with the commission with respect to either the wisdom or the efficiency of the plan suggested. In the first place, this 'before the war' plan was a complete failure so far as church extension was concerned, in the past when white churchmen had complete bodily control of their slaves. . . .

"The Journals of Virginia will verify the contention, that during the 'before the war' period, while the bishops and a large number of the clergy were always interested in the religious training of the slaves, yet as a matter of fact there was general apathy and indifference upon the part of the laity with respect to this matter.

"At various intervals resolutions were presented in the Annual Conventions with the avowed purpose of stimulating an interest in the religious welfare of the slaves. But despite all these efforts the Journals fail to record any great achievements along that line. . . . So faithful had been the work under such conditions that as late as 1879 there were less than 200 colored communicants reported in the whole state of Virginia." (*Church Advocate.*)

5. Charles C. Jones: "The Religious Instruction of the Negroes in the United States," Savannah, 1842. Cf. Atlanta University Publication, No. 8, passim.

6. Cf. Hart, *supra*. Note too the decrease in the proportion of free Negroes.

7. Note Dr. Cartwright's articles; DeBow's "Review", Vol. II, pp. 29, 184, 331 and 504. Cf. Fitzhugh, "Cannibals All."

8. Cf. Weeks, "Southern Quakers and Slavery," Balt. 1896; Ballagh, "Slavery in Virginia."

9. There has been in the North a generously conceived campaign in the last ten years to emphasize the good in the South and minimize the evil. Consequently many people have come to believe that men like Fleming and Murphy represent either the dominant Southern sentiment or that of a strong minority. On the contrary the brave utterances of such men represent a very small and very weak minority—a minority which is growing very slowly and which can only hope for success by means of moral support from the outside. Such moral support has not been generally given; it is Tillman, Vardaman and Dixon who get the largest hearing in the land and they represent the dominant public opinion in the South. The mass of public opinion there while it hesitates at the extreme brutality of these spokesmen is nearer to them than to Bassett or Fleming or Alderman.

10. Cf. "The Negro Church," Atlanta University Publication, No. 8. 212 pp. 1903.

11. Twenty good references on the ethical and religious aspect of slavery and the Negro problem are:

C. C. Jones, "The Religious Instruction of the Negroes in the United States," Savannah, 1842. 277 pp. 12mo.

R. F. Campbell, "Some Aspects of the Race Problem in the South," Pamphlet, 1899. Asheville, N. C. 31 pp. 8vo.

R. L. Dabney, "Defence of Virginia, and Through Her of the South," New York, 1867. 356 pp. 12mo.

Nehemiah Adams, "A South Side View of Slavery," Boston, 1854. viii, 7–214 pp. 16mo.

Richard Allen, First Bishop of the A. M. E. Church. "The life, experience and gospel labors of the Rt. Rev. Richard Allen." Written by himself. Phila., 1793. 69 pp. 8vo.

Matthew Anderson, "Presbyterianism and Its Relation to the Negro," Phila., 1897.

Geo. S. Merriam, "The Negro and the Nation," N. Y., 1906. 436 pp. 12mo.

M. S. Locke, "Anti-Slavery in America," 255 pp. 1901.

W. A. Sinclair, "The Aftermath of Slavery," etc., with an introduction by T. W. Higginson, Boston, 1905. 358 pp.

N. S. Shaler, "The Neighbor: The Natural History of Human Contrasts" (The problem of the African), Boston, 1904. vii, 342 pp. 12mo.

Atlanta University Publications:

Number 6, "The Negro Common School," 120 pp. 1901.

Number 8, "The Negro Church," 212 pp. 1903.

Number 9, "Notes on Negro Crime," 76 pp. 1904.

E. H. Abbott, "Religious life in America," A record of personal observation. N. Y.: *The Outlook,* 1902. xii, 730 pp. 8vo.

W. E. B. DuBois, "The Souls of Black Folk," Chicago, 1903.

Friends, "A Brief Testimony of the Progress of the Friends Against Slavery and the Slave-Trade," 1671–1787. Phila., 1843.

J. W. Hood, "One Hundred Years of the A. M. E. Zion Church."

S. M. Janney, "History of the Religious Society of Friends," Phila., 1859–1867.

D. A. Payne, "History of the A. M. E. Church," Nashville, 1891.

S. B. Weeks, "Anti-Slavery Sentiment in the South," Washington, D. C., 1898. "Southern Quakers and Slavery," Baltimore, 1896.

White, "The African Preacher."

12. Jesus Christ in Georgia

W.E.B. DuBois

The convict guard laughed.

"I don't know," he said, "I hadn't thought of that—"

He hesitated and looked at the stranger curiously. In the solemn twilight he got an impression of unusual height and soft dark eyes.

"Curious sort of acquaintance for the Colonel," he thought; then he continued aloud: "But that nigger there is bad; a born thief and ought to be sent up for life; is practically; got ten years last time—"

Here the voice of the promoter talking within interrupted; he was bending over his figures, sitting by the Colonel. He was slight, with a sharp nose.

"The convicts," he said, "would cost us $96 a year and board. Well, we can squeeze that so that it won't be over $125 apiece. Now, if these fellows are driven, they can build this line within twelve months. It will be running next April, Freights will fall fifty per cent. Why, man, you will be a millionaire in less than ten years."

The Colonel started. He was a thick, short man, with clean-shaven face, and a certain air of breeding about the lines of his countenance; the word millionaire sounded well in his ears. He thought—he thought a great deal; he almost heard the puff of the fearfully costly automobile that was coming up the road, and he said:

"I suppose we might as well hire them."

"Of course," answered the promoter.

The voice of the tall stranger in the corner broke in here:

"It will be a good thing for them?" he said, half in question.

The Colonel moved. "The guard makes strange friends," he thought to himself. "What's this man doing here, anyway?" He looked at him, or rather, looked at his eyes, and then somehow felt a warming toward him. He said:

"Well, at least it can't harm them—they're beyond that."

"It will do them good, then," said the stranger again. The promoter shrugged his shoulders.

"It will do us good," he said.

But the Colonel shook his head impatiently. He felt a desire to justify himself before those eyes, and he answered:

"Yes, it will do them good; or, at any rate, it won't make them any worse than they are."

Then he started to say something else, but here sure enough the sound of the automobile breathing at the gate stopped him and they all arose.

"It is settled, then," said the promoter.

"Yes," said the Colonel, signing his name and turning toward the stranger again.

"Are you going into town?" he asked with the Southern courtesy of white man to white man in a country town. The stranger said he was.

"Then come along in my machine. I want to talk to you about this."

They went out to the car. The stranger as he went turned again to look back at the convict. He was a tall, powerfully built black fellow. His face was sullen, with a low forehead, thick, hanging lips, and bitter eyes. There was revolt written about the mouth, and a hangdog expression. He stood bending over his pile of stones pounding listlessly.

Beside him stood a boy of twelve, yellow, with a hunted, crafty look. The convict raised his eyes, and they met the eyes of the stranger. The hammer fell from his hands.

The stranger turned slowly toward the automobile, and the Colonel introduced him. He could not exactly catch the foreign-sounding name, but he mumbled something as he presented him to his wife and little girl, who were waiting. As they whirled away he started to talk, but the stranger had taken the little girl into his lap, and together they conversed in low tones all the way home.

In some way, they did not exactly know how, they got the impression that the man was a teacher, and of course he must be a foreigner. The long cloak-like coat told this. They rode in the twilight through the half-lighted town, and at last drew up before the Colonel's mansion, with its ghostlike pillars.

The lady in the back seat was thinking of the guests she had invited to dinner, and wondered if she ought not to ask this man to stay. He seemed cultured, and she supposed he was some acquaintance of the Colonel's. It would be rather a distinction to have him there, with the Judge's wife and daughter and the Rector. She spoke almost before she thought:

"You will enter and rest awhile?"

The Colonel and the little girl insisted. For a moment the stranger seemed about to refuse. He said he was on his way North, where he had some business for his father in Pennsylvania. Then, for the child's sake, he consented. Up the steps they went, and into the dark parlor, and there they sat and talked a long time. It was a curious conversation. Afterward they did not remember exactly what was said, and yet they all remembered a certain strange satisfaction in that long talk.

Presently the nurse came for the reluctant child, and the hostess bethought herself:

"We will have a cup of tea—you will be dry and tired."

She rang and switched on a blaze of light. With one accord they all looked at the stranger, for they had hardly seen him well in the glooming twilight. The woman started in amazement and the Colonel half rose in anger. Why, the man was a mulatto, surely—even if he did not own the Negro blood, their practised eyes knew it. He was tall and straight, and the coat looked like a Jewish gabardine. His hair hung in close curls far down the sides of his face, and his face was olive, even yellow.

A peremptory order rose to the Colonel's lips, and froze there as he caught the stranger's eyes. Those eyes, where had he seen those eyes before? He remembered them long years ago—the soft tear-filled eyes of a brown girl. He remembered many things, and his face grew drawn and white. Those eyes kept burning into him, even when they were turned half away toward the staircase, where the white figure of the child hovered with her nurse, and waved goodnight. The lady sank into her chair and thought: "What will the Judge's wife say? How did the Colonel come to invite this man here? How shall we be rid of him?" She looked at the Colonel in reproachful consternation.

Just then the door opened and the old butler came in. He was an ancient black man with tufted white hair, and he held before him a large silver tray filled with a china tea service. The stranger rose slowly and stretched forth his hands as if to bless the viands. The old man paused in bewilderment, tottered and then, with sudden gladness in his eyes, dropped to his knees as the tray crashed to the floor.

"My Lord!" he whispered, "and My God!" But the woman screamed:

"Mother's china!"

The doorbell rang.

"Heavens! Here is the dinner party!" exclaimed the lady.

She turned toward the door, but there in the hall, clad in her night clothes, was the little girl. She had stolen down the stairs to see the stranger again, and the nurse above was calling in vain. The woman felt hysterical and scolded at the nurse, but the stranger had stretched out his arms, and with a glad cry the child nestled in them. "Of such," he whispered, "is the Kingdom of Heaven," as he slowly mounted the stairs with his little burden.

The mother was glad; anything to be rid of the interloper even for a moment. The bell rang again, and she hastened toward the door, which the loitering black maid was just opening. She did not notice the shadow of the stranger as he came slowly down the stairs and paused by the newel post, dark and silent.

The Judge's wife entered. She was an old woman, frilled and powdered into a caricature of youth, and gorgeously gowned. She came forward, smiling with extended hands, but just as she was opposite the stranger, a chill from somewhere seemed to strike her, and she shuddered and cried: "What a draft!" as she drew a silken shawl about her and shook hands cordially; she forgot to ask who the stranger was. The Judge strode in unseeing, thinking of a puzzling case of theft.

"Eh? What? Oh—er—yes—good-evening," he said, "good-evening."

Behind them came a young woman in the glory of youth, daintily silked, with diamonds around her fair neck, beautiful in face and form. She came in lightly, but stopped with a little gasp; then she laughed gaily and said:

"Why, I beg your pardon. Was it not curious? I thought I saw there behind your man"— she hesitated ("but he must be a servant," she argued)—"the shadow of wide white wings. It was but the light on the drapery. What a turn it gave me—so glad to be here!" And she smiled again. With her came a tall and haughty naval officer. Hearing his lady refer to the servant, he hardly looked at him, but held his gilded cap and cloak carelessly toward him; the stranger took them and placed them carefully on the rack.

Last came the Rector, a man of forty, and well clothed. He started to pass the stranger, stopped and looked at him inquiringly.

"I beg your pardon," he said, "I beg your pardon, I think I have met you?"

The stranger made no answer, and the hostess nervously hurried the guests on. But the Rector lingered and looked perplexed.

"Surely I know you; I have met you somewhere," he said, putting his hand vaguely to his head. "You—you remember me, do you not?"

The stranger quietly swept his cloak aside, and to the hostess' unspeakable relief moved toward the door.

"I never knew you," he said in low tones, as he went.

The lady murmured some faint excuse about intruders, but the Rector stood with annoyance written on his face.

"I beg a thousand pardons," he said to the hostess absently. "It is a great pleasure to be here—somehow. I thought I knew that man. I am sure I knew him, once."

The stranger had passed down the steps, and as he went the nurse-maid, lingering at the top of the staircase, flew down after him, caught his cloak, trembled, hesitated, and then kneeled in the dust. He touched her lightly with his hand and said, "Go, and sin no more."

With a glad cry the maid left the house with its open door and turned north, running, while the stranger turned eastward to the night. As they parted a long low howl rose tremulously and reverberated through the town. The Colonel's wife within shuddered.

"The bloodhounds," she said. The Rector answered carelessly.

"Another one of those convicts escaped, I suppose; really, they need severer measures." Then he stopped. He was trying to remember that stranger's name. The Judge's wife looked about for the draft and arranged her shawl. The girl glanced at the white drapery in the hall, but the young officer was bending over her, and the fires of life burned in her veins.

Howl after howl rose in the night, swelled and died away. The stranger strode rapidly along the highway and out into the deep forest. There he paused and stood waiting, tall and still. A mile up the road behind him a man was running, tall and powerful and black, with crime-stained face, with convict's stripes upon him and shackles on his legs. He ran and jumped in little short steps, and the chains rang. He fell and rose again, while the howl of the hounds rung harder behind him.

Into the forest he leaped and crept and jumped and ran, streaming with sweat; seeing the tall form rise before him, he stopped suddenly, dropped his hands in sullen impotence and sank panting to the earth. A bloodhound shot into the woods behind him, howled, whined and fawned before the stranger's feet. Hound after hound bayed, leapt and lay there; then silent, one by one, with bowed head, they crept backward toward the town.

The stranger made a cup of his hands and gave the man water to drink, bathed his hot head, and gently took the chains and irons from his feet. By and by the convict stood up. Day was dawning above the treetops. He looked into the stranger's face, and for a moment a gladness swept over the stains of his face.

"Why, you'se a nigger, too," he said.

Then the convict seemed anxious to justify himself.

"I never had no chance," he said furtively.

"Thou shalt not steal," said the stranger.

The man bridled.

"But how about them? Can they steal? Didn't they steal a whole year's work and then, when I stole to keep from starving—" he glanced at the stranger. "No, I didn't steal just to keep from starving. I stole to be stealing. I can't help stealing. Seems like when I sees things I just must—but, yes, I'll try!"

The convict looked down at his striped clothes, but the stranger had taken off his long coat—and put it around him, and the stripes disappeared. In the opening morning the black man started toward the low log farmhouse in the distance, and the stranger stood watching him. There was a new glory in the day. The black man's face cleared up and the farmer was glad to get him.

All day he worked as he had never worked before, and the farmer gave him some cold food toward night.

"You can sleep in the barn," he said, and turned away.

"How much do I git a day?" asked the man.

The farmer scowled:

"If you'll sign a contract for the season," he said, "I'll give you ten dollars a month."

"I won't sign no contract to be a slave," said the man doggedly.

"Yes, you will," said the farmer, threateningly, "or I'll call the convict guard." And he grinned.

The convict shrunk and slouched to the barn. As night fell he looked out and saw the farmer leave the place. Slowly he crept out and sneaked toward the house. He looked into the kitchen door. No one was there, but the supper was spread as if the mistress had laid it and gone out. He ate ravenously. Then he looked into the front room and listened. He could hear low voices on the porch. On the table lay a silver watch. He gazed at it, and in a moment was beside it, with his hand on it. Quickly he slipped out of the house and slouched toward the field. He saw his employer coming along the highway. He fled back stealthily and around to the front of the house, when suddenly he stopped. He felt the great dark eyes of the stranger and saw the same dark, cloaklike coat, where he was seated on the doorstep talking with the mistress of the house. Slowly, guiltily, he turned back, entered the kitchen and laid the watch where he had found it; and then he rushed wildly with arms outstretched back toward the stranger.

The woman had laid supper for her husband, and going down from the house had walked out toward a neighbor's. She was gone but a little while, and when she came back she started to see a dark figure on the doorsteps under the tall red oak. She thought it was the new Negro hand until he said in a soft voice:

"Will you give me bread?"

Reassured at the voice of a white man, she answered quickly in her soft Southern tones: "Why, certainly."

She was a little woman. Once she had been handsome, but now her face was drawn with work and care. She was nervous, and was always thinking, wishing, wanting for something. She went in and got him some cornbread and a glass of cool, rich buttermilk, and then came out and sat down beside him. She began, quite unconsciously, to tell him about herself—the things she had done, and had not done, and the things she had wished. She told him of her husband, and this new farm they were trying to buy. She said it was so hard to get niggers to work. She said they ought all to be in the chain gang and made to work. Even then some ran away. Only yesterday one had escaped.

At last she gossiped of her neighbors; how good they were and how bad.

"And do you like them all?" asked the stranger.

She hesitated.

"Most of them," she said; and then, looking up into his face and putting her hand in his as though he were her father, she said:

"There are none I hate; no, none at all."

He looked away and said dreamily:

"You love your neighbor as yourself?" She hesitated—

"I try—" she began, and then looked the way he was looking; down under the hill, where lay a little, half-ruined cabin.

"They are niggers," she said briefly.

He looked at her. Suddenly a confusion came over her, and she insisted, she knew not why—

"But they are niggers."

With a sudden impulse she rose, and hurriedly lighted the lamp that stood just within the door and held it above her head. She saw his dark face and curly hair. She shrieked in angry terror, and rushed down the path; and just as she rushed down, the black convict came running up with hands outstretched. They met in midpath, and before he could stop he had run against her, and she fell heavily to earth and lay white and still. Her husband came rushing up with cry and oath:

"I knew it," he said; "it is that runaway nigger." He held the black man struggling to the earth, and raised his voice to a yell. Down the highway came the convict guard with hound and mob and gun. They poured across the fields. The farmer motioned to them.

"He—attacked—my wife," he gasped.

The mob snarled and worked silently. Right to the limb of the red oak they hoisted the struggling, writhing black man, while others lifted the dazed woman. Right and left as she tottered to the house she searched for the stranger, with a sick yearning, but the stranger was gone. And she told none of her guest.

"No—no—I want nothing," she insisted, until they left her, as they thought, asleep. For a time she lay still listening to the departure of the mob. Then she rose. She shuddered as she heard the creaking of the limb where the body hung. But resolutely she crawled to the window and peered out into the moonlight; she saw the dead man writhe. He stretched his arms out like a cross, looking upward. She gasped and clung to the window sill. Behind the swaying body, and down where the little, half-ruined cabin lay, a single flame flashed up amid the far-off shout and cry of the mob. A fierce joy sobbed up through the terror in her soul and then sank abashed as she watched the flame rise. Suddenly whirling into one great crimson column it shot to the top of the sky and threw great arms athwart the gloom until above the world and behind the roped and swaying form below hung quivering and burning a great crimson cross.

She hid her dizzy, aching head in an agony of tears, and dared not look, for she knew. Her dry lips moved:

"Despised and rejected of men."

She knew, and the very horror of it lifted her dull and shrinking eyelids. There, heaven-tall, earth-wide, hung the stranger on the crimson cross, riven and bloodstained with thorn-crowned head and pierced hands. She stretched her arms and shrieked.

He did not hear. He did not see. His calm dark eyes all sorrowful were fastened on the writhing, twisting body of the thief, and a voice came out of the winds of the night, saying:

"This day thou shalt be with me in Paradise!"

13. Salvation

LANGSTON HUGHES

I was saved from sin when I was going on thirteen. But not really saved. It happened like this. There was a big revival at my Auntie Reed's church. Every night for weeks there had been much preaching, singing, praying, and shouting, and some very hardened sinners had been brought to Christ, and the membership of the church had grown by leaps and bounds. Then just before the revival ended, they held a special meeting for children, "to bring the young lambs to the fold." My aunt spoke of it for days ahead. That night I was escorted to the front row and placed on the mourners' bench with all the other young sinners, who had not yet been brought to Jesus.

My aunt told me that when you were saved you saw a light, and something happened to you inside! And Jesus came into your life! And God was with you from then on! She said you could see and hear and feel Jesus in your soul. I believed her. I had heard a great many old people say the same thing and it seemed to me they ought to know. So I sat there calmly in the hot, crowded church, waiting for Jesus to come to me.

The preacher preached a wonderful rhythmical sermon, all moans and shouts and lonely cries and dire pictures of hell, and then he sang a song about the ninety and nine safe in the fold, but one little lamb was left out in the cold. Then he said: "Won't you come? Won't you come to Jesus? Young lambs, won't you come?" And he held out his arms to all us young sinners there on the mourners' bench. And the little girls cried. And some of them jumped up and went to Jesus right away. But most of us just sat there.

A great many old people came and knelt around us and prayed, old women with jet-black faces and braided hair, old men with work-gnarled hands. And the church sang a song about the lower lights are burning, some poor sinners to be saved. And the whole building rocked with prayer and song.

Still I kept waiting to *see* Jesus.

Finally all the young people had gone to the altar and were saved, but one boy and me. He was a rounder's son named Westley. Westley and I were surrounded by sisters and deacons praying. It was very hot in the church, and getting late now. Finally Westley said to me in a whisper: "God damn! I'm tired o' sitting here. Let's get up and be saved." So he got up and was saved.

Then I was left all alone on the mourners' bench. My aunt came and knelt at my knees and cried, while prayers and songs swirled all around me in the little church. The whole congregation prayed for me alone, in a mighty wail of moans and voices. And I kept waiting serenely for Jesus, waiting, waiting—but he didn't come. I wanted to see him, but nothing happened to me. Nothing! I wanted something to happen to me, but nothing happened.

I heard the songs and the minister saying: "Why don't you come? My dear child, why don't you come to Jesus? Jesus is waiting for you. He wants you. Why don't you come? Sister Reed, what is this child's name?"

"Langston," my aunt sobbed.

"Langston, why don't you come? Why don't you come and be saved? Oh, Lamb of God! Why don't you come?"

Now it was really getting late. I began to be ashamed of myself, holding everything up so long. I began to wonder what God thought about Westley, who certainly hadn't seen Jesus either, but who was now sitting proudly on the platform, swinging his knickerbockered legs and grinning down at me, surrounded by deacons and old women on their knees praying. God had not struck Westley dead for taking his name in vain or for lying in the temple. So I decided that maybe to save further trouble, I'd better lie, too, and say that Jesus had come, and get up and be saved.

So I got up.

Suddenly the whole room broke into a sea of shouting, as they saw me rise. Waves of rejoicing swept the place. Women leaped in the air. My aunt threw her arms around me. The minister took me by the hand and led me to the platform.

When things quieted down, in a hushed silence, punctuated by a few ecstatic "Amens," all the new young lambs were blessed in the name of God. Then joyous singing filled the room.

That night, for the last time in my life but one—for I was a big boy twelve years old—I cried. I cried, in bed alone, and couldn't stop. I buried my head under the quilts, but my aunt heard me. She woke up and told my uncle I was crying because the Holy Ghost had come into my life, and because I had seen Jesus. But I was really crying because I couldn't bear to tell her that I had lied, that I had deceived everybody in the church, that I hadn't seen Jesus, and that now I didn't believe there was a Jesus any more, since he didn't come to help me.

14. My People! My People!

ZORA NEALE HURSTON

"My people! My people!" From the earliest rocking of my cradle days, I have heard this cry go up from Negro lips. It is forced outward by pity, scorn and hopeless resignation. It is called forth by the observations of one class of Negro on the doings of another branch of the brother in black. For instance, well-mannered Negroes groan out like that when they board a train or a bus and find other Negroes on there with their shoes off, stuffing themselves with fried fish, bananas and peanuts, and throwing the garbage on the floor. Maybe they are not only eating and drinking. The offenders may be "loud-talking" the place, and holding back nothing of their private lives, in a voice that embraces the entire coach. The well-dressed Negro shrinks back in his seat at that, shakes his head and sighs, "My people! My people!"

Now, the well-mannered Negro is embarrassed by the crude behavior of the others. They are not friends, and have never seen each other before. So why should he or she be embarrassed? It is like this: the well-bred Negro has looked around and seen America with his eyes. He or she has set himself to measure up to what he thinks of as the white standard of living. He is conscious of the fact that the Negro in America needs more respect if he expects to get any acceptance at all. Therefore, after straining every nerve to get an education, maintain an attractive home, dress decently, and otherwise conform, he is dismayed at the sight of other Negroes tearing down what he is trying to build up. It is said every day, "And that good-for-nothing, trashy Negro is the one the white people judge us all by. They think we're all just alike. My people! My people!"

What that educated Negro knows further is that he can do very little towards imposing his own viewpoint on the lowlier members of his race. Class and culture stand between. The humble Negro has a built-up antagonism to the "Big Nigger." It is a curious thing that he does not resent a white man looking down on him. But he resents any lines between himself and the wealthy and educated of his own race. "He's a nigger just like us," is the sullen rejoinder. The only answer to this is "My people! My people!"

So the quiet-spoken Negro man or woman who finds himself in the midst of one of these "broadcasts" as on the train, cannot go over and say, "Don't act like that, brother. You're giving us all a black eye." He or she would know better than to try that. The performance would not only go on, it would get better with the "dickty" Negro as the butt of all the quips. The educated Negro may know all about differential calculus and the theory of evolution, but he is fighting entirely out of his class when he tries to quip with the underprivileged. The bookless may have difficulty in reading a paragraph in a newspaper, but when they get down to "playing the dozens" they have no equal in America, and, I'd risk a sizable bet, in the whole world. Starting off in the first by calling you a seven-sided son-of-a-bitch, and pausing to name the sides, they proceed to "specify" until the tip-top branch of your family tree has been "given a reading." No profit in that to the upper-class Negro, so he minds his own business and groans, "My people! My people!"

It being a traditional cry, I was bound to hear it often and under many circumstances. But it is not the only folk label that I heard. "Race Pride"—"Race Prejudice"—"Race Man"—"Race Solidarity"—"Race Consciousness"—"Race."

"Race Prejudice" I was instructed was something bad that white people used on us. It seemed that white people felt superior to black ones and would not give Negroes justice for that reason. "Race Pride" was something that, if we had it, we would feel ourselves superior to the whites. A black skin was the greatest honor that could be blessed on any man. A "Race Man" was somebody who always kept the glory and honor of his race before him. Must stand ever ready to defend the Negro race from all hurt, harm and danger. Especially if a white person said "Nigger," "You people," "Negress" or "Darkies." It was a mark of shame if somebody accused: "Why, you are not a Race Man (or woman)." People made whole careers of being "Race" men and women. They were champions of the race.

"Race Consciousness" is a plea to Negroes to bear their color in mind at all times. It was just a phrase to me when I was a child. I knew it was supposed to mean something deep. By the time I got grown I saw that it was only an imposing line of syllables, for no Negro in America is apt to forget his race. "Race Solidarity" looked like something solid in my childhood, but like all other mirages, it faded as I came close enough to look. As soon as I could think, I saw that there is no such thing as Race Solidarity in America with any group. It is freely admitted that it does not exist among Negroes. Our so-called Race Leaders cry over it. Others accept it as a natural thing that Negroes should not remain an unmelting black knot in the body politic. Our interests are too varied. Personal benefits run counter to race lines too often for it to hold. If it did, we could never fit into the national pattern. Since the race line has never held any other group in America, why expect it to be effective with us? The upper-class Negroes admit it in their own phrases. The lower-class Negroes say it with a tale.

It seems that a Negro was asked to lead the congregation in prayer. He got down on his knees and began, "Oh, Lawd, I got something to ask You, but I know You can't do it."

"Go on, Brother Isham and ask Him."

"Lawd," Brother Isham began again, "I really want to ask You something but I just know You can't do it."

"Aw, Brother Isham, go on and tell the Lawd what you want. He's the Lawd! Ain't nothing He can't do! He can even lead a butt-headed cow by the horns. You're killing up time. Go 'head on, Brother Isham, and let the church roll on."

"Well then, Lawd, I ask You to get these Negroes together, but I know You can't do it." Then there is laughter and "My people! My people!"

Hearing things like this from my childhood, sooner or later I was bound to have some curiosity about my race of people.

What fell into my ears from time to time tended more to confuse than to clarify. One thing made a liar out of the one that went before and the thing that came after. At different times I heard opposite viewpoints expressed by the same person or persons.

For instance, come school-closing time and like formal occasions, I heard speeches which brought thunderous applause. I did not know the word for it at the time, but it did not take me long to know the material was traditional. Just as folk as the songs in church. I knew that because so many people got up and used the same, identical phrases: (a) The Negro had made the greatest progress in fifty years of any race on the face of the globe. (*b*) Negroes composed the most *beautiful* race on earth, being just like a flower garden with every color and kind. (*c*) Negroes were the bravest men on earth, facing every danger like lions, and fighting with demons. We must remember with pride that the first blood spilled for American Independence was that of the brave and daring Crispus Attucks, a Negro who had bared his black breast to the bullets of the British tyrants at Boston, and thus struck the first blow for American liberty. They had marched with Colonel Shaw during the Civil War and hurled back the forces of the iniquitous South, who sought to hold black men in bondage. It was a Negro named Simon who had been the only one with enough pity and compassion in his heart to help the Savior bear His cross upon Calvary. It was the Negro troops under Teddy Roosevelt who won the battle of San Juan Hill.

It was the genius of the Negro which had invented the steam engine, the cotton gin, the airbrake, and numerous other things—but conniving white men had seen the Negro's inventions and run off and put them into practice before the Negro had a chance to do anything about it. Thus the white man got credit for what the genius of the Negro brain had produced. Were it not for the envy and greed of the white man, the Negro would hold his rightful place—the noblest and the greatest man on earth.

The people listening would cheer themselves hoarse and go home feeling good. Over the fences next day it would be agreed that it was a wonderful speech, and nothing but the God's truth. What a great people we would be if we only had our rights!

But my own pinnacle would be made to reel and rock anyway by other things I heard from the very people who always applauded "the great speech," when it was shouted to them from the schoolhouse rostrum. For instance, let some member of the community do or say something which was considered either dumb or underhand: the verdict would be "Dat's just like a nigger!" or "Nigger from nigger leave nigger"—("Nothing from nothing leave nothing"). It was not said in either admiration or pity. Utter scorn was in the saying. "Old Cuffy just got to cut de fool, you know. Monkey see, monkey do. Nigger see de white man do something, he jump in and try to do like de white man, and make a great big old mess." "My people! My people!"

"Yeah, you's mighty right. Another monkey on de line. De white man, you understand, he was a railroad engineer, so he had a pet monkey he used to take along wid him all de time. De monkey, he set up there in de cab wid de engineer and see what he do to run de train. Way after while, figger he can run de train just as good as de engineer his own self. He was just itching to git at dat throttle and bust dat main line wide open. Well, one day de engineer jumped down at de station to git his orders and old monkey seen his chance. He just jumped up in de engineer's seat, grabbed a holt of dat throttle, and dat engine was splitting de wind down de track. So de engineer sent a message on ahead, say 'Clear de track. Monkey on de line!' Well, Brer Monk he was holding de throttle wide open and jumping up and down and laughing fit to kill. Course, he didn't know nothing about no side tracks and no switches and no schedules, so he was making a mile a minute when he hit a open switch and a string of box cars was standing on de siding. Ker-blam-er-lam-er-lam! And dat was de last of Brer Engine-driving Monk. Lovely monkey he was, but a damned poor engineer." "My people! My people!"

Everybody would laugh at that, and the laughter puzzled me some. Weren't Negroes the smartest people on earth, or something like that? Somebody ought to remind the people of what we had heard at the schoolhouse. Instead of that, there would be more monkey stories.

There was the one about the white doctor who had a pet monkey who wanted to be a doctor. Kept worrying his master to show him how, and the doctor had other troubles, too. Another man had a bulldog who used to pass the doctor's gate every day and pick a fight with the monkey. Finally, the doctor saw a way to stop the monkey from worrying him about showing him how to be a doctor. "Whip that bulldog until he evacuates, then bring me some of it, monkey. I'll take it and show you how to be a doctor, and then I'll treat it in a way so as to ruin that bulldog for life. He won't be no more trouble to you."

"Oh, I'll git it, boss. Don't you worry. I sho' wants to be a doctor, and then again, dat old bulldog sho' is worrisome."

No sooner did the bulldog reach the gate that day, than the monkey, which could not wait for the bulldog to start the fight as usual, jumped on the dog. The monkey was all over him like gravy over rice. He put all he had into it and it went on until the doctor came out and drove the dog off and gave the monkey a chance to bolt into the office with what he had been fighting for.

"Here 'tis, boss. It was a tight fight, but I got it."

"Fine! Fine!" the doctor told him. "Now, gimme that bottle over there. I'll fix that bulldog so he'll never be able to sit down again. When I get through with this, he'll be ruined for life."

"Hold on there, boss! Hold on there a minute! I wish you wouldn't do dat, boss."

"How come? You want to get rid of that old bulldog, don't you?"

"Dat's right, I sho' do."

"Well, why don't you want me to fix him, then?"

"Well, boss, you see it's like dis. Dat was a tight fight, a mighty tight fight. I could have been mistaken about dat bulldog, boss, we was all tangled up together so bad. You better leave dat fixing business alone, boss. De wrong man might git hurt."

There were many other tales, equally ludicrous, in which the Negro, sometimes symbolized by the monkey, and sometimes named outright, ran off with the wrong understanding of what he had seen and heard. Several white and Negro proposals of marriage were compared, and the like. The white suitor had said his love had dove's eyes. His valet had hurried to compliment his girl by saying she had dog's eyes, and so on.

There was a general acceptance of the monkey as kinfolks. Perhaps it was some distant memory of tribal monkey reverence from Africa which had been forgotten in the main, but remembered in some vague way. Perhaps it was an acknowledgment of our talent for mimicry with the monkey as a symbol.

The classic monkey parable, which is very much alive wherever the Negroes congregate in America, is the one about "My people!"

It seems that a monkey squatted down in the middle of a highway to play. A Cadillac full of white people came along, saw the monkey at play and carefully drove around him. Then came a Buick full of more white people and did the same. The monkey kept right on playing. Way after a while a T-model Ford came along full of Negroes. But instead of driving around the monkey, the car headed straight for him. He only saved his life by a quick leap to the shoulder of the road. He sat there and watched the car rattle off in the distance and sighed "My people! My people!"

A new addition to the tale is that the monkey has quit saying "My people!" He is now saying, "Those people! Those people!"

I found the Negro, and always the blackest Negro, being made the butt of all jokes,—particularly black women.

They brought bad luck for a week if they came to your house of a Monday morning. They were evil. They slept with their fists balled up ready to fight and squabble even while they were asleep. They even had evil dreams. White, yellow and brown girls dreamed about roses and perfume and kisses. Black gals dreamed about guns, razors, ice-picks, hatchets and hot lye. I heard men swear they had seen women dreaming and knew these things to be true.

"Oh, gwan!" somebody would chide, laughing. You know dat ain't so."

"Oh, now, he ain't lying," somebody else would take up the theme. "I know for my own self. I done slept wid yaller women and I done slept wid black ones. They *is* evil. You marry a yaller or a brown woman and wake her up in de night and she will sort of stretch herself and say, 'I know what I was dreaming when you woke me up. I was dreaming I had done baked you a chicken and cooked you a great big old cake, and we was at de table eating our dinner out of de same plate, and I was sitting on your lap and we was just enjoying ourselves to death!' Then she will kiss you more times than you ask her to, and go on back to sleep. But you take and wake up a black gal, now! First thing she been sleeping wid her fists balled up, and you shake her, she'll lam you five or six times before you can get her awake. Then when she do git wake she'll have off and ast you, 'Nigger, what you wake me up for? Know what I was dreaming when you woke me up? I dreamt dat you shook your old rusty black fist under my nose and I split your head open wid a axe.' Then she'll kick your feets away from hers, snatch de covers all over on her side, ball up her fists agin, and gwan back to sleep. You can't tell me nothing. I know." "My people!"

This always was, and is still, good for a raucous burst of laughter. I listened to this talk and became more and more confused. If it was so honorable and glorious to be black, why was it the yellow-skinned people among us had so much prestige? Even a child in the first grade could see that this was so from what happened in the classroom and on school programs. The light-skinned children were always the angels, fairies and queens of school plays. The lighter the girl, the more money and prestige she was apt, and expected, to marry. So on into high-school years, I was asking myself questions. Were Negroes the great heroes I heard about from the platform, or were they the ridiculous monkeys of everyday talk? Was it really honorable to be black? There was even talk that it was no use for Negro boys and girls to rub all the hair off of their heads against college walls. There was no place for them to go with it after they got all this education. Some of the older heads held that it was too much for Negroes to handle. Better leave such things for the white folks, who knew what to do with it. But there were others who were all for pushing ahead. I saw the conflict in my own home between my parents. My mother was the one to dare all. My father was satisfied.

This Negro business came home to me in incidents and ways. There was the time when Old Man Bronner was taken out and beaten. Mr. Bronner was a white man of the poor class who had settled in aristocratic Maitland. One night just after dark, we heard terrible cries back in the woods behind Park Lake. Sam Moseley, his brother Elijah, and Ike Clarke, hurried up to our gate and they were armed. The howls of pain kept up. Old fears and memories must have stirred inside of the grown folks. Many people closed and barred their doors. Papa and the men around our gate were sullen and restless as the cries churned over the woods and lake.

"Who do you reckon it is?" Sam Moseley asked.

"I don't know for sure, but some thinks it's Jim Watson. Anyhow, he ain't home yet," Clarke said, and all of them looked at each other in an asking way.

Finally Papa said, "Well, hold on a minute till I go get my rifle."

" 'Tain't no ifs and buts about it," Elijah Moseley said gravely, "We can't leave Jim Watson be beat to death like that."

Papa had sensed that these armed men had not come to merely stand around and talk. They had come to see if he would go with the rest. When he came out shoving the sixteen bullets into his rifle, and dropping more into his pocket, Mama made no move to stop him. "Well, we all got families," he said with an attempt at lightness. "Shoot off your gun, somebody, so de rest will know we ready."

Papa himself pointed his Winchester rifle at the sky and fired a shot. Another shot answered him from around the store and a huddle of figures came hurrying up the road in the dark.

"It's Jim Watson. Us got to go git him!" and the dozen or more men armed with double-barreled shotguns, breech-loaders, pistols and Papa's repeating Winchester hurried off on their grim mission. Perhaps not a single one of them expected to return alive. No doubt they hoped. But they went.

Mama gasped a short sentence of some sort and herded us all into the house and barred the door. Lights went out all over the village and doors were barred. Axes had been dragged in from woodpiles, grass-hooks, pitch-forks and scythes were ranked up in corners behind those barred doors. If the men did not come back, or if they only came back in part, the women and children were ready to do the best they could. Mama spoke only to say she wished Hezekiah and John, the two biggest boys, had not gone to Maitland late in the afternoon. They were not back and she feared they might start home and—But she did not cry. Our seven hounds with big, ferocious Ned in the lead, barked around the house. We huddled around Mama in her room and kept quiet. There was not a human sound in all the village. Nothing had ever happened before in our vicinity to create such tension. But people had memories and told tales of what happened back there in Georgia, and Alabama and West Florida that made the skin of the young crawl with transmitted memory, and reminded the old heads that they were still flinchy.

The dark silence of the village kept up for an hour or more. The once loud cries fell and fell until our straining ears could no longer find them. Strangest of all, not a shot was fired. We huddled in the dark and waited, and died a little, and waited. The silence was ten times more punishing than the cries.

At long last, a bubble of laughing voices approached our barn from the rear. It got louder and took on other dimensions between the barn and the house. Mama hissed at us to shut up when, in fact, nobody was saying a thing.

"Hey, there Little-Bits," Papa bellowed. "Open up!"

"Strike a light, Daught," Mama told my sister, feeling around in the dark to find Sarah's hand to give her the matches which I had seen clutched in her fingers before she had put out the light. Mama had said very little, and I could not see her face in the dark; somehow she could not scratch a match now that Papa was home again.

All of the men came in behind Papa, laughing and joking, perhaps more from relief than anything else.

"Don't stand there grinning like a chessy cat, Mr. Hurston," Mama scolded. "You ain't told me a thing."

"Oh, it wasn't Jim Watson at all, Lulu. You remember 'bout a week ago Old Man Bronner wrote something in de Orlando paper about H.'s daughter and W.B.G.'s son being seen sitting around the lakes an awful lot?"

"Yeah, I heard something about it."

"Well, you know those rich white folks wasn't going to 'low nothing like dat. So some of 'em waylaid him this evening. They pulled him down off of a load of hay he was hauling and drug him off back there in de woods and tanned his hide for him."

"Did y'all see any of it?"

"Nope, we could hear him hollering for a while, though. We never got no further than the lake. A white man, one of the G—— boys was standing in the bushes at de road. When we got ready to turn off round de lake he stepped out and spoke to us and told us it didn't concern us. They had Bronner down there tied down on his all-fours, and de men was taking turns wid dat bull whip. They must have been standing on tip-toes to do it. You could hear them licks clear out to de road."

The men all laughed. Somebody mocked Bronner's cries and moans a time or two and the crowd laughed immoderately. They had gone out to rescue a neighbor or die in the attempt, and they were back with their families. So they let loose their insides and laughed. They resurrected a joke or two and worried it like a bone and laughed some more. Then they just laughed. The men who spoke of members of their race as monkeys had gone out to die for one. The men who were always saying, "My skin-folks, but not kinfolks; my race but not my taste," had rushed forth to die for one of these same contemptibles. They shoved each other around and laughed. So I could see that what looked like ridicule was really the Negro poking a little fun at himself. At the same time, just like other people, hoping and wishing he was what the orators said he was.

My mother eased back in her chair and took a dip of snuff. Maybe she did not feel so well, for she didn't get tickled at all. After a while, she ordered us off to bed in a rough voice. Time was, and the men scattered. Mama sat right where she was until Hezekiah and John came home around ten o'clock. She gave them an awful going over with her tongue for staying out late, and then she eased to bed.

I was dredged up inside that night, so I did not think about the incident's general connection with race. Besides I had to go to sleep. But days later, it was called to my recollection again. There was a program at the Methodist Church, and Mrs. Mattie Moseley, it was announced, was to have a paper. She was also going to have a fine new dress to read it in. We all wanted to see the dress.

The time came and she had the dress on. The subject of her paper was, "What will the Negroes do with the whites?" I do not know what she decided was to be done. It seemed equally unimportant to the rest of the town. I remember that everybody said it was a fine subject. But the next week, the women talked about nothing else but the new wrist-watch she had on. It was the first one ever seen in our town.

But in me, the affair stirred up more confusion. Why bring the subject up? Something was moving around me which I had no hooks to grasp. What was this about white and black people that was being talked about?

Certainly nothing changed in the village. The townspeople who were in domestic service over in Maitland or Winter Park went to work as usual. The white people interested in Eatonville came and went as before. Mr. Irving Bacheller, the author, who had a show place in Winter Park, petted up Willie Sewell, who was his head gardener, in the same old way.

Bishop Whipple petted Elijah Moseley, and Mrs. Mars, who was his sister, did lots of things for Lulu Moseley, Elijah's wife. What was all the talk about? It certainly was puzzling to me.

As time went on, the confusion grew. By the time that I got to high school, I was conscious of a group that was neither the top nor the bottom of Negrodom. I met the type which designates itself as "the better-thinking Negro." I was thrown off my stride by finding that while they considered themselves Race Champions, they wanted nothing to do with anything frankly Negroid. They drew color lines within the race. The Spirituals, the Blues, *any* definitely Negroid thing was just not done. They went to the trouble at times to protest the use of them by Negro artists. Booker T. Washington was absolutely vile for advocating industrial education. There was no analysis, no seeking for merits. If it was old cuffy, down with it! "My People! My People!"

This irritated me until I got to the place where I could analyze. The thing they were trying to do went wrong because it lacked reason. It lacked reason because they were attempting to stand equal with the best in America without having the tools to work with. They were attempting a flight away from Negrodom because they felt that there was so much scorn for black skin in the nation that their only security was in flight. They lacked the happy carelessness of a class beneath them and the understanding of the top-flight Negro above them. Once, when they used to set their mouths in what they thought was the Boston Crimp, and ask me about the great differences between the ordinary Negro and "the better-thinking Negro," I used to show my irritation by saying I did not know who the better-thinking Negro was. I knew who the think-they-are-better Negroes were, but who were the better-thinkers was another matter. But when I came to understand what made them make their useless motions, and saw them pacing a cage that wasn't there, I felt more sympathy than irritation. If they want to establish a sort of fur-coat peerage, let 'em! Since they can find no comfort where they happened to be born, no especial talents to lift them, and other doors are closed to them, they have to find some pleasure somewhere in life. They have to use whatever their mentality provides. "My People! My People!"

But one thing and another kept the conflict going on inside me, off and on for years. Sometimes I was sure that the Negro race was all that the platform speakers said. Then I would hear so much self-deprecation that I would be deflated. Over and over I heard people shake their heads and explain us by the supposed prayer of a humble Negro, who got down on his knees and said: "Lawd, you know I ain't nothing. My wife, she ain't nothing. My chillun ain't nothing, and if you fool 'round us, Lawd, you won't be nothing neither."

So I sensed early, that the Negro race was not one band of heavenly love. There was stress and strain in-side as well as out. Being black was not enough. It took more than a community of skin color to make your love come down on you. That was the beginning of my peace.

Light came to me when I realized that I did not have to consider any racial group as a whole. God made them duck by duck and that was the only way I could see them. I learned that skins were no measure of what was inside people. So none of the Race clichés meant anything any more. I began to laugh at both white and black who claimed special blessings on the basis of race. Therefore I saw no curse in being black, nor no extra flavor by being white I saw no benefit in excusing my looks by claiming to be half Indian. In fact, I boast that I am the only Negro in the United States whose grandfather on the mother's side was *not* an Indian chief. Neither did I descend from George Washington, Thomas Jefferson, or any Governor of a Southern state. I see no need to manufacture me a legend to beat the facts.

I do not coyly admit to a touch of the tarbrush to my Indian and white ancestry. You can consider me Old Tar-Brush in person if you want to. I am a mixed-blood, it is true, but I differ from the party line in that I neither consider it an honor nor a shame. I neither claim Jefferson as my grandpa, nor exclaim, "Just look how that white man took advantage of my grandma!" It does not matter in the first place, and then in the next place, I do not know how it came about. Since nobody ever told me, I give my ancestress the benefit of the doubt. She probably ran away from him just as fast as she could. But if that white man could run faster than my grandma, that was no fault of hers. Anyway, you must remember, he didn't have a thing to do but to keep on running forward. She, being the pursued, had to look back over her shoulder every now and then to see how she was doing. And you know your ownself, how looking backwards slows people up.

In this same connection, I have been told that God meant for all the so-called races of the world to stay just as they are, and the people who say that may be right. But it is a well-known fact that no matter where two sets of people come together, there are bound to be some in-betweens. It looks like the command was given to people's heads, because the other parts don't seem to have heard tell. When the next batch is made up, maybe Old Maker will straighten all that out. Maybe the men will be more tangle-footed and the women a whole lot more faster around the feet. That will bring about a great deal more of racial and other kinds of purity, but a somewhat less exciting world. It might work, but I doubt it. There will have to be something harder to get across than an ocean to keep East and West from meeting. But maybe Old Maker will have a remedy. Maybe even He has given up. Perhaps in a moment of discouragement He turned the job over to Adolf Hitler and went on about His business of making more beetles.

I do not share the gloomy thought that Negroes in America are doomed to be stomped out bodaciously, nor even shackled to the bottom of things. Of course some of them will be tromped out, and some will always, be at the bottom, keeping company with other bottom-folks. It would be against all nature for all the Negroes to be either at the bottom, top, or in between. It has never happened with anybody else, so why with us? No, we will go where the internal drive carries us like everybody else. It is up to the individual. If you haven't got it, you can't show it. If you have got it, you can't hide it. That is one of the strongest laws God ever made.

I maintain that I have been a Negro three times—a Negro baby, a Negro girl and a Negro woman. Still, if you have received no clear cut impression of what the Negro in America is like, then you are in the same place with me. There is no *The Negro* here. Our lives are so diversified, internal attitudes so varied, appearances and capabilities so different, that there is no possible classification so catholic that it will cover us all, except My people! My people!

15. Religion

ZORA NEALE HURSTON

You wouldn't think that a person who was born with God in the house would ever have any questions to ask on the subject.

But as early as I can remember, I was questing and seeking. It was not that I did not hear. I tumbled right into the Missionary Baptist Church when I was born. I saw the preachers and the pulpits, the people and the pews. Both at home and from the pulpit, I heard my father, known to thousands as "Reverend Jno" (an abbreviation for John) explain all about God's habits, His heaven, His ways and means. Everything was known and settled.

From the pews I heard a ready acceptance of all that Papa said. Feet beneath the pews beat out a rhythm as he pictured the scenery of heaven. Heads nodded with conviction in time to Papa's words. Tense snatches of tune broke out and some shouted until they fell into a trance at the recognition of what they heard from the pulpit. Come "love feast"* some of the congregation told of getting close enough to peep into God's sitting-room windows. Some went further. They had been inside the place and looked all around. They spoke of sights and scenes around God's throne.

That should have been enough for me. But somehow it left a lack in my mind. They should have looked and acted differently from other people after experiences like that. But these people looked and acted like everybody else—or so it seemed to me. They plowed, chopped wood, went possum-hunting, washed clothes, raked up back yards and cooked collard greens like anybody else. No more ornaments and nothing. It mystified me. There were so many things they neglected to look after while they were right there in the presence of All-Power. I made up my mind to do better than that if ever I made the trip.

I wanted to know, for instance, why didn't God make grown babies instead of those little measly things that messed up didies and cried all the time? What was the sense in making babies with no teeth? He knew that they had to have teeth, didn't He? So why not give babies their teeth in the beginning instead of hiding the toothless things in hollow stumps and logs for grannies and doctors to find and give to people? He could see all the trouble people had with babies, rubbing their gums and putting wood-lice around their necks to get them to cut teeth. Why did God hate for children to play on Sundays? If Christ, God's son, hated to die, and God hated for Him to die and have everybody grieving over it ever since, why did He have to do it? Why did people die anyway?

---

* The "Love Feast" or "Experience Meeting" is a meeting held either the Friday night or the Sunday morning before Communion. Since no one is supposed to take Communion unless he or she is in harmony with all other members, there are great protestations of love and friendship. It is an opportunity to reaffirm faith plus anything the imagination might dictate.

It was explained to me that Christ died to save the world from sin and then too, so that folks did not have to die any more. That was a simple, clear-cut explanation. But then I heard my father and other preachers accusing people of sin. They went so far as to say that people were so prone to sin, that they sinned with every breath they drew. You couldn't even breathe without sinning! How could that happen if we had already been saved from it? So far as the dying part was concerned, I saw enough funerals to know that somebody was dying. It seemed to me that somebody had been fooled and I so stated to my father and two of his colleagues. When they got through with me, I knew better than to say that out loud again, but their shocked and angry tirades did nothing for my bewilderment. My head was full of misty fumes of doubt.

Neither could I understand the passionate declarations of love for a being that nobody could see. Your family, your puppy and the new bull-calf, yes. But a spirit away off who found fault with everybody all the time, that was more than I could fathom. When I was asked if I loved God, I always said yes because I knew that that was the thing I was supposed to say. It was a guilty secret with me for a long time. I did not dare ask even my chums if they meant it when they said they loved God with all their souls and minds and hearts, and would be glad to die if He wanted them to. Maybe they had found out how to do it, and I was afraid of what they might say if they found out I hadn't. Maybe they wouldn't even play with me any more.

As I grew, the questions went to sleep in me. I just said the words, made the motions and went on. My father being a preacher, and my mother superintendent of the Sunday School, I naturally was always having to do with religious ceremonies. I even enjoyed participation at times; I was moved, not by the spirit, but by action, more or less dramatic.

I liked revival meetings particularly. During these meetings the preacher let himself go. God was called by all of His praise-giving names. The scenery of heaven was described in detail. Hallelujah Avenue and Amen Street were paved with gold so fine that you couldn't drop a pea on them but what they rang like chimes. Hallelujah Avenue ran north and south across heaven, and was tuned to sound alto and bass. Amen Street ran east and west and was tuned to "treble" and tenor. These streets crossed each other right in front of the throne and made harmony all the time. Yes, and right there on that corner was where all the loved ones who had gone on before would be waiting for those left behind.

Oh yes! They were all there in their white robes with the glittering crowns on their heads, golden girdles clasped about their waists and shoes of jeweled gold on their feet, singing the hallelujah song and waiting. And as they walked up and down the golden streets, their shoes would sing, "sol me, sol do" at every step.

Hell was described in dramatic fury. Flames of fire leaped up a thousand miles from the furnaces of Hell, and raised blisters on a sinning man's back before he hardly got started downward. Hell-hounds pursued their ever-dying souls. Everybody under the sound of the preacher's voice was warned, while yet they were on pleading terms with mercy, to take steps to be sure that they would not be a brand in that eternal burning.

Sinners lined the mourner's bench from the opening night of the revival. Before the week was over, several or all of them would be "under conviction." People, solemn of face, crept off to the woods to "praying ground" to seek religion. Every church member worked on them hard, and there was great clamor and rejoicing when any of them "come through" religion.

The pressure on the unconverted was stepped up by music and high drama. For instance I have seen my father stop preaching suddenly and walk down to the front edge of the pulpit and breathe into a whispered song. One of his most effective ones was:

> *Run! Run! Run to the City of Refuge, children!*
> *Run! Oh, run! Or else you'll be consumed.*

The congregation working like a Greek chorus behind him, would take up the song and the mood and hold it over for a while even after he had gone back into the sermon at high altitude:

> Are you ready-ee? Hah!
> For that great day, hah!
> When the moon shall drape her face in mourning, hah!
> And the sun drip down in blood, hah!
> When the stars, hah!
> Shall burst forth from their diamond sockets, hah!
> And the mountains shall skip like lambs, hah!
> Havoc will be there, my friends, hah!
> With her jaws wide open, hah!
> And the sinner-man, hah!
> He will run to the rocks, hah!
> And cry, Oh rocks! Hah!
> Hide me! Hah!
> Hide me from the face of an angry God, hah!
> Hide me, Ohhhhhh!
> But the rocks shall cry, hah!
> Git away! Sinner man git away, hah!

(Tense harmonic chant seeps over the audience.)

> | | You run to de rocks, |
> |---|---|
> | CHORUS: | You can't hide |
> | SOLOIST: | Oh, you run to de rocks |
> | CHORUS: | Can't hide |
> | SOLOIST: | Oh, run to de mountain, you can't hide |
> | ALL: | Can't hide sinner, you can't hide. |
> | | Rocks cry I'm burning too, hah! |
> | | In the eternal burning, hah! |
> | | Sinner man! Hah! |
> | | Where will you stand? Hah! |
> | | In that great gittin'-up morning? Hah! |

The congregation would be right in there at the right moment bearing Papa up and heightening the effect of the fearsome picture a hundredfold. The more susceptible would be swept away on the tide and "come through" shouting, and the most reluctant would begin to waver. Seldom would there be anybody left at the mourners' bench when the revival meeting was over. I have seen my father "bring through" as many as seventy-five in one two-week period of revival. Then a day would be set to begin the induction into the regular congregation. The first thing was to hear their testimony or Christian experience, and thus the congregation could judge whether they had really "got religion" or whether they were faking and needed to be sent back to "lick de calf over" again.

It was exciting to hear them tell their "visions." This was known as admitting people to the church on "Christian experience." This was an exciting time.

These visions are traditional. I knew them by heart as did the rest of the congregation, but still it was exciting to see how the converts would handle them. Some of them made up new details. Some of them would forget a part and improvise clumsily or fill up the gap with shouting. The audience knew, but everybody acted as if every word of it was new.

First they told of suddenly becoming conscious that they had to die. They became conscious of their sins. They were Godly sorry. But somehow, they could not believe. They started to pray. They prayed and they prayed to have their sins forgiven and their souls converted. While they laid under conviction, the hell-hounds pursued them as they ran for salvation. They hung over Hell by one strand of hair. Outside of the meeting, any of the listeners would have laughed at the idea of anybody with hair as close to their heads as ni nety-nine is to a hundred hanging over Hell or anywhere else by a strand of that hair. But it was part of the vision and the congregation shuddered and groaned at the picture in a fervent manner. The vision must go on. While the seeker hung there, flames of fire leaped up and all but destroyed their ever-dying souls. But they called on the name of Jesus and immediately that dilemma was over. They then found themselves walking over Hell on a foot-log so narrow that they had to put one foot right in front of the other while the howling hell-hounds pursued them relentlessly. Lord! They saw no way of rescue. But they looked on the other side and saw a little white man and he called to them to come there. So they called the name of Jesus and suddenly they were on the other side. He poured the oil of salvation into their souls and, hallelujah! They never expect to turn back. But still they wouldn't believe. So they asked God, if he had saved their souls, to give them a sign. If their sins were forgiven and their souls set free, please move that big star in the west over to the east. The star moved over. But still they wouldn't believe. If they were really saved, please move that big oak tree across the road. The tree skipped across the road and kept on growing just like it had always been there. Still they didn't believe. So they asked God for one more sign. Would He please make the sun shout so they could be sure. At that God got mad and said He had shown them all the signs He intended to. If they still didn't believe, He would send their bodies to the grave, where the worm never dies, and their souls to Hell, where the fire is never quenched. So then they cried out "I believe! I believe!" Then the dungeon shook and their chains fell off. "Glory! I know I got religion! I know I been converted and my soul set free! I never will forget that day when the morning star bust in my soul. I never expect to turn back!"

The convert shouted. Ecstatic cries, snatches of chants, old converts shouting in frenzy with the new. When the tumult finally died down, the pastor asks if the candidate is acceptable and there is unanimous consent. He or she is given the right hand of fellowship, and the next candidate takes the floor. And so on to the end.

I know now that I liked that part because it was high drama. I liked the baptisms in the lake too, and the funerals for the same reason. But of the inner thing, I was right where I was when I first began to seek answers.

Away from the church after the emotional fire had died down, there were little jokes about some of the testimony. For instance a deacon said in my hearing, "Sister Seeny ought to know better than to be worrying God about moving the sun for her. She asked Him to move de tree to convince her, and He done it. Then she took and asked Him to move a star for her and He done it. But When she kept on worrying Him about moving the sun, He took and told her, says, 'I' I don't mind moving that tree for you, and I don't mind moving a star just to pacify your mind, because I got plenty of *them*. I aint got but one sun, Seeny, and I aint going to be shoving it around to please you and nobody else. I'd like mighty much for you to believe, but if you can't believe without me moving my sun for you, you can just go right on to Hell.'"

The thing slept on in me until my college years without any real decision. I made the necessary motions and forgot to think. But when I studied both history and philosophy, the struggle began again.

When I studied the history of the great religions of the world, I saw that even in his religion man carried himself along. His worship of strength was there. God was made to look that way too. We see the Emperor Constantine, as pagan as he could lay in his hide, having his famous vision of the cross with the injunction: *"In Hoc Signo Vinces,"* and arising next day not only to win a great battle, but to start out on his missionary journey with his sword. He could not sing like Peter, and he could not preach like Paul. He probably did not even have a good straining voice like my father to win converts and influence people. But he had his good points—one of them being a sword—and a seasoned army. And the way he brought sinners to repentance was nothing short of miraculous. Whole tribes and nations fell under conviction just as soon as they heard he was on the way. They did not wait for any stars to move, nor trees to jump the road. By the time he crossed the border, they knew they had been converted. Their testimony was in on Christian experience and they were all ready for the right hand of fellowship and baptism. It seems that Reverend Brother Emperor Constantine carried the gospel up and down Europe with his revival meetings to such an extent that Christianity really took on. In Rome where Christians had been looked upon as rather indifferent lion-bait at best, and among other things as keepers of virgins in their homes for no real good to the virgins, Christianity mounted. Where before, Emperors could scarcely find enough of them to keep the spectacles going, now they were everywhere, in places high and low. The arrow had left the bow. Christianity was on its way to world power that would last. That was only the beginning. Military power was to be called in time and time again to carry forward the gospel of peace. There is not apt to be any difference of opinion between you and a dead man.

It was obvious that two men, both outsiders, had given my religion its chances of success. First the Apostle Paul, who had been Saul, the erudite Pharisee, had arisen with a vision when he fell off of his horse on the way to Damascus. He not only formulated the religion, but exerted his brilliant mind to carry it to the most civilized nations of his time. Then Constantine took up with force where Paul left off with persuasion.

I saw the same thing with different details, happen in all the other great religions, and seeing these things, I went to thinking and questing again. I have achieved a certain peace within myself, but perhaps the seeking after the inner heart of truth will never cease in me. All sorts of interesting speculations arise.

So, having looked at the subject from many sides, studied beliefs by word of mouth and then as they fit into great rigid forms, I find I know a great deal about form, but little or nothing about the mysteries I sought as a child. As the ancient tent-maker said, I have come out of the same door wherein I went.

But certain things have seemed to me to be true as I heard the tongues of those who had speech, and listened at the lips of books. It seems to me to be true that heavens are placed in the sky because it is the unreachable. The unreachable and therefore the unknowable always seems divine—hence, religion. People need religion because the great masses fear life and its consequences. Its responsibilities weigh heavy. Feeling a weakness in the face of great forces, men seek an alliance with omnipotence to bolster up their feeling of weakness, even though the omnipotence they rely upon is a creature of their own minds. It gives them a feeling of security. Strong, self-determining men are notorious for their lack of reverence. Constantine, having converted millions to Christianity by the sword, himself refused the consolation of Christ until his last hour. Some say not even then.

As for me, I do not pretend to read God's mind. If He has a plan of the universe worked out to the smallest detail, it would be folly for me to presume to get down on my knees and attempt to revise it. That, to me, seems the highest form of sacrilege. So I do not pray. I accept the means at my disposal for working out my destiny. It seems to me that I have been given a mind and will-power for that very purpose. I do not expect God to single me out and grant me advantages over my fellow men. Prayer is for those who need it. Prayer seems to me a cry of weakness, and an attempt to avoid, by trickery, the rules of the game as laid down. I do not choose to admit weakness. I accept the challenge of responsibility. Life, as it is, does not frighten me, since I have made my peace with the niverse as I find it, and bow to its laws. The ever-sleepless sea in its bed, crying out "How long?" to Time; million-formed and never motionless flame; the contemplation of these two aspects alone, affords me sufficient food for ten spans of my expected lifetime. It seems to me that organized creeds are collections of words around a wish. I feel no need for such. However, I would not, by word or deed, attempt to deprive another of the consolation it affords. It is simply not for me. Somebody else may have my rapturous glance at the archangels. The springing of the yellow line of morning out of the misty deep of dawn, is glory enough for me. I know that nothing is destructible; things merely change forms. When the consciousness we know as life ceases, I know that I shall still be part and parcel of the world. I was a part before the sun rolled into shape and burst forth in the glory of change. I was, when the earth was hurled out from its fiery rim. I shall return with the earth to Father Sun, and still exist in substance when the sun has lost its fire, and disintegrated in infinity to perhaps become a part of the whirling rubble in space. Why fear? The stuff of my being is matter, ever changing, ever moving, but never lost; so what need of denominations and creeds to deny myself the comfort of all my fellow men? The wide belt of the universe has no need for finger-rings. I am one with the infinite and need no other assurance.

16. Letter from a Birmingham Jail

Martin Luther King, Jr.

My Dear Fellow Clergymen,

While confined here in the Birmingham city jail, I came across your recent statement[1] calling our present activities "unwise and untimely." Seldom, if ever, do I pause to answer criticism of my work and ideas. If I sought to answer all of the criticisms that cross my desk, my secretaries would be engaged in little else in the course of the day, and I would have no time for constructive work. But since I feel that you are men of genuine good will and your criticisms are sincerely set forth, I would like to answer your statement in what I hope will be patient and reasonable terms.

I think I should give the reason for my being in Birmingham, since you have been influenced by the argument of "outsiders coming in." I have the honor of serving as president of the Southern Christian Leadership Conference, an organization operating in every southern state, with headquarters in Atlanta, Georgia. We have some eighty-five affiliate organizations all across the South—one being the Alabama Christian Movement for Human Rights. Whenever necessary and possible we share staff, educational and financial resources with our affiliates. Several months ago our local affiliate here in Birmingham invited us to be on call to engage in a nonviolent direct-action program if such were deemed necessary. We readily consented and when the hour came we lived up to our promises. So I am here, along with several members of my staff, because we were invited here. I am here because I have basic organizational ties here.

Beyond this, I am in Birmingham because injustice is here. Just as the eighth-century prophets left their little villages and carried their "thus saith the Lord" far beyond the boundaries of their hometowns; and just as the Apostle Paul left his little village of Tarsus and carried the gospel of Jesus Christ to practically every hamlet and city of the Graeco-Roman world, I too am compelled to carry the gospel of freedom beyond my particular hometown. Like Paul, I must constantly respond to the Macedonian call for aid.

Moreover, I am cognizant of the interrelatedness of all communities and states. I cannot sit idly by in Atlanta and not be concerned about what happens in Birmingham. Injustice anywhere is a threat to justice everywhere. We are caught in an inescapable network of mutuality, tied in a single garment of destiny. Whatever affects one directly affects all indirectly. Never again can we afford to live with the narrow, provincial "outside agitator" idea. Anyone who lives in the United States can never be considered an outsider anywhere in this country.

You deplore the demonstrations that are presently taking place in Birmingham. But I am sorry that your statement did not express a similar concern for the conditions that brought the demonstrations into being. I am sure that each of you would want to go beyond the superficial social analyst who looks merely at effects, and does not grapple with underlying causes. I would not hesitate to say that it is unfortunate that so-called demonstrations are taking place in Birmingham at this time, but I would say in more emphatic terms that it is even more unfortunate that the white power structure of this city left the Negro community with no other alternative.

In any nonviolent campaign there are four basic steps: (1) collection of the facts to determine whether injustices are alive, (2) negotiation, (3) self-purification, and (4) direct action. We have gone through all of these steps in Birmingham. There can be no gainsaying of the fact that racial injustice engulfs this community.

Birmingham is probably the most thoroughly segregated city in the United States. Its ugly record of police brutality is known in every section of this country. Its unjust treatment of Negroes in the courts is a notorious reality. There have been more unsolved bombings of Negro homes and churches in Birmingham than any city in this nation. These are the hard, brutal and unbelievable facts. On the basis of these conditions Negro leaders sought to negotiate with the city fathers. But the political leaders consistently refused to engage in good faith negotiation.

Then came the opportunity last September to talk with some of the leaders of the economic community. In these negotiating sessions certain promises were made by the merchants—such as the promise to remove the humiliating racial signs from the stores. On the basis of these promises Rev. Shuttlesworth and the leaders of the Alabama Christian Movement for Human Rights agreed to call a moratorium on any type of demonstrations. As the weeks and months unfolded we realized that we were the victims of a broken promise. The signs remained. Like so many experiences of the past we were confronted with blasted hopes, and the dark shadow of a deep disappointment settled upon us. So we had no alternative except that of preparing for direct action, whereby we would present our very bodies as a means of laying our case before the conscience of the local and national community. We were not unmindful of the difficulties involved. So we decided to go through a process of self-purification. We started having workshops on nonviolence and repeatedly asked ourselves the questions, "Are you able to accept blows without retaliating?" "Are you able to endure the ordeals of jail?" We decided to set our direct-action program around the Easter season, realizing that with the exception of Christmas, this was the largest shopping period of the year. Knowing that a strong economic withdrawal program would be the by-product of direct action, we felt that this was the best time to bring pressure on the merchants for the needed changes. Then it occurred to us that the March election was ahead and so we speedily decided to postpone action until after election day. When we discovered that Mr. Connor was in the run-off, we decided again to postpone action so that the demonstrations could not be used to cloud the issues. At this time we agreed to begin our nonviolent witness the day after the run-off.

This reveals that we did not move irresponsibly into direct action. We too wanted to see Mr. Connor defeated; so we went through postponement after postponement to aid in this community need. After this we felt that direct action could be delayed no longer.

You may well ask, "Why direct action? Why sit-ins, marches, etc.? Isn't negotiation a better path?" You are exactly right in your call for negotiation. Indeed, this is the purpose of direct action. Nonviolent direct action seeks to create such a crisis and establish such creative tension that a community that has constantly refused to negotiate is forced to confront the issue. It seeks so to dramatize the issue that it can no longer be ignored. I just referred to the creation of tension as a part of the work of the nonviolent resister. This may sound rather shocking. But I must confess that I am not afraid of the word *tension*. I have earnestly worked and preached against violent tension, but there is a type of constructive nonviolent tension that is necessary for growth. Just as Socrates felt that it was necessary to create a tension in the mind so that individuals could rise from the bondage of myths and half-truths to the unfettered realm of creative analysis and objective appraisal, we must see the need of having nonviolent gadflies to create the kind of tension in society that will help men to rise from the dark depths of prejudice and racism to the majestic heights of understanding and brotherhood. So the purpose of the direct action is to create a situation so crisis-packed that it will inevitably open the door to negotiation. We, therefore, concur with you in your call for negotiation. Too long has our beloved Southland been bogged down in the tragic attempt to live in monologue rather than dialogue.

One of the basic points in your statement is that our acts are untimely. Some have asked, "Why didn't you give the new administration time to act?" The only answer that I can give to this inquiry is that the new administration must be prodded about as much as the outgoing one before it acts. We will be sadly mistaken if we feel that the election of Mr. Boutwell will bring the millennium to Birmingham. While Mr. Boutwell is much more articulate and gentle than Mr. Connor, they are both segregationists, dedicated to the task of maintaining the status quo. The hope I see in Mr. Boutwell is that he will be reasonable enough to see the futility of massive resistance to desegregation. But he will not see this without pressure from the devotees of civil rights. My friends, I must say to you that we have not made a single gain in civil rights without determined legal and nonviolent pressure. History is the long and tragic story of the fact that privileged groups seldom give up their privileges voluntarily. Individuals may see the moral light and voluntarily give up their unjust posture; but as Reinhold Niebuhr has reminded us, groups are more immoral than individuals.

We know through painful experience that freedom is never voluntarily given by the oppressor; it must be demanded by the oppressed. Frankly, I have never yet engaged in a direct action movement that was "well-timed," according to the timetable of those who have not suffered unduly from the disease of segregation. For years now I have heard the word "Wait!" It rings in the ear of every Negro with a piercing familiarity. This "Wait" has almost always meant "Never." It has been a tranquilizing thalidomide, relieving the emotional stress for a moment, only to give birth to an ill-formed infant of frustration. We must come to see with the distinguished jurist of yesterday that "justice too long delayed is justice denied." We have waited for more than 340 years for our constitutional and God-given rights. The nations of Asia and Africa are moving with jet-like speed toward the goal of political independence, and we still creep at horse and buggy pace toward the gaining of a cup of coffee at a lunch counter. I guess it is easy for those who have never felt the stinging darts of segregation to say, "Wait." But when you have seen vicious mobs lynch your mothers and fathers at will and drown your sisters and brothers at whim; when you have seen hate-filled policemen curse, kick, brutalize and even kill your black brothers and sisters with impunity; when you see the vast majority of your twenty million Negro brothers smothering in an airtight cage of poverty in the midst of an affluent society; when you suddenly find your tongue twisted and your speech stammering as you seek to explain to your six-year-old daughter why she can't go to the public amusement park that has just been advertised on television, and see tears welling up in her little eyes when she is told that Funtown is closed to colored children, and see the depressing clouds of inferiority begin to form in her little mental sky, and see her begin to distort her little personality by unconsciously developing a bitterness toward white people; when you have to concoct an answer for a five-year-old son asking in agonizing pathos: "Daddy, why do white people treat colored people so mean?"; when you take a cross-country drive and find it necessary to sleep night after night in the uncomfortable corners of your automobile because no motel will accept you; when you are humiliated day in and day out by nagging signs reading "white" and "colored"; when your first name becomes "nigger" and your middle name becomes "boy" (however old you are) and your last name becomes "John," and when your wife and mother are never given the respected title "Mrs."; when you are harried by day and haunted by night by the fact that you are a Negro, living constantly at tiptoe stance never quite knowing what to expect next, and plagued with inner fears and outer resentments; when you are forever fighting a degenerating sense of "nobodiness"; then you will understand why we find it difficult to wait. There comes a time when the cup of endurance runs over, and men are no longer willing to be plunged into an abyss of injustice where they experience the blackness of corroding despair. I hope, sirs, you can understand our legitimate and unavoidable impatience.

You express a great deal of anxiety over our willingness to break laws. This is certainly a legitimate concern. Since we so diligently urge people to obey the Supreme Court's decision of 1954 outlawing segregation in the public schools, it is rather strange and paradoxical to find us consciously breaking laws. One may well ask, "How can you advocate breaking some laws and obeying others?" The answer is found in the fact that there are two types of laws: there are *just* and there are *unjust* laws. I would agree with Saint Augustine that "An unjust law is no law at all."

Now what is the difference between the two? How does one determine when a law is just or unjust? A just law is a man-made code that squares with the moral law or the law of God. An unjust law is a code that is out of harmony with the moral law. To put it in the terms of Saint Thomas Aquinas, an unjust law is a human law that is not rooted in eternal and natural law. Any law that uplifts human personality is just. Any law that degrades human personality is unjust. All segregation statutes are unjust because segregation distorts the soul and damages the personality. It gives the segregator a false sense of superiority, and the segregated a false sense of inferiority. To use the words of Martin Buber, the great Jewish philosopher, segregation substitutes an "I-it" relationship for the "I-thou" relationship, and ends up relegating persons to the status of things. So segregation is not only politically, economically and sociologically unsound, but it is morally wrong and sinful. Paul Tillich has said that sin is separation. Isn't segregation an existential expression of man's tragic separation, an expression of his awful estrangement, his terrible sinfulness? So I can urge men to disobey segregation ordinances because they are morally wrong.

Let us turn to a more concrete example of just and unjust laws. An unjust law is a code that a majority inflicts on a minority that is not binding on itself. This is difference made legal. On the other hand a just law is a code that a majority compels a minority to follow that it is willing to follow itself. This is sameness made legal.

Let me give another explanation. An unjust law is a code inflicted upon a minority which that minority had no part in enacting or creating because they did not have the unhampered right to vote. Who can say that the legislature of Alabama which set up the segregation laws was democratically elected? Throughout the state of Alabama all types of conniving methods are used to prevent Negroes from becoming registered voters and there are some counties without a single Negro registered to vote despite the fact that the Negro constitutes a majority of the population. Can any law set up in such a state be considered democratically structured?

These are just a few examples of unjust and just laws. There are some instances when a law is just on its face and unjust in its application. For instance, I was arrested Friday on a change of parading without a permit. Now there is nothing wrong with an ordinance which requires a permit for a parade, but when the ordinance is used to preserve segregation and to deny citizens the First Amendment privilege of peaceful assembly and peaceful protest, then it becomes unjust.

I hope you can see the distinction I am trying to point out. In no sense do I advocate evading or defying the law as the rabid segregationist would do. This would lead to anarchy. One who breaks an unjust law must do it *openly*, *lovingly* (not hatefully as the white mothers did in New Orleans when they were seen on television screaming, "nigger, nigger, nigger"), and with a willingness to accept the penalty. I submit that an individual who breaks a law that conscience tells him is unjust, and willingly accepts the penalty by staying in jail to arouse the conscience of the community over its injustice, is in reality expressing the very highest respect for law.

Of course, there is nothing new about this kind of civil disobedience. It was seen sublimely in the refusal of Shadrach, Meshach and Abednego to obey the laws of Nebuchadnezzar because a higher moral law was involved. It was practiced superbly by the early Christians who were willing to face hungry lions and the excruciating pain of chopping blocks, before submitting to certain unjust laws of the Roman Empire. To a degree academic freedom is a reality today because Socrates practiced civil disobedience.

We can never forget that everything Hitler did in Germany was "legal" and everything the Hungarian freedom fighters did in Hungary was "illegal." It was "illegal" to aid and comfort a Jew in Hitler's Germany. But I am sure that if I had lived in Germany during that time I would have aided and comforted my Jewish brothers even though it was illegal. If I lived in a Communist country today where certain principles dear to the Christian faith are suppressed, I believe I would openly advocate disobeying these anti-religious laws. I must make two honest confessions to you, my Christian and Jewish brothers. First, I must confess that over the last few years I have been gravely disappointed with the white moderate. I have almost reached the regrettable conclusion that the Negro's great stumbling block in the stride toward freedom is not the White Citizens Counciler or the Ku Klux Klanner, but the white moderate who is more devoted to "order" than to justice; who prefers a negative peace which is the absence of tension to a positive peace which is the presence of justice; who constantly says, "I agree with you in the goal you seek, but I can't agree with your methods of direct action"; who paternalistically feels that he can set the timetable for another man's freedom; who lives by the myth of time and who constantly advised the Negro to wait until a "more convenient season." Shallow understanding from people of good will is more frustrating than absolute misunderstanding from people of ill will. Lukewarm acceptance is much more bewildering than outright rejection.

I had hoped that the white moderate would understand that law and order exist for the purpose of establishing justice, and that when they fail to do this they become dangerously structured dams that block the flow of social progress. I had hoped that the white moderate would understand that the present tension of the South is merely a necessary phase of the transition from an obnoxious negative peace, where the Negro passively accepted his unjust plight, to a substance-filled positive peace, where all men will respect the dignity and worth of human personality. Actually, we who engage in nonviolent direct action are not the creators of tension. We merely bring to the surface the hidden tension that is already alive. We bring it out in the open where it can be seen and dealt with. Like a boil that can never be cured as long as it is covered up but must be opened with all its pus-flowing ugliness to the natural medicines of air and light, injustice must likewise be exposed, with all of the tension its exposing creates, to the light of human conscience and the air of national opinion before it can be cured.

In your statement you asserted that our actions, even though peaceful, must be condemned because they precipitate violence. But can this assertion be logically made? Isn't this like condemning the robbed man because his possession of money precipitated the evil act of robbery? Isn't this like condemning Socrates because his unswerving commitment to truth and his philosophical delvings precipitated the misguided popular mind to make him drink the hemlock? Isn't this like condemning Jesus because His unique God-consciousness and never-ceasing devotion to his will precipitated the evil act of crucifixion? We must come to see, as federal courts have consistently affirmed, that it is immoral to urge an individual to withdraw his efforts to gain his basic constitutional rights because the quest precipitates violence. Society must protect the robbed and punish the robber.

I had also hoped that the white moderate would reject the myth of time. I received a letter this morning from a white brother in Texas which said: "All Christians know that the colored people will receive equal rights eventually, but it is possible that you are in too great of a religious hurry. It has taken Christianity almost two thousand years to accomplish what it has. The teachings of Christ take time to come to earth." All that is said here grows out of a tragic misconception of time. It is the strangely irrational notion that there is something in the very flow of time that will inevitably cure all ills. Actually time is neutral. It can be used either destructively or constructively. I am coming to feel that the people of ill will have used time much more effectively than the people of good will. We will have to repent in this generation not merely for the vitriolic words and actions of the bad people, but for the appalling silence of the good people. We must come to see that human progress never rolls in on wheels of inevitability. It comes through the tireless efforts and persistent work of men willing to be co-workers with God, and without this hard work time itself becomes an ally of the forces of social stagnation. We must use time creatively, and forever realize that the time is always ripe to do right. Now is the time to make real the promise of democracy, and transform our pending national elegy into a creative psalm of brotherhood. Now is the time to lift our national policy from the quicksand of racial injustice to the solid rock of human dignity.

You spoke of our activity in Birmingham as extreme. At first I was rather disappointed that fellow clergymen would see my nonviolent efforts as those of the extremist. I started thinking about the fact that I stand in the middle of two opposing forces in the Negro community. One is a force of complacency made up of Negroes who, as a result of long years of oppression, have been so completely drained of self-respect and a sense of "somebodiness" that they have adjusted to segregation, and, of a few Negroes in the middle class who, because of a degree of academic and economic security, and because at points they profit by segregation, have unconsciously become insensitive to the problems of the masses. The other force is one of bitterness and hatred, and comes perilously close to advocating violence. It is expressed in the various black nationalist groups that are springing up over the nation, the largest and best known being Elijah Muhammad's Muslim movement. This movement is nourished by the contemporary frustration over the continued existence of racial discrimination. It is made up of people who have lost faith in America, who have absolutely repudiated Christianity, and who have concluded that the white man is an incurable "devil." I have tried to stand between these two forces, saying that we need not follow the "donothingism" of the complacent or the hatred and despair of the black nationalist. There is the more excellent way of love and nonviolent protest. I'm grateful to God that, through the Negro church, the dimension of nonviolence entered our struggle. If this philosophy had not emerged, I am convinced that by now many streets of the South would be flowing with floods of blood. And I am further convinced that if our white brothers dismiss as "rabble-rousers" and "outside agitators" those of us who are working through the channels of nonviolent direct action and refuse to support our nonviolent efforts, millions of Negroes, out of frustration and despair, will seek solace and security in black nationalist ideologies, a development that will lead inevitably to a frightening racial nightmare.

Oppressed people cannot remain oppressed forever. The urge for freedom will eventually come. This is what happened to the American Negro. Something within has reminded him of his birthright of freedom; something without has reminded him that he can gain it. Consciously and unconsciously, he has been swept in by what the Germans call the *Zeitgeist*, and with his black brothers of Africa, and his brown and yellow brothers of Asia, South America and the Caribbean, he is moving with a sense of cosmic urgency toward the promised land of racial justice. Recognizing this vital urge that has engulfed the Negro community, one should readily understand public demonstrations. The Negro has many pent-up resentments and latent frustrations. He has to get them out. So let him march sometime; let him have his prayer pilgrimages to the city hall; understand why he must have sit-ins and freedom rides. If his repressed emotions do not come out in these nonviolent ways, they will come out in ominous expressions of violence. This is not a threat; it is a fact of history. So I have not said to my people "get rid of your discontent." But I have tried to say that this normal and healthy discontent can be channelized through the creative outlet of nonviolent direct action. Now this approach is being dismissed as extremist. I must admit that I was initially disappointed in being so categorized.

But as I continued to think about the matter I gradually gained a bit of satisfaction from being considered an extremist. Was not Jesus an extremist in love—"Love your enemies, bless them that curse you, pray for them that despitefully use you." Was not Amos an extremist for justice—"Let justice roll down like waters and righteousness like a mighty stream." Was not Paul an extremist for the gospel of Jesus Christ—"I bear in my body the marks of the Lord Jesus." Was not Martin Luther an extremist—"Here I stand; I can do none other so help me God." Was not John Bunyan an extremist—"I will stay in jail to the end of my days before I make a butchery of my conscience." Was not Abraham Lincoln an extremist—"This nation cannot survive half slave and half free." Was not Thomas Jefferson an extremist—"We hold these truths to be self-evident, that all men are created equal." So the question is not whether we will be extremist but what kind of extremist will we be. Will we be extremists for hate or will we be extremists for love? Will we be extremists for the preservation of injustice—or will we be extremists for the cause of justice? In that dramatic scene on Calvary's hill, three men were crucified. We must not forget that all three were crucified for the same crime—the crime of extremism. Two were extremists for immorality, and thusly fell below their environment. The other, Jesus Christ, was an extremist for love, truth and goodness, and thereby rose above his environment. So, after all, maybe the South, the nation and the world are in dire need of creative extremists.

I had hoped that the white moderate would see this. Maybe I was too optimistic. Maybe I expected too much. I guess I should have realized that few members of a race that has oppressed another race can understand or appreciate the deep groans and passionate yearnings of those that have been oppressed and still fewer have the vision to see that injustice must be rooted out by strong, persistent and determined action. I am thankful, however, that some of our white brothers have grasped the meaning of this social revolution and committed themselves to it. They are still all too small in quantity, but they are big in quality. Some like Ralph McGill, Lillian Smith, Harry Golden and James Dabbs have written about our struggle in eloquent, prophetic and understanding terms. Others have marched with us down nameless streets of the South. They have languished in filthy roach-infested jails, suffering the abuse and brutality of angry policemen who see them as "dirty nigger-lovers." They, unlike so many of their moderate brothers and sisters, have recognized the urgency of the moment and sensed the need for powerful "action" antidotes to combat the disease of segregation.

Let me rush on to mention my other disappointment. I have been so greatly disappointed with the white church and its leadership. Of course, there are some notable exceptions. I am not unmindful of the fact that each of you has taken some significant stands on this issue. I commend you, Rev. Stallings, for your Christian stance on this past Sunday, in welcoming Negroes to your worship service on a non-segregated basis. I commend the Catholic leaders of this state for integrating Springhill College several years ago.

But despite these notable exceptions I must honestly reiterate that I have been disappointed with the church. I do not say that as one of the negative critics who can always find something wrong with the church. I say it as a minister of the gospel, who loves the church; who was nurtured in its bosom; who has been sustained by its spiritual blessings and who will remain true to it as long as the cord of life shall lengthen.

I had the strange feeling when I was suddenly catapulted into the leadership of the bus protest in Montgomery several years ago that we would have the support of the white church. I felt that the white ministers, priests and rabbis of the South would be some of our strongest allies. Instead, some have been outright opponents, refusing to understand the freedom movement and misrepresenting its leaders; all too many others have been more cautious than courageous and have remained silent behind the anesthetizing security of the stained-glass windows.

In spite of my shattered dreams of the past, I came to Birmingham with the hope that the white religious leadership of this community would see the justice of our cause, and with deep moral concern, serve as the channel through which our just grievances would get to the power structure. I had hoped that each of you would understand. But again I have been disappointed. I have heard numerous religious leaders of the South call upon their worshippers to comply with a desegregation decision because it is the *law*, but I have longed to hear white ministers say, "Follow this decree because integration is morally *right* and the Negro is your brother." In the midst of blatant injustices inflicted upon the Negro, I have watched white churches stand on the sideline and merely mouth pious irrelevancies and sanctimonious trivialities. In the midst of a mighty struggle to rid our nation of racial and economic injustice, I have heard so many ministers say, "Those are social issues with which the gospel has no real concern," and I have watched so many churches commit themselves to a completely otherworldly religion which made a strange distinction between body and soul, the sacred and the secular.

So here we are moving toward the exit of the twentieth century with a religious community largely adjusted to the status quo, standing as a taillight behind other community agencies rather than a headlight leading men to higher levels of justice.

I have traveled the length and breadth of Alabama, Mississippi and all the other southern states. On sweltering summer days and crisp autumn mornings I have looked at her beautiful churches with their lofty spires pointing heavenward. I have beheld the impressive outlay of her massive religious education buildings. Over and over again I have found myself asking: "What kind of people worship here? Who is their God? Where were their voices when the lips of Governor Barnett dripped with words of interposition and nullification? Where were they when Governor Wallace gave the clarion call for defiance and hatred? Where were their voices of support when tired, bruised and weary Negro men and women decided to rise from the dark dungeons of complacency to the bright hills of creative protest?"

Yes, these questions are still in my mind. In deep disappointment, I have wept over the laxity of the church. But be assured that my tears have been tears of love. There can be no deep disappointment where there is not deep love. Yes, I love the church; I love her sacred walls. How could I do otherwise? I am in the rather unique position of being the son, the grandson and the great-grandson of preachers. Yes, I see the church as the body of Christ. But, oh! How we have blemished and scarred that body through social neglect and fear of being nonconformists.

There was a time when the church was very powerful. It was during that period when the early Christians rejoiced when they were deemed worthy to suffer for what they believed. In those days the church was not merely a thermometer that recorded the ideas and principles of popular opinion; it was a thermostat that transformed the mores of society. Wherever the early Christians entered a town the power structure got disturbed and immediately sought to convict them for being "disturbers of the peace" and "outside agitators." But they went on with the conviction that they were "a colony of heaven," and had to obey God rather than man. They were small in number but big in commitment. They were too God-intoxicated to be "astronomically intimidated." They brought an end to such ancient evils as infanticide and gladiatorial contest.

Things are different now. The contemporary church is often a weak, ineffectual voice with an uncertain sound. It is so often the arch-supporter of the status quo. Far from being disturbed by the presence of the church, the power structure of the average community is consoled by the church's silent and often vocal sanction of things as they are.

But the judgment of God is upon the church as never before. If the church of today does not recapture the sacrificial spirit of the early church, it will lose its authentic ring, forfeit the loyalty of millions, and be dismissed as an irrelevant social club with no meaning for the twentieth century. I am meeting young people every day whose disappointment with the church has risen to outright disgust.

Maybe again, I have been too optimistic. Is organized religion too inextricably bound to the status quo to save our nation and the world? Maybe I must turn my faith to the inner spiritual church, the church within the church, as the true *ecclesia* and the hope of the world. But again I am thankful to God that some noble souls from the ranks of organized religion have broken loose from the paralyzing chains of conformity and joined us as active partners in the struggle for freedom. They have left their secure congregations and walked the streets of Albany, Georgia, with us. They have gone through the highways of the South on tortuous rides for freedom. Yes, they have gone to jail with us. Some have been kicked out of their churches, and lost support of their bishops and fellow ministers. But they have gone with the faith that right defeated is stronger than evil triumphant. These men have been the leaven in the lump of the race. Their witness has been the spiritual salt that has preserved the true meaning of the gospel in these troubled times. They have carved a tunnel of hope through the dark mountain of disappointment.

I hope the church as a whole will meet the challenge of this decisive hour. But even if the church does not come to the aid of justice, I have no despair about the future. I have no fear about the outcome of our struggle in Birmingham, even if our motives are presently misunderstood. We will reach the goal of freedom in Birmingham and all over the nation, because the goal of America is freedom. Abused and scorned though we may be, our destiny is tied up with the destiny of America. Before the Pilgrims landed at Plymouth we were here. Before the pen of Jefferson etched across the pages of history the majestic words of the Declaration of Independence, we were here. For more than two centuries our foreparents labored in this country without wages; they made cotton king; and they built the homes of their masters in the midst of brutal injustice and shameful humiliation—and yet out of a bottomless vitality they continued to thrive and develop. If the inexpressible cruelties of slavery could not stop us, the opposition we now face will surely fail. We will win our freedom because the sacred heritage of our nation and the eternal will of God are embodied in our echoing demands.

I must close now. But before closing I am impelled to mention one other point in your statement that troubled me profoundly. You warmly commended the Birmingham police force for keeping "order" and "preventing violence." I don't believe you would have so warmly commended the police force if you had seen its angry violent dogs literally biting six unarmed, nonviolent Negroes. I don't believe you would so quickly commend the policemen if you would observe their ugly and inhuman treatment of Negroes here in the city jail; if you would watch them push and curse old Negro women and young Negro girls; if you would see them slap and kick old Negro men and young boys; if you will observe them, as they did on two occasions, refuse to give us food because we wanted to sing our grace together. I'm sorry that I can't join you in your praise for the police department.

It is true that they have been rather disciplined in their public handling of the demonstrators. In this sense they have been rather publicly "nonviolent." But for what purpose? To preserve the evil system of segregation. Over the last few years I have consistently preached that nonviolence demands that the means we use must be as pure as the ends we seek. So I have tried to make it clear that it is wrong to use immoral means to attain moral ends. But now I must affirm that it is just as wrong, or even more so, to use moral means to preserve immoral ends. Maybe Mr. Connor and his policemen have been rather publicly nonviolent, as Chief Pritchett was in Albany, Georgia, but they have used the moral means of nonviolence to maintain the immoral end of flagrant racial injustice. T. S. Eliot has said that there is no greater treason than to do the right deed for the wrong reason.

I wish you had commended the Negro sit-inners and demonstrators of Birmingham for their sublime courage, their willingness to suffer and their amazing discipline in the midst of the most inhuman provocation. One day the South will recognize its real heroes. They will be the James Merediths, courageously and with a majestic sense of purpose facing jeering and hostile mobs and the agonizing loneliness that characterizes the life of the pioneer. They will be old, oppressed, battered Negro women, symbolized in a seventy-two-year-old woman of Montgomery, Alabama, who rose up with a sense of dignity and with her people decided not to ride the segregated buses, and responded to one who inquired about her tiredness with ungrammatical profundity: "My feet is tired, but my soul is rested." They will be the young high school and college students, young ministers of the gospel and a host of their elders courageously and non-violently sitting-in at lunch counters and willingly going to jail for conscience's sake. One day the South will know that when these disinherited children of God sat down at lunch counters they were in reality standing up for the best in the American dream and the most sacred values in our Judeo-Christian heritage, and thusly, carrying our whole nation back to those great wells of democracy which were dug deep by the Founding Fathers in the formulation of the Constitution and the Declaration of Independence.

Never before have I written a letter this long (or should I say a book?). I'm afraid that it is much too long to take your precious time. I can assure you that it would have been much shorter if I had been writing from a comfortable desk, but what else is there to do when you are alone for days in the dull monotony of a narrow jail cell other than write long letters, think strange thoughts, and pray long prayers?

If I have said anything in this letter that is an overstatement of the truth and is indicative of an unreasonable impatience, I beg you to forgive me. If I have said anything in this letter that is an understatement of the truth and is indicative of my having a patience that makes me patient with anything less than brotherhood, I beg God to forgive me.

I hope this letter finds you strong in the faith. I also hope that circumstances will soon make it possible for me to meet each of you, not as an integrationist or a civil rights leader, but as a fellow clergyman and a Christian brother. Let us all hope that the dark clouds of racial prejudice will soon pass away and the deep fog of misunderstanding will be lifted from our fear-drenched communities and in some not too distant tomorrow the radiant stars of love and brotherhood will shine over our great nation with all of their scintillating beauty.

Yours for the cause of Peace and Brotherhood,
Martin Luther King, Jr.

Note

¹Public Statement by Eight Alabama Clergymen

April 12, 1963

We the undersigned clergymen are among those who, in January, issued "An Appeal for Law and Order and Common Sense," in dealing with racial problems in Alabama. We expressed understanding that honest convictions in racial matters could properly be pursued in the courts, but urged that decisions of those courts should in the meantime be peacefully obeyed.

Since that time there had been some evidence of increased forbearance and a willingness to face facts. Responsible citizens have undertaken to work on various problems which cause racial friction and unrest. In Birmingham, recent public events have given indication that we all have opportunity for a new constructive and realistic approach to racial problems.

However, we are now confronted by a series of demonstrations by some of our Negro citizens, directed and led in part by outsiders. We recognize the natural impatience of people who feel that their hopes are slow in being realized. But we are convinced that these demonstrations are unwise and untimely.

We agree rather with certain local Negro leadership which has called for honest and open negotiation of racial issues in our area. And we believe this kind of facing of issues can best be accomplished by citizens of our own metropolitan area, white and Negro, meeting with their knowledge and experience of the local situation. All of us need to face that responsibility and find proper channels for its accomplishment.

Just as we formerly pointed out that "hatred and violence have no sanction in our religious and political traditions," we also point out that such actions as incite to hatred and violence, however technically peaceful those actions may be, have not contributed to the resolution of our local problems. We do not believe that these days of new hope are days when extreme measures are justified in Birmingham.

We commend the community as a whole, and the local news media and law enforcement in particular, on the calm manner in which these demonstrations have been handled. We urge the public to continue to show restraint should the demonstrations continue, and the law enforcement official to remain calm and continue to protect our city from violence.

We further strongly urge our own Negro community to withdraw support from these demonstrations, and to unite locally in working peacefully for a better Birmingham. When rights are consistently denied, a cause should be pressed in the courts and in negotiations among local leaders, and not in the streets. We appeal to both our white and Negro citizenry to observe the principles of law and order and common sense.

C. C. J. Carpenter, D.D., LL.D.
Bishop of Alabama

Joseph A. Durick, D.D.
Auxiliary Bishop, Diocese of Mobile, Birmingham

Rabbi Hilton L. Grafman
Temple Emanu-El, Birmingham, Alabama

Bishop Paul Hardin
Bishop of the Alabama-West Florida Conference

Bishop Holan B. Harmon
Bishop of the North Alabama Conference of the Methodist Church

George M. Murray, D.D., LL.D.
Bishop Coadjutor, Episcopal Diocese of Alabama

Edward V. Ramage
Moderator, Synod of the Alabama Presbyterian Church in the United States

Earl Stallings
Pastor, First Baptist Church, Birmingham, Alabama

17. Black Man's History

MALCOLM X

I want to thank Allah for coming and giving to us our leader and teacher here in America, The Honorable Elijah Muhammad. I want to thank Brother Benjamin at the outset for doing a wonderful job of opening up our eyes and giving us a good preliminary basic understanding of the means and the objectives of The Honorable Elijah Muhammad, and also I am thankful to Allah for bringing so many people out here tonight, especially just before Christmas. You know, it's next to a miracle when you get this many of our people together so close to Christmas interested in anything whatsoever that's serious. And actually what this shows is the change that's taking place among the so-called Negroes not only here in New York but throughout the entire world. Today dark mankind is waking up and is undertaking a new type of thinking, and it is this new type of thinking that is creating new approaches and new reactions that make it almost impossible to figure out what the black man is going to do next, and by black man we mean, as we are taught by The Honorable Elijah Muhammad, we include all those who are nonwhite. He teaches us that black is the basic color, that black is the foundation or the basis of all colors. And all of our people who have not yet become white are still black, or at least part of the Black Nation, and here at Muhammad's Mosque when you hear us using the term "black" we mean everbody who's here, regardless of your complexion. If you're here at the Mosque you're black, because the only ticket you need to get into Muhammad's Mosque is to be black. So if you got in you know you're black. You may not have known that you were black before you came here. In fact, very few of our people really look upon themselves as being black. They think of themselves as practically everything else on the color spectrum except black. And no matter how dark one of our people may be, you rarely hear him call himself black. But now that The Honorable Elijah Muhammad has been teaching among the so-called Negroes, you find our people of all complexions going around bragging that "I'm a black man." This shows you that a new teaching is taking place and there is new thinking among the so-called Negroes. Yet just yesterday you would have to admit that it was very difficult to get our people to refer to themselves as black. Now all of a sudden our people of all complexions are not apologizing for being black but bragging about being black. So there's a new thinking all over America among the so-called Negroes. And the one who is actually the author of this new thinking is The Honorable Elijah Muhammad. It is what he is teaching that is making our people, for the first time, proud to be black, and what's most important of all, for the first time it makes our people want to know more about black, want to know why black is good, or what there is about black that is good.

I might stop right here to point out that some of you may say, "I came up here to listen to some religion, about Islam, but now all I hear you talk about is black." We don't separate our color from our religion. The white man doesn't. The white man never has separated Christianity from white, nor has he separated the white man from Christianity. When you hear the white man bragging, "I'm a Christian," he's bragging about being a white man. Then you have the Negro. When he is bragging about being a Christian, he's bragging that he's a white man, or he wants to be white, and usually those Negroes who brag like that, I think you have to agree, in their songs and the things they sing in church, they show that they have a greater desire to be white than anything else. My mother was a Christian and my father was a Christian and I used to hear them when I was a little child sing the song "Wash Me White as Snow." My father was a black man and my mother was a black woman, but yet the songs that they sang in their church were designed to fill their hearts with the desire to be white. So many people, especially our people, get resentful when they hear me say something like this. But rather than get resentful all they have to do is think back on many of the songs and much of the teachings and the doctrines that they were taught while they were going to church and they'll have to agree that it was all designed to make us look down on black and up at white.

So the religion that we have, the religion of Islam, the religion that makes us Muslims, the religion that The Honorable Elijah Muhammad is teaching us here in America today, is designed to undo in our minds what the white man has done to us. It's designed to undo the type of brainwashing that we have had to undergo for four hundred years at the hands of the white man in order to bring us down to the level that we're at today. So when you hear us often refer to black in almost a boastful way, actually we're not boasting, we're speaking of it in a factual sense. All we're doing is telling the truth about our people. Whenever you exalt black, that's not propaganda; when you exalt white, *that's* propaganda. Yet no one can give biological evidence to show that black actually is the stronger or superior of the two if you want to make that kind of comparison. So never think ill of the person whom you hear representing The Honorable Elijah Muhammad if an overemphasis seems to be placed on the word black, but rather sit and analyze and try to get an understanding.

The Honorable Elijah Muhammad teaches us that of all the things that the black man, or any man for that matter, can study, history is the best qualified to reward all research. You have to have a knowledge of history no matter what you are going to do; anything that you undertake you have to have a knowledge of history in order to be successful in it. The thing that has made the so-called Negro in America fail, more than any other thing, is your, my, lack of knowledge concerning history. We know less about history than anything else. There are black people in America who have mastered the mathematical sciences, have become professors and experts in physics, are able to toss sputniks out there in the atmosphere, out in space. They are masters in that field. We have black men who have mastered the field of medicine, we have black men who have mastered other fields, but very seldom do we have black men in America who have mastered the knowledge of the history of the black man himself. We have among our people those who are experts in every field, but seldom can you find one among us who is an expert on the history of the black man. And because of his lack of knowledge concerning the history of the black man, no matter how much he excels in the other sciences, he's always confined, he's always relegated to the same low rung of the ladder that the dumbest of our people are relegated to. And *all* of this stems from his lack of knowledge concerning history. What made Dr. George Washington Carver a *Negro* scientist instead of a scientist? What made Paul Robeson a *Negro* actor instead of an actor? What made, or makes, Ralph Bunche a *Negro* statesman instead of a statesman? The only difference between Bunche and Carver and these others I just mentioned is they don't know the history of the black man. Bunche is an expert, an international politician, but he doesn't know himself, he doesn't know the history of the black people. He can be sent all over the world by America to solve problems for America, or to solve problems for other nations, but he can't solve problems for his own people in this country. Why? What is it that ties our people up in this way? The Honorable Elijah Muhammad says that it boils down to just one word—history.

When you study the history of Bunche, his history is different from the history of the black man who just came here from Africa. And if you notice, when Bunche was in Atlanta, Georgia, during the summer NAACP Convention, he was Jim Crowed, he was segregated, he was not allowed to go in a hotel down there. Yet there are Africans who come here, black as night, who can go into those cracker hotels. Well, what is the difference between Bunche and one of them? The difference is Bunche doesn't know his history, and they, the Africans, do know their history. They may come here out of the jungles, but they know their history. They may come here wearing sheets with their heads all wrapped up, but they know their history. You and I can come out of Harvard but we don't know our history. There's a basic difference in why we are treated as we are: one knows his history and one doesn't know his history! The American so-called Negro is a soldier who doesn't know his history; he's a servant who doesn't know his history; he's a graduate of Columbia, or Yale, or Harvard, or Tuskeegee, who doesn't know his history. He's confined, he's limited, he's held under the control and the jurisdiction of the white man who knows more about the history of the Negro than the Negro knows about himself. But when you and I wake up, as we're taught by The Honorable Elijah Muhammad, and learn our history, learn the history of our kind, and the history of the white kind, then the white man will be at a disadvantage and we'll be at an advantage.

The only thing that puts you and me at a disadvantage is our lack of knowledge concerning history. So one of the reasons, one of the missions, one of the objectives of The Honorable Elijah Muhammad here in America is not only to teach you and me the right religions but to teach you and me history. In fact, do you know that if you and I know history we know the right religion? The only way that you can become confused, that you can become mixed up and not know which religion belongs to God, is if you don't know history. In fact, you have to know history to know something about God. You have to know history to know something about God's religion. You have to know history to know something about God's people. You have to know history to know something about God's plans and God's purposes, and, as I say, the only people who don't know history are the American so-called Negroes. If you know history, for example, you know when you look at this religion right here [writes "Christianity" on the blackboard] the only way you can explain it is to have a knowledge of history.

Why is it called Christianity? It is called Christianity, they say, because it was named after a man called Christ who was born two thousand years ago. Now you know, brothers and sisters, God is an old God, and the world is an old world. The universe has been here a long time. I think all of you would agree that the universe has been here longer than two thousand years. Then you'll also agree that the universe was made by God Himself, that God created the universe. God created the people who are on this earth, God wouldn't create a universe, God wouldn't set a thing up in the sky that makes nine planets rotate around it, all of them inhabited, you and I inhabiting the planet earth upon which we live—God wouldn't have done all this and not given people a religion. God put His religion here at the creation of the universe. In fact, God's religion is older than the universe. Now then, since you agree to this and you'll agree also that Christ was born two thousand years ago, this couldn't have been God's religion. Your knowledge of history tells you that God couldn't call His religion Christianity because Christianity is only two thousand years old. So if this is the case, then what was God's religion called *before* the birth of Christ? Can you see the importance of history? Why, if you didn't know history you'd think that Christianity was God's religion, and you'd be running around here wondering why everybody doesn't practice it. Because some people have a better knowledge of history than others do, it is only the people whose knowledge of history is limited who jump up and say that Christianity is the name of God's religion. If Christianity hasn't *always* been the name of God's religion it isn't *now* the name of God's religion. God doesn't change the name of His religion; God doesn't change His religion; God doesn't change His mind; God's mind is made up from the beginning. He doesn't have to change His mind because He knows all there is to know all the way down the wheel of time. He never has to change His mind, His mind is made up, His knowledge is complete, all encompassing. Do you understand? So once you can see, and I think you can, then it's almost impossible for God to call *Christianity* His religion.

What should God call His religion? Christians are the ones who call God's religion Christianity, but God was here before Christians came on the scene. They tell you that Christians began back there with the Romans, with one of the Roman Emperors who accepted the teachings of some of Jesus' disciples and then named what the disciples taught "Christianity." But Jesus didn't call it Christianity, it wasn't named until two or three hundred years after Jesus was dead. Right or wrong? Any history book will tell this, any theologian knows this, and the only Negroes who will contend this are those who don't know history, and most Negroes don't know history. Most Negroes will contend this, but when you tell it to the white man he shuts his mouth because he knows that this is true.

Then those who have studied a little deeper will say, "Before God called it Christianity it was called Judaism"—isn't this what they say? Named after a man called Judah. This doesn't follow logically. If Christianity was named after Christ was born, and before Christ was born the religion was called Judaism, then that means that it got its name from a son of Jacob whose name was Judah. But history tells us that Jacob was bending down before Judah was born, which shows us that Jacob's religion couldn't have been Judaism, and Isaac was Jacob's father and he was bending down also before Jacob, his son, was born. Isaac was Judah's grandfather and Abraham was Judah's great-grandfather, meaning that Abraham was on the scene long before Judah, and you couldn't call Abraham's religion Judaism because there was no such thing as Judaism in Abraham's day. There was no such thing as Judaism in Isaac's day, or in Jacob's day. Do you understand? So what was God's religion before they called it Judaism? This is something that the white man has never taught you and me. The white man is afraid to let you and me know what's God's religion was called in Abraham's day because Abraham is supposed to have been the father of all of them. He is supposed to have been the progenitor of all of them. He is supposed to have been one of God's first servants. One of the first to submit to God is supposed to have been Abraham. Now if you can see this, then find out what Abraham's religion was.

The Honorable Elijah Muhammad teaches us that Abraham's religion was the religion of Islam. Islam only means complete submission to God, complete obedience to God. Abraham obeyed God. Abraham obeyed God so much so that when God told Abraham to take his son and sacrifice him—stick a dagger in his heart, isn't that what he said?—Abraham took his only son up on the mountain. He was going to sacrifice him to God, showing that he believed in Islam. What does Islam mean? Obey God. Submit to God. So that this name [writes "Islam"], if you'll notice, has no connection, no association, with the death of a man. This is not a man's name, this doesn't come from a man. Buddhism is named after a man called Buddha; Confucianism is named after a man called Confucius—right or wrong? Likewise with Judaism and Christianity. But Islam is not connected with any name. Islam is independent of any name. Islam is an act which means submit completely to God, or obey God. And when you say your religion is Islam that means you're a Muslim. So to clarify this what must you do? You must have a knowledge of history. If you don't have a knowledge of history you'll run around calling yourself a Christian when you're serving God, or you'll run around saying your religion is Judaism and you'll swear you're serving God. If your religion is Christianity you're following Christ, if your religion is Judaism you're following Judah, if your religion is Buddhism you're following Buddha, do you understand? And they are all dead, and if you follow them you'll die too. This is where it all leads you. Wherever your leaders go, that's what happens to you. Now we who follow The Honorable Elijah Muhammad, we believe in Islam, we don't believe in Muhammad.

He teaches us the religion of Islam. Do you understand the difference? These people who follow Christ [pointing to the cross painted on the blackboard], they believe in Christ; they believe Christ is God—Oh yes, they do—that he was born of the Blessed Virgin, didn't have a father, was just a spirit, and then came into the world and was crucified, rose from the dead, and went up into space. They believe that, but they believe it because they don't know history. But if you notice, the Jews have a better knowledge of history than the Christians do, do they not? The Christians' history only goes back two thousand years; the history of the Jews goes back beyond four thousand years. Can you see this? And the Muslim history goes back . . . there is no limit to the Muslim history. If you notice, the Christians can only go back to what they call the Greek Empire. That's what they call the Occidental, the beginning of the Occident, the Greek Empire, the Roman Empire, and so forth. The Jews have a knowledge of history that goes back into Egypt and Babylon. You notice how one goes back further than the other. But now the Muslims' history goes back . . . it has no limit. There are no chains on how far you can go back when you are a Muslim. The Christians and the Jews combined go back to whom? To Adam, and they stop right there. And they say beyond him there was nothing happening. The greater their knowledge of history is—this has an influence on the type of religion that they accept. Do you understand?

All praise is due to Allah. Another example: What makes the royal family of Europe, or any country, differ from the peasant? Royalty knows its ancestry, royalty knows its history, this is what makes them royal. You can't have a king who can't trace his history back to his forefathers. The only way you can be king is to be born a king. If you take away his history, and he doesn't know who his forefathers were, what does he become? A peasant—a common ordinary man. Same with the Jews and Christians. It's because the Jews have the longest record of history that they can call themselves the Chosen People. The Christians can't call themselves the Chosen People because their history is not long enough. They can't go back to the time when the choice was being made. The Hebrews, the so-called Jews, can go back so far they can lay claim to that which is actually not theirs. But the reason they can claim it is that nobody else they are dealing with can go back far enough to disprove them. Except the Muslims—do you understand? So The Honorable Elijah Muhammad's mission is to teach the so-called Negroes a knowledge of history, the history of ourselves, our own kind, showing us how we fit into prophecy, Biblical prophecy. When you go to one of the churches you will notice that it is named after some word in their Bible: Big Rock Baptist Church, or Drinking at the Well Baptist Church, Friendship Baptist Church, Union Baptist, Israel Baptist, Jacob's Ladder Baptist. They find some kind of old funny word in their Bible to name their whole religion after. Their whole doctrine is based on a verse in the Bible: "He rose."

The Honorable Elijah Muhammad bases what he teaches not on a verse but on the entire book. And from beginning to end, he says, he can open up the Book and prove that the Bible agrees with him, and then use the Bible to prove that what they are teaching in the church is wrong. You know that's saying something.

For instance, he says that in Genesis, the fifteenth chapter and the thirteenth verse, just to give you an example: "And he said unto Abram, Know of a surety that thy seed shall be a stranger in a land that is not theirs, and shall serve them; and they shall afflict them four hundred years; and also that nation, whom they shall serve, will I judge: and afterward shall they come out with great substance." Now The Honorable Elijah Muhammad says that explains his teachings right there, because he teaches that the so-called Negro is the one that the Bible is talking about. Who have spent four hundred years and are strangers in a land that is not theirs? And you can't deny that we are strangers here. I don't think any of you will deny that we are strangers here. We are not in a country where we are made to feel at home. We'll put it that way. There is hardly any Negro in his right mind who can say he feels at home in America. He has to admit that he is made to feel like a stranger. Right or wrong? Well, this is what God said to Abraham would happen in this day and time. Remember, Abraham's religion was Islam. Abraham wasn't a Jew, Abraham wasn't a Christian, Abraham wasn't a Buddhist, Abraham was a Muslim, which means he obeyed God. God told him, yes, He said, your people are going into bondage, they're going to become slaves, they're going to be afflicted, they'll be strangers in a land far from home for four hundred years. The Honorable Elijah Muhammad says you and I are the seed of Abraham, we're the descendants of Abraham. Now the preacher in the church, he tells you that the Jews are the seed of Abraham. One of them is right and one of them is wrong; either Mr. Muhammad is right and the preacher is wrong, or the preacher is right and Mr. Muhammad is wrong. This is what we are putting on the line today.

Who is the seed of Abraham? Is it this blue-eyed, blond-haired, pale-skinned Jew? Or is it the so-called Negro—you? Who is it? And what makes it so pitiful, many of our people would rather believe that the Jews are God's Chosen People than to believe that they are God's Chosen People. They would rather believe that God is going to save the Jews than believe that God is going to save them. They would rather believe that the Jew is better than anybody else. This is a Negro. Nobody else would put everybody else above him but the Negro. No one likes to place himself below everybody else but the Negro. I mean the American Negro. Remember, God said that the people would be strangers. The Jews aren't strangers. The Jews know their history, the Jews know their culture, the Jews know their language; they know everything there is to know about themselves. They know how to rob you, they know how to be your landlord, they know how to be your grocer, they know how to be your lawyer, they know how to join the NAACP and become the president—right or wrong? They know how to control everything you've got. You can't say they're lost. But the poor so-called Negro, he hasn't control over anything. He doesn't control the NAACP, he can't control the Urban League, he can't control CORE, he can't control his church, he can't control his own schools, he can't control his own businesses in his own community. He can't even control his own mind. He's lost and lost control of himself and gone astray.

But he fits the picture here that the Bible says concerning our people in the last day: "Know of a surety that thy seed shall be a stranger in a land that is not theirs, and shall serve them." And you have served the white man; he hasn't served you and me. Why, the Jew hasn't served anybody here. You are the one that's serving: "And they shall afflict them four hundred years; and also that nation, whom they shall serve, will I judge: and afterward shall they come out with great substance." Ofttimes when you say this to the so-called Negroes they'll come up and tell you that this is the Jew. But if you'll notice, when Jesus was talking to the Jews, way back here in John, he told them that they shall know the truth and it will make them free. The Jews popped up and said: "How are you going to say that we shall be made free? We have never been in bondage to anyone." Isn't that what the Jews told Jesus? Now look at it. If the Jews said to Jesus, two thousand years after Moses supposedly led the Hebrews out of bondage, that they had never been in bondage—now you know the Jews had Moses' history, they knew who Moses was—how could they stand up and tell Jesus they had never been in bondage? Not *these* things that you *call* Jews. They weren't in Egypt, *they* weren't the people that Moses led out of Egypt, and the Jews know this. But the Bible is written in such a tricky way, when you read it you think that Moses led the Jews out of bondage. But if you get a Jew in a good solid conversation today and you know how to talk to him, he'll have to admit this, that it wasn't out of Egypt's land that Moses brought them, that it wasn't out of bondage that Moses brought them—it was out of somewhere else—and where Moses really brought them is their secret, but, thanks to Almighty God, The Honorable Elijah Muhammad knows their secret, and he told it to us and we're going to tell it to you.

If the Bible said that God is going to judge that nation, the nation that enslaved His people, how would He keep from destroying His own people? The same Bible is a book of history and in the eighteenth chapter of the book of Deuteronomy, in the eighteenth verse, God told Moses: "I will raise them up a Prophet"—talking about you and me—I'll raise them up a prophet just like thee—a prophet like Moses whose mission it would be to do for you and me the same thing that Moses did back then. It would be a prophet like Moses. In fact, when you get down to Malachi, He lets it be known that just before He comes to judge that nation, the name of the prophet or messenger whom He would send among the people would be Elijah. It says: Before the coming of that great and dreadful day I shall send you Elijah and Elijah's job will be to turn the hearts of the children to the fathers and the hearts of the fathers to the children. What does this mean, turn the hearts of the children to the fathers? The so-called Negro are childlike people—you're like children. No matter how old you get, or how bold you get, or how wise you get, or how rich you get, or how educated you get, the white man still calls you what? Boy! Why, you are a child in his eyesight! And you *are* a child. Anytime you have to let another man set up a factory for you and you can't set up a factory for yourself, you're a child; anytime another man has to open up businesses for you and you don't know how to open up businesses for yourself and your people, you're a child; anytime another man sets up Schools and you don't know how to set up your own schools, you're a child. Because a child is someone who sits around and waits for his father to do for him what he should be doing for himself, or what he's too young to do for himself, or what he is too dumb to do for himself. So the white man, knowing that here in America all the Negro has done—I hate to say it, but it's the truth—all you and I have done is build churches and let the white man build factories.

You and I build churches and let the white man build schools. You and I build churches and let the white man build up everything for himself. Then after you build the church you have to go and beg the white man for a job, and beg the white man for some education. Am I right or wrong? Do you see what I mean? It's too bad but it's true. And it's history. So it shows that these childlike people—people who would be children, following after the white man—it says in the last day that God will raise up Elijah, and Elijah's job will be to turn the hearts of these children back toward their fathers. Elijah will come and change our minds; he'll teach us something that will turn us completely around. When Elijah finds us we'll be easy to lead in the wrong direction but hard to lead in the right direction. But when Elijah gets through teaching the Lost Sheep, or the Lost People of God, he'll turn them around, he'll change their minds, he'll put a board in their back, he'll make them throw their shoulders back and stand upright like men for the first time. It says he'll turn the hearts of these children toward their fathers and the hearts of the fathers toward the children. This is something that The Honorable Elijah Muhammad is doing here in America today. You and I haven't thought in terms of our forefathers. We haven't thought of our fathers. Our fathers, brother, are back home. Our fathers are in the East. We're running around here begging the Great White Father. You never hear of black people in this country talking or speaking or thinking in terms of connecting themselves with their own kind back home. They are trying to make contact with the white man, trying to make a connection with the white man, trying to connect, trying to make a connection with a kidnapper who brought them here, trying to make a connection with, actually, the man who enslaved them. You know that's a shame—it's pitiful—but it's true.

The Honorable Elijah Muhammad says that when Elijah comes, the Book says when Elijah comes, what Elijah will do is to teach these people the truth. And the truth that Elijah will teach the people would be so strong it will make all that other stuff that the preachers are talking about sound like a fairy story. Elijah will open the people's eyes up so wide that from then on a preacher won't be able to talk to them—and this is really true. Do you know, people have come to Muhammad's Mosque and no matter whether they believed in what Mr. Muhammad was saying or not they never could go back and sit in church. This is true. What The Honorable Elijah Muhammad does is to turn on the light, and when he turns on the light it enables us to see and think for ourselves. He shows us that what the white man has taught us concerning history has actually been a distortion. He's never given you and me true facts about history, neither about himself nor about our people. You know I read a book one day called *The Four Cities of Troy*. You can go to the library, some libraries, and check it out. What was this based on? To show you what a *liar* the white man is. When I say liar: you have white people who are scientists and keep truth in their own circles, and they never let you—they never let the masses—know anything about this truth that they keep in the circle. They got something else that they invent and put out for the masses to believe, but they themselves keep knowledge in a circle. So in this particular book it pointed out that some archaeologists were delving in the ruins of the ancient city of Troy, and it's the practice of archaeologists to dig, so in digging down into the ruins of Troy they dug deeper than they intended to, and they ran into the ruins of another city that had been there so much longer than this city of Troy that it had gone down beneath the sands of time, and they had built this city of Troy on top of it. When these archaeologists were delving into the ruins of the ancient city they learned that there were ruins of a city more ancient than that. So they started frantically digging into that one and dug some more until they found another one and before they got through digging they had dug down and they had discovered that civilizations in that area had been there so far back into history that at different times in history some of the cities had been destroyed, had become completely covered up with sand and dirt, until another people came along and didn't even know it was there and built another civilization on top of it. This happened four different times—to give you some idea of what the white man knows concerning the length of time man has been on this earth—and still that white man would jump up in your face and try to make you believe that the first man was made six thousand years ago named Adam. And a lot of Negroes will want to know what you are talking about—Adam—that's what God called him—God took some dirt and breathed on it and told Adam, "Come forth," and there he was. Now you know that's a shame. It's all right to believe when you were a little baby that God made a little doll out of the sand and mud and breathed on it and that was the first man. But here it is 1962 with all this information floating around in everybody's ears—you can get it free. Why, you should open up your minds and your heads and your hearts and realize that you have been led by a lie. Today it's time to listen to nothing but naked, undiluted truth. And when you know the truth, as Jesus said: "The truth will make you free." Abraham Lincoln won't make you free. Truth will make you free. When you know the truth, you're free. Also you have your archaeologists, anthropologists, other forms of historians who agree that they don't know how long man has been on earth, but they do know that man has been on earth longer than six thousand years. They know that man was not made just six thousand years ago. They know this now but a long time ago they didn't know it. There was a time when they believed that a man had fewer ribs than a woman. You can believe that because they said that God made Eve from one of Adam's ribs—so Adam had a rib missing. And they actually ran around here believing for many years that man had one less rib, and they were shook up when they got into the science of anatomy and discovered that man—all his ribs were there! They began to wonder then what happened in the Bible?

How long has man been here? In the Bible in the first chapter of Genesis and the twenty-sixth verse, after God had made everything else it says: "And God said, Let us make man." Let me write what God said here on the board . . . Look what God said, brothers. I don't think you ever *looked* at this. It says: "And God said, Let us make man." The key word here is what? Yes, what does "us" mean? More than one. Who was God talking to? If God was all by Himself, no one was there but Him, who was He talking to when He said, "Let us make man"? Who was there with God who was about to help Him make this man? When God was getting ready to make the sun He didn't say, "*Let us* make some sun!" He said, "Let there be light." And here is the sun, a ball of fire 2,679,785 miles in circumference, 853,000 miles in diameter, 14,072 degrees hot, and God said, "Let there be," and that big ball of fire popped up there in the universe, with no help. Now you know something is wrong. It should be harder to make that than a man: a huge ball of fire 2,679,785 miles in circumference, 14,072 degrees hot—that's a whole lot of heat. And God said, "Let there be," and that just jumped up in the universe. He didn't ask for no help: "Let there be this and let there be that." He had so much power that everything He wanted came into existence; as soon as He said "be," there it was. But when He got to man something happened, someone else was there, wasn't there? That's something to think about. We'll let you think about it for a minute . . .

The white man's world is a newer world than the black man's world. If this man said that they were about to make man, and he said we would make him how—in our image—this shows you that there's somebody there with him—in *our* likeness—there is somebody there with him. "Let us make man in our image, in our likeness. Let us make him look like us. He won't be the same as we are, he'll be in our image." That's God talking, right? He's talking to somebody. You know, I'm thankful to Allah for raising up The Honorable Elijah Muhammad and making us see these things that we could never see before. The birth of the white race has always been a secret. The Honorable Elijah Muhammad says that the birth of the white race is shrouded in the story of Adam. The story of Adam hides the birth of the white race, and because you and I have never been taught to look into a thing and analyze a thing we took the story of Adam exactly as it was. We thought that God made *a* man named Adam six thousand years ago. But today The Honorable Elijah Muhammad teaches us that that man, Adam, was a white man; that before Adam was made the black man was already here. The white man will even tell you that, because *he* refers to Adam as the first one. He refers to the Adamites as those who came from that first one. He refers to the pre-Adamites as those who were here before Adam. Right or wrong? Those people who were here before Adam. And he always refers to these people as "aborigines," which means what? BLACK FOLK!!!! You never find a white aborigine. Aborigines are called natives, and they're always dark-skinned people. You and I are aborigines. But you don't like to be called an aborigine; you want to be called an American. Aborigine actually means, "from the beginning." It's two Latin words, "ab" meaning "from"; "origine" meaning "the beginning"; and aborigine is only the term applied to those dark-skinned people who have been on this earth since the beginning of the universe. You know that's going way back. What do you mean, since the beginning of the universe?

The Honorable Elijah Muhammad teaches us that, just as we pointed out a moment ago, the black man has been here a long time. He never has had a beginning. But the white man has never had a knowledge of the history of the black man. It's like a father and a son. If the father is fifty years old and the son is only ten, the father knows everything there is to know about his son because he was here before his son was born; the son only knows what has happened during his own ten years. He only knows what went on before his arrival from what his father tells him. It's the same way with the black man and the white man: the black man's been here a long time, but the white man has been here a short time. Now the white man only knows about himself, what he's been told, and he hasn't been told anything. He came to himself up in the caves of Europe, and he can't get any information that goes beyond the cave. And since you and I fell into his trap and were made deaf, dumb, and blind by him, we don't have access now to any information that the white man doesn't know about. So we think that the beginning of the white man meant the beginning of everything, us too. We're not aware that we were here before he was made. Can you understand that? The Honorable Elijah Muhammad teaches us that sixty-six trillion years ago—trillion, how much is trillion? Not hundreds, nor thousands, nor millions, nor billions, but sixty-six trillion years ago—the black man was here. We have the sun which is the center of the universe; 36,000,000 miles from the sun is the planet we call Mercury, and 67,200,000 miles from the sun is the planet called Venus, and 93,000,000 miles from the sun is the planet here that you and I live on called Earth, 141,500,000 miles out here is a planet called Mars, and 483,000,000 miles from the sun is a planet called Jupiter, 886,000,000 miles from the sun is a planet called Saturn, and on down the road a piece are a couple more planets. So right here this planet that you and I live on called Earth, that rotates around the sun, The Honorable Elijah Muhammad teaches us that sixty-six trillion years ago our people were living on this planet: the black man was living on this planet. But in those days it was larger than it is now, and the planet Mars, that was off here beyond it, had an effect upon our planet then in the same manner that the moon affects us today. At that time there was no moon up there. Where was the moon? The moon was down here, the moon was part of this planet, the moon and this planet were one planet, and the black man was living here then. He was a scientist, he was a wise black man. Black men have always been wise, black men have always been the wisest beings in the universe, and among these beings, black beings, there is one who is supreme; he is referred to as the Supreme Being, do you understand?

So The Honorable Elijah Muhammad tells us that a wise black scientist, sixty-six trillion years ago, began to argue with the other scientists because he wanted the people of Earth to speak a certain language, and since they wouldn't agree he wanted to destroy civilization. So this scientist drove a shaft into the center of the Earth and filled it with high explosives and set it off. He was trying to destroy civilization; he was trying to destroy the black man. But you can't destroy the black man; the black man can't destroy himself. The black man has the most powerful brain in the universe. So there is no intelligence more powerful than the intelligence of the black man. And because of this the black man can't even create a *thought* that would destroy him. He is indestructible. You can blow up everything and the black man will still be here. You just can't get away from him, brother. So The Honorable Elijah Muhammad said he filled the Earth, the planet, with high explosives and set it off, and when it was exploded the piece that you and I today call the moon was tossed out here into space and it rotated around the Earth. It still rotates around the Earth; it came from the Earth; it was blasted right off the Earth. And as it was blasted right off the Earth, it turned over and over and over and all of the water that was on it stayed with the Earth. So that the piece that was blasted out there has no water on it today, and because it has no water on it it has no civilization on it, has no life on it. You can't have life where there's no water; water is the source of life. Where there's no water there's no life; where there's no life there's no civilization. Can you understand that? So this dead piece, called the moon by us today, turning over and over and over, lost all of its water, all of the water coming with *this* piece. The Honorable Elijah Muhammad told us that this piece, that the Earth, that we remained on, shifted, dropped thirty-six thousand miles in the pocket that we remained in. And as it dropped and all of the water came with it, that left a situation in which today the Earth that we now live on weighs six sextillion tons. The weight of it is six sextillion tons. And as it makes its way around the sun, the strong power of the sun's rays striking the equator causes the planet to turn on its own axis at the speed of 1037⅓ miles per hour. And he teaches us that the square mileage of the Earth is 196,940,000 square miles which means only 57,255,000 square miles of land stuck up out of 139,685,000 square miles of water. Three-fourths of the Earth's surface is covered with water. Part of the water that left the moon is here with the Earth. So you say since it's the natural law for water to seek its own level, why doesn't it overrun the land? The Honorable Elijah Muhammad says that as the Earth speeds around the sun turning on its axis 1037⅓ miles per hour it creates gravity and the strong attracting power of the sun pulls on the waters of the Earth, drawing them up into the Earth's atmosphere in a fine mist that the naked eye can hardly detect. As this water gathers into the Earth's atmosphere it then distills and comes back to Earth. When it gets heavier than the atmosphere in which it is, it distills and comes back to the Earth in the form of water, rain, hail, or snow. All of the water that you see coming out of the sky went up into the sky. Everything that's coming down on the Earth got up there by leaving the Earth. Do you understand? And he teaches us that it comes back down in the form of hail or rain or snow or whatever else you have, depending upon the temperature of the current atmosphere that it was in. He says that at night the gravitational pull of the moon takes over, and, because the power of the moon is not as great as that of the sun, once the attracting power of the sun is absent at night the moon takes over, but since it can't pull the waters up like the sun does, it still has that magnetic pull and it causes the waves that you see out there on the ocean to churn. It is the moon that does that; the moon makes the waves go up and down. It never lets them level out. If they leveled out the water would overrun the land. It also causes the shifting of the tide. This is the pull of the moon upon the waters of the Earth. If it weren't for the attracting powers of the sun and the moon upon the Earth, the waters would overrun the land and drown out civilization. All of this was done by man himself, not some Mystery God. A black man set this up. And you and I have been running around in the trap that the white man put us in, thinking that the only one who can do anything is a Mystery God and what the Mystery God doesn't do the white man does.

The Honorable Elijah Muhammad says that all the time that this was going on there was no white man. The white man was nowhere on the scene. He says that when the moon was blasted away and we came along with the Earth, one tribe was in fact destroyed. Prior to the time that the explosion took place there were thirteen tribes. In the explosion set off sixty-six trillion years ago the thirteenth tribe was destroyed, and then all of the time down through the wheel of time since then there were twelve tribes until six thousand years ago. And six thousand years ago, a scientist named Yacub created another tribe on this Earth.

Understand, prior to the time the explosion took place, there were thirteen tribes, but the thirteenth tribe was destroyed in that explosion and then six thousand years ago another tribe came on the scene. It was made different from all of the twelve tribes that were here when it arrived. A new tribe, a weak tribe, a wicked tribe, a devilish tribe, a diabolical tribe, a tribe that is devilish by nature. So that before they got on the scene, The Honorable Elijah Muhammad says that when we came with the Earth, the oldest city on the Earth is the Holy City, Mecca, in Arabia. Mecca is the oldest city on Earth. Mecca is the city that is forbidden. No one can go there but the black man. No one can go there but the Muslims. No one can go there but the believer. No one can go there but the righteous. And at Mecca are kept the records of history that go on back to the beginning of time. He says that fifty thousand years ago another scientist named Shabazz became angry with the scientists of his day. He wanted to bring about a tougher people. He wanted the people to undergo a form of life that would make them tough and hard, and the other scientists wouldn't agree with him. So this scientist named Shabazz took his family and wandered down into the jungles of Africa. Prior to that time no one lived in the jungles. Our people were soft; they were black but they were soft and delicate, fine. They had straight hair. Right here on this Earth you find some of them look like that today. They are black as night, but their hair is like silk, and originally *all* our people had that kind of hair. But this scientist took his family down into the jungles of Africa, and living in the open, living a jungle life, eating all kinds of food had an effect on the appearance of our people. Actually living in the rough climate, our hair became stiff, like it is now. We undertook new features that we have now. The Honorable Elijah Muhammad says that the only hair that the black man has today that looks now like it looked prior to fifty thousand years ago is your and my eyebrows. Right here, you notice, all Negroes have straight—I don't care how nappy their hair is—they have straight eyebrows. When you see a nappy-hair-eyebrowed Negro [chuckle] you got somebody. But all of this took place back in history, and everything The Honorable Elijah Muhammad teaches is based on history. Now then, where does the white man come in?

The Honorable Elijah Muhammad says that the wise black man who was a master of science never wrote his history like it is written today, of the past. The wise black man in that day wrote his history in the future. The Honorable Elijah Muhammad says that the circumference of the Earth is 24,896 miles, approximately 25,000 miles. So when he says the wise black man of the East writes history a year for every mile, he writes history to last for 25,000 years—not in the past, but in the future. He says that on this Earth there are wise black men who can tune in and tell what's going to happen in the future just as clear—they can see ahead just as clear—as they can see in the past. And every 25,000 years he says that civilization reaches its peak, or reaches its perfection. At this time the wise black man can hear a pin drop anywhere on the planet Earth. And they sit down and write history to last for 25,000 years. After this history expires they put it in a vault at the Holy City, Mecca, and write a new history. This has been going on and on and on. So, in the year one of the cycle in which we now live, he says that in the East there are twenty-four wise men. They're spoken of in the Bible as twenty-four elders or twenty-four prophets or twenty-four scientists or twenty-four imams. Twelve of them are major and twelve of them are minor. So The Honorable Elijah Muhammad says that these twenty-three men are called together by this one, which makes twenty-four. And these twenty-four, these twenty-three presided over by the twenty-fourth, are spoken of in the Book of Revelation where John said he had a vision in heaven where there was a throne, and around the throne were twenty-four seats and on the seats sat twenty-four elders. These twenty-four elders are called angels. They are actually twenty-four wise black men who live right here on this Earth, but no one knows who they are. At the end of every 25,000 years this one calls all of them into conference, and they sit down at the Holy City, Mecca, and he informs them that the history of the past 25,000 years has expired and it's time to write a new history. So these twenty-four, these scientists, begin to tune in on the population of the planet Earth and he says that back in his day—at that time there were five billion people on this Earth—all of them black, not a white man in sight—five billion people—not a white man in sight, so he says that when these twenty-four scientists begin to tune in, they look down through the wheel of time. They can tell not only what the people on this Earth are thinking, but they can tell what their children are thinking, what the unborn children's children are thinking, what the unborn children's children's children are thinking. They can look right down through the wheel of time and tell minute-by-minute, hour-by-hour, day-by-day, week-by-week, month-by-month, year-by-year, for 25,000 years exactly what is going to take place. And they discovered that in the year 8400 to come it would register that among five billion black people, seventy percent would be satisfied and thirty percent would be dissatisfied. And out of that thirty percent would be born a wise black scientist named Yacub, and Yacub would teach among these thirty percent dissatisfied from whom he would come, and create a new race, start a new world, and a new civilization that would rule this Earth for six thousand years to come. So they brought these findings back to the king and they were put in a book. And by the way, that which is written to last for 25,000 years is called the Holy Koran.

The Honorable Elijah Muhammad said that this was put into the history and then when the year 8400 came, Yacub was born. When Yacub reached the age of six years he was playing in the sand one day with two pieces of metal, two pieces of steel, at which time he discovered what is known as the law of magnetism: that unlike attracts and like repels. Two objects that are alike repel each other like two women repel each other, but man and woman attract each other. Unlike attracts and like repels. Yacub discovered this. So Yacub knew that all he had to do was make a man unlike any other man on this Earth and because he would be different he would attract all other people. Then he could teach this man a science called tricknology, which is a science of tricks and lies, and this weak man would be able to use that science to trick and rob and rule the world. So Yacub turned to his uncle and said, "When I grow up I'm going to make a man who will rule you." And Yacub's uncle said, "What can you make other than that which will cause bloodshed and wickedness in the land?" And Yacub pointed to his head and said, "I know that which you know not." Yacub was born with a determined idea to make this man because it had been predicted 8400 years prior to his birth that he would be born to do this work. So he was born with this idea in him, and when his uncle realized that this was he about whom it had been prophesied his uncle submitted. The Honorable Elijah Muhammad said that Yacub went to school in the East; he studied the astronomical sciences, mathematical sciences, and the germination of man. He discovered that in the black man there are two germs. In the black man there's a brown man. In the black man, or the black germ, which is a strong germ, there's a weak germ, a brown germ. Yacub was the first one to discover this and Yacub knew that by separating that brown one from the black one, and then by grafting the brown one from the black one so that it became lighter and lighter, it would eventually reach its lightest stage which is known as white. And when it got to that stage it would be weak, and because it was weak it would be susceptible to wickedness. And then Yacub could take that weak man that he made and teach him how to lie and rob and cheat and thereby become the ruler of all of the rest of the world.

So The Honorable Elijah Muhammad teaches us that Yacub began to preach at the age of sixteen. He began to preach all over Arabia in the East. He preached among the thirty percent who were dissatisfied and got many of them to follow him. As they began to listen to Yacub's teachings and believe them, his teachings spread, his followers grew, and it created confusion in the land. So The Honorable Elijah Muhammad says that so much confusion came into existence over there that they threw Yacub's followers in jail, and as fast as they would throw them in jail they taught more people. So the teachings spread in jail. Finally Yacub was put in jail, under an alias. And one day, The Honorable Elijah Muhammad says, the thing began to get out of hand and the authorities went to the king and told him that they couldn't control these people, but that they had the leader of the people in jail right now, and the king said, "Take me to him."

And when the king went to the jail where Yacub was, he greeted Yacub with "As-Salaam-Alaikum, Mr. Yacub"—I know you're Mr. Yacub—and Yacub said, "Wa-Alaikum-Salaam"—I am Yacub! And the king said, "Look, I came to make an agreement with you. I know that you are the one that it is written or predicted would be on the scene in this day and would create a new race, and there is nothing we can do to stop you. But in order for us to have peace we want to make an agreement with you. In order to stop the confusion and for there to be some peace in the land, we want you to agree to take all who will follow you and exile yourselves out on an island in the Aegean Sea."

Yacub told them, "I'll go. But you've got to give me everything that I will need to bring into existence a new civilization. You've got to give me everything I'll need. You've got to supply me with everything I need for the next twenty years." And The Honorable Elijah Muhammad says that the king agreed with Yacub, the government of that day agreed to supply Yacub and his followers with everything they needed for twenty years. And he says that he gets this from the Bible where it says Jacob wrestled with the angel. Jacob was Yacub, and the angel that Jacob wrestled with wasn't God, it was the government of that day. "Angel" only means "a power," or somebody with power. When a man has his wings clipped, you say that he has lost his power, lost his position. So wings only mean a position of power entrapped him. So when it says Jacob wrestled with an angel, "angel" is only used as a symbol to hide the one he was really wrestling with. Jacob was wrestling with the government of that day. He made the government of that day give him everything he needed to last him and his followers for twenty years, just like The Honorable Elijah Muhammad is telling the government of this day that they've got to give us everything that we need in our own separate territory to last us for twenty to twenty-five years. You say, well, The Honorable Elijah Muhammad teaches us that Yacub agreed, the government agreed, Yacub took all of his followers down to the sea. The Honorable Elijah Muhammad says that Yacub took 59,999 of his followers down to the seaside, with himself making 60,000. He piled them in boats and took them out to an island in the Aegean Sea called Pelan. In the Bible it's called Patmos. When you read in the Book of Revelation where John, on the island of Patmos, heard the word of the Lord, that is Yacub. What was John doing on the island of Patmos? John was Yacub. John was out there getting ready to make a new race, he said, for the word of the Lord. What was the word of the Lord? The word was that in the year 8400 a new man would be made, a new race would be made. And when Yacub and his followers got out there his followers realized that Yacub was wiser than any man of his day, and they recognized him as a god; he was a god to them. So when you get to the place in the Bible where it says, "And God said, 'Let us make man,'" that was Yacub too, not the Supreme Being. It wasn't the Supreme Being who made the sun who said, "Let us make man." When the Supreme Being made the sun he said, "Let there be light." He said He was supreme, He was independent, He needed no help, no associates. But when it came to making a man, that god said, "Let us make man." He didn't speak with independence, because there were two different gods. God the Supreme Being made the light. His word is "be"; that's how He makes things. But Yacub, who was a lesser god, said to 59,999 of his followers, "Let us make man, let us make a man in our image, in our likeness. We're going to make a white man." It was Yacub talking: "Make him in our image and in our likeness, and give him dominion over the fowl of the air and the fish of the sea and the creatures of the land. And we'll call him Adam." It's only a name for the white man. The white man has taken mastery over the air, his airplanes rule the sky, his submarines and ships rule the sea, his armies rule the land. This was the man that was made six thousand years ago and the purpose for making him was so he could rule the world for six thousand years. That's the white man.

The Honorable Elijah Muhammad says that first thing Yacub did was to get his ministers, doctors, nurses, and cremators together. He gave them the laws because he had to set up a birth control law. He told the doctors whenever two black ones come to him to get married to stick a needle in their veins, take some blood, and go back and tell them that their blood doesn't match so that they can't marry. He also said when a black one and a brown one come, let them get married, or if two brown ones come let them get married. Then he told the nurse nine months after they're married, when you're ready to deliver their child, if it's a black child, put a needle in its brain and feed it to a wild animal or give it to the cremator. Let it be destroyed. But if it's a brown child, take that child to the mother and tell her that this is going to be a great man when he grows up because he's lighter than the others. Tell her that the child you destroyed was an angel baby and it went up to heaven to prepare a place for her when she dies. Same old lie they tell you today—when a little baby dies they tell you it went to heaven. When a baby dies he goes to the same place a man goes when he dies—right down into the ground. Is that right or wrong? So The Honorable Elijah Muhammad has taught us that Yacub right there set up his birth control law. Within two hundred years they had killed off all of the black babies on the island. Everything black on the island had been destroyed. And then Yacub only lived 150 years. But he left laws and rules and regulations behind, for his followers to go by. And after they had destroyed all of the black on the island of Pelan, they began to work on the brown germ. They saved the yellow and destroyed the brown, because you see in the black there's brown and in the brown there's yellow. Can you see how it goes? The darkest one always has a lighter one in it. So in the black man there's a brown man, in the brown man there's a yellow man, in the yellow man there's what? A white man. Oh yes. Getting weaker all the time. So it took two hundred years to destroy the black. And then they worked on the brown for two hundred years. And in two hundred years all the brown was destroyed and all they had on the island of Pelan was a yellow or mulatto-looking civilization. And then they went to work on it and began to destroy it. So that after six hundred years of destruction on the island of Pelan, they had grafted away the black, grafted away the brown, grafted away the yellow, so that all they had left was a pale-skinned, blue-eyed, blond-haired thing that you call a man. But actually the Bible calls him the devil. That's the devil that the Bible is talking about: old Lucifer, Satan, or the serpent. Because the lighter they got, the weaker they got. As they began to get lighter and lighter they grew weaker and weaker. Their blood became weaker, their bones became weaker, their minds became weaker, their morals became weaker. They became a wicked race; by nature wicked. Why by nature?

The Book says concerning the devil: "He was conceived in inequity and born in sin." What does this mean? At the outset the nurses had to kill the little black babies, but after a while it got so that the mother, having been brainwashed, hated that black one so much she killed it herself. Killed it herself, and saved the light one. And right on down for six hundred years. In order for the white one to come into existence, the darker one was always murdered, murdered, MURDERED! This went right into the nature of the child that was being born. The mother wanted a light baby when the child was being conceived. This went right into the baby. The mother hated black when the child was being conceived. This went right into the baby. So that at the end of the six hundred years, after planting the seed of inequity right into the brain, right into the mind, right into the heart, right into the nature of these people, by the time they got the white man, they had someone who by nature hated everything that was darker than he was. Why, they had to murder off the black to get to the brown. They had to murder off the brown in order to get to the yellow. They had to murder off the black, brown, and yellow in order to get to the white. And right to this very day the white man *by nature* wants to murder off the black, brown, and yellow. You don't have to teach him to kill the black man. He does it for sport. He does it for kicks. He does it because it's his nature to do it. Do you understand that?

So in six hundred years now they got a devil on the scene, a blue-eyed devil, blond-haired. Oh yes, they were out here on the island of Pelan. Yacub was dead. Yacub was their father but he never saw them. They never saw him. Yacub was their god. When the Bible says no man had seen God, that's what it means. No white man has seen their god. None of them saw Yacub because Yacub only lived to be 150 years old. This doesn't mean that no man can see God the Supreme Being. Why, the Book of Revelation says when He comes every eye will see Him. So The Honorable Elijah Muhammad says after these devils got grafted—now we're not going to call them white any more. We call them what they are. White, that's their color, but devil, that's what they are. These aren't white people. You're not using the right language when you say the white man. You call it the devil. When you call him devil you're calling him by his name, and he's got another name—Satan; another name—serpent; another name—snake; another name—beast. All these names are in the Bible for the white man. Another name—Pharaoh; another name—Caesar; another name—France; French; Frenchman; Englishman; American; all those are just names for the devil.

So after they were out there six hundred years, after they were made and grafted and Yacub was dead, then they packed up their bags and made it back to civilization. Yacub had left them some laws to go by. He left them a science called "tricknology": how to divide and conquer. Yacub told these people in his book: "All you got to do to take over the world is lie. Go back among the black people. Take your woman and send her to the black man's woman and let her lie about the neighbor across the street. And then send another woman to that woman to lie on this woman to that woman. And when they get through spreading those lies and they all start fighting and killing one another, you tell them to let you be the mediator." This is the trick the white man used. It all comes from Yacub. You see, he's an underdog. He's a minority, and the only way a minority can rule a majority is to *divide* the majority. This is the trick that the white man was born to execute among dark mankind here on this Earth. Yacub said, "When you go back among them, lie about them to each other, and when they start fighting, ask them to let you be the mediator. And as soon as you become the mediator then you're the boss." The white man has done this trick everywhere. Here in America to the Indians. He sent one priest to the Indians in New York and another priest to the Indians in Pennsylvania and both of them would tell lies to both Indians, and the Indians who had never been at war with each other would start beating the tom-toms, the war drums, and then as they got ready to fight the priest would run in and say, "Let me be the mediator."

So he told the New York Indians, you just move out to Minnesota; and the Pennsylvania Indians, you move out to Oklahoma. That would leave the whole states of New York and Pennsylvania for the white man. You see how he does it? He's all over the world. He's a mediator. He's an instigator and a mediator. He instigates division and dissension and as soon as they start fighting one another he says, "OK, I'll settle it." If you don't think so look all over the world right now. Every place on this earth you have a division: South Korea-North Korea, South Vietnam-North Vietnam. Right or wrong? He is the one that makes this decision. He doesn't let anybody get together, but when it comes to his kind he's united. United States means all white people are united. United States of Europe, or European Common Market—they want to get together. But when you start talking about a United States of Asia, or a United States of Africa, why he says, "Oh no, too many different languages [chuckle]. You all don't have anything in common." You see how he does it? He always discourages unity among others but he encourages unity among his own kind. "United We

Stand," that doesn't mean *you*. That means the white man. The white man is the one who stands united.

So The Honorable Elijah Muhammad says that these devils went back into Arabia. When they got there they started telling lies, started confusion, and in six months' time they had turned heaven into hell. Oh yeah, they had so much fighting going on among our people, brother, it became hell. We never did fight each other we loved each other, we were in harmony with each other. And when these devils came back into our midst they turned our paradise into a hell. So it was taken to the king and the king looked into the book and said, "Why, these are Yacub's people." He said, "They were made to do what they're doing and the only way to have peace is to get rid of all of them. Put them all to death." So the king gave the order for all of the devils to be rounded up. And by devils I mean all those blue-eyed, blond-haired, white things. He gave orders for them to be rounded up there in the East, and they were rounded up. They were rounded up and taken down to the edge of the Arabian Desert. They were stripped naked, stripped of everything except their language. The Honorable Elijah Muhammad says that we put lambskin aprons around their waists to hide their nakedness. We put them in chains and marched them across the hot sands of the Arabian Desert. This is what the black man did to the white man, brothers. This is what the gods did to the devils. Actually, if you think I don't know what I'm talking about, those of you who are Masons, you go through this and don't understand it. When you go in, they put a lambskin apron around your waist. They put you in what's called the "cable tow." Right or wrong? And then they make you jump up and down on an electric mat. Make you take off your shoes and put the juice in the mat and make you jump up and down. Why? What are they getting at? That's all a sign of what happened to the white man six thousand years ago. It just doesn't have anything to do with you, but you're supposed to be walking on hot sands when you jump up and down. Right or wrong? You've all been in some of that stuff. They tell you that's crossing the hot sand. And if you walk up to a Negro Mason and you ask him, "When you crossed the hot sand were you walking or riding?" he'll say, "I was walking." He's a fool. Because he was riding. He was riding horseback. He was riding on a camel. It was the white man that was in chains. It was the white man that had the apron around him. It was the white man that was walking the white sand. We walked them at high noon. We wouldn't even let them walk at night. We stopped at night. And you know how hot the sun and the sands are in Arabia. We expected the white man to die when we were running him out of the East. But that fool lived, brother [chuckle]. He lived. A lot of them died on the desert. And I might come back—all of this is tied up in the Masonic ritual. When a man gets initiated into the higher degrees of that order he goes through this. They put on the chains, they put on the aprons, and they darken him up and pretend to be driving him across. Then when he gets up to the top order in those degrees, they tell him what it means. The white man, they tell the white man what it means: a white Shriner, a white Mason, what it means. A Negro never learns what it means. But it actually points back toward the time when the white man, who is the devil, or Adam, as they say, was cast out of the Garden. When the Bible says Adam sinned and was cast out of the Garden, this is what is meant. And an angel was put at the East gate to keep him from coming back in. When the white man was run out of the East by the Muslims six thousand years ago into the caves of Europe, the people called Turks were put there at the Straits of the Dardanelles, with swords, and any old devil that they caught trying to come back across the water—WHOP!!!—off went his head. The Book tells you that the angel had a flaming sword, and any time any of them tried to come back across they were put to death.

The Honorable Elijah Muhammad says that the white man went down into the caves of Europe and he lived there for two thousand years on all fours. Within one thousand years after he had gotten there he was on all fours, couldn't stand upright. You watch an old cracker today. Crackers don't walk upright like black people do. Every time you look at them, they're about to go down on all fours. But those who have had some education, they straighten up a little bit because they're taught how to straighten up. But a black man can be the most dumb, illiterate thing you can find anywhere, and he still walks like a million dollars because by nature he's upright, by nature he stands up. But a white man has to be stood up. You have to put a white man on the square. But the black is born on the square.

Can we prove it? Yes. You notice in the East, dark people carry things on their heads, don't they? Just throw it up there and walk with it, showing you they have perfect poise, perfect balance. It just comes natural to them. You and I lost our poise. We, you, can't even wear a hat on your head, hardly, today [chuckle]. The Honorable Elijah Muhammad says that within one thousand years after the white people were up in the caves they were on all fours. And they were living in the outdoors where it's cold, just as cold over there as it is outside right now. They didn't have clothes. So by being out there in the cold their hair got longer and longer. Hair grew all over their bodies. By being on all fours, the end of their spine begin to grow. They grew a little tail that came out from the end of their spine . . . Oh yes, this was the white man, brother, up in the caves of Europe. He had a tail that long. You ever notice that anything that walks on all fours has a tail? That which straightens up doesn't have a tail, because when you get down, you see, you just make that spine come right on out. And just like a dog, he was crawling around up there. He was hairy as a dog. He had a tail like a dog. He had a smell like a dog. And nothing could get along with him but another dog. The Honorable Elijah Muhammad says that all the beasts up in Europe wanted to kill the white man. Yeah, they tried to kill the white man. They were after the white man. They hated the white man. So, he says, what the white man would do, he'd dig a hole in the hill, that was his cave. And his mother and his daughter and his wife would all be in there with the dog. The only thing that made friends with the white man was the dog. Everything else hated him. He'd sit outside of the cave at night in a tree with rocks in his hand, and if any beast came up and tried to get in the cave at his family, he'd throw rocks at it, or he'd have a club that he'd swing down and try to drive it away with it. But the dog stayed in the cave with his family. It was then that the dog and the white man amalgamated. The white woman went with the dog while they were living in the caves of Europe. And right to this very day the white woman will tell you there is nothing she loves better than a dog. They tell you that a dog is a man's best friend. A dog isn't a black man's best friend. God is the black man's best friend. But a dog is the white man's best friend. They lived in that cave with those dogs and right now they got that dog smell. They got that dog . . . They are dog lovers. A dog can get in a white man's house and eat at his table, lick out of his plate. They'll kiss the dog right on the nose and think nothing of it. You're not a dog kisser. You don't see black people kissing or rubbing noses with dogs. But little white children will hug dogs and kiss dogs and *eat* with dogs. Am I right or wrong? You-all have been inside their kitchens cooking their food, and making their beds, you *know* how they live. The dog will live right in the white man's house, better than you can; you try and break your way in there and they'll put a rope around your neck [chuckle], but the dog has got free run of the whole house. He's the white man's best friend.

The Honorable Elijah Muhammad says that they lived up there for two thousand years, and at the end of two thousand years the scientists in the East, realizing that it was originally predestined that the white race would rule for six thousand years, and that they had already lost two thousand years in the caves of Europe, sent a prophet up there, from Mecca, to teach the white race, the race of devils, how to become civilized again, and become upright, and come back and rule the way they had originally been meant to. The name of that prophet was Moses. Moses never went down into Egypt. Moses went into the caves of Europe and civilized the white man. It was Moses who raised the devil from a dead level to a perpendicular and placed him on the square. Moses taught the white man how to cook his food. Moses taught the white man how to build a house for himself. He taught the white man also some of the tricknology that Yacub had originally meant for him, and it was Moses who put the white man back on the road toward civilization. He told him that he was supposed to rule for six thousand years, but that much of the time had already been lost, and at the end of time one would come who would destroy the whole white race. Moses taught them this. And this is why when the Jews, two thousand years later, were looking for the Messiah, they thought that Jesus was the Messiah and they put him to death because they knew when the Messiah came he was going to destroy that whole race of devils. The Jews knew this, so they put him to death thinking that they could stop him from destroying them. But actually, they made a mistake because Jesus two thousand years ago wasn't the Messiah. Their time wasn't up two thousand years ago. Their time would not be up until two thousand years later, the day and time that we're living in right now.

So, brothers and sisters, my time has expired. I just wanted to point out that the white man, a race of devils, was made six thousand years ago. This doesn't mean to tell you that this implies any kind of hate. They're just a race of devils. They were made six thousand years ago, they were made to rule for six thousand years, and their time expired in the year 1914. The only reason God didn't remove them then was because you and I were here in their clutches and God gave them an extension of time—not *them* an extension of time, but they received an extension of time to give the wise men of the East the opportunity to get into this House of Bondage and "awaken" the Lost Sheep. Once the American so-called Negroes have been awakened to a knowledge of themselves and of their own God and of the white man, then they're on their own. Then it'll be left up to you and me whether we want to integrate into this wicked race or leave them and separate and go to our own. And if we integrate we'll be destroyed along with them. If we separate then we have a chance for salvation. So on that note, in the name of Allah, and His Messenger The Honorable Elijah Muhammad, I bring my talk to a close, "As-Salaam-Alaikum."

With your hands outstretched in this manner, follow silently in the closing Muslim prayer:

In the name of Allah, the Beneficent, the Merciful,
All praise is due to Allah, the Lord of the Worlds,
The Beneficent, the Merciful,
Master of this Day of Judgment in which we now live,
Thee do we serve and Thee do we beseech for thine aid.
Guide us on the right path,
The path upon which Thou hast bestowed favors,
Not the path upon which Thy wrath is brought down

Nor of those who go astray after they have heard Thy teaching.
Say: He Allah is one God
Allah is He upon whom nothing is independent but
Upon whom we all depend.
He neither begets nor is He begotten and none is like Him.
I bear witness there is none to be served but Allah,
And I bear witness that The Honorable Elijah Muhammad is
His True Servant and Last Apostle . . . Amen

18. God in Black Theology

JAMES H. CONE

The reality of God is presupposed in black theology. Black theology is an attempt to analyze the nature of that reality, asking what we can say about the nature of God in view of God's self-disclosure in biblical history and the oppressed condition of black Americans.

If we take the question seriously, it becomes evident that there is no simple answer to it. To speak of God and God's participation in the liberation of the oppressed of the land is a risky venture in any society. But if the society is racist and also uses God-language as an instrument to further the cause of human humiliation, then the task of authentic theological speech is even more dangerous and difficult.

It is *dangerous* because the true prophet of the gospel of God must become both "anti-Christian" and "unpatriotic." It is impossible to confront a racist society, with the meaning of human existence grounded in commitment to the divine, without at the same time challenging the very existence of the national structure and all its institutions, especially the established churches. All national institutions represent the interests of society as a whole. We live in a nation which is committed to the perpetuation of white supremacy, and it will try to exterminate all who fail to support this ideal. The genocide of the Amerindian is evidence of that fact. Black theology represents that community of blacks who refuse to cooperate in the exaltation of whiteness and the degradation of blackness. It proclaims the reality of the biblical God who is actively destroying everything that is against the manifestation of black human dignity.

Because whiteness by its very nature is against blackness, the black prophet is a prophet of national doom. He proclaims the end of the "American Way," for God has stirred the soul of the black community, and now that community will stop at nothing to claim the freedom that is three hundred and fifty years overdue. The black prophet is a rebel with a cause, the cause of over twenty-five million American blacks and all oppressed persons everywhere. It is God's cause because God has chosen the blacks as God's own people. And God has chosen them not for redemptive suffering but for freedom. Blacks are not elected to be Yahweh's suffering people. Rather we are elected because we are oppressed against our will and God's, and God has decided to make our liberation God's own undertaking. We are elected to be free now to do the work for which we were called into being—namely, the breaking of chains. Black theologians must assume the dangerous responsibility of articulating the revolutionary mood of the black community. This means that their speech about God, in the authentic prophetic tradition, will always move on the brink of treason and heresy in an oppressive society.

The task of authentic theological speech is *difficult* because all religionists in society claim to be for God and thus for humankind. Even executioners are for God. They carry out punitive acts against certain segments of society because "decent" citizens need protection against undesirables. That is why blacks were enslaved and Amerindians exterminated—in the name of God and freedom. That is why today blacks are forced into ghettos and shot down like dogs if they raise a hand in protest.

When George Washington, Thomas Jefferson, Lyndon Johnson, Richard Nixon, and other "great" Americans can invoke the name of God at the same time that they are shaping society for whites only, then black theology knows it cannot approach the God-question too casually. It must ask, "How can we speak of God without being associated with oppressors?" White racism is so pervasive that oppressors can destroy the revolutionary mood among the oppressed by introducing a complacent white God into the black community, thereby quelling the spirit of freedom.

Therefore if blacks want to break their chains, they must recognize the need for going all the way if liberation is to be a reality. The white God will point to heavenly bliss as a means of detouring blacks away from earthly rage. Freedom comes when we realize that it is against our interests, as a self-determining black community, to point out the "good" elements in an oppressive structure. *There are no assets to slavery!* Every segment of society participates in black oppression. To accept the white God, to see good in evil, is to lose sight of the goal of the revolution—the destruction of everything "masterly" in society. "All or nothing" is the only possible attitude for the black community.

Must We Discard God-Language?

Realizing that it is very easy to be co-opted by the enemy and the enemy's God-language, it is tempting to discard all references to God and seek to describe a way of living in the world that could not possibly be associated with "Christian" murderers. Some existentialist writers—Camus and Sartre—have taken this course, and many black revolutionaries find this procedure appealing. Reacting to the ungodly behavior of white churches and the timid, Uncle Tom approach of black churches, many black militants have no time for God and the deadly prattle about loving your enemies and turning the other cheek. Christianity, they argue, participates in the enslavement of black Americans. Therefore an emancipation from white oppression means also liberation from the ungodly influences of white religion.

This approach is certainly understandable, and the merits of the argument warrant a serious investigation. As black theologians seeking to analyze the meaning of black liberation, we cannot ignore this approach. Indeed, it is quite intellectually tempting. Nevertheless two observations are in order at this juncture.

(1) Black theology affirms that there is nothing special about the English word "God" in itself. What is important is the dimension of reality to which it points. The word "God" is a symbol that opens up depths of reality in the world. If the symbol loses its power to point to the meaning of black liberation, then we must destroy it. Black theology asks whether the word "God" has lost its liberating power. Must we say that as a meaningful symbol the word "God" is hopelessly dead and cannot be resurrected?

Certainly black theology realizes that, when a society performs ungodly acts against the poor in the name of God, there may come a time when the oppressed might have to renounce all claims to that kind of "faith" in God in order to affirm authentic faith in God. Sometimes because of the very nature of oppressed existence, the oppressed must define their being by negating everything oppressors affirm, including belief in the God of oppressors. The oppressed must demonstrate that all communications are cut off. In Camus's words:

There is, in fact, nothing in common between a master and a slave; it is impossible to speak and communicate with a person who has been reduced to servitude.[1]

Oppressed and oppressors cannot possibly mean the same thing when they speak of God. The God of the oppressed is a God of revolution who breaks the chains of slavery. The oppressors' God is a God of slavery and must be destroyed along with the oppressors. The question then, as black theology sees it, is not whether blacks believe in God, but whose God?

(2) In response to those inclined to discard God-language, black theology also believes that the destiny of blacks is inseparable from the religious dimensions inherent in the black community. Theologically, one way of describing this reality is to call it general revelation. This means that all human beings have a sense of the presence of God, a feeling of awe, and it is precisely this experience that makes them creatures who always rebel against domestication. The black community is thus a religious community, a community that views its liberation as the work of the divine.

It is important to note that every significant black liberation movement has had its religious dimensions. Black liberation as a movement began with the pre-Civil War black churches which recognized that Christian freedom grounded in Jesus Christ was inseparable from civil freedom. That is why black preachers were the leaders in the struggle for the abolition of slavery, and why southern slave owners refused to allow the establishment of independent black churches in the south. It is true, however, that the post-Civil War black church lost its emphasis on civil freedom and began to identify Christianity with moral purity. But this does not mean that religion is irrelevant altogether; it only means that religion unrelated to black liberation is irrelevant.

To try to separate black liberation from black religion is a mistake, because black religion is authentic only when it is identified with the struggle for black freedom. The influence of Marcus Garvey, Elijah Muhammed, Malcolm X, and Martin Luther King, Jr., demonstrates the role of religion in the black community.

It is not the task of black theology to remove the influence of the divine in the black community. Its task is to interpret the divine element in the forces and achievements of black liberation. Black theology must retain God-language despite its perils, because the black community perceives its identity in terms of divine presence. Black theology cannot create new symbols independent of the black community and expect blacks to respond. It must stay in the black community and get down to the real issues at hand ("cutting throats" to use LeRoi Jones's phrase) and not waste too much time discussing the legitimacy of religious language.

The legitimacy of any language, religious or otherwise, is determined by its usefulness in the struggle for liberation. That the God-language of white religion has been used to create a docile spirit among blacks so that whites could aggressively attack them is beyond question. But that does not mean that we cannot kill the white God, so that the presence of the black God can become known in the black-white encounter. The white God is an idol created by racists, and we blacks must perform the iconoclastic task of smashing false images.

Hermeneutical Principle for the Doctrine of God

Every doctrine of God is based on a particular theological methodology. For instance, Karl Barth's theological point of departure is the word of God as revealed in the man Jesus. We know who God is, according to Barth, because we know who Christ is. To look for the knowledge of God other than in Christ is to look in the wrong place, and thus end up constructing images which reflect human pride rather than divine revelation. "The knowledge of God occurs in the fulfillment of the revelation of His Word by the Holy Spirit."[2]

Paul Tillich, on the other hand, does not share Barth's kerygmatic emphasis. His theological methodology is a "method of correlation," in which he seeks to relate the changeless gospel to changing cultural situations. Culture, according to Tillich, is indispensable for God-talk.

Relying heavily on existential philosophy and its analysis of the human condition (a condition best described by the word "estrangement"), Tillich describes God as being-itself, which provides the only answer to human estrangement from self and neighbor. Because being-itself is free from the threat of nonbeing or nothingness, it is the source of human courage—the ability to affirm being in spite of the presence of nonbeing. Therefore "God" is a symbolic word pointing to the dimension of reality which is the answer to the human condition.

Inasmuch as the perspective of black theology differs from that of both Barth and Tillich, there is also a difference in its approach to the doctrine of God. The point of departure of black theology is the biblical God as related to the black liberation struggle. It asks, "How do we *dare* speak of God in a suffering world, a world in which blacks are humiliated because they are black?" This question, which occupies the central place in our theological perspective, forces us to say nothing about God that does not participate in the emancipation of black humanity. God-talk is not Christian-talk unless it is *directly* related to the liberation of the oppressed. Any other talk is at best an intellectual hobby, and at worst blasphemy.

There are, then, two hermeneutical principles which are operative in the black theology analysis of the doctrine of God.

(1) The Christian understanding of God arises from the biblical view of revelation, a revelation of God that takes place in the liberation of oppressed Israel and is completed in the incarnation, in Jesus Christ. This means that whatever is said about the nature of God and God's being-in-the-world must be based on the biblical account of God's revelatory activity. We are not free to say anything we please about God. Although scripture is not the only source that helps us to recognize divine activity in the world, it cannot be ignored if we intend to speak of the Holy One of Israel.

(2) The doctrine of God in black theology must be of the God who is participating in the liberation of the oppressed of the land. This hermeneutical principle arises out of the first. Because God has been revealed in the history of oppressed Israel and decisively in the Oppressed One, Jesus Christ, it is impossible to say anything about God without seeing him as being involved in the contemporary liberation of all oppressed peoples. The God in black theology is the God of and for the oppressed, the God who comes into view in their liberation. Any other approach is a denial of biblical revelation.

New Wine in New Wineskins

Because black theology is the theology of black liberation, it must break with traditional theological speech when that speech softens the drive for black self-determination. It cannot run the risk of putting "new wine into old wineskins" (Mark 2:22). When Jesus used the phrase, he was referring to the kingdom of God and its relationship to the conventional Judaism of his time.

When black theologians analyze the doctrine of God, seeking to relate it to the emerging black revolution in America, they must be especially careful not to put this new wine (the revelation of God as expressed in black power) into old wineskins (white folk-religion). The black theology view of God must be sharply distinguished from white distortions of God. This does not mean that black theology rejects white theology entirely. Unfortunately, this cannot be done, for oppression always means that the communication skills of an oppressed community are determined to a large degree by the oppressors. That is precisely the meaning of oppression! Because black theologians are trained in white seminaries, and white thinkers make decisions about the structure and scope of theology, it is not possible for black religionists to separate themselves immediately and completely from white thought.

When Jesus spoke of the gospel as new wine, it did not mean a total rejection of Judaism. What he meant was that the revolutionary message could not be restricted to the possibilities available in the old structure.

Similarly, because our knowledge of Christianity came from white oppressors, the black theology view of God is in part dependent on white theologians, but this does not mean white theologians set the criteria for black theology. Liberation means that the oppressed must define the structure and scope of reality for themselves; they do not take their cues from oppressors. If there is one brutal fact that the centuries of white oppression have taught blacks, it is that whites are incapable of making any valid judgment about human existence. The goal of black theology is the destruction of *everything* white, so that blacks can be liberated from alien gods.

The God of black liberation will not be confused with a bloodthirsty white idol. Black theology must show that the black God has nothing to do with the God worshiped in white churches whose primary purpose is to sanctify the racism of whites and to daub the wounds of blacks. Putting new wine in new wineskins means that the black theology view of God has nothing in common with those who prayed for an American victory in Vietnam or who pray for a "cool" summer in the ghetto.

The refusal of black theology to put new wine in old wineskins also means that it will show that the God of the black community cannot be confused with the God of white seminaries. With their intellectual expertise, it is inevitable that white scholars fall into the racist error of believing that they have the right to define what is and what is not orthodox religious talk. Because they have read so many of their own books and heard themselves talk so often, it is not surprising that they actually believe most of the garbage they spout out about God. They therefore think that all authentic God-talk must meet their approval before it can be called theology. But black theology rejects their standards, for we know they speak for oppressors, and thus will inevitably analyze the nature of God in the interests of white society as a whole.

Black theology must also be suspicious of so-called white revolutionary theologians. What is most disturbing about their self-proclaimed identification with black power is their inability to let *us* speak for ourselves. They still insist on defining what black power is, and not only in private conversations but also in print. And to make it worse, they invariably miss the whole point of black power. They should know by now that, in view of white brutality against blacks and church participation in it, no white person who is halfway sensitive to black self-determination should have the audacity to speak for blacks. That is the problem! *Too many whites think they know how we feel about them.* If whites were really serious about their radicalism in regard to the black revolution and its theological implications in America, they would keep silent and take instructions from blacks. Only blacks can speak about God in relationship to their liberation. And those who wish to join us in this divine work must be willing to lose their white identity—indeed, destroy it.

Black theology also rejects any identification with the "death of God" theology. The death-of-God question is a white issue which arises out of the white experience. Questions like "How do we find meaning and purpose in a world in which God is absent?" are questions of an affluent society. Whites may wonder how to find purpose in their lives, but our purpose is forced upon us. We do not want to know how we can get along without God, but how we can survive in a world permeated with white racism.

God Is Black

Because blacks have come to know themselves, as *black*, and because that blackness is the cause of their own love of themselves and hatred of whiteness, the blackness of God is the key to our knowledge of God. The blackness of God, and everything implied by it in a racist society, is the heart of the black theology doctrine of God. There is no place in black theology for a colorless God in a society where human beings suffer precisely because of their color. The black theologian must reject any conception of God which stifles black self-determination by picturing God as a God of all peoples. Either God is identified with the oppressed to the point that their experience becomes God's experience, or God is a God of racism.

As Camus has pointed out, authentic identification

> [Is not] a question of psychological identification—a mere subterfuge by which the individual imagines that it is he himself who is being offended. . . . [It is] identification of one's destiny with that of others and a choice of sides.[3]

Because God has made the goal of blacks God's own goal, black theology believes that it is not only appropriate but necessary to begin the doctrine of God with an insistence on God's blackness.

The blackness of God means that God has made the oppressed condition God's own condition. This is the essence of the biblical revelation. By electing Israelite slaves as the people of God and by becoming the Oppressed One in Jesus Christ, the human race is made to understand that God is known where human beings experience humiliation and suffering. It is not that God feels sorry and takes pity on them (the condescending attitude of those racists who need their guilt assuaged for getting fat on the starvation of others); quite the contrary, God's election of Israel and incarnation in Christ reveal that the *liberation* of the oppressed is a part of the innermost nature of God. Liberation is not an afterthought, but the essence of divine activity.

The blackness of God means that the essence of the nature of God is to be found in the concept of liberation. Taking seriously the Trinitarian view of the Godhead, black theology says that as Creator, God identified with oppressed Israel, participating in the bringing into being of this people; as Redeemer, God became the Oppressed One in order that all may be free from oppression; as Holy Spirit, God continues the work of liberation. The Holy Spirit is the Spirit of the Creator and the Redeemer at work in the forces of human liberation in our society today. In America, the Holy Spirit is black persons making decisions about their togetherness, which means making preparation for an encounter with whites.

It is the black theology emphasis on the blackness of God that distinguishes it sharply from contemporary white views of God. White religionists are not capable of perceiving the blackness of God, because their satanic whiteness is a denial of the very essence of divinity. That is why whites are finding and will continue to find the black experience a disturbing reality.

White theologians would prefer to do theology without reference to color, but this only reveals how deeply racism is embedded in the thought forms of their culture. To be sure, they would *probably* concede that the concept of liberation is essential to the biblical view of God. But it is still impossible for them to translate the biblical emphasis on liberation to the black-white struggle today. Invariably they quibble on this issue, moving from side to side, always pointing out the dangers of extremism on both sides. (In the black community, we call this "shuffling.") They really cannot make a decision, because it has already been made for them.

How scholars would analyze God and blacks was decided when black slaves were brought to this land, while churchmen sang "Jesus, Lover of My Soul." Their attitude today is no different from that of the bishop of London who assured slaveholders that:

> *Christianity, and the embracing of the Gospel, does not make the least Alteration in Civil property, or in any Duties which belong to Civil Relations; but in all these Respects, it continues Persons just in the same State as it found them. The Freedom which Christianity gives, is a Freedom from the Bondage of Sin and Satan, and from the dominion of Man's Lust and Passions and inordinate Desires; but as to their outward Condition, whatever that was before, whether bond or free, their being baptized and becoming Christians, makes no matter of change in it.*[4]

Of course white theologians today have a "better" way of putting it, but what difference does that make? It means the same thing to blacks. "Sure," as the so-called radicals would say, "God is concerned about blacks." And then they would go on to talk about God and secularization or some other white problem unrelated to the emancipation of blacks. This style is a contemporary white way of saying that "Christianity . . . does not make the least alteration in civil property."

In contrast to this racist view of God, black theology proclaims God's blackness. Those who want to know who God is and what God is doing must know who black persons are and what they are doing. This does not mean lending a helping hand to the poor and unfortunate blacks of society. It does not mean joining the war on poverty! Such acts are sin offerings that represent a white way of assuring themselves that they are basically "good" persons. Knowing God means being on the side of the oppressed, becoming *one* with them, and participating in the goal of liberation. *We must become black with God!*

It is to be expected that whites will have some difficulty with the idea of "becoming *black* with God." The experience is not only alien to their existence as they know it to be, it appears to be an impossibility. "How can whites become black?" they ask. This question always amuses me because they do not really want to lose their precious white identity, as if it is worth saving. They know, as everyone in this country knows, blacks are those who say they are black, regardless of skin color. In the literal sense a black person is anyone who has "even one drop of black blood in his or her veins."

But "becoming black with God" means more than just saying "I am black," if it involves that at all. The question "How can white persons become black?" is analogous to the Philippian jailer's question to Paul and Silas, "What must I do to be saved?" The implication is that if we work hard enough at it, we can reach the goal. But the misunderstanding here is the failure to see that blackness or salvation (the two are synonymous) is the work of God, not a human work. It is not something we accomplish; it is a gift. That is why Paul and Silas said, "Believe in the Lord Jesus and you will be saved."

To *believe* is to receive the gift and utterly to reorient one's existence on the basis of the gift. The gift is so unlike what humans expect that when it is offered and accepted, we become completely new creatures. This is what the Wholly Otherness of God means. God comes to us in God's blackness, which is wholly unlike whiteness. To receive God's revelation is to become black with God by joining God in the work of liberation.

Even some blacks will find this view of God hard to handle. Having been enslaved by the God of white racism so long, they will have difficulty believing that God is identified with their struggle for freedom. Becoming one of God's disciples means rejecting whiteness and accepting themselves as they are in all their physical blackness. This is what the Christian view of God means for blacks.

The Love and Righteousness of God

The theological statement "God is love" is the most widely accepted assertion regarding the nature of God. All theologians would agree that it is impossible to speak of the Christian understanding of God without affirming the idea of love as essential to the divine nature. Anders Nygren's *Agape and Eros*[5] is the classic treatment of the subject, and he shows, perhaps conclusively, that *agape* is inseparable from the authentic Christian view of God. When religionists deviated from the *agape* motif, the result was always a distortion of the authentic Christian conception of God.

Though religionists have agreed that love is indispensable to the Christian view of God's nature, there has been much disagreement on how the idea of the *wrath* of God is reconciled with the love of God.

Marcion was one of the first to face this problem head-on. According to him, it is impossible to reconcile the Old Testament idea of the righteous God with the New Testament idea of the God of love.[6] The concept of law (*nomos*) is a complete denial of love (*agape*). Marcion's solution was to insist that the gospel of Christ is completely new and thus has nothing to do with the concept of righteousness (including wrath) as presented in the Old Testament. This led him to posit two Gods, the Creator God of the Old Testament who stressed obedience to the law of righteousness, and the Redeemer God of the New Testament who is the "good" God, the God of love. Interpreting Marcion's view, Nygren writes:

The message of Christ is marked by the spontaneous love and mercy of the Highest God, shown to strangers, unmotivated and uncalculated. In the Old Testament, on the other hand, man's relation to God is dominated by the idea of retribution, of reward and punishment.[7]

It was to be expected that the church would reject Marcion's view: the early Christian community did not understand its existence as being completely new in the sense of negating the God of the Old Testament. The early Christians believed that they were the authentic continuation of the old Israel, not its denial. Jesus, therefore, did not destroy the Old Testament; he fulfilled it.

Although the church rejected Marcion's sharp dichotomy between the Old Testament view of God's righteousness and the New Testament view of God's love in Jesus Christ, there is still much confusion about the precise relationship between the two "symbols"[8] when applied to God's nature. The most common procedure is to emphasize God's love as the dominant motif of Christianity and then interpret God's righteousness in the light of it. But this approach fails to take seriously the concept of God's righteousness and tends to make God's love mere sentimentality. By emphasizing the love of God to the exclusion of a meaningful encounter of God's righteousness, we could argue that the approach is basically Marcionite, except that Marcion was more honest. Marcion claimed that the idea of righteousness is *basic* to the Old Testament view of God, and he was right in this. He further suggested that the idea of love as revealed in Christ is a negation of the Old Testament view of righteousness, and he was wrong in this.

Most religionists, although rejecting the Marcion dichotomy, proceed to analyze the concept of the love of God without relating it to God's righteousness. Marcion's position presents us with two alternatives. Either we agree with him and his view of the two Gods, Righteousness and Love, or we affirm the basic oneness of God's righteousness and love, and that means that God's love is inexplicable without equal emphasis on God's righteousness and vice versa. Contemporary theology seems to want to have its cake and eat it too—that is, reject the Marcionite view and also accept a view of love that ignores righteousness, and that is not possible.

Gordon Kaufmann's work, *Systematic Theology: A Historicist Perspective*, seems to be open to this criticism. Particularly concerned about protecting the idea of love in God's nature, Kaufmann says that it is improper to speak of the "wrath" of God as an expression of the being of God. Love is essential, but the idea of wrath is an expression of human disobedience and can be understood only by looking at human nature, not God's nature:

The wrath of God is a symbol more appropriate to discussion of the nature (and plight) of man than God. . . . The man hanging on the cross . . . reveals God's nature as long-suffering love, not vengeance or wrath in any sense. . . . I Hence, in our direct exposition of the doctrine of God such symbols as "wrath" would only be misleading and should be avoided: God reveals himself as love and faithfulness, and this it is that we must seek to grasp here.[9]

Black theology agrees that the idea of love is indispensable to the Christian view of God. The exodus, the call of Israel into being as the people of the covenant, the gift of the promised land, the rise of prophecy, the second exodus, and above all the incarnation reveal God's self-giving love to oppressed humanity.

We do not read far in the biblical tradition without recognizing that the divine-human fellowship is to be understood exclusively in terms of what God does for humankind and not what humankind does for itself or for God. That is why Nygren is correct in describing

God's *agape* as the "initiation of the fellowship with God,"[10] and why it is appropriate for Barth to emphasize the complete freedom of God in the divine-human encounter. If the incarnation means anything in Christian theology, it must mean that "God so loved the world that he gave his only Son, that whoever believes in him should not perish but have eternal life" (John 3:16).

The love of God is the heart of the Christian gospel. As the writer of I John puts it, "God is love" (4:8, 16). Commenting on the theological implications of this phrase, C. H. Dodd writes:

> *To say "God is love" implies that all His activity is loving activity. If He creates, He creates in love; if He rules, He rules in love; if He judges, He judges in love. All that He does is the expression of His nature which is—to love.*[11]

Black theology, then, asks not whether love is an essential element of the Christian interpretation of God, but whether the love of God itself can be properly understood without focusing equally on the biblical view of God's righteousness. Is it possible to understand what God's love means for the oppressed without making *wrath* an essential ingredient of that love? What could love possibly mean in a racist society except the righteous condemnation of everything racist? Most theological treatments of God's love fail to place the proper emphasis on God's wrath, suggesting that love is completely self-giving without any demand for obedience. Bonhoeffer called this "cheap grace":

> *Cheap grace means grace as a doctrine, a principle, a system. It means forgiveness of sins proclaimed as a general truth, the love of God taught as the Christian "conception" of God.*[12]

The difficulty with Kaufmann's view and others like his is not so much his explicit statements but their false implications. By removing wrath as a symbol of the nature of God, his interpretation weakens the central biblical truth about God's liberation of the oppressed from oppressors. A God without wrath does not plan to do too much liberating, for the two concepts belong together. A God minus wrath seems to be a God who is basically not against anything. All we have to do is behave nicely, and everything will work out all right.

Such a view of God leaves us in doubt about God's role in the black-white struggle. Blacks want to know whose side God is on and what kind of decision God is making about the black revolution. We will not accept a God who is on everybody's side—which means that God loves everybody in spite of who they are, and is working (through the acceptable channels of society, of course) to reconcile all persons to the Godhead.

Black theology cannot accept a view of God which does not represent God as being for oppressed blacks and thus against white oppressors. Living in a world of white oppressors, blacks have no time for a neutral God. The brutalities are too great and the pain too severe, and this means we must know where God is and what God is doing in the revolution. There is no use for a God who loves white oppressors *the same as* oppressed blacks. We have had too much of white love, the love that tells blacks to turn the other cheek and go the second mile. What we need is the divine love as expressed in black power, which is the power of blacks to destroy their oppressors, here and now, by any means at their disposal. Unless God is participating in this holy activity, we must reject God's love.

The interpretation of God's love without righteousness also suggests that white "success" is a sign of God's favor, of God's love. Kaufmann's view is open to the ungodly assumption that all is well with the way whites live in the world, because God loves them, and their material success is the evidence. But according to black theology, it is blasphemy to say that God loves white oppressors unless that love is interpreted as God's wrathful activity against them and everything that whiteness stands for in American society. If the wrath of God is God's almighty no to the yes of human beings, then blacks want to know where the no of God is today in white America. We believe that the black community's no as expressed in the black revolution is God's no, showing God's rejection of oppressors and acceptance of the oppressed.

Kaufmann's view also suggests that there is knowledge of God as God is *in se*. Theologically this seems impossible. We can know God only in relationship to the human race, or more particularly in God's liberating activity in behalf of oppressed humanity. The attempt to analyze God independently of God's liberating work is analogous to the theological attempt to understand human nature *before* the fall. The fall itself renders such knowledge impossible: there is no way to get behind the human condition as we know it to be.

The limitation of human knowledge is equally true in regard to God as God is *in se*. We are not permitted to transcend our finiteness and rise to a vision of God unrelated to the human condition. If this is true, what merit is there in saying that God's wrath is not a part of the divine nature? If God is a God of the oppressed of the land, as the revelation of Christ discloses, then wrath is an indispensable element for describing the scope and meaning of God's liberation of the oppressed. The wrath of God is the love of God in regard to the forces opposed to liberation of the oppressed.

Love without righteousness is unacceptable to blacks: this view of God is a product of the minds of enslavers. By emphasizing the complete self-giving of God in Christ, without seeing also the content of righteousness, oppressors could then demand that the oppressed do likewise. If God freely enters into self-donation, then in order to be godlike we must give ourselves to our oppressors in like manner. If God has loved us in spite of our revolt against God, then to be like God we too must love those who revolt against or enslave us. For blacks this would mean letting whites crowd us into ghettos where rats and filth eat away at our being, and not raising a hand against them.

This view of love places no obligation on white oppressors. The existing laws of society protect them, and their white skins are badges of acceptance. In fact, they are permitted to do whatever they will against blacks, assured that God loves them as well as the ones they oppress. Love means that God will accept white oppressors, and blacks will not seek reprisal.

Black theology rejects this view, saying that those who oppress others are in no position to define what love is. How could white scholars know that love means turning the other cheek? They have never had to do so. Only those who live in an oppressed condition can know what their love-response ought to be to their oppressors. Their oppressors certainly cannot answer that question for them!

This means that all white intellectual disputation about blacks and God is a religious lie. If oppressors themselves, who claim to be followers of the love-ethic, would actually practice what they preach, then the oppressed condition would no longer exist. There is something demonic about whites who have the protection of the state but advise blacks to go the second mile for them. They have not moved even an inch for blacks: how can they claim to be speaking from a common perspective called Christianity?

It takes a special kind of reasoning to conclude that God's love means that God is no respecter of persons in a society filled with hate, where some think they have the right to define the course of human history for all. Ungodly in their very relationship to blacks, they want to tell us what God's love means. There is only one explanation for this attitude. They are white and can think only in white thought-patterns, even in reference to God. How else do we explain that the white theological view of God's love invariably complements or shores up outrageous socio-political structures that want blacks to be complacent and obedient to white enemies? Can they really expect blacks to take them seriously?

The oppressor's view of God's love is rejected by black theologians because they represent a people that shares Frantz Fanon's feelings about the world:

> All the native has seen in his country is that they can freely arrest him, beat him, starve him: and no professor of ethics, no priest has ever come to be beaten in his place, nor to share their bread with him. As far as the native is concerned, morality is very concrete; it is to silence the settler's defiance, to break his flaunting violence—in a word, to put him out of the picture.[13]

Black theology will accept only a love of God which participates in the destruction of the white oppressor. With Fanon, black theology takes literally Jesus' statement, "the last will be first, and the first last." Black power "is the putting into practice of this sentence."[14]

Blacks cannot adhere to a view of God that will weaken their drive for liberation. This means that in a racist society, we must insist that God's love and God's righteousness are two ways of talking about the same reality. Righteousness means that God is addressing the black condition; love means that God is doing so in the interests of both blacks and whites. The blackness of God points to the righteousness of God, as well as to the love of God.

Paul Tillich, in another connection, has placed a similar emphasis. Though he refuses to say that wrath is a part of God's being, it is to his credit that he has insisted that divine love and justice should not be separated:

> Justice is that side of love which affirms the independent right to object and subject within the love relation. [Because love is the reunion of the estranged, it] does not destroy the freedom of the beloved and does not violate the structures of the beloved's individual and social existence.[15]

This means that justice is the structure necessary for the human expression of human freedom. To be God, God must protect both the freedom and the structure of human behavior. That is why Tillich rejects sentimental misinterpretations of love as emotion, which suggest that there is a conflict between divine love and its relationship to power and justice. The three are inseparable, according to Tillich:

> It must be emphasized that it is not divine power as such which is thought to be in conflict with the divine love. The divine power is the power of being-itself, and being-itself is actual in the divine life whose nature is love. A conflict can be imagined only in relation to the creature who violates the structure of justice and so violates love itself. When this happens . . . judgment and condemnation follow. . . . Condemnation then is not the negation of love but the negation of the negation of love.[16]

What, then, can we conclude about the meaning of God's love in a racist society? Using blackness as the point of departure, black theology believes that God's love of humankind is revealed in God's willingness to become black. God's love is incomprehensible apart from blackness. This means that to love blacks God takes on black oppressed existence, becoming one of us. God is black because God loves us; and God loves us because we are black.

Righteousness is that side of God's love which expresses itself through black liberation. God makes black what humans have made white. Righteousness is that aspect of God's love which prevents it from being equated with sentimentality. Love is a refusal to accept whiteness. To love is to make a decision against white racism. Because love means that God meets our needs, God's love for white oppressors could only mean wrath—that is, a destruction of their whiteness and a creation of blackness.

For black theology love cannot be discussed in the abstract. It must be concrete because black suffering is concrete. Black suffering is whites making decisions about our place in the world, telling us what we can or cannot do in society. Love must be brought down to this level, the reality of white inhumanity against the black community. As Fanon says, "no phraseology can be a substitute for reality."[17] That is why black theology says that God's love is God's liberation of blacks as expressed in black power.

Traditional Theological Language and the Black God

One of the major tasks of black theology is that of making sense out of the traditional theological talk about God. It asks, in regard to every theological assertion, "What are its implications for the oppressed?" Or, more specifically, "Does it have any meaning in the struggle for black liberation in America?" Believing that the biblical God is made known through the liberation of the oppressed, the black theology analysis of God begins with an emphasis on God's blackness.

But now we must ask, How is the concept of the blackness of God related to such traditional divine symbols as creator, transcendence, immanence, and providence?

1. *God as Creator.* The biblical view of God as creator is expressed in the priestly assertion, "In the beginning God created the heavens and the earth" (Genesis 1:1). To speak of God as creator means that the world and everything that is *is* because of the creative will of God. In traditional theological language, God as creator expresses aseity—that is, the total independence of God from creation. God is self-existent, meaning that the source of God's existence is found in God.

In order to emphasize the absolute sovereignty of God over creation, traditional theology introduced the idea of creation out of nothing (*ex nihilo*). The purpose is to deny that God used an eternal substance (as in Plato) in the creation of the universe. The existence of an eternal substance would compromise the complete lordship of God over creation. God is fully free, Being without limitations.

Black theology is not interested in debating the philosophical and theological merits of God's aseity except as it can be related to the earthly emancipation of the oppressed. What has the idea of God's self-existence to do with the existence of the oppressed? First it is necessary to point out that the biblical view of God as creator is not a paleontological statement about the nature and origin of the universe, but a theological assertion about God and God's relationship to the oppressed of the land.

It is important to remember that the priestly narrative was put together during the Babylonian exile as an attempt to make theological sense of the history of Israel as an oppressed people. Therefore, it is impossible to remain faithful to the biblical viewpoint without seeing the doctrine of creation as a statement about God and the oppressed of the land. God as creator means that humankind is a creature; the source of its meaning and purpose in the world is not found in oppressors but in God. This view of God undoubtedly accounts for the exclusivism of Israel in a situation of political oppression.

Though white theologians have emphasized that God as creator is a statement about the divine-human relationship, they have not pointed out the political implications of this theological truth for blacks. God as creator has not been related to the oppressed in society. If creation "involves a bringing into existence of something that did not exist before,"[18] then to say God is creator means that *my being* finds its source in God. *I am black because God is black!* God as creator is the ground of my blackness (being), the point of reference for meaning and purpose in the universe.

If God, not whiteness, is the ground of my being, then God is the only source for reference regarding how I should behave in the world. Complete obedience is owed only to God, and every alien loyalty must be rejected. Therefore, as a black person living in a white world that defines human existence according to white inhumanity, I cannot relax and pretend that all is well with black humanity. Rather it is incumbent upon me by the freedom granted by the creator to deny whiteness and affirm blackness as the essence of God.

That is why it is necessary to speak of the black revolution rather than reformation. The idea of reformation suggests that there is still something "good" in the system itself, which needs only to be cleaned up a bit. This is a false perception of reality. The system is based on whiteness, and what is necessary is a replacement of whiteness with blackness. God as creator means that oppressed humanity is free to revolutionize society, assured that acts of liberation are the work of God.

2. *Immanence and Transcendence of God.*   The immanence of God means that God always encounters us in a situation of historical liberation. That is why Christianity is called a historical religion. God is not a symbol referring to the interior religious experiences of humankind. Nor is God to be thought of in the manner of the deist philosophers, who pictured God as performing the initial act of creation but refraining from any further involvement in the world. According to biblical religion, God is involved in the concrete affairs of human history, liberating the oppressed. Therefore to ask, "Who is God?" is to focus on what God is doing; and to look at what God is doing is to center on human events as they pertain to the liberation of suffering humanity.

God, then, is not that pious feeling in our hearts, nor is God a being "out there" or "up there." It is not possible to speak of the reality of the divine in scientific categories. Like the symbol transcendence, immanence is not a causal term. It refers to the depths of liberation in human society, affirming that God is never less than our experience of liberation.

The immanence of God is the infinite expressing itself in the finite. It is God becoming concrete in finite human existence. We are able to speak of the divine because the divine is revealed in the concreteness of this world. The immanence of God forces us to look for God in the world and to make decisions about the Ultimate in terms of present historical reality. We cannot postpone our decision about God or condition it in terms of a future reality. The finality of God is God's involvement in human now-experiences. For blacks this means that God has taken on blackness, has moved into the black liberation struggle.

Though black theology stresses the immanence of God, it does not deny the reality of God's transcendence. The transcendence of God prevents us from deifying our own experiences, which results in pantheism. God is neither nature nor our highest aspirations. God is always more than our experience of God. This means that truth is not limited to human capabilities. It is this reality that frees the rebel to give all for the liberation struggle without having to worry about the Western concept of winning.

When blacks say that "all is in God's hand," this should not be equated with the trite expression "We should do nothing." It should be taken to mean that blacks are now free to be for the black community, to make decisions about their existence in the world without an undue preoccupation with white ideas about "odds" (we have all the guns) or victory (you cannot win). Ultimately (and this is what God's transcendence means) black humanity is not dependent on our power to win. Despite the empirical odds, our involvement in our liberation is not pointless; it is not absurd. It refers to the depth and meaning of our being-in-the-world.

It is interesting that, although white "Christians" say they adhere to the meaning of Jesus Christ's existence in the world, they are especially concerned about "winning." The military budget of this country is evidence of this fact. When confronted with the uncompromising demands of the black community, they quickly remind us that they have all the guns, as if that fact itself is supposed to make blacks "stay in their place." Being "Christian," they should know that Jesus was crucified because he did not "stay in his place."

In fact, that is what authentic Christian existence is all about, *the refusal to stay in one's place*. Of course, this may mean physical death, but death is beside the point when one knows that there is a depth to existence that transcends death. The death and resurrection of Christ were an expression of God's transcendence—that is, human beings do not have to live on the basis of mere physical existence. They are free to transcend it, free to encounter the presence of the infinite, which transcends physical reality. This is why blacks do not have to cling to physical life as if it were the ultimate.

Like immanence, transcendence is not a special concept. God is not "above" or "beyond" the world. Rather transcendence refers to human purpose as defined by the infinite in the struggle for liberation. For blacks this means that their humanity is not defined by sociological reports and scientific studies. There is a transcendent value in blackness that makes us all human and to which blacks must appeal as ultimate. Human dignity transcends human calculation.

Whites try to tell blacks what is "best" for them in scientific terms—as if blackness were subject to white measurements. But to the surprise of whites, blacks reject their definitions, because blacks know that they are not "things" to be computerized and limited according to white predeterminations. We are *free*, free to defy the oppressor's laws of human behavior, because we have encountered the concreteness of the divine in our liberation, which has revealed to us the transcendence of our cause beyond all human definitions.

The tension between the transcendence and immanence of God is what Paul Tillich calls the risk of faith. To speak of God is to speak, on the one hand, of the presence of the infinite in the finite concrete world. On the other hand, the infinite can never be reduced to the finite. Though the infinite is not equated with finite existence, yet because human beings can encounter the infinite only in their finiteness, they must speak of the finite as if it were the ultimate. Tillich calls this "the infinite tension between the absoluteness of its claim and the relativity of its life."[19]

Relating this to black humanity, black theology interprets it to mean that our struggle for liberation is the infinite participating in the concrete reality of human existence. But because God is always more than our experience of God, the reality of God cannot be limited to a particular human experience. However, just because God is more than our encounter of the divine in a particular moment of liberation, this should not be interpreted to mean that we must qualify our assertions about God. Just the opposite. Because God is not less than our experience of the divine, we must speak with an absoluteness that does not compromise with evil, despite the relativity of our claims.

3. *Providence.*   It is difficult to talk about divine providence when men and women are dying and children are tortured. Richard Rubenstein pointed out the dangers of this concept in his excellent book *After Auschwitz*.[20] Whether or not we agree with his conclusion about the death of God, we can appreciate his analysis, based as it is on his identification with an oppressed people. Like black theology, Rubenstein refuses to affirm any view of God which contributes to the oppression of the Jewish people. If God is the Lord of history, directing the course of events toward a final goal, and if the Jews are God's elected people, then there is no way to avoid divine responsibility for the death of six million Jews in Germany, according to Rubenstein. Therefore, rather than accept a view of God that incorporates Jewish blood in the divine plan, he concludes that God is dead. The argument is cogent and certainly advances the death-of-God theology beyond white Christian views as represented in the thinking of William Hamilton and Thomas Altizer.

Rubenstein was not the first to recognize the difficulty of reconciling human suffering and divine participation in history. Without focusing on the God of history, the writer of Job recognized this problem. In more recent writing Albert Camus and the existentialists have dealt with it also. In the thinking of Camus, if God is omnipotent and permits human suffering, then God is a murderer. That is why he quotes Bakunin with approval: "If God did exist, we would have to abolish Him."

Traditional Christian theology somehow fails to take this problem seriously. Although agreeing that human suffering is a reality which appears to conflict with God's love, theologians still insist on quoting Paul with approval: "We know that in everything God works for good with those who love him, who are called according to his purpose" (Romans 8:28).

Emil Brunner's view of divine providence is perhaps representative. He begins by distinguishing between God as creator and God's providential care of the world. Avoiding both pantheism and deism, he writes:

> There is an existence which is not that of God, but is a creaturely existence, one therefore which is distinguished from the existence of God. Without a certain independent existence the creature cannot stand over against God, and if it does not do so, then it is not a creature as contrasted with the Creator. Even if we do not speak of a creatio continua we imply that even now God does not cease to create an existence distinct from His own, a manner of existence which is different from His. If this be so, then there is also an activity of God in and on this existence which is distinct from himself, in and on the world He has created, which is not the activity of the Creator, but of the Preserver, the Ruler.[21]

After distinguishing providence from God's activity as creator, Brunner proceeds to define the meaning of divine providence. Providence, he says, means that "all that is, and all that happens, takes place within the knowledge and the will of God." There is nothing that happens that does not fit into God's ultimate plan:

> All that happens is connected with the divine Purpose; all is ordered in accordance with, and in subordination to, the divine plan and the final divine purpose.[22]

If providence means what Brunner says, it is difficult, if not impossible, to avoid the conclusion that all human suffering is in accordance with the divine plan. This would mean that the death of six million Jews, the genocide of Amerindians, the enslavement and lynching of blacks, and every other inhumanity, happened "within the knowledge and will of God." Only oppressors can make such a claim.

Of course, my opponents could reply that this view of providence does not mean that God *wills* human suffering. It simply means that God permits it in order to protect human freedom. It means further that, although there is oppression in this world, God does not let humankind have the last word about human existence, but translates human evil into the divine purpose. Quoting Paul with approval, Brunner says, "I reckon that the sufferings of this present time are not worthy to be compared with the glory which shall be revealed in us" (Romans 8:18). The believer looks beyond suffering to the final goal which it must serve; compared with that promised glory, suffering does not count. Suffering becomes the way to eternal life. No human suffering is overlooked by God, and thus providence means that it is redeemable. Thus "the real solution to the problem of theodicy is redemption."[23]

Despite the emphasis on future redemption in present suffering, black theology cannot accept any view of God that even *indirectly* places divine approval on human suffering. The death and resurrection of Jesus does not mean that God promises us a future reality in order that we might tolerate present evil. The suffering that Jesus accepted and which is promised to his disciples is not to be equated with the easy acceptance of human injustice inflicted by white oppressors. God cannot be the God of blacks *and* will their suffering. To be elected by God does not mean freely accepting the evils of oppressors. The suffering which is inseparable from the gospel is that style of existence that arises from a decision to *be* in spite of non-being. It is that type of suffering that is inseparable from freedom, the freedom that affirms black liberation despite the white powers of evil. It is suffering in the struggle for liberation.

Providence, then, is not a statement about the future. It does not mean that all things will work out for the best for those who love God. Providence is a statement about present reality—the reality of the liberation of the oppressed. For blacks it is a statement about the reality of blackness and what it means in the liberation struggle against whites. As Tillich says:

Faith in providence is faith "in spite of"—in spite of the . . . meaninglessness of existence. . . . [Special providence] gives the individual the certainty that under any circumstances, under any set of conditions, the divine "factor" is active and that therefore the road to his ultimate fulfillment is open.[24]

Black theology interprets this to mean that in spite of whiteness a way is open to blackness, and we do not have to accept white definitions.

It is within this context that divine omnipotence should be interpreted. Omnipotence does not refer to God's absolute power to accomplish what God wants. As John Macquarrie says, omnipotence is "the power to let something stand out from nothing and to be."[25] Translating this idea into the black experience, God's omnipotence is the power to let blacks stand out from whiteness and to be. It is what happens when blacks make ready for the black-white encounter with the full determination that they shall have their freedom or else. In this situation, divine providence is seeing divine reality in the present reality of black liberation—no more, no less.

Notes

1. Albert Camus, *The Rebel,* trans. by Anthony Bower, Vintage Book V30 (New York: Random House, 1956), p. 283.

2. Barth, *Church Dogmatics,* vol. 2, part 1, trans. by T. H. L. Parker, W. B. Johnston, Harold Knight, J. L. M. Haire (Edinburgh: T. & T. Clark, 1957), p. 3.

3. Camus, *The Rebel,* pp. 16, 17.

4. Quoted in H. Richard Niebuhr, *The Social Sources of Denominationalism* (Cleveland: Meridian Books, 1929), p. 249.

5. Trans. by P. S. Watson (Philadelphia: The Westminster Press, 1953).

6. This follows Nygren's view of Marcion; *Agape and Eros,* pp. 316–34.

7. Ibid., p. 321.

8. I use "symbols" instead of "attributes" because I agree with Tillich and others who suggest that the phrase "attributes of God" is misleading. It suggests the idea of a property which God has. God is not an object, and thus cannot be referred to as such. "Symbol," though it has its weakness, is a better word for expressing the Being of God in the world.

9. Kaufmann, *Systematic Theology: A Historicist Perspective* (New York: Charles Scribner's Sons, 1968), p. 154.

10. Nygren, *Agape and Eros,* p. 80.

11. C. H. Dodd, *The Johannine Epistles* (New York: Harper and Brothers, 1946), p. 110.

12. Dietrich Bonhoeffer, *The Cost of Discipleship* (New York: The Macmillan Co., 1961), p. 35.

13. Frantz Fanon, *The Wretched of the Earth,* trans. by Constance Farrington (New York: Grove Press, 1963), p. 36.

14. Ibid., p. 40. Of course, Fanon was speaking in the context of decolonization.

15. Tillich, *Systematic Theology,* vol. 1 (University of Chicago Press, 1951), p. 282.

16. Ibid., p. 283.

17. Fanon, *The Wretched,* p. 36.

18. Kaufmann, *Systematic Theology,* p. 140.

19. Tillich, *Dynamics of Faith* (New York: Harper and Brothers, 1957), p. 57.

20. New York: Bobbs-Merrill Co., 1966.

21. Brunner, *The Christian Doctrine of Creation and Redemption,* trans. by Olive Wyon (Philadelphia: The Westminster Press, 1952), p. 149.

22. Ibid., p. 155.

23. Ibid., p. 183.

24. Tillich, *Systematic Theology,* vol. 1, pp. 264, 267.

25. Macquarrie, *God and Secularity* (Philadelphia: The Westminster Press, 1967), p. 123.

19. Womanist Theology: Black Women's Experience as a Source for Doing Theology, with Special Reference to Christology

JACQUELYN GRANT

Introduction

This essay is an exploration into the experiences of Black women for the purpose of providing alternative sources for doing theology.

Black theology and other third world theologies of liberation have shown through their challenge of the methodologies of classical theologies that experience of the dominant culture has been the invisible crucible for theologizing. They have demonstrated that theology is not unrelated to socio-political realities of existence; and that historically it has been used to maintain the social and political advantages of the status quo. The portrayal of the universal God was such that an affirmation of this God meant a simultaneous negation of all others' cultural perceptions of the divinity, as well as a negation of those very cultures. Nowhere was this more clear than in the area of Christian foreign missions where conversion to Christianity implicitly meant deculturalization and acceptance of the western value system on the part of Asians, Africans, and Latin Americans. Upon conversion, one had to withdraw from indigenous ways of imaging the divine reality, and embrace foreign, western ways which often served to undergird oppressive religious, social and political structures.

This is true not only in the foreign missions field but also in the western world; it is reflected in the ways in which oppressors deal with oppressed people within their own territory. We see this with respect to third world people in the first world context as well as with respect to women.

An illustration emerging out of Black theology and Feminist theology will make the point. Theologians in both these theological camps propose an alternative understanding, for example, of Christian love.

James Cone in an early work makes a distinction between a non-threatening love of many Christians and the radical love of Jesus which demands justice.

"Womanist Theology: Black Women's Experience as a Source for Doing Theology, with Special Reference to Christology" by Jacquelyn Grant. Reprinted with permission from *The Journal of Interdenominational Theological Center*, 13, Spring 1986, Atlanta, GA.

There is no place in Christian theology for sentimental love—love without risk or cost. Love demands all, the whole of one's being. Thus, for the black [person] to believe the Word of God about [God's] love revealed in Christ, he/she must be prepared to meet head-on the sentimental "Christian" love of whites, which would make him/her a nonperson.[1]

Cone insists that one cannot practice Christian love and at the same time practice racism. He argues:

It seems that whites forget about the necessary interrelatedness of love, justice, and power when they encounter Black people. Love becomes emotional and sentimental. This sentimental, condescending love accounts for their desire to "help" by relieving the physical pains of the suffering blacks so they can satisfy their own religious piety and keep the poor powerless. But the new blacks, redeemed in Christ, must refuse their "help" and demand that blacks be confronted as persons. They must say to whites that authentic love is not "help," not giving Christmas baskets, but working for political, social, and economic justice, which always means a redistribution of power. It is a kind of power which enables the blacks to fight their own battles and thus keep their dignity. "Powerlessness breeds a race of beggars."[2]

Black people do not need a love which functions contrary to the establishment of Black personhood. This understanding of love was just recently affirmed by Black theologians (lay and clergy, professional and non-professional) in Southern Africa in their challenge to the church through *The Kairos Document*. They cautioned, "we must also remember that the most loving thing we can do for both the oppressed and for our enemies who are oppressors is to eliminate the oppression, remove the tyrants from power and establish a just government for the common good of all the people."[3] Here, love is not defined in the interest of those who wish to maintain the present status quo. But it is defined from the point of view of those on the underside of history—the victims of the oppressors' power.

In a similar vein, feminists challenge traditional understandings of love. Valerie Saiving Goldstein expresses her suspicions of traditional theological works in the following way:

I am no longer certain as I once was that, when theologians speak of "man," they are using the word in its generic sense. It is, after all, a well-known fact that theology has been written almost exclusively by men. This alone should put us on guard, especially since contemporary theologians constantly remind us that one of man's strongest temptations is to identify his own limited perspective with universal truth.[4]

Lifting up the Christian notion of sin and love, Goldstein suggests that it would be equally unsatisfactory to impose universal understanding on those concepts. The identification of these notions with self-assertion and selflessness respectively, functions differently in masculine experience and feminine experience. She explains further:

Contemporary theological doctrines of love have, I believe, been constructed primarily upon the basis of masculine experience and thus view the human condition from the male standpoint. Consequently, these doctrines do not provide an adequate interpretation of the situation of women—nor, for that matter, of men, especially in light of certain fundamental changes now taking place in our own society.[5]

Because of their feminine character, for women love takes the form of nurturing, supporting and servicing their families. Consequently, if a woman believes

> the theologians, she will try to strangle other impulses in herself. She will believe that, having chosen marriage and children and thus being face to face with the needs of her family for love, refreshment, and forgiveness, she has no right to ask anything for herself but must submit without qualification to the strictly feminine role.[6]

For women, too, the issue is one of personhood—are women to deny who they are in order to be saved?

Goldstein then argues that when experience in theology is scrutinized, we will discover that because it has been synonymous with masculine experience, it is inadequate to deal with the situation of women.

In other words, Black theologians and feminist theologians have argued that the universalism which classical theologians attempt to uphold represents merely the particular experiences of the dominant culture. Blacks identify that experience as White experience; and women identify it as male experience. The question then is, if universalism is the criterion for valid theology, how is such a universalism achieved?

What I will be exploring here is how Black women's experiences can provide some insights into this question. In doing so, Black women not only join Blacks and feminists in their challenge of theology but they also provide an internal critique for Black men as well as for White women. In this paper, I will focus primarily upon Black women's experience as related to the development of feminist theology. (In a rather limited way, I have addressed the issue of Black women's experiences and Black theology in an article entitled "Black Theology and the Black Woman."[7] That subject certainly has not been exhausted, and shall be treated in more substantive ways in the future.)

But here I am interested in engaging feminist theology with reference to its constructive efficacy for Black women given the peculiarities of their experiences. The results will be the beginnings of a theology from a Black woman's perspective with special reference to Christology.

In order to create a common starting point, let's begin with a synopsis of the basic tenets of Feminist theology. First, Feminist theology seeks to develop a *wholistic theology*. Feminist theology rejects the traditional forms of oppressive and one-sided, male-dominated theologies which arise out of patriarchal religion(s).[8] Women have begun to see that their continuous oppression in the church and society has its basis in these patriarchal religion(s). Historically, the theologies of religions have emerged out of the experiences of men, making the theologies representative thereof. Because humanity is comprised of both men and women Feminist theologians seek to develop a more wholistic perspective in theology.

Second, in seeking to produce a wholistic perspective in theology Feminist theologians call for the *eradication of social/sexual dualisms* in human existence which are inherent in patriarchy. A patriarchy is characterized by male-domination and female submission and subordination. In such a society, men are considered strong, intelligent, rational and aggressive; women are considered weak, irrational, and docile.

A third function of Feminist theology is to *conceptualize new and positive images of women*. Throughout history, including the history of theology, women have been portrayed in negative ways. They have been sources of evil (snakes), authors of trickery (witches), and stimulants (therefore causes) for the sexual perversions of men (temptresses and prostitutes). These negative images must be changed to reflect reality.

Finally, Feminist theology must *evaluate male articulated understandings of the Christian faith*. Doctrines developed in a system of patriarchy merely perpetuate patriarchal structures. As the patriarchal theological system is challenged, so are the doctrines, e.g., God, Jesus Christ, the Fall and the Church.

Emerging Black Feminist Perspective

It has been argued by many Blacks that the women's liberation movement is a White middle-class movement. Therefore, it is believed to be totally irrelevant to the situation of Black women since the majority of them are not middle-class.

Brenda Eichelberger gives several reasons for Black women's non-involvement in feminist causes. Among them are such things as class differences, the lack of Black women's knowledge about the real issues involved and the suspicion that the middle-class White women's movement is divisive to the Black community which claims prior allegiance.[9] In spite of these and other negative responses to the White women's liberation movement, there has been a growing feminist consciousness among many Black women and some Black men. This consciousness is coupled by the increased willingness of Black women to undertake an independent analysis of sexism, thereby creating an emerging Black perspective on feminism. Black feminism grows out of Black women's tri-dimensional reality of race/sex/class. It holds that full human liberation cannot be achieved simply by the elimination of any one form of oppression. Consequently, real liberation must be "broad in the concrete";[10] it must be based upon a multi-dimensional analysis.

Recent writings by secular Black feminists have challenged White feminist analysis and Black race analysis, particularly by introducing data from Black women's experience that has been historically ignored by White feminists and Black male liberationists.

In only a few of them do Black women employ only a gender analysis to treat Black women's reality. Whereas Ntozake Shange focuses chiefly upon sexism, Michelle Wallace, like Alice Walker, presumes that White racism has had an adverse effect upon the Black community in a way that confuses and reinforces the already existing sexism. Sharon Harley, Rosalyn Terborg-Penn, Paula Giddings and Gloria Wade-Gayles all recognize the inclusiveness of the oppressive reality of Black women as they endure racism, sexism and economic oppression. Barbara Smith, Gloria Hull, Bell Hooks and Angela Davis particularly explore the implications of this tri-dimensional oppression of Black women. In so doing, Black women have either articulated Black feminist perspectives or developed grounds for doing so.[11] These perspectives, however, have not led to the resolution of tensions between Black women and White women, and they even have brought to the forefront some tensions between Black women and Black men.

On the contrary, the possibly irreparable nature of these tensions is implied in Walker's suggestion that the experience of being a Black woman or a White woman is so different that another word is required to describe the liberative efforts of Black women. Her suggestion that the word "womanist" is more appropriate for Black women is derived from the sense of the word as it is used in Black communities:

Womanist, from womanish. (Opp. of "girlish," i.e., frivolous, irresponsible, not serious.) A Black feminist or feminist of color. From the Black folk expression of mothers to female children, "You acting womanish," i.e., like a woman. Usually referring to outrageous, audacious, courageous or willful behavior. Wanting to know more and in greater depth than is considered "good" for one. Interest in grown-up doings. Acting grown up. Being grown up. Interchangeable with another black folk expression: "You trying to be grown." Responsible. In charge. Serious.[12]

Womanists were Sojourner Truth, Jarena Lee, Amanda Berry Smith, Ida B. Wells, Mary Church Terrell, Mary McCloud Bethune and countless others not remembered in any historical study. A womanist then is a strong Black woman who has sometimes been mislabeled as domineering castrating matriarch. A womanist is one who has developed survival strategies in spite of the oppression of her race and sex in order to save her family and her people. Walker's womanist notation suggests not "the feminist," but the active struggle of Black women that makes them who they are. For some Black women that may involve being feminine as traditionally defined, and for others it involves being masculine as stereotypically defined. In any case, womanist means being and acting out who you are and interpreting the reality for yourself. In other words, Black women speak out for themselves. As a Black feminist critic Barbara Christian explains, referring to Audre Lorde's poem about the deadly consequence of silence, Black women must speak up and answer in order to validate their own experience. This is important even if only to ourselves. It is to the womanist tradition that Black women must appeal for the doing of theology.

The Beginnings of a Womanist Theology with Special Reference to Christology

Womanist theology begins with the experiences of Black women as its point of departure. This experience includes not only Black women's activities in the larger society but also in the churches, and reveals that Black women have often rejected the oppressive structure in the church as well.

These experiences provide a context which is significant for doing theology. Those experiences had been and continue to be defined by racism, sexism and classism and therefore offer a unique opportunity and a new challenge for developing a relevant perspective in the theological enterprise. This perspective in theology which I am calling womanist theology draws upon the life and experiences of some Black women who have created meaningful interpretations of the Christian faith.

Black women must do theology out of their tri-dimensional experience of racism/sexism/classism. To ignore any aspect of this experience is to deny the wholistic and integrated reality of Black womanhood. When Black women say that God is on the side of the oppressed, we mean that God is in solidarity with the struggles of those on the underside of humanity, those whose lives are bent and broken from the many levels of assault perpetrated against them.

In a chapter entitled "Black Women: Shaping Feminist Theory," Hooks elaborates on the interrelationship of the threefold oppressive reality of Black women and shows some of the weaknesses of White feminist theory. Challenging the racist and classist assumptions of White feminism, Hooks writes:

Racism abounds in the writings of white feminists, reinforcing white supremacy and negating the possibility that women will bond politically across ethnic and racial boundaries. Past feminist refusal to draw attention to and attack racial hierarchy suppressed the link between race and class. Yet class structure in American society has been shaped by the racial politics of white supremacy.[13]

This means that Black women, because of oppression determined by race and their subjugation as women, make up a disproportionately high percentage of the poor and working classes. However, the fact that Black women are a subjugated group even within the Black community and the White women's community does not mean that they are alone in their oppression within those communities. In the women's community poor White women are discriminated against, and in the Black community, poor Black men are marginalized. This suggests that classism, as well as racism and sexism, has a life of its own. Consequently, simply addressing racism and sexism is inadequate to bring about total liberation. Even though there are dimensions of class which are not directly related to race or sex, classism impacts Black women in a peculiar way which results in the fact that they are most often on the bottom of the social and economic ladder. For Black women doing theology, to ignore classism would mean that their theology is no different from any other bourgeois theology. It would be meaningless to the majority of Black women, who are themselves poor. This means that addressing only issues relevant to middle-class women or Blacks will simply not do. The daily struggles of poor Black women must serve as the gauge for the verification of the claims of womanist theology. Anna Julia Cooper makes a relevant point:

Women's wrongs are thus indissolubly linked with all undefended woes, and the acquirement of her "rights" will mean the supremacy of triumph of all right over might, the supremacy of the moral forces of reason, and justice, and love in the government of the nations of earth.[14]

Black women's experience must be affirmed as the crucible for doing womanist theology. It is the context in which we must decide theological questions. More specifically, it is within the context of this experience that Black women read the Bible. A (brief) look at Black women's use of the Bible indicates how it is their experiences which determine relevant questions for them.

The Bible in the Womanist Tradition

Theological investigation into the experiences of Christian Black women reveals that Black women considered the Bible to be a major source of religious validation in their lives. Though Black women's relationship with God preceded their introduction to the Bible, this Bible gave some content to their God-consciousness.[15] The source for Black women's understanding of God has been twofold: first, God's revelation directly to them, and secondly, God's revelation as witnessed in the Bible and as read and heard in the context of their experience. The understanding of God as creator, sustainer, comforter, and liberator took on life as they agonized over their pain, and celebrated the hope that as God delivered the Israelites, they would be delivered as well. The God of the Old and New Testament became real in the consciousness of oppressed Black women. Of the use of the Bible, Fannie Barrier Williams quite aptly said:

> *Though the Bible was not an open book to the Negro before emancipation, thousands of the enslaved men and women of the negro race learned more than was taught to them. Thousands of them realized the deeper meanings, the sweeter consolations and the spiritual awakenings that are part of the religious experiences of all Christians.*[16]

In other words, though Black people in general and Black women in particular were politically impotent, religiously controlled, they were able to appropriate certain themes of the Bible which spoke to their reality. For example, Jarena Lee, a nineteenth-century Black woman preacher in the African Methodist Episcopal Church, constantly emphasized the theme "Life and Liberty" in her sermons which were always biblically based. This interplay of scripture and experience was exercised even more expressly by many other Black women. An ex-slave woman revealed that when her experience negated certain oppressive interpretations of the Bible given by White preachers, she, through engaging the biblical message for herself, rejected them. Consequently, she also dismissed white preachers who distorted the message in order to maintain slavery. Her grandson, Howard Thurman, speaks of her use of the Bible in this way:

> *"During the days of slavery," she said, "the master's minister would occasionally hold services for the slaves. Alas the white minister used as his text something from Paul. 'Slaves be obedient to them that are your masters . . . as unto Christ.' Then he would go on to show how, if we were good and happy slaves, God would bless us. I promised my Maker that if I ever learned to read and if freedom ever came, I would not read that part of the Bible."*[17]

What we see here is perhaps more than a mere rejection of a White preacher's interpretation of the Bible: it is an exercise in internal critique of the Bible. The liberating message of the gospel is seen as over against the oppressive elements in the Bible.

The truth which the Bible brought was undeniable, though perception of it was often distorted in order to support the monstrous system of oppression. Sarcastically responding to this tendency, Fannie Barrier Williams admonished, "do not open the Bible too wide." Biblical interpretation, realized Williams, a non-theologically trained person, had at its basis the prior agenda of White America. She therefore argued:

> *Religion, like every other force in America, was first used as in instrument and servant of slavery. All attempts to Christianize the negro were limited by the important fact that he was property of valuable and peculiar sort and that the property value must not be disturbed, even if his soul were lost. If Christianity could make the negro docile, domestic and less an independent and fighting savage, let it be preached to that extent and no further.*[18]

Such false, pernicious, demoralizing gospel could only be preached if the Bible was not opened wide enough, lest one sees the liberating message of Jesus as summarized in Luke 4:18. The Bible must be read and interpreted in the light of Black women's own oppression and God's revelation within that context. Womanist must, like Sojourner, "compare the teachings of the Bible with the witness" in them.[19]

To do Womanist theology, then, we must read and hear the Bible and engage it within the context of our own experience. This is the only way that it can make sense to people who are oppressed. Black women of the past did not hesitate in doing this and we must do no less.

Jesus in the Womanist Tradition

Having opened the Bible wider than many White people, Black people, in general, and Black women in particular, found a Jesus who they could claim, and whose claim for them was one of affirmation of dignity and self-respect.

In the experience of Black people, Jesus was "all things."[20] Chief among these however was the belief in Jesus as the divine co-sufferer, who empowers them in situations of oppression. For Christian Black women in the past, Jesus was their central frame of reference. They identified with Jesus because they believed that Jesus identified with them. As Jesus was persecuted and made to suffer undeservedly, so were they. His suffering culminated in the crucifixion. Their crucifixion included rapes, and husbands being castrated (literally and metaphorically), babies being sold, and other cruel and often murderous treatments. But Jesus' suffering was not the suffering of a mere human, for Jesus was understood to be God incarnate. As Harold Carter observed of Black prayers in general, there was no difference made between the persons of the trinity, Jesus, God, or the Holy Spirit. All of these proper names for God were used interchangeably in prayer language. Thus, Jesus was the one who speaks the world into creation. He was the power behind the Church.[21] Black women's affirmation of Jesus as God meant that White people were not God. One old slave woman clearly demonstrates this as she prayed:

"Dear Massa Jesus, we all uns beg Ooner [you] come make us a call dis yere day. We is nutting but poor Etiopian women and people ain't tink much 'bout we. We ain't trust any of dem great high people for come to we church, but do' you is de one great Massa, great too much dan Massa Linkum, you ain't shame to care for we African people."[22]

Implicit in the description "nothing but poor Black women" and what follows is the awareness of the public devaluation of Black women. But in spite of that Jesus is presented as a confidant who could be trusted while White people could not be trusted. This woman affirmed the contribution of Abraham Lincoln to the emancipation of Blacks, but rejected Mr. Lincoln as her real or ultimate master. Quite a contrast to the master's (slave owner's) perception of his/herself.

This slave woman did not hesitate to identify her struggle and pain with those of Jesus. In fact, the common struggle made her know that Jesus would respond to her beck and call.

Come to we, dear Massa Jesus. De sun, he hot too much, de road am dat long and boggy (sandy) and we ain't got no buggy for send and fetch Ooner. But Massa, you 'member how you walked dat hard walk up Calvary and ain't weary but tink about we all dat way. We know you ain't weary for to come to we. We pick out de torns, de prickles, de brier, de backslidin' and de quarrel and de sin out of you path so dey shan't hurt Ooner pierce feet no more.[23]

The reference to "no buggy" to send for Jesus, brings to mind the limited material possessions of pre- and post-Civil War Blacks. In her speech, "Ain't I a Woman," Sojourner Truth distinguished between White women's and Black women's experiences by emphasizing that Black women were not helped into carriages as were White women.[24] In the prayer, this woman speaks of that reality wherein most Blacks didn't even have carriages or buggys. For had she owned one, certainly she'd send it to fetch Jesus. Here we see the concern for the comfort and the suffering of Jesus. Jesus suffers when we sin—when we backslide or when we quarrel. But still Jesus is identified with her plight. Note that Jesus went to the cross with this Black woman on his mind. He was thinking about her and all others like her. So totally dedicated to the poor, the weak, the downtrodden, the outcast that in this Black woman's faith, Jesus would never be too tired to come. As she is truly among the people at the bottom of humanity, she can make things comfortable for Jesus even though she may have nothing to give him—no water, no food—but she can give tears and love. She continues:

Come to me, dear Massa Jesus. We all uns ain't got no good cool water for give when you thirsty. You know Massa, de drought so long, and the well so low, ain't nutting but mud to drink. But we gwine to take de munion cup and fill it wid de tear of repentance, and love clean out of we heart. Dat all we hab to gib you good Massa.[25]

The material or physical deprivation experienced by this woman did not reduce her desire to give Jesus the best. Being a Black woman in the American society meant essentially being poor, with no buggy, and no good cool water. Life for Black women was indeed bad, hot and at best muddy. Note that there is no hint that their condition results from some divine intention. Now, whereas I am not prepared to say that this same woman or any others in that church the next day would have been engaged in political praxis by joining such movements as Nat Turner's rebellion or Denmark Vesey's revolt, it is clear that her perspective was such that the social, political and economic orders were believed to be sinful and against the will of the real master, Jesus.

For Black women, the role of Jesus unraveled as they encountered him in their experience as one who empowers the weak. In this vein, Jesus was such a central part of Sojourner Truth's life that all of her sermons made him the starting point. When asked by a preacher if the source of her preaching was the Bible, she responded, "No honey, can't preach from de Bible—can't read a letter."[26] Then she explained, "When I preaches, I has jest one text to preach from, an' I always preaches from this one. My text is, 'When I found Jesus!' "[27] In this sermon Sojourner Truth recounts the events and struggles of life from the time her parents were brought from Africa and sold "up an' down, an' hither an' yon . . ."[28] to the time that she met Jesus within the context of her struggles for dignity of Black people and women. Her encounter with Jesus brought such joy that she became overwhelmed with love and praise:

Praise, praise, praise to the Lord! An I begun to feel such a love in my soul as I never felt before—love to all creatures. An then, all of a sudden, it stopped, an I said, Dar's de white folks that have abused you, an beat you, an abused your people—think o them! But then there came another rush of love through my soul, an cried out loud—Lord, I can love even de white folks![29]

This love was not a sentimental, passive love. It was a tough, active love that empowered her to fight more fiercely for the freedom of her people. For the rest of her life she continued speaking at abolition and women's rights gatherings, and condemned the horrors of oppression.

The Womanist Traditions and Christological Reflections

More than anyone, Black theologians have captured the essence of the significance of Jesus in the lives of Black people which to an extent includes Black women. They all hold that the Jesus of history is important for understanding who he was and his significance for us today. By and large they have affirmed that this Jesus is the Christ, that is, God incarnate. They have argued that in the light of our experience, Jesus meant freedom.[30] They have maintained that Jesus means freedom from the sociopsychological, psychocultural, economic and political oppression of Black people. In other words, Jesus is a political messiah.[31] "To free [humans] from bondage was Jesus' own definition of his ministry."[32] This meant that as Jesus identified with the lowly of his day, he now identifies with the lowly of this day, who in the American context are Black people. The identification is so real that Jesus Christ in fact becomes Black. It is important to note that Jesus' blackness is not a result of ideological distortion of a few Black thinkers, but a result of careful christological investigation. Cone examines the sources of Christology and concludes that Jesus is Black because "Jesus was a Jew." He explains:

> It is on the basis of the soteriological meaning of the particularity of his Jewishness that theology must affirm the christological significance of Jesus' present blackness. He is black because he was a Jew. The affirmation of the black Christ can be understood when the significance of his past Jewishness is related dialetically to the significance of his present blackness. On the other hand, the Jewishness of Jesus located him in the context of the Exodus, thereby connecting his appearance in Palestine with God's liberation of oppressed Israelites from Egypt. Unless Jesus were truly from Jewish ancestry, it would make little theological sense to say that he is the fulfillment of God's covenant with Israel. But on the other hand, the blackness of Jesus brings out the soteriological meaning of his Jewishness for our contemporary situation when Jesus' person is understood in the context of the cross and resurrection. Without negating the divine election of Israel, the cross and resurrection are Yahweh's fulfillment of his original intention for Israel . . .[33]

The condition of Black people today reflects the cross of Jesus. Yet the resurrection brings the hope that liberation from oppression is immanent. The resurrected Black Christ signifies this hope.

Cone further argues that this christological title, "The Black Christ," is not validated by its universality, but, in fact, by its particularity. Its significance lies in whether or not the christological title "points to God's universal will to liberate particular oppressed people from inhumanity."[34] These particular oppressed peoples to which Cone refers are characterized in Jesus' parable on the Last Judgment as "the least." "The least in America are literally and symbolically present in Black people."[35] This notion of "the least" is attractive because it descriptively locates the condition of Black women. "The least" are those people who have no water to give, but offer what they have, as the old slave woman cited above says in her prayer. Black women's experience in general is such a reality. Their tri-dimensional reality renders their particular situation a complex one. One could say that not only are they the oppressed of the oppressed, but their situation represents "the particular within the particular."

But is this just another situation that takes us deeper into the abyss of theological relativity? I would argue that it is not, because it is in the context of Black women's experience where the particular connects up with the universal. By this I mean that in each of the three dynamics of oppression, Black women share in the reality of a broader community. They share race suffering with Black men; with White women and other Third World women, they are victims of sexism; and with poor Blacks and Whites, and other Third World peoples, especially women, they are disproportionately poor. To speak of Black women's tri-dimensional reality, therefore, is not to speak of Black women exclusively, for there is an implied universality which connects them with others.

Likewise, with Jesus Christ, there was an implied universality which made him identify with others—the poor, the woman, the stranger. To affirm Jesus' solidarity with the "least of the people" is not an exercise in romanticized contentment with one's oppressed status in life. For as the resurrection signified that there is more to life than the cross of Jesus Christ, for Black women it signifies that their tri-dimensional oppressive existence is not the end, but it merely represents the context in which a particular people struggle to experience hope and liberation. Jesus Christ thus represents a three-fold significance; first he identifies with the "little people," Black women where they are; secondly, he affirms the basic humanity for these, "the least"; and thirdly, he inspires active hope in the struggle for resurrected, liberated existence.

To locate the Christ in Black people is a radical and necessary step, but understanding of Black women's reality challenges us to go further. Christ among the least must also mean Christ in the community of Black women. William Eichelberger was able to recognize this as he further particularized the significance of the Blackness of Jesus by locating Christ in Black women's community. He was able to see Christ not only as Black male but also Black female.

God in revealing Himself and His attributes from time to time in His creaturely existence has exercised His freedom to formalize His appearance in a variety of ways. . . . God revealed Himself at a point in the past as Jesus the Christ a Black male. My reasons for affirming the Blackness of Jesus of Nazareth are much different from that of the white apologist. . . . God wanted to identify with that segment of mankind which had suffered most, and is still suffering. . . . I am constrained to believe that God in our times has updated His form of revelation to western society. It is my feeling that God is now manifesting Himself, and has been for over 450 years, in the form of the Black American Woman as mother, as wife, as nourisher, sustainer and preserver of life, the Suffering Servant who is despised and rejected by men, a personality of sorrow who is acquainted with grief. The Black Woman has borne our griefs and carried our sorrows. She has been wounded because of American white society's transgressions and bruised by white iniquities. It appears that she may be the instrumentality through whom God will make us whole.[36]

Granted, Eichelberger's categories for God and woman are very traditional. Nevertheless, the significance of his thought is that he is able to conceive of the Divine reality as other than a Black male messianic figure.

Even though Black women have been able to transcend some of the oppressive tendencies of White male (and Black male) articulated theologies, careful study reveals that some traditional symbols are inadequate for us today. The Christ understood as the stranger, the outcast, the hungry, the weak, the poor, makes the traditional male Christ (Black and White) less significant. Even our sisters of the past had some suspicions about the effects of a male image of the divine, for they did challenge the oppressive use of it in the church's theology. In so doing, they were able to move from a traditional oppressive Christology, with respect to women, to an egalitarian Christology. This kind of egalitarian Christology was operative in Jarena Lee's argument for the right of women to preach. She argued ". . . the Saviour died for the woman as well as for the man."[37] The crucifixion was for universal salvation, not just for male salvation or, as we may extend the argument to include, not just for white salvation. Because of this, Christ came and died, no less for the woman as for the man, no less for Blacks as for Whites. For Lee, this was not an academic issue, but one with practical ramifications.

> *If the man may preach, because the Saviour died for him, why not the woman? Seeing he died for her also. Is he not a whole Saviour instead of half one? as those who hold it wrong for a woman to preach, would seem to make It appear.*[38]

Lee correctly perceives that there is an ontological issue at stake. If Jesus Christ were a Saviour of men then it is true the maleness of Christ would be paramount.[39] But if Christ is a Savior of all, then it is the humanity—the wholeness—of Christ which is significant.

Sojourner was aware of the same tendency of some scholars and church leaders to link the maleness of Jesus and the sin of Eve with the status of women and she challenged this notion in her famed speech "Ain't I A Woman?"

> *Then that little man in black there, he says women can't have as much rights as men, 'cause Christ wasn't a woman! Where did your Christ come from? Where did your Christ come from? From God and a woman. Man had nothing to do with Him.*
>
> *If the first woman God ever made was strong enough to turn the world upside down alone, these women together ought to be able to turn it back, and get it right side up again! And now they is asking to do it, the men better let them.*[40]

I would argue, as suggested by both Lee and Sojourner, that the significance of Christ is not his maleness, but his humanity. The most significant events of Jesus Christ were the life and ministry, the crucifixion, and the resurrection. The significance of these events, in one sense, is that in them the absolute becomes concrete. God becomes concrete not only in the man Jesus, for he was crucified, but in the lives of those who will accept the challenge of the risen Saviour—the Christ. For Lee, this meant that women could preach; for Sojourner, it meant that women could possibly save the world; for me, it means today, this Christ, found in the experience of Black women, is a Black woman.

Conclusion

I have argued that Black women's tri-dimensional reality provides a fertile context for articulating a theological perspective which is wholistic in scope and liberating in nature. The theology is potentially wholistic because the experience out of which it emerges is totally interconnected with other experiences. It is potentially liberating because it rests not on one single issue which could be considered only a middle-class issue relevant to one group of people, but it is multi-faceted. Thus, the possibility for wholistic theology is more likely. Feminist theology as presently developed is limited by virtue of the experience base for feminist theology. That is, when feminists say that experience is the crucible for doing [feminist] theology, they usually mean White women's experience. With few exceptions, feminist thinkers do their analysis primarily, and in some circles exclusively, based on the notion that because sexism is the longest and most universal form of oppression, it should claim priority.[41]

Black women, by and large, have not held this assumption. Many have claimed that because of the pervasiveness of racism, and because of its defining character for Black life in general, racism is most important. Though Sojourner Truth never did develop a sophisticated social analysis she was aware of the fact that she (and her people) were poor because she was Black, and perhaps poorer because she was woman. I say "perhaps" simply because in the slave economy one could argue that there was relatively little distinction between the property status of slaves by virtue of gender; women were no less property than men. As properly, they were a part of the material distributed, rather than participants in the inequitable (system of) material distribution. Thus as indicated above in the Black woman's prayer, material possessions of Blacks were limited. In a sense one could say that by virtue of one's race, one was slave and by virtue of that status one was poor.

Still as we see the issues today, class distinctions which have emerged even in the Black community, and sex differences, which have taken on new forms of institutionalization, must be addressed. For liberation to become a reality, race, sex and class must be deliberately confronted. Interconnected as they are, they all impinge greatly on the lives of Black women. Overwhelming as are these realities, black women do not feel defeated. For Jarena Lee observed the hope of the struggle is based on the faith that Jesus died (and was raised) for the woman as well as the man. This realization gave inspiration for the struggle. Black women today inside and outside of the church still bring an optimistic spirit as reflected in the conclusion of Maya Angelou's poem, "Still I Rise":

Out of the hut of history's shame
I rise
Up from a past that's rooted in pain
I rise
I'm a Black ocean, leaping and wide,
Welling and swelling, I bear in the tide
Leaving behind nights of terror and fear
I rise
Into a daybreak that's wondrously clear
I rise
Bringing the gifts that my ancestors gave
I am the dream and the hope of the slave.
I rise.
I rise.
I rise.[42]

Notes

1. James H. Cone, *Black Theology and Black Power* (New York: Seabury Press, 1969), 53–54.

2. Ibid., 54–54.

3. The Kairos Theologians, *The Kairos Document: Challenge to the Church*, 2d ed. (Braarufontein, South Africa: Skotaville Publishers, 1985; Grand Rapids, Mich.: Eerd-mans, 1986), 24–25.

4. Valerie Saiving Goldstein, "The Human Situation of a Feminine," *Journal of Religion* 40 (April 1960): 100.

5. Ibid.

6. Ibid.

7. Jacquelyn Grant, "Black Theology and the Black Woman" in *Black Theology: A Documentary History 1966–1979*, ed. Gayraud S. Wilmore and James H. Cone (Maryknoll, N.Y.: Orbis Books, 1979; and rev. ed. vol. 1, 1993).

8. See Sheila D. Collins, *A Different Heaven and Earth: A Feminist Perspective on Religion* (Valley Forge, Pa.: Judson Press, 1974); Mary Daly, *Beyond God the Father: Toward a Philosophy of Women's Liberation* (Boston: Beacon Press, 1973); Mary Daly, *The Church and the Second Sex: With a New Feminist Post Christian Introduction by the Author* (New York: Colophon Books/Harper & Row, 1975).

9. Brenda Eichelberger, "Voice of Black Feminism," *Quest: A Feminist Quarterly* III (Spring, 1977): 16–23.

10. This phrase is used by Anna Julia Cooper, *A Voice From the South* (1852; reprint, Westport Conn.: Negro Universities Press, 1969), cited by Bell Hooks, *Ain't I A Woman: Black Women and Feminism* (Boston: South End Press, 1981), 193–194. I use it here to characterize Black women's experience. To be concerned about Black Women's issues is to be *concrete*. Yet because of their interconnectedness with Black men (racism), White women (sexism) and the poor (classism), it is also to be, at the same time, concerned with broad issues.

11. See Ntozake Shange, *For Colored Girls Who Have Considered Suicide When the Rainbow is Enuf* (New York: MacMillan, 1975); Michelle Wallace, *Black Macho and the Myth of the Superwoman* (New York: Dial Press, 1978); Alice Walker, *The Color Purple* (New York: Harcourt Brace Jovanovich, 1982); and *In Search of Our Mothers' Gardens* (San Diego, Calif.: Harcourt Brace Jovanovich, 1983); Sharon Harley and Rosalyn Terborg-Penn, eds., *Afro-American Women* (New York: Kennikat Press, 1978); Paula Giddings, *When and Where I Enter* (New York: William Morrow & Co., 1984); Gloria Wade-Gayles, *No Crystal Stair: Visions of Race and Sex in Black Women's Fiction* (New York: Pilgrim Press, 1984); Bell Hooks, *Feminist Theory: From Margin to Center* (Boston: South End Press, 1984); Barbara Smith, Gloria Hull, and Patricia Scott, *All the Women are White, and All the Blacks are Men, But Some of Us are Brave* (Old Westbury, N.Y.: Feminist Press, 1982); Angela Y. Davis, *Women, Race and Class* (New York: Vintage Books, 1981).

12. Walker, *In Search of Our Mothers' Gardens*, xi.

13. Hooks, *Feminist Theory*, 3.

14. Cooper, *A Voice From The South*, 91

15. Cecil Wayne Cone, *Identity Crisis In Black Theology* (Nashville: African Methodist Episcopal Church Press, 1975), passim, especially chapter III.

16. Ben James Loewenberg and Ruth Bogin, eds., *Black Women in Nineteenth-Century American Life: Their Words, Their Thoughts, Their Feelings* (University Park, Pa.: Pennsylvania State University Press, 1976), 267.

17. Howard Thurman, *Jesus and the Disinherited* (Nashville: Abingdon Press, 1949), 30–31.

18. Loewenberg and Bogin, *Black Women in Nineteenth-Century*, 265.

19. Olive Gilbert, *Sojourner Truth: Narrative and Book of Life* (1850 and 1875; reprint Chicago: Johnson Publishing Co. 1970), 83.

20. Harold A. Carter, *The Prayer Tradition of Black People* (Valley Forge: Judson Press, 1976), 50. Carter, in referring to traditional Black prayer in general, states that Jesus was revealed as one who "was all one needs!"

21. Ibid.

22. Ibid., 49.

23. Ibid.

24. Sojourner Truth, "Ain't I A Woman?" in *Feminism: The Essential Historical Writings*, ed. Miriam Schneir (New York: Vintage Books, 1972).

25. Carter, *The Prayer Tradition*, 49.

26. Gilbert, *Book of Life*, 118.

27. Ibid., 119.

28. Ibid.

29. Ibid.

30. James Deotis Roberts, *A Black Political Theology* (Philadelphia: Westminster Press, 1974), 138. See especially chapter 5. See also Noel Leo Erskine, *Decolonizing Theology: A Caribbean Perspective* (Maryknoll, N.Y.: Orbis, 1980), 125.

31. Roberts, *A Black Political Theology*, 133.

32. Albert B. Cleage, Jr., *The Black Messiah* (New York: Sheed & Ward, 1969), 92.

33. James H. Cone, *God of the Oppressed* (New York: Seabury Press, 1975), 134.

34. Ibid., 135.

35. Ibid., 136.

36. William Eichelberger, "Reflections on the Person and Personality of the Black Messiah," *The Black Church II* (n.d.): 54.

37. Jarena Lee, *The Life and Religious Experiences and Journal of Mrs. Jerema Lee: A Colored Lady Giving an Account of Her Call to Preach* (Philadelphia, Pa.: n.p., 1836), 15–16.

38. Ibid., 16.

39. There is no evidence to suggest that Black women debated the significance of the maleness of Jesus. The fact is that Jesus Christ was a real, crucial figure in their lives. However, recent feminist scholarship has been important in showing the relation between the maleness of Christ and the oppression of women.

40. Truth, "Ain't I A Woman," in Schneir, ed., *Feminism*, 94.

41. This question is explored further in Jacquelyn Grant, "The Development and Limitation of Feminist Theology: Toward an engagement of black women's religious experience and white women's religious experience" (Ph.D. diss., Union Theological Seminary, New York, 1985).

42. Maya Angelou, *And Still I Rise* (New York: Random House, 1978), 42.

20. Women in Islam

AMINAH BEVERLY MCCLOUD

And one of His signs is that He created mates for you from yourselves that you may find rest in them, and He put between you love and compassion; most surely there are signs in this for a people who reflect.

—Sura Rum 30:21.

Discourses on the Status of Muslim Women

Muslim women and their roles in communities continue to be a major concern of both scholarly and everyday inquiry. To non-Muslims, Muslim women have been the subject of speculation, consternation, and ridicule for decades. As one Muslim teacher and scholar has noted:

Old ideas about the place of women in Islam have hardly changed. The most difficult task I have faced in years of teaching Islam is how to provide an accurate account of the role of women in face of the deep prejudices of not only my students but also my colleagues. . . . And given the background of the students, it was natural for them to come into class convinced, on some level of their awareness, that Eastern women, and especially Muslim women, are the most oppressed and downtrodden women on earth, and that although Islam may have something interesting to say on some level, it certainly has nothing to offer on the level of women's role in society.[1]

Scholarly works have called Muslim women's existence and ways of being in the world as oppressed and voiceless, and have explored these characteristics in a variety of communities, elaborating a discourse replete with negative stereotypes. Western women feel that their "work on" Muslim women is a model of excellence.

Our knowledge of women in Islamic society has benefited from the burgeoning studies on women in the West. This interest has resulted in excellent monographs, essay collections, scholarly and popular articles, and translations of works by Muslim women into Western languages, particularly English.[2]

Muslim women, however, are generally unflattered by such scholarship. For example, Leila Ahmed had complained that

The peculiar practices of Islam with respect to women had always formed part of the Western narrative of the quintessential otherness and inferiority of Islam.[3]

Broadly speaking, the thesis of the discourse on Islam blending a colonialism committed to male dominance with feminism—the thesis of the new colonial discourse of Islam centered on women—was that Islam was innately and immutably oppressive to women, that the veil and segregation epitomized that oppression, and that these customs were the fundamental reasons for the general and comprehensive backwardness of Islamic societies.[4]

This is not to imply that Muslim women in many Muslim cultures are not struggling to break bonds that prevent them from intellectual pursuits and physical mobility. Yet whereas many social scientists asserted a need to liberate Muslim women from their families, husbands, children, history, and culture, liberation for Muslim women is mostly conceived of in terms of the veil, often called *hijab*, and their role in the home. Muslim women scholars, fighting patriarchy have devoted considerable energy to clarifying the emergence of *hijab* as defining for Muslim women. Fatima Mernissi has explored this issue at length.

The hijab—literally "curtain"—"descended," not to put a barrier between a man and a women . . . The descent of the hijab is an event dating back to verse 53 of Surah 33, which was revealed during year 5 of the Hejira (627 A.D.).

"O you who believe! Enter not the Prophet's house for a meal without waiting for the proper time, unless permission be granted you. But when you are invited, enter; and when your meal is ended, then disperse. Linger not for conversation. Lo, that would cause annoyance to the Prophet, and he would be shy of (asking) you (to go); but Allah is not shy of the truth. And when you ask of them (the wives of the Prophet) anything, ask it of them from behind a curtain. That is purer for your hearts and for their hearts."[5]

Mernissi further illustrates another major use of the word *hijab* in *Qur'an* in *Sura 41 ayah 5*:

And they say, "Our hearts are (fortified) within a covering against that (Book) towards which you call us. We are deaf in the ear and there exists a barrier between us and you. So carry on your work (according to your creed) and surely you are the workers (in accordance with our own doctrines)."[6]

In light of these Qur'anic passages, Mernissi concludes:

So it is strange indeed to observe the modern course of this concept. . . . The very sign of the person who is damned, excluded from the privileges and spiritual grace to which the Muslim has access, is claimed in our day as a symbol of Muslim identity, manna for the Muslim woman.[7]

Muslim women scholars are not alone in seeking to clarify the identity of women although the emphases and roles outlined are sometimes different. Afzular Rahman asserts that

It seems quite fair and rational to say that the circle of operation of woman in general is the home, while the field of work of man is outside the home. In other words, the basic and

fundamental function of woman is to run the home. She is equipped with such natural gifts and capabilities as are suitable for the bringing up, nursing, education and training of children.[8]

But woman is not called upon that scale and with that urgency to undertake social and collective obligations which would entail her leaving her household duties . . . it is more important for a woman to continue doing her household duties than to participate in collective worship.[9]

Dr. Hasan Al-Turabi, a Sudanese scholar and statesman, has contributed significantly to the issue of women and gender relations in a pamphlet entitled, *Women in Muslim Society and Islam*. Some of Dr. Al-Turabi's key observations are cited below.

Men purposefully attempt to keep women weak, and the jealousy which they entertain in respect to women induces them to multiply the means for restraining and monopolizing them. They dominate the property and life of women out of vanity and arrogance.

The greatest injustice visited upon women is their segregation and isolation from the general society. Sometimes the slightest aspect of her public appearance is considered a form of obscene exhibitionism. Even her voice is bracketed in the same category. Her mere presence at a place where men are also present is considered shameful promiscuity. She is confined to her home in a manner prescribed in Islam only as a penal sanction for an act of adultery. She is so isolated on the pretext that she should devote herself exclusively to the care of her children and the service of her husband. But how can she qualify for attending to domestic family affairs or for the rearing of children in satisfactory manner without being herself versed through education or experience, in the moral and functional culture of the wider society?

So far as the familiar Hijab is concerned, it refers to the special regulations pertaining to the Prophet's wives due to their status and situation. They occupied a position different from all other women, and their responsibilty was therefore stiffened. God ordained that their reward, as well as their punishment would be double that for any other woman.

The verses of the same Sura ordained that the wives of the Prophet draw a curtain (to ensure privacy in the prophet's room which naturally attracted many visitors of all sorts), and that they dress up completely without showing any part their bodies including face and hands to any man; though all other Muslim women were exempted from these restrictions.[10]

Along similar lines, Rashid al-Ghanushi finds that in a close review of different *tafseers* (commentaries on the *Qur'an* and *hadith*), the view of women that is elaborated is incompatible with predominant cultural views.[11]

In attempting to sort out the controversial literature on the status of Muslim women, the most obvious questions to raise include: What actually does the *Qur'an* say about women? If there is a difference between the Qur'anic discourse and the cultural practices of Muslims, why is this so, given the fact that Muslims understand the *Qur'an* to be the word of God? If Muslims believe the *Qur'an* to be the authority for the social life, how could they misinterpret it so seriously?

In order to answer these important questions, Muslim women scholars are beginning to meticulously investigate what the *Qur'an* says and what has happened. In a text entitled, *Qur'an and Woman*, Amina Wadud-Mushin has made the following observations:

Compatible mutually supportive functional relationships between men and women can be seen as part of the goal of the Qur'an with regard to society. However, the Qur'an does not propose or support a singular role or single definition of a set of roles, exclusively, for each gender across every culture.[12]

Man and woman are two categories of the human species given the same or equal consideration and endowed with the same or equal potential. . . . The Qur'an encourages all believers, male and female, to follow their belief with actions, and for this it promises them a great reward.[13]

The roles of women who have been referred to in the Qur'an fall into one of three categories: (1) A role which represents the social, cultural, and historical context in which that individual lived—without compliment or critique from the text. (2) A role which fulfills a universally accepted (i.e., nurturing or caretaking) female function, to which exceptions can be made—and have been made even in the Qur'an itself. Finally, (3) A role which fulfills a non-gender-specific function.[14]

Why is the contemporary discourse on women (there are no texts on men) so full of conflicting claims? Leila Ahmed has observed that "discourses shape and are shaped by specific moments in specific societies," which means that we have to look to Islamic history for an answer to this question.

Converts brought traditions of thought and custom with them. For instance (to give just one example of how easily and invisibly scriptural assimilation could occur), in its account of the creation of humankind the Qur'an gives no indication of the order in which the first couple was created from Adam's rib. In Islamic traditionalist literature, however, which was inscribed in the period following the Muslim conquests, Eve, sure enough, is referred to as created from a rib.[15]

The adoption of the veil by Muslim women occurred by similar process of seamless assimilation of the mores of the conquered people. . . . During Muhammed's (pbuh) lifetime and only toward the end at that, his wives were the only Muslim women required to veil. After his death and following the Muslim conquest of the adjoining territories, where upper-class women veiled, the veil became a commonplace item of clothing among Muslim upper-class women, by a process of assimilation that no one has yet ascertained in much detail.[16]

Dr. Al-Turabi has offered similar observations along these lines:

Throughout history, Muslims have experienced a significant deviation from the general ideals of life as taught by Islam. . . . Whenever weakness creeps into the faith of Muslim men, they tend to treat women oppressively and seek to exploit them. This is a natural tendency, and is amply demonstrated by the fact that most of the rulings of the Qur'an regarding women were set down as restrictions on men—to prevent them from transgressing against women, as is their natural disposition and their actual practice in most societies.

This discriminatory attitude of interpretation is very widespread. Yet another aspect of this tendentious jurisprudence is to generalize the provisions of the Qur'an and the Sunna that were meant to apply exclusively to the Prophet or his wives due to their unique position.[17]

While we do not have all the pieces to this puzzle, some Muslim scholars are examining Islamic history, philosophy, and commentaries on the *Qur'an* and *hadith* to find answers. Interpretations of the Qur'anic message, like all interpretations, are an exercise in power and knowledge. In the early days of Islam, debate and controversy filled the air, and from this atmosphere schools of thought formed. Eventually, we were left with five schools of legal thought, a few well-known philosophers, and one interpretation of the *Qur'an*. As Dr. Al-Turbi writes:

> *Although the message of Islam spread in [Arab, Persian, and Indian] societies from early times, the teaching and inculcation of Islamic cultural values was not coextensive with the horizontal expansion. Consequently, some pre-Islamic values and prejudices, have contiued to persist despite the domination of Islamic forms.*
>
> *By attaching an Islamic value to these practices, they sought to give them legitamacy and sanctity, because the values of Islam were accepted as sacred and supreme. This explains the unabated influence, on the minds of many otherwise good Muslims, of attitudes abhorent to Islam.*[18]

In the end, Muslim women were encased in a mold called "Muslim woman" which was ahistorical, silent, and without a strong Qur'anic basis.

Islam in the Lives of African American Women

Before we examine how African-American women walk into this fourteen-hundred-year-old history, we need to know a few things about them. We must first address the issue of silence, on which bell hooks has aptly commented in her work *Talking Back*.

> *This emphasis on woman's silence may be an accurate remembering of what has taken place in the households of women from WASP backgrounds in the United States, but in black communities . . . women have not been silent. Their voices can be heard. Certainly for black women, our struggle has not been to emerge from silence into speech but to change the nature of our speech, to make a speech that compels listeners, one that is heard.*[19]

African-American women as a whole have not seen themselves as silenced by their circumstances, though many times they have been hostage to the need to survive. They have always carefully chosen what they share, because the "sharing is always an issue of survival." African-American women have had to constantly fight the issues of racism, and even though they are aware of sexism, racism has been the commanding force. As hooks points out,

> *Many black women insist that they do not join the feminist movement because they cannot bond with white women who are racist. . . .*
>
> *At times, the insistence that feminism is really "a white female thing that has nothing to do with black women" masks black female rage towards white women, a rage rooted in the historical servant-served relationship where white women have used power to dominate, exploit, and oppress. Many black women share this animosity, and it is evoked again and again when white women attempt to assert control over us.*[20]

African-American women have, in large numbers, spurned the women's liberation movement and the feminist movement even though they have gained a little from both. African-American women have been formed socially by racism. Their spiritually has rarely been examined except through narratives of heroic deeds—usually either for family or the race.

The first Islamic encounter for African-American women was predominately in communities, where 'asabiya was the focus. During the first half of the twentieth century, for most African-American Muslim women, who generally had not encountered their Muslim sisters from the Muslim world, there is an ambiguous gender relationship. Women have a lot of say in nation-building—they are present, sometimes in quasi-leadership capacities, keeping the mini-nations informed and intact. At the same time, however, they are subject to the attitudes about women held by the men. For example, even though Clara Muhammad tended the Nation of Islam in its early days when Elijah Muhammad was jailed or running from the police, she is rarely written about, and leads no organizations within the Nation. For women in the Moorish Science Temple and the First Mosque of Pittsburgh, subordination of women is not so clearly a problem, but we have no written accounts of the first women and their lives. Women wear a modest dress and cover their heads, but do not seem to feel oppressed; rather, their dress is viewed as a difference that aligns them with a worldview, an identity other than slavery, and God.

The second half of the twentieth century brings a wave of Muslim immigrants into contact with already established African-American Islamic expressions. Along with these Muslim immigrants comes the notion of "Muslim woman," which includes silence, submissiveness, and absence. For some African-American Muslim women and for some of those moving into Islam, this notion is enticing, while for others it is the beginning of a new struggle.

The notion "Muslim woman" refers directly to dress and adab. The Muslim woman is one who looks Muslim, wearing a scarf that covers her hair, neck, and bosom. Her dress touches the ground, her sleeves close at the wrist, and whether she wears a blouse and pants or a dress her clothing must be loose enough so that it does not show her form. The Muslim woman is obedient to her husband, takes constant care of her children, and is soft spoken. She does not want much, is content, and understands that this behavior is pleasing to God. Her obligations as a Muslim are marginalized. If she does not look like a Muslim woman she is not a Muslim woman, even if she prays five times daily, pays zakat, fasts during Ramadan, and saves to make hajj. This conception of Muslim woman has determined life for many African-American Muslim women for decades, though not all have accommodated this notion its entirety.

In the last decade, I have been asked the question, "Why Islam?" hundreds of times. It seems to me that the attraction of Islam for women, especially African-American women, is best summarized by Leila Ahmed, who informs us that

> even as Islam instituted, in the initiatory society, a hierarchical structure as the basis of relations between men and women, it also preached, in its ethical voice . . . the moral and spiritual equality of all human beings.[21]
>
> It is because Muslim women hear this egalitarian voice that they often declare (generally to the astonishment of non-Muslims) that Islam is non-sexist.[22]

African-American women come to Islam from various educational, social, and economic positions, and their reasons for choosing Islam reflect that diversity. How they lived their previous lives is important for understanding their accommodations and struggles in Islam.

Some women, with college educations and opportunities for self-empowerment, come to Islam after the study of several worldviews and/or participation in other traditions. The following remarks from interviews express some of the paths traveled by African-American women toward their encounter with Islam:

One thing is clear. Christianity is one of the roots of black folk's problems in this country. It's got black folk thinkin' that white folk are God. As long as black folk are singin' and shoutin' in church thinkin' that some White god is gonna save them they will not and can never fight to preserve their humanity. Jesse Jackson tells everybody to say, "I am somebody"—hell, the White man already knows we are somebody. That's why he is kickin' our asses on every level he can.

—Ayesha

Everywhere I read there was some mention of Islam or Muslims. I figured I should check it out; this was very different, wide enough for everybody. More like one huge culture with little communities. God, I already knew about, Muhammad was new but since nobody was worship-pin' him he was no problem. Most of all the Qur'an didn't ask me to love those who did evil. This was cool.

—Sayeeda

I remember reading Carlos Castaneda and trying to understand the opening of the universe in the mind with the mind-altering drugs. I was too scared to take anything, though, but I got a great imagination and it was working overtime. What was clear though was a different connection with nature and the universe than what I was being taught in school. What some people thought should result in "love," I kinda got the feeling that we have a responsibility to nature.

—Fareeda

After spending all my childhood and some of my adult years in Catholicism I knew that what Scriptures say and what people do don't always go together. Islam seemed to be a way for me to be religious just between me and God. There was the stress on community but my personal connection with God didn't depend on anybody else. You know what I mean—there was no confession: God knows and expects me to straighten it out.

—Maryam

Other women come to Islam through direct contact with Muslims. Several women talked about meeting Muslim women in public places. They were most aware of the difference in attitude.

I was in the welfare office talkin' to this sister and she was tellin' me wasn't no sense in gettin' mad with these people 'cause all this was just a moment. People who treated other people like this weren't long for this earth. She said it like it was understood and she knew somethin' deep.

—Fatimah

Muslim men also play a role in attracting women to Islam. Muslim men, both immigrant and African-American, engage in African-American women in conversations about Islam and Muslim women. Often the end result of these conversations is a move into Islam.

I guess I kinda raised myself. They thought I was bright and pretty so if I kept quiet nobody paid me much attention. I liked high school but I just didn't fit—too light to be black and too black to be white. I read all the time—black literature, history, autobiography. My family only paid attention to the fact that I read, wasn't in trouble, and was cute. I wanted to be a doctor—family doctor. So when at fifteen I met this Muslim brother who was about thirty, good-looking, and smart. I listened to what he had to say because he listened to what I had to say and didn't treat me like a kid. He was attentive and Islam was exotic.

—Sandra

Further reflections on their lives reveal considerations of life in America.

College taught the history, philosophy, and literature of Europeans. We learned how primitive, undeveloped, and backward Africans and other people of color were.

—Ameena

Even though my folks walked picket lines and experienced white folks calling them dirty names, throwin' things at them, puttin' their dogs on 'em, they still felt they had to prove they were human. They feel that if they act like white folks they will be accepted by white folks. So they make sure their English is proper. The things we were taught to want and need were European. My folks thought that the key to equality was to be jus' like 'em. They never thought that they were o.k. jus' bein' who they are.

—Rabiyyah

Welfare means you are totally unable to care for yourself, your children. The person on welfare is made to be nobody and is kept in the system by force. I will clean toilets, anything, before I go on welfare and if there is nothing out there to do, I will make stuff and sell it. . . . I know that this country has put a system into motion that feeds on poor people and rather than educate them to be independent of it, it makes more dependencies. It constantly penalizes people who try to get out of it so that it can stay alive.

—Joan

In Catholic school, the black children always know that they are different because the priests and nuns tell you in so many ways. They always assume that you are in the special lunch program or that you can't participate in something because of money, they don't ask. When it comes to things like band or the orchestra black kids don't get to go because they are always assigned to gym or sports. Everybody thinks that all black people can do is play games. If you are smart it's unique 'cause black folks aren't supposed to know anything either. In class, the teachers are always cutting you off before you're finished or interpreting what you mean like you can't say what you mean. . . . My mother taught us that any kind of work is work. I might think that I'm too educated for certain types of work by if the alternative is welfare, then to the toilets

—Leila

As mentioned in previous chapters, the move into Islam—affirming the *shahadah*—is accompanied by a move into a community. These two levels of contract—one with God and the other with community—are reflected in spirituality and personal space transformation. On the spiritual level, the move into Islam demands a level of consciousness of God—an awareness of *deen* (religion). The God-centeredness of Islam and *wa'ezudeeni Islamiyyah* (Islamic consciousness) are instilled by the performance of *salat*, reading the *Qur'an*, and the use of everyday phrases such as *al-hamdullilah, insha Allah, as-salaamu alaikum, ma'shallah*, and so on. African-American Muslim women describe this God-consciousness in a number of ways. For example, *sawm* (fasting) clears one's sight and tunes one's hearing to one's environment. The discipline of the fast from sunrise to sunset for thirty days while working (in or outside of the home) or attending school, and residing in a culture where the fast has no meaning is one space of spiritual nourishment.

During Ramadan, I see things differently. It is as though everyone has to be their real selves. People, the people I work with can pretend all the other months of the year except Ramadan. I can see right through them and see who they really are. Ramadan always shocks me with the evil I can see clearly.

—Rasheeda

As I am just talking now I use inshallah all the time. Using it makes me remember that nothing I can plan can happen without God's will.

—Ameena

In Islam, my soul has a focus. I know that there is no one who can save me. I must obey God and wait until the last day to see what I have really done in this life. So I try and sometimes fail to keep this on my mind. I pray to stay on the path.

—Deborah

Listening to the Qur'an on tape is something I do everyday. The recitation always brings tears and moves my heart. I don't see how anyone could hear the Qur'an and not be moved. I am learning a new surah a month. When I get to the long ones I guess it will take years, but I will get it done.

—Bahirah

In addition to personal spiritual strivings, women also participate in classes and less formal groups for Qur'anic and Arabic studies. These sessions generally are focused on some portion of the *Qur'an* chosen for study and comment on what God intends to be learned from it. Here women seek interpretation from each other using hadith literature and each other's knowledge. Women have little or no opportunity to share their knowledge with the men, but often continue in these sessions for years. One group in Chicago, called Bushra, has had ongoing meetings for fifteen consecutive years. Women's groups have expanded in the past ten years out of local communities to regional organizations, but a major focus remains spirituality.

While women have nurtured their own spirituality, both personally and in groups, the move into Islam on the community level has its own indoctrination. The following remarks indicate some of the difficulties encountered in this indoctrination.

Befo' I could ketch my breath, they were telling me about all the layers of clothes I had to wear so nobody could lust after me.

—Hassannah

I literally cried when I was told I couldn't listen to my music because it was vulgar. But I refused to get rid of the records. I just had to look at all those memories. Some sisters "snatched" down pictures of my family off the walls and I freaked out!

—Aisha

I had to learn to go to bed early in order to make the morning prayer and learn the prayer at the same time in Arabic. I used to worry if I had memorized it correctly or if I was mispro-nouncing words. At first I was scared to make prayer at work because everybody had already started acting funny around me so I waited until I got home and then I worried about hav-ing missed the prayer. There was so much to learn that I worried all the time. The only time I could relax was when my menstrual cycle was on.

—Latifah

I went to the masjid to look around, went to some of the classes. Most of the sisters were either my age and real kids or women not paying me any attention. I look back on it and wish I had just joined the other teenagers. Instead I decided that I was a black woman and was bright enough to be on my own. When he showed me what the Qur'an said about men being the maintainers and protectors of women and that Muslim men could have four wives, I thought I was mature enough to handle it. When I met his wife she was nice and thought I was there to learn about Muslim women, not to marry her husband. Well, I became a co-wife, second wife, pregnant, high school drop out, family outcast, you name it, all before I turned sixteen. The women at the masjid would not talk to me. I figured and my husband told me they were envious so I just studied Islam and Arabic on my own. My life was hell except for reading the Qur'an and prayer.

—Sharifah

People are people no matter what religious community they belong to. Some are there for secu-rity, others seeking knowledge and some just 'cause they think it's a happening. You have to decide why you are there if this presents a problem for you and then go with it. We have sis-ters who were born Muslim and it is the only way of life they know and we have some who are making mistakes with brothers as they try to find out how they want to be Muslims. Some come into Islam trying to make it Christianity and are confused as they find out it isn't. Its hard to be Muslim in America in the center of a weird kind of Christianity mixed up with all kinds of other things.

—Jamiliah

What is life like in these Muslim communities for African-American women? According to many Muslim women it is average American life with a spiritual twist. What does this mean? African-American Muslim women experience all the joys and struggles that their African-American and Muslim sisters experience. These women struggle in the culture of the United States, where women of all social classes struggle; in African-American culture, where women are torn between fighting racism and sexism; and finally in a budding Muslim culture that inherited the Muslim world's misrepresentation of gender relations in Islam. They push against three layers of mire, and are making dents. Those women who struggle with sexism and male domination see Muslim women as necessarily in the service of their mates, but not in a diminutive way.

> *Muslim women must see themselves as the backbone of the family and society. If their homes are peaceful, their husbands content, their children loved and safe, then their [own] lives can be productive. There are many ways women can influence men without being out there, up front.*
>
> —Maryam

> *It is inherent in the genetic make-up of the black female to seek to satisfy the black male, to help him meet his goals and to demand good treatment from him.*
>
> —Minister Ava Muhammad[23]

> *The woman in Islam's role is very important, because she has the responsibility, as the Mother of Civilization and first teacher, of teaching these good manners to the (her) children, to continue this polite society.*
>
> —Nyasha Muhammad[24]

In a widely read and discussed article, "Women of the Veil: Islamic Militants Pushing Women Back to an Age of Official Servitude," two non-Muslim female journalists for the *Atlantic Journal-Constitution* sparked the ire of African-American Muslim women from all over the country. Led by women in Warithudeen Muhammad's communities, these women rejected the claim that Islam degrades women and makes them servants:

> *We urge all Muslim women from all over the world—those born in the religion of Islam and those who have converted to it—to speak out and defend their choice [of Islam] in spirit, word, and in action.*[25]

African-American Muslim women who struggle against male dominance do so within a framework that does not mimic Western feminism. These women seek valid Qur'anic interpretation. As Mildred El-Amin argues,

> *Many Muslims interpret 4:34 to mean devout obedience to the husband; there is no Qur'anic foundation for this interpretation. Devout obedience is due Allah alone; all human beings are subject to error and ignorance.*[26]

In contrast to many Muslim societies, African-American Muslim women spend a great deal of time in the *masjid*, organizing educational programs, doing good in community activities, attending classes, and praying. Like the women of the earliest Muslim communities, most African-American Muslim women attend *Jum'ah* prayer when possible. Separation from men is put into effect differently in different communities. All communities provide for the privacy of women. In two communities I visited—Masjid Ar-Raham on Chicago's West side, and the First Cleveland Mosque in Cleveland—the Imams made concerted efforts to give the women a sense of belonging to the *masjid*, and acknowledged that what women contribute is very important. In those communities, where the Imam is elected based on knowledge of the *Qur'an* and *hadith*, women participate in the community selection. Women also participate in the selection of some of the sites for the *masjid*.

African-American Muslim women have tended on the whole to be better acclimated to various sectors of the work force, though less well educated in professional fields, than their Middle Eastern and Southeast Asian sisters. While the government has seriously restricted Muslim women's educational levels in a number of Muslim communities in the world, racism, religious bias, and sexism in the United States have placed an overwhelming burden on Muslim women. The secular nature of American society is often used to force Muslim women out of positions of high visibility. Most African American women find a great deal of bias and hostility directed toward them, no matter what their status or occupation. Many women are forced either to compromise their appearances in order to maintain employment in mainstream professions, or turn to home businesses for income.

Religious discrimination, particularly toward Islam, is widespread in the United States, but this has not prevented large numbers of African American women from turning to Islam as a way of life. Highly visible as "religious artifacts," African American Muslim women in public spaces are the constant objects of hostilities. In contrast, immigrant Muslim women receive either compliments or other positive regard for their difference in the same public spaces. There seems to be some sort of expectations that Muslim women from the Muslim world will look different, while difference in the appearance of African American Muslim women is not accepted.

Among women in various communities there are points of convergence and divergence on any number of issues. In general, African American Muslim women live in a closed society that is highly charged with rumor, innuendo, envy, love, nurturing, and spirituality. These women strive to overcome the negative in search of the positive—most times.

Notes

1. Sachiko Murata, *The Tao of Islam: A Source Book on Gender Relationships in Islamic Thought*, (New York: State University of New York Press, 1992), 1.

2. Wiebeke Walther, *Women in Islam from Medieval to Modern Times* (New York: Markus Weiner Publishing, Inc., 1993), 3.

3. Leila Ahmed, *Women and Gender in Islam*, (New Haven, Connecticut: Yale University Press, 1992), 149.

4. *Ibid.*, 151–52.

5. Fatima Mernissi, *The Veil and the Male Elite*, trans. Mary Jo Lakeland (New York: Addison-Wesley Publishing Company, Inc., 1991), 85. The remainder of this quote says ". . . but between

two men." I assume this is an error in translation, because the ayah clearly is speaking about a curtain between visitors and the Prophet's wives.

6. *Ibid.*

7. *Ibid.*

8. Afzular Rahman, *Role of Muslim Women in Society* (London: Seerah Foundation, 1986), 1.

9. *Ibid..,* 2.

10. Hasa Al-Turabi, *Women in Muslim Society and Islam* (London: Milestone, 1973).

11. Rashid al-Ghanushi, *Al-Mara a-Muslim fi Tunis Bain Tawjeehat al-Qur'an was Wagi al-Mujtama al-Tunisi (The Muslim Women of Tunisia between the Directives of Qur'an and the Reality of the Tunisia Society)* (Kuwait: Dar al-Qalam, 1988). Some other recent texts that explore issues around women include: Abdul-Halim Abu Shaqa, *Tahreer al-Mara fi Asr al-Risala (The Liberation of Women in the Era of Revelation: A Comprehensive Study of Qur'an, Sahih Burkari, and Sahih Muslim Texts)* (Kuwait: Dar al-Kuwait, 1990); al-Turabi, *Al-Mara Bin Taa'lim al-Sharia's was Takalid al-Mujtama (Women between the teaching of Sharia and the Customs of Society)* (Sudan.)

12. Amina Wadud-Mushin, *Woman and the Qur'an* (Kuala Lumpur, Malaysia: Penerbit Fajar Bakit Sdn. Bhd., 1992), 8.

13. *Ibid.,* 15.

14. *Ibid.,* 29.

15. Ahmed, *Women and Gender in Islam* 4.1 also note that there is no Eve in the *Qur'an.*

16. *Ibid.,* 5.

17. Hasan Al-Turabi

18. Hasan Al-Turabi.

19. bell hooks, *Talking Back* (Boston: South End Press, 1989), 6.

20. *Ibid.,* 79.

21. Ahmed, *Women and Gender in Islam,* 238.

22. Ibid., 239.

23. From *Final Call,* 10 May 1993.

24. From *Muhammad Speaks Continues,* December 1992.

25. Ayesha Mustafa, editor, *Muslim Journal,* 24 July 1993, 20.

26. Mildred El-Amin, *Family Roots,* (Chicago: International Ummah Foundation), 1991, 29.

Index